'This is a superb text, one that builds on what political scientists have learned and yet integrates and illuminates it. *Politics: A Unified Introduction to How Democracy Works* makes sense of the political world and how it really works in modern democratic politics, and I heartily recommend it'.
– *Christopher Wlezien, University of Texas at Austin, USA.*

'This book is lively, engaging and accessible to anyone who has even a passing interest in politics, policy and government. The chapters cover a wide range of important issues, concepts and foundational ideas in politics'.
– *Zareh Ghazarian, Monash University, Australia.*

'This book is a marvellous and useful introduction to modern political science. Professor Ian Budge has produced a fresh approach to study and analyse "Democratic Politics". By means of "predictive theory" the student can understand and explain the political process in full. I am convinced that this introduction fills a void and is an asset for any student of political science, whether a freshman or advanced in this field'.
– *Hans Keman, VU University Amsterdam, The Netherlands.*

'For any student interested in a systematic and rigorous introduction to a science of politics, this book is a must-read'.
– *Edoardo Bressanelli, King's College London, UK.*

'Terrific systematic presentation which specifies the conditions under which contemporary democracies operate clearly and concisely both for students and the general public'.
– *Jean Blondel, Founding Professor, Department of Government, University of Essex, UK, and Founding Director of the European Consortium for Political Research (ECPR).*

Politics

This comprehensive introduction to politics provides an essential template for assessing the health and workings of present-day democracy by exploring how democratic processes bring public policy into line with popular preferences. Incorporating the latest findings from Big Data across the world, it provides a crucial framework showing students how to deploy these findings for themselves, providing a straightforward, practical orientation to the scope and methods of modern political science.

Key features:

- Everyday politics is explained through concrete applications to democracies across the world.
- Predictive theories illuminate what goes on at various levels of democracy.
- The book outlines – in easy-to-understand terms – the basic statistical approaches that drive empirically informed analysis.
- Rich textual features include chapter summaries, reviews, key points, illustrative briefings, key concepts and project and essay suggestions, with relevant reading all clearly explained in 'How to use this book'.
- The book provides a firm basis for institutional and normative analyses of democratic politics.
- The concluding section reviews other approaches to explaining politics, assessing their strengths and weaknesses.

Politics is an essential resource for students of political science and is of key interest to economics, public policy analysis and more broadly the social sciences.

Ian Budge is emeritus professor in the Department of Government, University of Essex, UK, and well known internationally as the author of numerous research articles and textbooks on democratic politics.

Preface

Politics

A Unified Introduction to How Democracy Works

Ian Budge

 Routledge
Taylor & Francis Group

LONDON AND NEW YORK

First published 2019
by Routledge
2 Park Square, Milton Park, Abingdon, Oxon OX14 4RN

and by Routledge
52 Vanderbilt Avenue, New York, NY 10017

Routledge is an imprint of the Taylor & Francis Group, an informa business

© 2019 Ian Budge

British Library Cataloguing-in-Publication Data
A catalogue record for this book is available from the British Library

Library of Congress Cataloging-in-Publication Data
Names: Budge, Ian, author.
Title: Politics : a unified introduction to how democracy works / Ian Budge.
Description: Abingdon, Oxon ; New York, NY : Routledge, 2019. | Includes bibliographical references and index.
Identifiers: LCCN 2018059937 | ISBN 9780367025083 (hardback) |
    ISBN 9780367025090 (pbk.) | ISBN 9780429399176 (master ebook) |
    ISBN 9780429678301 (Mobipocket/Kindle) | ISBN 9780429678318
    (ePub) | ISBN 9780429678325 (web PDF)
Subjects: LCSH: Political science. | Political science—Philosophy. |
    Democracy.
Classification: LCC JA66 .B78 2019 | DDC 320—dc23
LC record available at https://lccn.loc.gov/2018059937

ISBN: 978-0-367-02508-3 (hbk)
ISBN: 978-0-367-02509-0 (pbk)
ISBN: 978-0-429-39917-6 (ebk)

Typeset in Sabon
by Apex CoVantage, LLC

Preface
Explaining politics systematically

Globalization has moved the goalposts for political science, from a focus on politics within individual countries to a concern with what their shared processes and institutions (elections, governments, political parties, democracy itself) have in common across the world.

So far as political textbooks are concerned, this has prompted a shift from an 'Introduction to British (or American, Russian or Indian) Politics' to general introductions to politics, or books on 'comparative government'. Generally focusing on politics in democracies, these take off from the common-sense view that elections, governments based on the election results, parliaments and supporting institutions like the civil service and courts, are central to the democratic process. Individual chapters are devoted to each of these. Discussions of similarities and contrasts between countries are increasingly based on the standardized data now available. Thus, we are able to compare how long governments last in various countries and see how duration is related to the number of parties in the legislature or to fixed or varying dates for elections, as well as other factors.

Country comparisons thus provide a basis for generalizations and explanations of democratic differences which go beyond a simple appeal to their different national histories and geographical location. Ideological appeals may generate similar types of party (greens, socialists, liberals) across national boundaries. Differing numbers of parties in the legislature may be associated with different ways of aggregating their votes into their share of legislative seats. Vast numbers of statistical studies have been made of these and other relationships, which foster generalizations about democratic processes and outcomes in general rather than how they operate in particular countries.

However, there is still something missing so far as a complete and satisfactory explanation of politics is concerned. It is difficult to put thousands of studies together and say what they really add up to. We lack any coherent picture of how one outcome relates to another. This causes problems when we get into details. For example, is it better for democracy to have long-lived or short-lived governments? Long-lived ones might produce greater stability, but short-lived ones could be more responsive to popular wishes. Does relative stability make any difference at all? Most discussions seem to think it does and that stability is more important than (possibly) improved responsiveness. Contrasting examples can be found on both sides, so the argument is usually left inconclusive.

This is partly because one feature of political science, as of the social sciences in general, is the existence of so many weak relationships between concurrent processes running over the same period of time. National football teams may tend to be successful at times when governing parties get re-elected. While the resulting euphoria may contribute somewhat to re-election, it is hard to argue for it as a strong influence, even if it passes statistical tests of significance showing that the relationship is not simply a result of measurement error.

The problem of everything being connected (weakly) with everything else is compounded by the fact that thousands of analyses based on diverse groupings of countries produce contradictory results. Someone, somewhere, will have found a basis for a particular interpretation of events, even if it is contradicted by others. But which really explains what gets done politically?

Many introductions to politics confine themselves to simply reviewing current concepts and explanations. In contrast, this book aims at cutting through conflicting explanations and weak but statistically significant relationships, which leave readers unclear about what is really going on – and which are particularly confusing for those being introduced to the subject for the first time. The discussion here clarifies things by basing itself on successful predictive 'process' theories – concise and clear statements about how collective actors like political parties or governments behave. (You can find several examples in Chapter 7.) Such theories give rise to precise expectations about what such actors will do next. The truth of the theory can then be judged on how often it gets this right. Of course, such truths are never final. If another well-specified theory comes along which predicts outcomes better than the first, then it can be put in its place. The point is, however, that we work with the best available explanation (up to now) of how things work, and this gives a unique and detailed account which cuts through explanatory ambiguities and weak relationships.

Predictive theories have to be clear and concise in order to generate predictions (often numeric ones) in the first place. The incrementalist theory of ministries' budget allocations, for example, states that next year's allocation will closely resemble last year's, owing to (specified) constraints on change. The theory can be readily tested against actual departmental allocations year by year. And it tells us a lot about bureaucratic behaviour (Chapter 14) and 'policy inertia', which in turn plays a central role in the theory of democratic processes presented in Part I. (Of course, it can be extended and improved – see Table 14.2.) None of this subverts traditional institutional accounts of how elections, parties and governments operate. It simply fills in crucial details which are usually lacking.

By constructing predictive theories on plausible lines and then checking them against independent evidence, we can do a great deal to explain democratic processes, especially since the theories form a mutually supportive 'web of explanation' (Chapter 8). Each explanation feeds into and supports the others because they share many underlying assumptions, both about the way behaviours and processes can be measured and what political explanations should concentrate on. Often left implicit in the specific theory itself, focused as it is on a particular process or event (party policy formation, for example), these working assumptions are common to most mainstream work in the field. Systematic political science as understood here 'integrates the working assumptions of that body of political research from which a set of interrelated predictive explanations of political processes can be generated and validated – in particular for democratic policymaking'. The predictive theories we use to explain democracy in fact derive from the vast body of previous research whose working assumptions we summarize, relate and put together as 'systematic political science' in a series of clear, numbered statements (Chapters 8 and 19).

Basing our work on this previous research also gives us a focus. Democracy's defining characteristic lies in trying to match public policy to popular preferences for it. One can of course approach public policy in other ways – assessing its moral worth or its effectiveness in achieving its stated goals. However, the bulk of research on democracy, whether qualitative or quantitative, concerns itself directly or indirectly with the extent to which its institutions and processes produce a correspondence between popular preferences and policy outputs. That provides a clear frame of reference for the discussion here, paralleling 'supply and demand' for private goods and services in economics. Public goods, however, are more complicated to envisage and deliver. So the whole of the book is devoted to the processes and actors that do this.

Having a detailed understanding of how representative democracy actually functions at various levels paradoxically makes it easier to go on to other kinds of theoretical and conceptual approaches to political analysis. These might be analysing democracy from a class-based or power-based point of view, asking such questions as 'Who benefits?' or 'Who rules?' or 'Can democracies really produce morally good policies?'

To answer any such questions correctly, however, we must know how democracy works in the first place. Otherwise, any analysis misses its mark, as it is not talking about real democracies as they actually operate in the present day – which is what this book aims to do. Far from excluding other approaches to political analysis, it aims to provide them with a firmer basis for pursuing their own concerns. An end review (Part V) assesses the main explanatory approaches to politics and relates them to each other.

Integrating the main explanatory theories of democracy with each other, and relating them to the methods and evidence used to assess them, makes it easier for students to appreciate the scope and methods of modern political science, and gives them a firm grip on its basic assumptions – and through them on the way democratic politics work. The discussion will also be useful to teachers and researchers seeking to orientate themselves to new developments within the discipline, as well as to interested readers outside it. To strengthen democracy, we need to understand its politics better. Hopefully this book helps.

Sources and resources

A powerful argument for the use of predictive explanation in political research can be found in

Michael D. Ward, Brian D. Greenhill, and Kristin M. Bakke (2010) The Perils of Policy by P-Value: Predicting Civil Conflicts. *Journal of Peace Research*, 47(4), 363–375.

A focus on policy-preference correspondence as the central democratic feature we want to explain is advocated in

G. Bingham Powell Jr. (2000) *Elections as Instruments of Democracy* (New Haven, Yale University Press).

Michael Saward (1998) *The Terms of Democracy* (Cambridge, Polity Press).

Contents

Briefing summary

Chapter 5 Electors' policy thinking: from a joined-up left-right perspective to issue-by-issue reactions

Chapter 6 Party policy thinking: framing policy targets and election-based estimates of majority preferences

Chapter 7 Matching public policy to popular preferences

Chapter 8 The 'web of explanation': relating process theories to each other within a general political science context

Part II – Rules: rules designate – but may misrepresent – majority preferences, thus biasing policy outcomes

Chapter 9 Majority choice of policies: voting paradoxes and attempted solutions

Chapter 10 General elections and election systems: finalizing the collective choice of policies

Part III – Protagonists: parties and governments shape popular preferences and reflect them in public policies

Chapter 11 Citizens, parties and governments: interactive preference formation

Chapter 12 Political parties: ideological policy carriers

Chapter 13 Governments: prime participants in policymaking

Chapter 14 Ministries: separating out policy areas

Part IV – States: collective action without binding rules

Chapter 15 Globalization and world democracy

Part V – Explanation: explaining politics by specifying its processes more exactly so as to predict outcomes

Chapter 16 Generating 'Big Data': sources, procedures, error checks

Chapter 17 Simplifying 'Big Data': dimensions, majorities and the (missing?) middle

Chapter 18 Managing 'Big Data': theoretical explanation and statistical analysis

Figures

Part II

Part III

Part IV

Part V

Tables

Acknowledgements

The heroes of this book are the originators of the predictive explanations of democratic processes at its heart. Michael D. McDonald first proposed that party alternation in government would keep implemented policy close to the centre where electors are – an idea later developed in collaboration with Hans Keman, Paul Pennings and Ian Budge. Chris Wlezien had earlier seen 'thermostatic' interactions between politicians and citizens as the major way of bringing policy closer to citizen preferences in inter-election periods, a theory later elaborated and applied with Stuart N. Soroka.

A context for such thinking was Stein Rokkan's developmental theory of party systems, emphasizing the social cleavages which gave parties a stable ideological character and divided them into 'families'. Rokkan later developed these ideas with Derek Urwin and Stein Kuhnle. They were operationalized and applied to Big Data collected across the world largely on the initiative of Hans-Dieter Klingemann, building in part on the textual analyses pioneered by David Robertson and the surveys inspired by the Michigan School of Angus Campbell, Philip Converse, Warren Miller and Donald Stokes.

Party behaviour inside governments and bureaucracies has been systematized in the predictive decision trees developed by Hans Kerman and Ian Budge, who also developed the 'inward-looking factional theory' of party policymaking in conjunction with Lawrence Ezrow and Michael D. McDonald. Of course, a whole host of researchers from all around the world, too numerous to cite individually here, have either collaborated on these developments or facilitated them in their own research, building up a 'systematic political science' in the process, which has particularly focused on the questions of democratic representation pioneered by G. Bingham Powell Jr. The analyses covered in this book would not have been possible without their work over the last half century.

As this book centres mainly on their published and refereed research findings, it is indebted to the publishers who have allowed tables and figures illustrating them to be reproduced here: Table 5.1, Preference clustering produced by considering two issues together which do not produce a clear or stable majority view, and Table 3.1, Government policy alternations in 17 post-war democracies after general elections, are both from Ian Budge, Hans Keman, Michael D. McDonald and Paul Pennings, *Organising Democratic Choice* (Oxford: OUP, 2012); Table 6.3, The comprehensive range of policy categories into which manifesto sentences can be assigned and counted, Table 6.4, Mean percentage distribution of manifesto sentences over 56 policy categories within various party families in 24 OECD countries 1945–1998, Table 6.5, Scoring left-right positions on the emphases that party manifestos give to the topic, and Figure 6.2, Mean party left-right positions 1945–1998, are from Ian Budge, H. D. Klingemann and Andrea Volkens, *Mapping Policy Preferences* (Oxford: OUP, 2001); Figure 12.5, Left-right movements by British Labour, Liberal and Conservative parties 1945–2005, is taken from H. D. Klingemann et al., *Mapping Policy Preferences II*; Table 12.1, Dominant policy characteristics discriminating election programmes of a particular party family from all others, is from Andrea Volkens et al. (eds), *Mapping Policy Preferences From Texts* (Oxford, OUP, 2013). Figure 7.4, Theoretical expectations for the size of policy equilibrium intervals under varying conditions of speed of policy change and frequency of alternation in government, comes from Ian Budge et al., *Organizing Democratic Choice* (Oxford, OUP, 2012), Table 14.4, Ministries ranked in order of preference for each party family.

The following figures are all from Ian Budge and Hans Keman, *Parties and Democracy* (Oxford, OUP, 1990):

14.1 The acquisition of ministries by an agrarian party in a coalition government

14.2 The acquisition of ministries by a conservative party in a coalition government

14.3 The acquisition of ministries by a liberal party in a coalition government

14.4 The acquisition of ministries by a religious party in a coalition government

14.5 The acquisition of ministries by a socialist party in a coalition government

Thanks are due to Oxford University Press for its permission to reproduce all of the above and to Cambridge University Press for Table 17.1, The two leading dimensions from a factor analysis of election programmes over 20 post-war democracies from 1948 to 1980, from Ian Budge, David Robertson and Derek J. Hearl (eds), *Ideology, Strategy and Party Change* (Cambridge, CUP, 1987) – and for Figure 12.3, Postdictions of the factional or alternative model of party policy change, presented as a decision tree and Figure 12.4, A simulation of the three-party policy dynamics from the assumptions of the integrated factional theory, both from Ian Budge, Lawrence Ezrow and Michael D. McDonald, 'Ideology, party factionalism and policy change: An integrated dynamic theory', *British Journal of Political Science* 2010 (40): 781–804.

Translating such a mass of material into this book has been a massive task initiated by Linda Day and mainly carried out by Becky Fray, who essentially acted as technical editor of the manuscript. It has been carried to completion by Kit Coutts, and Stephen Litherland to whom I owe a debt of gratitude for stepping in to finish the task at a crucial moment.

Patrick Leslie has contributed directly to text and tables. I also owe some of these to colleagues, above all Hans Keman, Michael D. McDonald, Lawrence Ezrow and Judith Bara.

Sage advice and criticism has come from John Bartle, Donald Searing and Michael Freeman.

After all this help, there should be no mistakes, but any that remain are clearly mine – hopefully not too many at this stage (and perhaps useful in suggesting new projects for readers?). I would be grateful to have them pointed out to me for correction in later editions.

About the author

Ian Budge is a political scientist who has pioneered the use of quantitative methods in studying party democracy across countries. He has been a professor at the European University Institute, Florence (1982–1985), and a visiting professor at various institutions in five other countries and is currently emeritus professor of the Department of Government, University of Essex.

Seminal publications from his research include Ian Budge et al., *Ideology, Strategy and Party Change* (1987, 2008), Ian Budge et al., 'Ideology, party factionalism and policy change: An integrated dynamic theory' (*British Journal of Political Science* 40, 2010, 781–804), and Ian Budge (with various authors), *Mapping Policy Preferences* (2001, 2006, 2013: winner of the American Political Science Association Award, 2003).

Budge has also pioneered other areas of political research, anticipating the autonomous development of Scottish politics in *Scottish Political Behaviour* (1966) with Derek Urwin, developments in voting behaviour in *Party Identification and Beyond* (1976) ed. with Ivor Crewe and Dennis Farlie, the saliency theory of party competition (with Farlie) in *Explaining and Predicting Elections* (1983) and developments in direct democracy in *The New Challenge of Direct Democracy* (1996).

His achievements have been recognized in essays by leading scholars in a volume reviewing his work (*Democratic Politics and Party Competition*, ed. Judith Bara and Albert Weale, Routledge 2006) as well as by numerous research awards over his career. The citation written by an international jury for his European Achievement Award (2013) noted his 'outstanding contribution to European Political Science . . . through international research projects . . . scholarly production and institutional service'.

How to use this book

This book innovates in several ways as an introduction to politics – ways which make it easier for readers with different backgrounds and levels of knowledge to use it for their own purposes. The overview of political science introduced in Chapter 8 and reviewed in detail in Chapter 19 helps readers immediately grasp the full range and working assumptions of the discipline and the coverage of this book. This overall summary also forms a convenient reference point to go back to after reading individual chapters or parts of the book. That is helped by summarizing what they discuss in the shape of individual **propositions** reported at the end of each chapter and numbered in terms of their sequence in the overall summary. In this way, they can be instantly located at the appropriate place within the general book discussion.

Propositions

Concise statements of some part of a chain of reasoning.

The summary is useful not only in helping readers orientate themselves but also for putting in context the specific predictive theories introduced in the corresponding chapter (for example, the 'thermostatic' theory of hostile popular reactions to government policy proposals (Chapter 3) or the 'incrementalist' theory of slow change in budgetary allocations (Chapter 14)). The shared working assumptions behind all the specific predictive theories – often, confusingly, left unstated in other discussions – are here explicitly laid out. Together they provide a unified exposition of the research approach and coverage of much of modern political science. This should help even beginners with no prior knowledge of the subject to quickly form an initial idea of it and go on to apply its ideas and thinking to the political problems which most interest them.

Besides a starting overview of their contents, most chapters present specific, validated theories which form the basis of their discussion. Why do particular political parties pursue the policy targets they do when in government? That is accounted for by the factional theory of party position taking in Chapter 12. Why do governments form, which allow them to do this? This is discussed in the theories of government formation presented as decision trees in Chapter 13 and developed further in Chapter 14. How is the correspondence between public policy and majority preferences guaranteed under a democratic setup? Most of Part I is devoted to expounding how. The theories there make assumptions about the behaviour of democratic actors such as parties and governments, assumptions that are further developed and checked out for relevance and accuracy in Part III

(Protagonists). While such predictive 'process' theories are too specialized to feature in the general overview of systematic political science (Chapters 8 and 19), they can be related to each other within the 'web of explanation' presented in Figure 8.1, which shows how each complements the others within the overall account of democratic processes provided by alternation theory (Chapter 7).

These discussions go from the very basics of political science to some of its most far-flung research frontiers. They thus confront problems which have often perplexed scholars and provoked controversy and debate. The philosophy behind our discussion is always to confront difficult points directly (such as the exact extent to which policies and other aspects of politics can be assigned numbers or represented as points in **policy space**). However, we allow this neither to hold up the overall discussion unduly nor to block the development of its general argument.

Policy space

One or more lines or 'dimensions' representing policy positions.

The main principle guiding the presentation is thus to advance quickly but explain everything in sufficient detail that even beginners can grasp the concepts and arguments involved. For example, every new key term and concept is explicitly defined in the margin not only when first introduced but also when used later, to avoid overloading the general discussion in the text. Inserts provide briefings on specialized points, such as the different types of voting systems used in general elections (Chapter 10, Briefing 10.1). And there are supporting graphs, tables and decision trees throughout, with their own notes.

Fast moving but clear and comprehensive are thus leading characteristics of the presentation. It never discusses the consequences and expectations derived from any theoretical explanation without having first expounded its basic concepts and assumptions. This also applies to the whole plan of the book set forth in the Table of Contents. The Preface has already specified our theoretical approach. The Introduction (Chapter 1) goes on to outline the political context. Part I focuses on the democratic processes whereby public policy supply meets popular majority demand through party alternation in government. In Part II we see how the rules for adding up individual votes in elections may affect this matching process and even influence the kinds of public policy which emerge. Part III examines the behaviour of individual actors and checks out whether the assumptions made about them in Part I are correct. From traditional states, we move in Part IV to the prospects for world democracy, as the only way at international level to solve the problems of collective action identified for individual countries in Chapter 2. Finally, in Part V we examine the extent and ways in which modern political science can adequately examine, predict and explain political processes and events. The conclusion is that it can, using predictive theorizing checked against Big Data as the main tool. The assumptions and approaches involved in doing so are reviewed again in our summary of systematic political science in Chapter 19.

While each chapter deals with a different aspect of democratic politics, they have as far as possible a similar structure. They begin with an introduction and overview, anticipating major themes in the more detailed discussion. There are marginal definitions of new or technical terms in the text: frequent free-standing numbered briefings, graphs, tables and summaries, often with their own supporting notes. Chapters conclude with an end-summary, which is followed by the numbered propositions relating that chapter to the overall summary of underlying assumptions (Chapters 8 and 19). These help to place the more focused and specialized discussion of the chapter within the general context of current political research.

The way to use all these aids and shortcuts for your own purposes is to plan your route through the book in advance. If you want a comprehensive introduction to modern political science before taking a course, or without taking one, the best strategy is to read the text right through. The ordering of chapters is planned for this, so you go from context (Preface and Introduction) to the overall democratic process (Part I), the rules which regulate it (Part II), its main institutional players (Part III), its international context (Part IV) and approaches and methods for studying politics (Part V).

Often, however, you will have more specific purposes in mind – for example, how governments and bureaucracy work. In that case, read Chapters 13 and 14. If your interests are more in data gathering and estimation, Chapter 16 should be the focus. Most topics on which college students might be asked to do papers or essays appear as separate chapters. If you have a choice of topic, or can volunteer one, you might score by setting up a predictive theory for some political process or actor yourself. To see how this is done, Chapter 18 and the review of assumptions and specific theories in Chapter 19 should help.

The way you organize your reading of an individual chapter may vary with the time you have. With enough time, there is nothing like reading the text right through. For those with less time and a tight focus, start with the summary and bullet points at the beginning; read the summary at the end; go over the summaries of theories presented in the tables and diagrams; then read the bits of the text relevant to you. Chapters are divided into sections to make this easy.

Do not, in any case, try to cope with all the material in the chapter at a first reading. Stick to the text, ignoring the briefings for the time being. The briefings are designed to be free-standing. Their purpose is to explain details and references in the main text which you might not understand or which you might want to follow up on – *after* reading the chapter text. The same is true of tables and graphs. They are all commented on and summarized in the text, so on a first or quick reading, stick to the text. The more specialized material inside and around a chapter is useful for writing essays and pursuing the topic in relevant articles or books and on the internet – to which references are also supplied at the end of each chapter.

In writing papers, use this book as a starting point, but do not just reproduce its arguments and material; rather, engage with them, question them (with reasonable arguments) and expand on them. Some of the points made in the book have provoked considerable debate in their time. So never be afraid of challenging them yourself – but always with reasonable and well-founded arguments of your own or with specially collected counter-evidence. Predictive theories are meant to be checked and tested and hopefully replaced with better ones. That is the process through which knowledge develops. So try them out yourself – and possibly earn publication in your own right!

Chapter 1

Introduction

Politics and policy – what do we want to explain and how?

What do we want to explain?

States

Governments recognized as initiating or regulating some or all activities within a particular territory.

Electorates

The body of citizens registered to vote in state elections.

Political parties

Organizations which run blocs of candidates for election to public office based on a policy programme and organize them to continuously support it.

Politics covers everything to do with the management of countries, regions or states, including the bodies (**electorates**, **political parties** and **interest groups**) seeking to influence this – going down to local levels and up to the organizations and alliances that states form with other states. (Examples are the EU, the North Atlantic Treaty Organization (NATO) and the United Nations (UN)). The terms 'nation', 'country' and 'state' are used interchangeably in ordinary conversation and media commentary, though they focus attention on different aspects of the territorial units into which our world is divided – population, land and institutions respectively.

The government is the body that ultimately manages and co-ordinates the activities going on within its state boundaries and which deals with other governments. Sometimes the government simply authorizes other bodies (e.g. businesses) to perform certain activities. In other cases, it performs them itself.

A government's decisions about what it will do or allow others to do and how this is to be carried out, are termed policies. Individual citizens are generally less concerned with the policies themselves than their end products, from jobs and food to roads, transport, policing and cleaning. The effect of particular policies on the various types of goods and services produced, however, is more in the sphere of economics than of political science. From our point of view, the major outputs of governments come in the shape of policies. These constitute the main focus of this book, although to explain them, we have to detail the institutions and processes producing them and the way these work.

Governments always keep the ultimate authorization and control of public policy in their own hands, however, much they may delegate. This is particularly true about enforcing the rules they lay down or the decisions they make. Enforcement may involve the use of force by soldiers or police, imprisoning people or imposing fines or penalties.

Interest groups

Organizations which seek to promote policies without running candidates in elections.

If a government has to resort to these actions too often, it is probably failing and may have to give way to an alternative government. Nevertheless, the ability to take extreme measures or to authorize their use by others within the territory is what marks out a government and distinguishes it from other political actors. A major basis for a government's ability to initiate or authorize policies and other activities is its recognition by other governments as the established government in its own territory. Occasionally part of the territory may break away and set up its own government and state organization. This is rare because such breakaways are not readily recognized by other states, which fear for their own territorial integrity.

The traditional function of the state is to provide internal and external security for its own population and, by extension, to organize (and pay for) collective works vital to the population, such as flood defences or irrigation. In practice most contemporary states originate from conquests in which a ruler – whether native or foreign – imposed themselves on the inhabitants of a given territory and levied taxes in return for protection. The ruler also regulated them in other ways that supported the ruler's power (e.g. in terms of religion). Boundaries were fixed when the rulers in two or more adjoining territories could not defeat the other(s) and so agreed on mutual boundary recognition. Sometimes such agreements were and are broken, resulting in wars.

Bureaucracy

Government advisors and administrators, often organized in specialized bodies, who formulate policy proposals and implement them when authorized by government to do so.

The need to control and defend territory makes the army the most basic state institution. Armies, however, 'march on their stomachs'. They need to be efficiently fed, housed, transported and equipped. This creates the need for a supporting organization which can do this. In an established territorial unit, this commissariat rapidly turns into a **bureaucracy** which can organize production and raise taxes for the central government. These activities in turn require regularity and certainty – at a basic level, peasants need to know how much of the crop to put aside for taxes and have to be allowed to keep enough for survival. If everything is extorted from them, they flee or die, undermining the tax base for the next year. General policies and rules have to be established to avoid this – and where they are disputed, adjudicated. This gives rise to **courts and tribunals** separate from the regular bureaucracy, as well as police to enforce their decisions.

Courts and tribunals

Organizations staffed by legal and administrative specialists formally independent of government and bureaucracy, which settle disputes by reference to established laws and policies.

Force is most effective where it is accepted as justified by (most of) the population. Governments traditionally relied on religion, often organized and controlled through a territorial church, to justify their actions. This presented state and government as part of the divinely established order which people should support and submit to.

In the nineteenth century, religious appeals were supplemented by nationalism. This set of beliefs presented the people (or the dominant majority) within the state territory as a nation (i.e. a grouping bound together by a unique language, culture and destiny), which could be fully realized only through their own government and political institutions. To the traditional trinity of state institutions – army, bureaucracy and church – were added schools and media assimilating the whole population to the dominant language and culture.

States joined with other states in international alliances to expand or defend these, by force if necessary. With the growth of world communications, dissident movements within states united internationally to oppose or change existing policies – often supported by other states which saw benefits to themselves, territorial or otherwise, in disturbing the established order elsewhere.

Politics today thus has a strong international dimension, with states having become so interdependent in terms of trade, social and economic well-being and above all through easy, long-distance communication (the continued developments known as globalization) that politics inside any one state will be strongly affected by what is going on elsewhere. Nevertheless, states remain the most cohesive political unit in the world today, particularly in terms of how day-to-day politics are organized and the type of policies they produce. Differences in the type of political regime – particularly between democracy and other forms of rule – run mostly between states.

That is the reason why our discussion focuses on politics inside states, though we come back to interstate or 'international' relations in Part IV. We begin, however, with internal politics. Here a multitude of institutions and other bodies play a part, shaping political processes and state policies by their interactions.

It follows from what has been said that modern states have all developed the traditional institutions – army, bureaucracy, law courts, police – without which they could not function. The most basic distinction between states, however, is whether politics is handled exclusively by these traditional institutions – alone and apart from the mass of the population – or whether other institutions have been added to express and impose popular policy preferences upon them. Such institutions include **political parties** and **mass media** not wholly directed by the state; regular competitive elections, parliaments determined by election results; and governments responsive to such parliaments. Other refinements include independent courts and judiciary with some control over the police; autonomous interest groups and **unions**; and possibly also local and regional governments and legislatures with devolved powers. There might also be direct votes on policy in referendums and initiatives.

All of these democratic institutions result from a second wave of institution building within states, in the late nineteenth century and the twentieth century. The prime stimulus was the invention of mass political parties by social groups (workers, farmers, minorities) which felt ignored under the existing setup. By asserting their claim to direct state policy in line with the views of their supporters and then competing in free elections for control of policymaking, mass parties rendered the population proactive in making the political decisions which affected them, rather than simply having to submit to policies made by their rulers.

The mass party transformed the political situation in three ways. In contrast to earlier factions – which opposed each other only at elite level, often covertly and exclusively within the traditional institutions – mass parties created state-wide organizations which grouped supporters into

---

Political parties

Organizations which run blocs of candidates for election to public office based on a policy programme and organize them to continuously support it.

Mass media

Ways of communicating messages to a large population through printed words, electronic transmissions or other means.

Unions

Bodies of workers in particular areas of the economy with welfare and political functions.

local branches. Such branches collected money to finance party activities – giving the party a financial base independent of state subsidies. They also rallied and organized supporters in elections contested between parties, in order to get the maximum number of party candidates elected to the legislature and thus empowered to push party policy there.

Originally intended as a way of deciding on state policy independently of the mass of the population, legislatures were subverted by requirements for candidates to openly support the party's policy programme in the election and to vote for it in the legislature when elected to it. Mass parties thus instituted a direct link between popular voting in the election and the choice of government and policy. Moreover, they '**framed**' policy for voters, who might otherwise have been confused by a variety of vague possibilities. Parties helped produce a clear, popular decision by presenting voters with relatively well-defined policy choices in elections.

Democracy can thus be defined as a state which guarantees a *necessary* connection between public policy and popular preferences for it. This distinguishes democratic states from others where a benevolent dictator may well decide to give the people what they want – but with no guarantee that this will continue. The institutional mechanisms of democracy – competing parties, free and controlling **elections**, responsive parliaments and governments – all guarantee this link. Democracies, to exist as democracies at all, have to follow these essential practices. This makes it easier to generalize about political processes across the majority of countries in the world which *are* democracies (roughly 115 out of 177, or 65%).

In contrast, non-democratic regimes – where decision-making takes place inside the traditional state institutions without reference to popular preferences – keep power sharing limited through a variety of means. The most common is a straight military dictatorship, based on the army, which relies mainly on force to obtain popular compliance. Others are theocracies, where a traditional ruler founds a claim to sole power on religious, mostly Islamic, teachings. Others again have a single mass party in which all important officers and bureaucrats have to enrol, which has local branches and runs in elections. The catch, however, is that the official party is the only one to run. The party structure is thus aimed at persuading the populace to follow government decisions rather than the other way around.

Because we can generalize about the essential features of democracy but not the variety of methods used in other systems, we focus on democratic politics in this book. There is a clear analogy here with economics which concentrates on the way markets work, ignoring the variety of controlled or **command economies** that exist, since these are run in such diverse ways.

Where one person or one grouping impose their will on the rest of the population, public policy certainly has a potential for emerging more directly and clearly than where there is democratic and collective decision-making. One problem here is knowing what the majority popular preference, which should guide decision-making, actually is. We begin our analysis of democratic processes with such problems of popular collective

---

Framing

Defining the possible courses of action to be considered on an issue.

Elections

Regular events where most or all the adult population choose between competing candidates who will select and form a government which pursues certain policies.

Command economy

An economy subject to centralized government planning rather than market influences.

---

action, which are discussed in most of Part I. The other parts go on to discuss the rules which govern collective voting on decisions, the actors which generate these, and the ways we study them.

As pointed out in the Preface, the most effective way to explain politics is to formulate clear explanatory theories of the behaviour and processes involved and check out whether the predictions they make are correct when judged against the appropriate evidence about what actually did happen. Now we look in more detail at how we can do this.

Explaining democratic policymaking

Social movements

Groupings like churches or labour unions that mobilize sections of the population, often politically.

Opinion groupings

Citizens who share a common public concern (e.g. on climate change).

Conceptual framework

A set of background assumptions about the theory, process or behaviour being examined.

Regime (political)

The arrangements which exist for choosing governments and policies within a state.

Democracies produce rather different types of policy, depending on how they choose to organize their collective decision-making (Part II). What they have in common, however, is an intent to match their policies to citizen preferences for them. Since preferences may differ between states, they provide the main explanation of why policies differ between countries and time periods. The processes by which we can achieve this policy-preference correspondence are what we want to explain – our 'independent variables' in technical terms. Many actors (governments, political parties, **social movements** and **opinion groupings**) are involved in this matching process. So to get a full understanding of it, we also need to understand why they act (and can also be *guaranteed* to act) in the way they do.

The best road to understanding is through developing, and then checking, a clear predictive theory of the processes involved, such as party policymaking. This is because the explanation it provides has to be clear and precise to make an exact prediction at all. We are also able to say whether such theories are correct or not in terms of the predictions they make being upheld by independent evidence (for example, by a party actually choosing the type of policy the theory says it will, under various conditions).

Our discussion will go into a lot of detail about predictive theories and how to formulate them. Some chapters base themselves directly on specific theories of the processes and behaviours they discuss. Others, particularly in Part V, concern themselves principally with the measures and techniques used to create and check such theories and the wider **conceptual framework** they draw their basic assumptions from.

Here we need only emphasize that the first essential step in all theorizing is to identify clearly, as directly and simply as possible, what you want to explain. In this case, the 'dependent variable' in statistical terms is the guaranteed correspondence between popular preferences and public policy which democratic processes should produce. Focusing so sharply on this central feature cuts through centuries of controversy about what democracy 'really' is, to identify the unique characteristic which distinguishes it from other types of **regimes**.

In contrast to states where a single party dominates the government and uses it to stay in control, democracies meet popular preferences by alternating parties with different policy targets in control of government.

As they slowly change policy towards their own position, the actual public policies being implemented mostly end up in the middle, which is the majority popular preference for them. We detail how this process works in Part I, where we also present this 'alternation theory' in five precise propositions. We also examine the expectations these generate about what should happen if the explanation is correct and check their accuracy against independent evidence.

This alternation theory starts from assumptions about the way parties behave and governments form. These are partly upheld if predictions from the overall theory of which they form part are successful. But they can also be examined in their own right, as an explanation, for example, of how political parties decide on the policy they will adopt. We present and evaluate theories about all the major participants in the democratic process in various chapters of Part III. Going down to precise details helps readers see how in practice clear predictive theories about political processes can be formulated and checked for credibility and how they feed into each other in a mutually supportive 'web of explanation' (Figure 8.1).

The strength of specific predictive theories is their tight focus on one aspect of what a particular **actor** does or the outcome that a process produces. That is what renders theory precise and clear. No one such presentation, however, can cover all the assumptions about politics which we have reviewed in this Introduction – for example, about states being the major context within which political action occurs. If every theoretical statement went that far back in its chain of reasoning, it would rapidly become overextended and unclear.

However, all the specific theories about party and government policy behaviour do share basic working assumptions which they use as a springboard for their own, more focused reasoning. So it is worthwhile to state these connectedly and together so we can see how they define the systematic political science approach adopted in this book. We do this in Chapters 8 and 19 in the shape of concise statements ('**propositions**') defining **concepts** like state and government and the relationships between them, along with **methodological** assumptions about how to estimate and represent them. Each chapter draws on some of these assumptions. To further clarify how they fit into our overall discussion, we cite relevant ones at the end of each chapter and number them, as in the overall summary in Chapters 8 and 19. To illustrate this procedure, we now cite the propositions coming into this Introduction. This summary of the main points made above should form a handy reminder for readers of the major features of our discussion here.

Actors (political)

Participants in political processes who can be individuals, organizations or groupings like electors.

Propositions

Concise statements of some part of a chain of reasoning.

Concepts

A theoretical entity or idea.

Methodological

Anything related to ways of estimating or representing processes, behaviour or relationships, often in numbers.

Systematic working assumptions coming into this discussion

1 States form the basic unit or context for political research.
2 States are governments with supporting (quasi-)military, administrative and other institutions, recognized by other governments as

providing public goods and services (including the regulation of non-state activities) within specified territorial boundaries.

9   States vary in the extent to which decisions about policy and who is to make it are shared widely among citizens.

10   The most extensive sharing occurs in democracies, since by definition these have to guarantee that public policies necessarily reflect the preferences of citizens for them.

11   This guarantee is provided by free, regular and competitive elections of governments and/or policies open to all groups and individuals, where votes reveal citizen preferences and authorize those preferences as either policymaking governments or directly as state policy.

12   Democracies are the only states with such key political procedures in common across the world. Hence, they are the only states whose policymaking processes can be analysed and explained at a general level by political science.

13   Ideally, explanations should take the form of predictive theories consisting of propositions or equations which can be checked for predictive success against observed outcomes or behaviour.

14   The unifying focus of such theories – extending from preference formation and expression to policymaking and implementation – is on the extent of policy-preference correspondence and how it is achieved.

These propositions state in a clear and concise form the main points made in the Introduction here about what we are trying to explain (Proposition 14), within what context (Propositions 1–12) and how (Proposition 13). You can check them against the text to see where and why they come into our discussion. The numbers they have been given link them to the overall summary in Chapters 8 and 19. You can go on to read this right away and familiarize yourself with the whole systematic approach used in the book. Or you can build up to that by reading through the chapters which follow, each of which presents and explains its own set of (sometimes overlapping) propositions. In the end, these all figure in the overall summary in Chapter 19, which provides a concise statement of what systematic political science is all about.

Sources and resources

Erik Moberg (2015) *Towards a Science of States: Their Evolution and Properties* (Lovestad Sweden, Moberg Publications,) www.amazon.co.uk

Stein Rokkan (1975) *Dimensions of State-Formation and Nation-Building* in C. Tilly (ed) *The Formation of National States in Western Europe* (Princeton, NJ, Princeton University Press).

Part I

Processes

Elections alternate party-based governments with different preferences and priorities, thus bringing public policies into line with centrist majority preferences in the long run

Part I overview

The ultimate focus of our discussion is on how democracies fulfil their promise of bringing public policy into line with expressed popular preferences for it. This is the political equivalent of economists' concern with providing the goods and services that consumers want (often in fact described as consumer democracy).

The markets' balancing of supply and demand is greatly helped, however, by the circulation of money and the price mechanism. Suppliers get a price for their goods, which they can then spend on other goods for their own consumption. Tangible individual benefits are thus gained from buying or selling goods and services in a way which does not apply to public policy. The main distinguishing feature of the public goods which policies deliver – for example, clean air from environmental legislation, security or public health – is that they are provided for all, even for individuals who might refuse to pay for them. Here the government steps in to make sure everyone *will* pay, by sanctioning anyone who does not (e.g. tax evaders).

If everyone can ultimately be coerced into accepting and paying for policies and the public goods they provide, how do we know that they really want to have them? We can ask them, but often individuals are a bit hazy themselves about how their private preferences for security, good services and schools, efficient healthcare and so on can be translated

Policies

Government decisions about what it will do (or allow others to do) and how.

Parties

Organizations which run blocs of candidates for election to public office based on a policy programme and organize them to support it on a continuing basis.

Collective action

An action undertaken by numbers of people together.

Governments

The body which ultimately controls the activities going on within its state boundaries.

Left-right

Welfare state, government intervention, and peaceful internationalism on the left and traditional morality, freedom, and internal and national security on the right.

Ministry

A section of the administration which deals with a particular policy area under a politically approved minister.

into public policies, particularly into the alternatives offered by the **parties** (Figure 3.1). When we democratically decide on a policy, we want to make sure it is one really preferred by the majority – but also the one most acceptable to minorities, if possible. This points to minimizing the gap between what each individual wants and the policy actually adopted. How do we do that? We suggest it is through election processes which switch government control between parties and thus keep actual policy in the middle, which is what most electors and voters also prefer.

How this works out in detail, we explain in the following chapters, which are all about shaping **collective action** through policy proposals and then deciding whether and how to implement them. Deciding on policy is helped by having a common frame of reference for all actors involved – citizens, parties and **governments**. In Chapter 4 we look at how this is provided (up to a point!) by viewing policies and preferences in **left-right** terms – which is the frame of reference most political actors and commentators (and political scientists!) commonly use. However, a left-right interpretation of democratic politics has its limits. We see in Chapter 5 how it breaks down in some areas and how democratic processes can bring majority preferences and public policies into line without general left-right divisions underpinning them.

This is important because it shows that democracy does not depend on special assumptions to make it work. Normal election processes and government alternation, along with slow policy change, are enough to drive it. We pick up all these points in Chapter 7 and relate them to each other in a series of clear, numbered statements – adding up to a predictive theory – about how democracy works to bring public policy into line with popular preferences.

Part II fills in the details by looking at the rules regulating election processes and their effects in promoting a clear understanding of majority preferences on the one hand and substantive policies which reflect them on the other.

Part III looks at the various collective actors involved in aggregating and transmitting preferences and demands – starting with the public and the political parties and their combined and individual effects and going on to the governments and **ministries** which translate these into public actions.

Part IV looks at the state itself as an actor in the international arena and how its internal processes interact with those of other **states**, often through interstate organizations, which have the potential to turn into democracies themselves.

Having covered the main **processes** and **institutions** shaping policies and collective action, our discussion moves in Part V to consider how we can study them better. The traditional division between empirical theory on the one hand, which seeks to explain how and why things are as they are, and moral and normative political theory on the other, which deals with the goals we *should* be aiming for, is less sharp here than it often seems. This is because the normative goal of democracy is clear:

States

Governments recognized by other governments as providing public goods, including regulation within specified territorial boundaries.

Processes

Any series of events which leads to political outcomes (e.g. elections).

Institutions

Organizations with rules shaping their procedures and outcomes.

to produce public policies as close as possible to popular preferences for them. If policies did not follow popular preferences, it would not *be* a democracy. Because we are mostly studying democratic politics in this book, we are less bothered by moral dilemmas than we would be if we were considering the general question of what the ideal policies would be.

Having surveyed the whole field of democratic politics and the way it is studied, we summarize our conclusions as numbered propositions in Chapter 19 to help readers bring everything together. Readers may find this presentation useful to fix points in their mind or even as a preview of earlier chapters. Where there are problems unresolved by current research, our discussion frankly identifies them. So the chapter also constitutes a useful springboard for the further studies and analyses or even essays which readers might want to undertake. Hopefully this book will stimulate your enthusiasm for doing so, thus enhancing the appeal of democracy by helping citizens understand it better.

Chapter 2

Why politics? Making policies to provide public goods

Chapter overview

Part I describes the key democratic processes, centring on elections, parties and changing governments, which initiate public policymaking and bring it into line with popular preferences. This chapter kicks off the discussion by considering why collective action – that is, action involving co-operation between individuals or groups – has to be promoted by the state and how this is done by governments making **policy** decisions about what action to undertake. Governments are formed by political parties which produce rival policy programmes published at election time. In choosing parties, voters also endorse their programme as a basis for government action. This is useful because without the party programmes it would be even harder for electors to link up public policy to what they want for themselves and their families. This all provides a basis for identifying majority preferences for policies, which we consider in Chapter 3.

The following are the specific topics covered in this chapter:

- The different concerns of the three main social sciences: sociology, economics and politics.
- Policy and its relationship with government action.
- Public goods and the universal provision of services.
- Problems of collective action in funding public goods and services.
- The need for state and government intervention.
- Slowness of real policy change ('inertia') and its consequences.
- Expert versus popular decision-making.

Policy

A government's decisions about what it will do or allow others to do and how.

Politics, political science and public policy

If you are seriously praying for a miracle, you go to church. If you are inviting friends for supper, you go shopping. If you want traffic-calming measures on the road in front of your house, you contact the town hall.

All these actions form part of our social behaviour, involving collective institutions (church, supermarket, local administration) and interactions with other people. For convenience, society is studied by different sets of specialists organized into separate university departments and professional bodies. General social behaviour is covered by sociologists; production and distribution of goods by economists; and public policy and its implementation by political scientists.

Of course, separating out these specialists and the kind of behaviour they study is a bit artificial. Why is the church you go to allowed to function in the first place? Do you have only small shops near you or a large supermarket? The decision whether to allow the practice of a particular religion (think Scientology) or have supermarkets in the town centre is political. It is a policy that has been adopted consciously or unconsciously by elected authorities. Conversely, the road your house is on might be private, in which case you would phone your service manager rather than the local town hall.

Most roads, however, are run by public authorities, because the transport infrastructure is too important to be left haphazardly to private institutions. So by and large electorates, parties and governments agree that roads must be politically overseen to provide a guarantee that they will be there when needed. This 'policy' of public supervision and maintenance of most roads is an end process of collective decision-making by authoritative political bodies. Policies and the processes by which they are made is the area of social life covered by political science.

Governments could, in principle, decide to do everything and take over all the churches and supermarkets themselves. Or they could decide to give all of them free rein. Both 'decisions about decisions' would be public policies. This example shows there are no eternally fixed limits between market, society and politics or between the areas studied by economists, sociologists and political scientists respectively.

In practice, however, representative democracies leave the provision of most goods and services to the market and keep out of religion as far as they can. Democracy is the normal way people organize politics in most world countries today. So in practice there is considerable scope for analysing markets, society and politics separately, though the boundaries between them may vary quite a lot in different countries.

Public goods and free-riders: the need for the state to enforce policies

There are, however, some areas of communal life where political intervention is absolutely necessary since without it some vital service would not be provided. An example would be a clean water supply. If citizens in some area got together on a voluntary basis to build a water system, they might all be persuaded to do it, both for personal convenience and to avoid outbreaks of disease from contaminated water. But it is likely that there would be one or two individuals who would not help – or even refuse to pay. They might reason that the water would be provided anyway, so they, individually, could benefit without helping or paying. Or they could refuse help or payment on the grounds that they were quite happy the way they were and didn't want a connection with the new supply. If enough people took these positions, the project might never get off the ground. Yet cholera and typhoid threaten everyone, including those drinking clean water. Stopping the threat from these, as well as providing the clean water, is a public good.

The peculiarity of a public good is that it is a service or a benefit which, if provided at all, has to be provided for everyone. Manufactures such as chairs and tables, or services such as restaurant meals, can be sold individually and charged individually. Those who choose not to pay do not get them. Security from foreign attack, or street lighting, cannot be parcelled up into bits and sold individually. If you have an army, it protects everyone. If you walk on the streets at night, you get the benefit of lighting whether you have paid for it or not.

Public goods are therefore ones which nobody can be excluded from using even if they do not contribute. While some – possibly even a majority – might contribute voluntarily out of a feeling of solidarity, some will opt out. These 'free-riders' reason that they will get the benefit anyway, so they might as well keep their money to spend on themselves and thus maximize their personal benefits.

Under these circumstances, how do you keep the army and the administration going and prevent crime epidemics? You force individuals into line by *making* them contribute to public schemes. Or, more indirectly, you make them pay taxes which the government then spends on institutions like the military, the health inspectorate or on programmes of public works like roads, sewage or even weapons development.

Decisions about spending limited public money on one of these areas rather than another and how to organize payment and action on them over time – possibly a long time – are policies. All governments inherit a lot of policies from their predecessors, so they are often not making new decisions. They may just continue to implement the old policies, which in itself is a form of endorsement even if the decision to carry on with them is taken by default.

Talking about the boundaries between public and private action is appropriate here because the central political decision is how far our lives should be regulated by political decisions and how far things should be left to private initiatives. Individually, we should all like to do what we want. However, our freedom might be others' constraint. If we could just build as we wanted, we could cut off our neighbours' air and light – and possibly, if everyone built to their own taste, convert a pleasant neighbourhood into a densely packed slum.

Besides, we require help from others to satisfy our own preferences and needs – healthcare, for example. We could make a collective decision to leave this to the market, with patients paying doctors and hospitals and possibly taking out health insurance. However, concern for those who

Briefing 2.1

Are public goods defined by only being able to be delivered universally, or are they services which governments have *decided* to deliver universally?

The question is whether public goods need by their very nature to be delivered universally or whether universal delivery simply stems from government decisions to do it that way. This may all seem a bit academic. But if things like security and roads could all be delivered privately and for individual payment, this would undermine arguments for having states and governments at all, as all social needs could be provided privately.

Many services which states choose to deliver universally have been delivered privately at some point. A good example is individual healthcare. Each individual could buy it, either on the spot or through subscribing to health insurance. Of course, those who couldn't pay wouldn't get care. But this is true of all goods and services provided by the market. If states provide such healthcare for all 'free at the point of need' 'free-riders' (individuals who get benefits but refuse to pay for them) pose problems. These have to be avoided by the state taxing everyone to pay for the benefit. That in turn could have been avoided by leaving individual healthcare to the market.

However, public health – avoiding epidemics by having clean water and providing decent sewage – seems by its nature to have to be provided for all. If not, some people will infect others. So all have to be included in the schemes and made to pay. The same applies to defence and security. If you have an army, it has to defend whole territories with all the individuals in them and not exclude some (even though they might have been willing to pay for their own security guards).

Given this, it does seem that we need state and government to provide and force payment for certain services if they are to be provided at all. However, many services and goods which are provided and paid for universally by the state could be provided by other means, leaving it open for governments to decide how they prefer to organize delivery in most areas.

cannot pay – and also the desire to avoid epidemics and foster public health in ways beneficial to ourselves – might lead us to provide free care for everyone, paid for by taxes and compulsory insurance. Or we could have a mix of provisions.

Because resources like land and money are limited, and what we do has repercussions on others, we have to find some way of regulating our social behaviour to avoid negative effects and even produce positive benefits. This is where the state and government action come in.

Of course, one form of regulation is to refrain from political regulation! On the whole, we leave it to shops and stores to provide clothing because that seems the best way to satisfy people's needs. And freedom (e.g. to practise your preferred religion) is a basic democratic principle. However, action in other areas, like public health, law and order, transport infrastructure, building regulations and so on, is generally decided politically because we cannot avoid taking some collective action on them, if we want to avoid negative consequences for all.

Policy inertia and the speed of real change

Taking collective action is not easy. For one thing, it often involves drastic alterations to existing procedures and routines. State administrators and bureaucracies don't like this. Legislation probably has to be changed, contracts renegotiated, entitlements to government payments or services altered (e.g. social security payments). Collective action involves a lot of people, and changing it involves even more. The people currently involved – administrators, families, recipients – tend to react against the immediate disadvantages of change rather than support the ultimate benefits. Even if these are well publicized and discussed, they may be hard to work out and rather indefinite and distant, while the costs are more obvious and immediate.

This helps explain why new policies are often so violently opposed by the groups immediately affected. Once the government has announced and defined a new policy, the first popular reactions are usually critical and hostile. This may lead opponents to organize sit-ins, picket lines, strikes and street demonstrations, as well as to write in newspapers and appear on radio and TV to emphasize how mistaken the policy is. These **thermostatic reactions** against the new measure often force governments to suspend their proposals while they negotiate a compromise with affected groups – or even abandon their attempt at change altogether.

Thermostatic reactions

Expressions of popular support for or (more often) hostility towards government policy proposals.

Policy inputs

Administrative and financial arrangements necessary to put a policy into effect.

Along with much technical, legal and administrative hassle, therefore, attempts to change policy will often provoke popular opposition. It is no wonder that governments, even ones committed to some change, tend to carry on with most existing policy. This means that **policy inputs** such as the money spent on the entitlements deriving from a policy or the rules being applied to distribute them rarely change much from year to year. Thus, the best predictor of next year's expenditure on a policy is usually this year's expenditure – a phenomenon which goes by the general name of 'incrementalism'. In the extreme case, policies may not change at all, leading to total 'policy inertia'. Where such inertia covers a set of policies spanning a whole area of social life, like health provision or welfare, we get slow-moving 'policy regimes' – sets of detailed policies inspired by some unifying principle such as ensuring 'free delivery at the point of need' for healthcare or the 'universal benefit' in the case of welfare.

Because of all these constraints on change, it has been calculated that policy expenditures will only move from where they are towards a new target set by government, at an annual rate of 10%–15% of the current gap between what it wants and what is actually being done. This means that a government lasting two years – the normal length of time for most

Coalitions

Governments formed by two or more parties.

coalitions – will only be able to change policy in its preferred direction by less than a third of the current gap. A government lasting four years (usual for single-party governments) would get only half that gap bridged by the time it faces another election. If it loses the election, its successor may well reverse its policy back to what it was before. This ensures a constant zigzagging of policy in disputed areas as governments and parties succeed each other in control. This helps keep the policy actually being applied somewhere in the middle: between parties. We will see that most citizens actually prefer it to be there, so inertia helps keep public policy close to citizen preferences.

Where a policy is not controversial and carries on in much the same way from government to government, it has probably been a compromise between the parties in the first place and so also ends up close to citizen preferences. We shall explore these possibilities in more detail in Chapter 3.

Policies and parties: election and government programmes

Ideology

A set of assumptions about the world leading to certain kinds of political action.

What drives policy change in the first place? In modern democracies, it is primarily due to political parties having policy objectives and programmes different from those of other parties – and sometimes quite sharply opposed to them. The party programmes derive from the principles that the party was founded to promote in the first place – its **ideology** – as we explain in Chapter 12. This is often associated with the aspirations and interests of particular groups in society – churches, **social classes**, regions and so on which took the initiative in originally starting the party up. Party programmes spring out of the party's attempts to apply general principles derived from their ideologies to current problems in various policy areas. For example, if it believes that the state should take a more active role in society to help deprived groups linked to it, its programme would probably also recommend more intervention in schools, if educational standards are being discussed a lot at that moment. If, on the other hand, the party believes that business freedom and initiative are generally being eroded by 'big government', it might advocate more scope for private education.

Social classes

A grouping of individuals sharing the same work and life experiences.

Parties

Organizations which run candidates for political office based on a policy programme and organize them to support it on a continual basis.

Parties have to publish such programmes ('manifestos' or platforms) because one thing they will be judged on in **general elections** is their plan for the next four or five years if they participate in government. The party also needs a plan for internal reasons: to motivate its supporters to give them their support in the election. Without a lot of people willing to take to the air in support, to contact voters and get them to polling stations and/or to give money, the party is not going to win parliamentary seats nor probably enter government. If they do so, they also need to have an overall plan, so its ministers and representatives can co-ordinate their policy responses in the face of demands for immediate action, foreign crises, political scandals and all the continual bustle and confusion of

(General) elections

Regular events where most

or all the adult population choose between competing party candidates.

Investigative journalism

An enquiry by a newspaper or media programme into some political or social activity.

Policy space

One or more measured lines or 'dimensions' which allow governments, parties and electors to be located according to their policy preferences.

---

day-to-day politics, which obscure the overall picture once they are in government.

The parties are the only political or social bodies who step back periodically to review the whole national and world situation and suggest what to do about it, in a reasonably coherent and comprehensive way. They do this for their own reasons and because it is forced on them by the regular occurrence and recurrence of elections. Their election programmes do, however, provide a focus for national debate and discussion of policies in various areas. **Investigative journalism** in newspapers and media programmes may also focus attention on specific problems. But only parties put these together as a whole and assess overall priorities. As a result, the broad alternatives they offer, particularly in terms of more state intervention and expenditure in various areas as opposed to encouraging other bodies (business, volunteers) to take action, help electors and citizens to clarify and focus their own opinions better and to make clearer choices when they vote. We go into this in Chapter 3. With a near monopoly on the production of such 'Five-Year Plans', the parties play the main role in simplifying and structuring political debate. We shall see the effects of this in Chapter 6, which considers how party structuring of policies and issues enables us to visualize them as dimensions defining some kind of **policy space** within which we can locate parties and electors in relation to each other (e.g. in left-right terms). This enables us to clarify and improve our own theories and analyses, as we shall see. However, these can also be explained and applied more generally without making strong 'spatial' assumptions. We do this in Chapter 3.

Deciding collectively on policies for collective action

Parties simplify decision-making by reducing the main policy issues to a choice between the parties themselves and their published priorities and programmes. Even so, individuals find it difficult to know which would most advance their own ambitions for their family and society. Collective decision-making is always difficult and seems even more so amid the confusion of voices and competing proposals in democracies' 'free marketplace of ideas'.

Because this debate also involves conflict and argument – spilling over into accusations of personal incompetence and character failings, which many ordinary people find distressing – one obvious question is, why should we make decisions in this messy way anyway? Why should everyone be involved if this means that problems and policies have to be simplified, and divisive elections held? Why not just leave decisions to experts who will find the best technical solution for everyone?

Unfortunately, several thousand years have shown that leaders who claim to have some special inspiration or expertise generally make worse decisions than elected ones. Shutting off controversy often leads to unjust and inefficient outcomes. If all voices are not heard, some citizens are passed over, while others are well placed to secure enormous benefits for themselves.

Underlying general debate and discussion of policies is the notion that, just like the free market, public interests are most efficiently identified by affected individuals and groups themselves. A person's interests are what they want. The idea that your 'real' interests are best identified from outside, by someone else, has to be distrusted because it so easily leads to tyranny and other people's preferences and interests being imposed upon you.

Democracy therefore involves the maximum possible allowance for discussion, comment and, if necessary, argument. If anyone is initially mistaken about where their true interest lies, discussion should reveal this to them. If in the end, however, a person or group remains unconvinced by the counterarguments, their preferences must then get accepted as a valid expression of what is best for them.

Democracy is not just about discussion and debate but also about deciding. To this end, regular elections are held to select both policies and the party which should implement them. It is in fact the parties – groups of individuals who run for office with a common programme – who define election choices through both their differing policy platforms and other attributes and who recruit the personnel for both legislatures and governments.

Their participation at all levels of politics – electoral, legislative and governmental – helps provide the '*necessary* correspondence between acts of government and the equally weighted felt interests of citizens with regard to these acts', which is the defining characteristic of democracy. This 'necessary' correspondence is made by ensuring that public policy responds to the election result, in ways we shall examine below.

Organizing a clear general discussion of policies and issues and attracting individual votes are both difficult. In the next chapter, we will see more exactly how a framework for discussion is provided by the parties and how this leads to the evolution of a majority preference and its implementation by legislatures and governments.

End-summary

This chapter has focused on the need for collective action and for states to promote and deliver it in the shape of policies. In particular, the discussion shows the following:

- Many problems facing us can be solved only by individuals acting together.
- When they do undertake such 'collective action', they tend to produce 'public goods' like clean air and security, which nobody can be excluded from using.
- As a result, some individuals (free-riders) may refuse to help or pay for them as they will get them anyway without costs or effort.

- Their opt-out could prevent the service from being delivered at all.
- To ensure that it *is* delivered, the state government and administration have to get everyone to help or pay, coercing them, if necessary, through the courts, police and prisons.
- The easiest way to undertake state action is to collect taxes, then decide on what tax-supported collective action is needed.
- These decisions ('policies') are best made in democracies by collective discussion so that everybody's interests are considered.
- Such decisions are rendered manageable by political parties putting forward alternative policy packages for the next four to five years in the shape of published election programmes. These platforms or 'manifestos' spell out a medium-term and reasonably comprehensive action plan which the party will seek to promote if it participates in government.
- Electors then vote for their preferred party in the general election, in this way advancing its prospects of government participation and of its policies being implemented – as we shall see in the next chapter.

Systematic working assumptions coming into this discussion

These points boil down to three more general propositions which link up with the ones at the end of the Introduction to form part of the general summary presented in Chapters 8 and 19. They are numbered in the order they appear there – after Propositions 1 and 2 in the Introduction which talked about states:

3   Public goods and services are those provided universally so that no one can be individually charged for them or excluded from benefiting.

4   Only states can guarantee the provision of public goods and services through their unique ability to finance them by taxes and other means.

5   Government decisions about what public goods and services to provide and how to provide them are recorded as state laws and policies to guide the actions of the state and other bodies and the behaviour of individual citizens.

Sources and resources

A good review from a political perspective is:

K. Morrels (2009) Governance and the Public Good. *Public Administration*, 87(3), pp. 538–556.
Wikipedia provides an updated and ongoing discussion of public goods at https://wikipedia.org/wiki/publicgood

Suggestions for class papers

1   Can public goods be provided only by states? Why or why not?
2   Why do some states provide more public goods than others?
3   Are some goods inherently public by nature and others private? Why or why not?
4   What is the difference (if any) between acting for 'the public good' and providing public goods?
5   How far is competition between individuals for goods in the private sphere replaced by competition between groups for goods in the public sphere?

Suggestions for class projects

1   Analyse the manifesto data set (Tables 6.3 and 6.4) to establish how much political parties aim at providing actual public goods and concrete services as opposed to regulating other bodies?
2   How much do different types of government activity vary over time in your country? How can the variation you discover be explained?
3   To what extent do governments in different countries do different things? What explanations for their differences emerge from your analysis?

Chapter 3

How popular preferences develop

Chapter overview

This chapter directly tackles the central question for democracy: how can we get the government to pursue the policies people want? This is all the more difficult because ordinary citizens may not have clear ideas about what they *do* want in the public sphere, or even on what general problems they wish to be tackled first.

Parties and **governments** help out here by 'framing' preferences – that is, identifying problems and proposing priorities and strategies to which citizens can react – first by voting for a party on general grounds in an election and then by supporting or opposing specific government proposals made between elections. The way citizen preferences form and the way policies are suggested and implemented by parties and governments are thus closely linked. The paradox is that parties have relatively extreme views on policy but are still supposed to act in government in ways congenial to the majority of citizens, whose views are less extreme.

Our discussion here covers the election and inter-election processes which ensure that long-term policy evolves in line with citizen preferences. This is mainly secured by party alternation in government. Major shifts in both **policy** and preferences can occur if parties do not alternate much.

The chapter ends by considering the consequences of these processes for the 'necessary connection' between preferences and policy that democracy seeks to make. The specific topics covered by this chapter are as follows:

- Distinguishing between party and government policy 'targets' and the current policy actually being implemented.
- 'Policy inertia' – slowness in changing actual implemented policy in line with government targets for it.
- How popular preferences are framed by party and government policy proposals.
- Expressing policy preferences through general election voting.
- Government and policy '**mandates**'.
- Change and stability in governments and their consequences.

Parties

Organizations which run blocs of candidates for public office on the basis of a policy programme and organize them to support it on a continuing basis.

Governments

The body that ultimately controls the activities that go on its territory.

Policy

Government decisions about what it will do (or allow others to do) and how.

Mandate

Both an authorization and a requirement for the government to ensure that something gets done.

How do electors (helped by parties) decide what they want?

Parties, elections and government change

Parties are the main carriers of policies into government. They only get into government in the first place if they persuade sufficient numbers of citizens to vote for them – and by extension for their policies. So governments – whether they are formed by one party or by several (coalitions) – can already claim some popular support for what they try to do.

Governments have stronger popular support if they are formed by a single party which gets a majority (50% + 1) of votes. If one party gets substantially more votes than any other – that is, is the undisputed plurality party – it can also claim strong support for its **policy targets** and can then act like a majority party. This is particularly the case if the **election rules** give the popular plurality party a majority of support in the legislature. Where they do not, the plurality party and its targets take the lead in a government formed of two or more parties (a coalition), where it may have to agree to compromise on policies with its partners.

Policy targets

What governments want policy to be, as opposed to the policies currently implemented.

Election rules

Stipulate how vote winners are to be identified.

Government targets and actual policy

Elections normally change the party composition of governments since people often feel negatively affected by some of the things the current government has done since the last election and vote against it – a reaction termed 'the costs of governing'. This regularly reduces popular support for the governing parties by over 2% of their previous votes on average. That in turn may result in an opposition party getting the majority or plurality in the next general election or in new parties having to be brought into an existing coalition to boost support. They will then negotiate changes in policy. All this means that government policy targets will usually change after an election – often from one policy position to its opposite.

However, the government's targets for policy are not exactly the same as those that the state administration and bureaucracy are actually enforcing during their period in office. This is because of the barriers and constraints on policy change that we noted in the last chapter (**policy inertia**). These drastically limit the speed at which existing policy can be altered. So existing policies are generally only halfway modified in line with a target before the target itself changes, due to an election and the change of government which it brings. Policy is now modified in another – often an opposite – direction, which may slowly bring it closer to the policy in place before the last government took over.

Policy inertia

Slowness in changing the policies currently applied in line with government targets.

Slow change and frequent reversals of targets thus keep the actual policy which is being implemented closer to the previous state of affairs than the current government would prefer it to be. This suits many citizens and electors who prefer to stick with the way things are – the status quo – even if they do not particularly benefit from it. They feel that any change will probably make life more difficult for them.

Because of the gap between policy targets and the policy being implemented on the ground, actual policy thus falls between the different parties' targets for it and is closer than any of these to electoral aspirations. Election and government alternation thus bring popular preferences and real policy closer together, preventing too much change in one direction or another. This meets the democratic requirement for a 'necessary connection' between the two, as we detail below.

Inter-election framing of policy preferences

Framing

Defining the possible courses of action to be considered on an issue.

The connection between preferences and policy is reinforced between elections by the negative reactions which specific government proposals for change encounter once they start to stimulate popular responses. We explain this reaction below (Figure 7.2). Our discussion starts from the need for popular preferences to have some context within which they can be specified and expressed. These are provided at a general or 'macro' level by the different policy priorities that parties put forward at general elections. At the more detailed level of policymaking between elections, government attempts to implement their priorities provide a more specific frame for popular reactions.

Difficulties of forming preferences

Asking electors to decide on what policies they want is the first step in making collective, democratic decisions. It is not at all easy, however. Ordinary citizens, who may not be particularly well-educated or experts, are asked to choose between policies such as going to war in Afghanistan or Syria or relying on less extreme diplomatic measures. On the domestic or 'internal' side, they might be required to decide whether to provide state support for healthcare as opposed to taking out private insurance for it. Citizens are neither diplomats nor doctors, so how do they decide?

It is much easier when people are acting as consumers, choosing whether to use their money to buy a refrigerator or washing machine, or food or clothing in a supermarket. In these cases, they have personal experience and immediate performance to guide their decisions. So economists can assume that consumers are at least reasonably informed about the choices they make – even if these are often deflected and distorted by influences from the supply side like availability (who thought of buying tablets before they were made?) – or advertising, which usually aims at making you buy more of the available goods than you strictly need.

Public policy debate is mostly concerned with advertising intangible policies, which may cause unanticipated and often unforeseen consequences far in the future. No wonder many citizens prefer the current situation to unknown alternatives when they are given a straight choice. At least they know about it, and for most it is not intolerable.

Party framing of public decisions: an overview

The difficulties of linking up what you want immediately, for yourself and your family, with the public policies on offer are illustrated in Figure 3.1.

The central point this makes is that citizens need help in making the translation between the perfectly clear private aspirations they have for themselves and their family – centring on good service delivery and personal security (Box 1) – and the public alternatives on offer (Box 2). Help is provided by the political parties – directly, when they offer choices between general policy priorities in general elections (Box 3), and indirectly, when the governments they form make specific policy proposals for change between elections (Box 7) and implement them (Box 8). Both their election and inter-election proposals frame citizen preferences – that is, present them with reasonably clear actions on policy, which they can agree or disagree with. This enables the public to express themselves in terms of general policies which would otherwise be difficult for them to do.

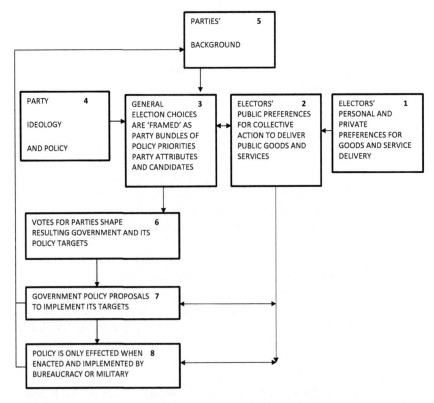

FIGURE 3.1 How electors' preferences are bounded and defined by political parties in general elections and between elections

Briefing 3.1

Notes to Figure 3.1 on party framing of policy decisions

The boxes in Figure 3.1 represent the various choice situations that voters and electors find themselves in. Electors' private preferences (Box 1) are relatively unconstrained politically because they are framed by their personal and family needs and ambitions (mainly for good public service delivery and personal security). Immediately they are expressed in the public domain (Box 2); however, they have to be translated into collective and political alternatives. Electors who go on to vote in general elections then have to relate their preferred courses of action to the policy priorities that parties commit themselves to, among other things (Box 3). These priorities are defined partly by party **ideology** (Box 4) and their history (Box 5). *Electoral* preferences – private and public – have to be sharply distinguished from *voters'* election choices between parties' policy alternatives. The aggregated votes that parties receive in an election (Box 6) are publicly declared and recorded. So they form a record of the last general election, which takes on a life of its own independent of electors' current preferences, giving government parties a 'mandate' for effecting their policy targets and priorities (Box 7). These are operationalized as specific proposals for change in current policies (e.g. for cutting welfare payments by 10%). This then provides a specific context within which electors can formulate a preference for or (more usually) against the specific proposal (Box 2), leading to discussion and often protests and criticisms, which result in it being modified. While the government parties lose support, they continue to be associated with the proposal, which goes into their record (Box 5) and affects evaluations of them and voting in future elections.

Election and inter-election framing

Ideology
A set of assumptions about the world, leading to certain kinds of political action.

There are thus two processes described in the figure through which citizens can express public preferences – a process whereby electors react to the proposals continually being made by governments to alter existing policies in line with their overall programme (Box 7) and an election process through which parties collect votes and form governments – not only based on their policy programme but also through the personal appeal of their candidates and their general record (Boxes 3, 4, 5).

Once governments *are* formed, however, they have to implement their general targets through specific proposals, which often involve moving back to policies in operation before the previous government started changing them. By this time, however, many electors have accepted the existing situation as the status quo, find it quite tolerable and oppose changing it from fear of unknown consequences. Thus, a majority usually opposes specific government proposals.

This 'cycle' of increasing support for the opposition and then decreasing support as it becomes the new government is part of the 'costs of governing' through which parties in government incur a regular decline in votes of around 2% between one election and the next. This vote loss is the major explanation of why parties alternate in government and thus why policies change. We examine these processes in more detail in Chapter 7.

Meanwhile, the different party programmes and government proposals and actions provide a concrete way for people to express agreement or disagreement with policy priorities and their implementation (Figure 3.1: Boxes 3, 7). In other words, government actions and party programmes provide a frame for expressing public preferences in a concrete way, for or against the policies they offer. Without parties, this would be lacking.

Electors and voters: different bases of choice

The cycle of preference formation and expression shown in Figure 3.1 thus starts off with general elections and the choices they involve. Importantly, there are three types of participants involved in electoral decision-making: parties, voters and electors. The terms 'elector' and 'voter' are often used interchangeably, as though there was no real difference between them. But of course there is. Not all electors vote, for a start. The number of people actually voting in elections may vary from 30% to just over 80% of those eligible to do so. Thus, **voters** make up only a part of the body of **citizens** or **electors**.

Voter

An elector who actually votes in the election.

Another crucial difference is that voters have to make different choices from electors when confronted with deciding on what public policies they want. Both start off from their own personal and private preferences, shown as Box 1 in Figure 3.1. These naturally involve their family, work and social situation: the way they live, how much they have to spend and so on. They want to have good schools for their children, less crime, more money, a clean environment – everything that improves their family and personal situation. The more policy decisions move on to a general level and away from specific decisions about one's own family and circumstances, however, the harder it is to decide what their personal consequences will be.

Citizen

A person with political rights inside a state.

Elector

A citizen registered to vote in state elections.

As the figure illustrates, individuals do not come straight to a decision on what public policy they support. Indeed, they may always be a bit undecided about the course of action they really prefer and switch views, depending on how the question is put to them or on what aspect of an issue comes to mind when they answer. There is a difficult transition to make from their personal preference for better education, more money and less crime, for example (Box 1), to a general public preference about what policy government should adopt (e.g. a police officer attached to each school to improve discipline, as opposed to more money for teaching). Opinions might well differ on which is a better policy for schools even if individuals share the same private preference for better education in general.

Most members of the public do not volunteer their views on such matters spontaneously, either because they have not heard or thought much about them or find it difficult to relate them to their everyday life. The opinions we hear reported usually come from opinion polls, in which a more or less representative sample of electors are contacted and asked various questions (often covering a wide range of matters besides politics). Thus, electors' answers are more or less framed by the pollsters – that is, they are asked to respond to specific questions about current issues, often being presented with different positions on an issue ('for' or 'against' spending more money on schools, for example). Sometimes they may be asked to put themselves on a five-point or ten-point scale between fully agreeing and disagreeing with a proposal. More rarely they may be asked an 'open' question, such as 'What do you think is the most important problem facing the country?' where they can respond more freely but still within the limits of the question. Electors' opinions, therefore, are rarely spontaneous, as when people phone in with a ready formed opinion on a radio show. In the case of surveys, electors may never have considered the issue before. Framing the discussion for electors by making them answer a questionnaire runs the risk that the questions and answers may be biased – that is, designed to push them towards certain kinds of answers. Most polls make their framing of the discussion as neutral as possible since their own success depends heavily on a reputation for honesty and reliability. Polls also have the advantage of covering a wide cross section of electors, not the particular kind of person who voluntarily participates in public discussions. Such a person is generally not typical of the general public.

The framing provided by poll questions actually helps ordinary people express themselves by focusing their mind on specific topics. In a similar way, people who have never really considered particular problems may well form an opinion for and against various lines of action in response to government proposals. For example, people who have always taken it for granted that they can take their children walking in a nearby wood may react violently against government plans to sell off woodland. The government proposal provides a frame in two ways: stimulating them to develop an opinion in the first place and relating their private preference to public policy by opposing the proposal – just as a pollster's questionnaire does when it is put to them.

Electoral opinions and preferences are therefore rarely spontaneous and self-generating. Rather, they come out of an interaction between the individual's predispositions and the stimulus provided by polls, parties, governments or other agencies.

General elections

Regular events where most of the adult population choose between competing party candidates.

In **general elections**, however, voters can express their preferences only by voting for candidates of one of the parties – out of the two to six which have a credible chance of taking the presidency or being in parliament. In many cases, there is a gap between the party policies available (boost spending on education, cut government spending) and voters' private preferences (better schools, less crime) with no guarantee that simply spending more will improve the service. Perhaps better organization is required? There is a party to argue each case. But how should voters choose between them? Perhaps one decides on the basis of which party actually supplied the better service last time it was in government or of the candidates available now and their reputation for competence.

Inconsistency between issue preferences – another problem for policy voting!

As Figure 3.1 shows, it is difficult for electors and voters to make a connection between their private preference and public policy proposals even in regard to one area (what exactly to do to improve the quality of education, for example). Linking preferences and public policy is made even more difficult, however, because a policy preferred by a majority in one area may have implications for the policy preferred in another area. The most obvious inconsistency is where a majority wants more to be spent on education but also wants less government spending in general. Educational improvements have to be paid for, and the most obvious way is through raising taxes – which is generally unpopular. The majority preferences seem to be inconsistent here and do not add up to a clear message about what governments should do. Whichever line they follow (cutting taxes and education or raising taxes to spend more on education) is inconsistent with the overall majority preference for cutting taxes *and* spending more in areas of concern.

Governments and parties often try to resolve the problem by promising to press ahead with other policies in other areas. A favourite is 'growing the economy', so increased money coming into the government will let them both cut the rate of tax *and* allow more spending on education! In practice they often borrow or print more money to do this. Citizens are thus not necessarily more inconsistent than governments in seeing less taxes and more spending as compatible. But it does create difficulties in forming a clear overall majority preference which governments can then respond to.

Thus, when electors come to vote, they cannot act on their public preferences – let alone their private ones – directly. Instead, they have to choose between party 'bundles' of policies, which may include spending more money on the police but also cutting other services, such as education, to pay for this. How this policy target is then related to having a police officer attached to every school and better education in general is problematic even for expert policy analysts.

Simplifying election decisions

As a result, voters often give up on any detailed assessment of the issues at stake in an election or of their consequences. Instead, they turn to 'decision aids' or shortcuts – means of assessing likely issue effects without going into much detail about them. They may, for example, see all issues in terms of a general opposition between progressive forces and self-interested ones and hence vote for one party and its policy programme because it has a progressive record (or alternatively a history of defending certain interests). These are the background factors in Box 5 of Figure 3.1. An alternative – given the difficulty of figuring out long-term effects – might be to abandon any concern with the issues and choose a party because it seems more united and competent in government or because the local candidate has more experience in education.

This raises the possibility that when people vote in general elections, they may not have policy or political issues in mind at all, even though the outcome will determine – for the next three to five years at any rate – what government policy will be. The fact that policies, through the choice of a party to vote for, may be decided on non-policy grounds seems at first blush to subvert the democratic ideal of making a 'necessary connection' between popular preferences for policy and the actual policy that government implements. We will see later that various factors operate – particularly over the medium to long term – to bring them together again. But certainly, there may be little correspondence in the short term between popular preferences and government targets. This stems partly from the difficulties facing voters who want to make up their minds on the issues alone.

General elections are 'general'

These difficulties do not arise wholly from the complexity of the issues themselves and voters' conceptual limitations in confronting them. In large part, they stem from the fact that most democracies bring electors into the decision process only once every three to five years, at a general election. This election then decides everything, from which policies are to be chosen to which candidates are to sit in the legislature and which party or parties are to form the government. It is no wonder that many voters give up on issues and policies and just choose parties based on which potential leadership team is best suited to govern in the current situation (which may involve wars, economic crisis, corruption or scandals). Even though these other factors got them elected, however, the government will still claim its policies have been endorsed by the people and go on to try to implement them.

General elections – in the short term at any rate – are thus an imperfect way of ensuring that governments do what electors want. We can contrast the situation that general elections create for voters with policy elections (referendums), where electors are asked to vote for or against some policy decision, such as staying in or out of the EU. Here voting is clearly focused on policy rather than personalities or government – and it directly links voters' preferences on the matter to what the state should do. Most contemporary democracies, however, decide most policy through general elections, not referendums, and some do not hold referendums at all.

The contrast between general elections and policy-based elections provides a first example of the tremendous influence that rules and procedures have on outcomes. Rules are supposed to be impartial and unbiased. But the whole course of policy might be changed if one set of rules were substituted for another (a series of referendums on the main issues and policies rather than a general election deciding on all of these, along with the choice of government, for example). So important are institutional rules in shaping policy outcomes that we focus on them in Part II.

When expressing their preferences in reply to survey questions, electors are in a choice situation rather like that created by policy elections. Surveys and polls ask them to record their opinions for or against a particular policy proposal, just as they are asked to do in a referendum. They do not have to evaluate parties, candidates and governments at the same time. Voters in the general-election situation are, on the other hand, required to do all these things. It is the different situation within which they must record their opinion which primarily distinguishes voters from electors, even though they are also composed of different, if overlapping, sets of people.

Voters translate all these considerations into a final vote (Box 6 in Figure 3.1), with the aid of 'shortcuts' such as the party record (Box 5) and ideology (Box 4). The distribution of votes between the parties then determines (if one gets a majority) or influences (if there is no clear majority) which party or parties will form the government and what they will do there (Boxes 7 and 8).

Voting and the 'mandate'

In this way, the actual vote distribution (the percentages of votes received by each of the parties) takes on a life of its own, independently of the motives of the individuals who actually cast the votes. Not only does it shape the government, but parties also claim that it gives an endorsement to their policy targets, which they are now authorized by the people to pursue in government. In constitutional terms, they have both a 'government mandate' and a 'policy mandate' which they are free to effect over the next three to five years.

Briefing 3.3

Government and policy mandates

A mandate both authorizes and obliges a party to do the things it has previously said it would do (or at least see that they get done). A government mandate is broader than a policy one in that it authorizes and obliges the party with a majority or plurality after the election to form and run a government, which involves deciding many policies.

A policy mandate is more focused and specialized. It authorizes and obliges parties to implement (or see implemented) the policies that they said in their election programme they would effect if they got into the government. This assumes of course that (1) voters choose between parties based on their policies and (2) the party has enough control of government to push its policies through rather than having to compromise with coalition partners.

Why majority preferences are always between party policy positions and at the 'centre'

We have noted that a majority of electors generally favour the policies being implemented at the moment because they know about them and because any change may bring new costs and risks. This kind of support for existing policies puts them between most party positions, closest to a 'centre' party if there is one. As we have already seen in the Introduction, political parties were all founded by some social or opinion grouping to represent their own point of view and protect their interests. In Chapter 12 (Table 12.1) we shall see how this basic 'ideological' position – stressing issues of interest to its founding group – continues to characterize parties all their life.

However, the electorate as a whole is made up of a number of party support groupings, often with opposing views. One groups' point of view tends to be opposed or balanced by another. Hence, the policy preferred by the electorate as a whole – composed as it is of all these opinion groupings – lies in the middle, between the party positions. If we think of preferences as being distributed along a line between 'opposition' and 'support' for a project or over a space defined by all the party policy positions, we can say that the popular majority position is almost bound to be between them. Thus, if actual government policy alternates between party policy targets, as first one and then another takes control over time, it is likely to be pulled back towards or through the centre after each election change in control. We shall go into this process in more detail after we introduce the ideas underlying 'spatial representations' of policy – that is, policy spaces – in the next chapter. But the general picture is clear enough. In the next section, we go into more detail about the party side of this process, because parties repeatedly introduce new 'targets' for government to pursue.

How far do parties and governments actually represent popular preferences?

The grounds for claiming an 'authorization to govern' are clear enough in the case of a majority party. If more than 50% have voted for it, there can be little doubt about its popularity and support, at least at the time of the election. Given that individuals have mixed motives for voting, there may be more doubt about whether all its policy targets have been equally strongly endorsed. At least, however, they have not actually deterred the majority from voting for that party, and no other party is in a strong position to argue that its policies have better support.

Presidential elections

Elections in which the chief executive is elected directly.

True majority parties with over 50% of votes are, however, rare outside **presidential elections**. Only about 10% of general elections actually produce them. In some cases, a coalition of parties compete in elections with a common programme. If they get a majority, they can fairly claim to have the same authorization or 'mandate' for their programme as a single party.

Parliamentary elections

Elections in which candidates are selected to sit in parliament and choose a government.

Far more common, however, under '**parliamentary**' arrangements are elections where each party has campaigned on its own and none has got 50% of votes. Indeed, the largest may have got no more than 30% or 40%. Even with such low support, certain election rules may still give the largest party a parliamentary majority in terms of seats. If, for example, legislative seats are each tied to a particular district or constituency, these can be awarded to a party candidate who has 1% of the constituency vote more than the candidate's nearest rival. So with three parties competing in the constituency and the distribution of votes being 34–33–33, the first party wins the seat. If this is repeated in a majority of constituencies, the first party will then get more than 50% of the seats in parliament, even with 34% of the vote. This is another example of the effects which rules may exert (Chapter 10).

Other rules, however, award seats in parliament proportionately to party shares of the national vote. In such a case, no party gains a majority – not even of legislative seats. So the question arises in acute form: which party represents the popular majority and is therefore democratically entitled to have its policies taken as reflecting electoral preferences and put into effect over the next four to five years? The obvious candidate is the party with most votes – the 'plurality' party – even though a popular majority might be said to have voted against its policies by choosing its competitors. On the other hand, it could be argued that the largest bloc of voters has chosen this party, so its combined preferences should be respected.

Since lots of votes have not been cast purely on policy grounds but mainly in favour of competence and having a strong and stable government, there is in fact some evidence that if the election were rerun, the plurality party – as the best suited to do this – might indeed get a majority. This strengthens the case for considering it and its policies as the popular choice.

Given that some doubt remains, however, an obvious solution is to compromise and form a joint or coalition government with another party or parties. Compromising across the broad range of policies might even end up pleasing citizens more than if the plurality party had just pursued its own programme, since majority preferences for policy generally fall between those of the parties. Compromising on targets will also tend to make them more like the established policies being pursued at the moment with which electors are happier (because they know more about their actual effects).

Alternating targets for actual policy

A majority or plurality party has received the most public support and can therefore be regarded as authorized by the electorate both to form a government and set its policy targets. Given the extent of non-policy voting and the possible mismatch between party policy and citizen preferences for limited or no change, such governments may introduce new targets which are not generally supported. Indeed, that is a likely possibility. Parties base themselves on particular groups, often with special interests which they follow through in terms of policy. Rarely are these shared by everyone. In fact, they are likely to be opposed by other groups and their party representatives. Party policy is thus likely to go further in one direction or another than most people want. When used to set government policy targets these are also likely to go further than the majority wishes.

How does actual policy come to conform to popular preferences for it in this paradoxical situation where a moderate population is supposed to be represented by more extreme parties? There are in fact three ways in which they can be brought closer:

- The kind of 'thermostatic' reaction discussed above is one way. This is the common situation where the government announces some policy initiative, thus providing a framework within which affected people can react – possibly to an issue they had never thought much about. Generally there is more immediate opposition to government proposals for changing current policies than support for them. This is because the groups most obviously affected are the ones benefiting from current arrangements. The benefits of any change are usually long term and less clear. So there is usually more opposition to any new proposal than support for it, forcing a governmental retreat from its target towards some compromise with current arrangements. In turn, this brings new targets and policies closer to the majority preference for them.
- This kind of compromise and retreat by government from its policy target to something closer to current policy underlines the more general point: that targets and actual policies are not the same. The government inherits an existing set of policies which are being applied by the **bureaucracy**. It may wish to change them, but existing procedures still have to be enforced and applied right up to the point at which legislation is passed or administrative practices changed by the relevant ministry. Popular opposition and **interest group** pressures may all prolong these processes. So even if a target passes through all the necessary stages to get official authorization, it may well start to be implemented only two or three years into the government's term of office.
- Even then, it cannot be put into force all at once. Existing entitlements, such as those to benefit payments, have to be respected (one cannot simply stop existing pension payments even if they will not be paid to new entrants to the scheme). Contractual obligations have to be fulfilled (e.g. a half-built aircraft carrier cannot just be abandoned). Buildings rejected under previous planning law cannot now be suddenly permitted wholesale, without thought for other consequences.

Bureaucracy

A group of government advisers and administrators organized in specialized groups, dealing with particular policy areas.

Interest groups

Organizations that promote policies without running candidates in elections.

All these obstacles slow down the rate of implementing new targets to only about one-tenth of the gap between the target and the actual policy each year. Before the new policy can be fully implemented, a new general election needs to be called and a new government formed. In the likely event that its party composition differs from the old one, its policy targets will change – possibly to ones diametrically opposed to the previous half-implemented schemes. When the new targets start actually being effected two to three years after the election, they will have the effect of pulling policy closer to what it was and closer to popular preferences again.

Change of policy thus depends mostly on changes of government. From Table 3.1 we can see this is quite frequent. Governments often switch between parties with different policy orientations. In most countries, in fact, there is something like a 50/50 chance of government change between 'right-wing' and 'left-wing' parties after every general election – like tossing a coin to decide if the party government and its policies will alter. This is understandable given the variety of policy and non-policy factors that affect election outcomes.

There are thus two dynamic processes at work limiting policy change and ensuring that currently enacted policy keeps fairly close to previously enacted policy and hence to popular preferences. There is a long-term

TABLE 3.1 Government policy alternations in 17 post-war democracies after general elections

Country	N	Proportion of governments standing to the right of centre	Government switches from left to right or vice versa
Australia	16	0.73	3 of 17
Austria	13	0.47	3 of 12
Belgium	15	0.27	5 of 14
Canada	14	0.57	7 of 13
Denmark	19	0.42	8 of 19
Finland	10	0.55	5 of 9
France	10	0.80	4 of 9
Germany	12	0.50	5 of 11
Ireland	14	0.64	7 of 13
Italy	10	0.70	4 of 9
Netherlands	13	0.62	7 of 12
New Zealand	15	0.73	7 of 14
Norway	11	0.45	4 of 10
Sweden	15	0.20	5 of 14
Switzerland	12	0.50	3 of 12
UK	13	0.62	5 of 12
US	11	0.55	4 of 10
Total	223	0.55	--------

Notes: Column 4 of Table 3.1 reports the number of changes in direction from right to left or vice versa, and the total number of opportunities to switch directions after an election, in 17 democracies, from 1945 to 2012. The question is whether the number of switches is significantly greater or less than could be expected in a series of 50/50 chance selections. A large number of switches indicates too many direction changes to be a chance-like outcome, as if nearly every time a left-wing government forms, it would necessarily be followed by a government of the right. A small number of switches indicates too few direction changes for the outcomes to be chance, because they show that a government on the left or right has too much staying power to be something that chance forces would produce. The actual number of switches shown in the table supports the idea that government changes, along with change in their policy orientations, occur largely by chance.

Source: Budge et al. (2012) *Organizing Democratic Choice* (Oxford, OUP), 278

process of change in governments due to general elections. This affects the overall process of policy formation and implementation and ensures that change in them is limited over the long term.

In between elections, the population is likely to react adversely (thermostatically) to government proposals and either block them or force them back towards what is already being done. This continuing inter-election process is linked to the election-by-election process in the sense that the government offends more and more people with its policy proposals and hence loses votes at the election – even if there are a lot of other factors contributing to vote loss as well.

Changing policies and altering policy regimes

Status quo

The situation as it exists.

Policy regimes

The body of established policies being implemented in a particular area, such as welfare or defence, which do not alter much from year to year.

Budgetary allocations

The money given by governments to ministries in different policy areas.

All of this makes democratic politics seem inherently static and immobile in policy terms. Something like the same policy always emerges no matter how hard the relatively extreme parties try to break away from it.

This is generally true but not entirely so. Given time, a government can implement all of its targets even if year-by-year change is slow. The crucial thing is to have enough time in government – 10 to 15 years at least. Government alternation, heavily affected by chance events, allows this to happen – but not very often. There is a high probability of change between general elections. But this also implies that there is a low probability of being in office after two elections and an even lower probability of staying in office after three elections – 10 to 15 years. If the same government continues, it can keep on enforcing its policies even in the teeth of opposition. By doing so, it will eventually end up with its targets being more or less fully effected even though the next election reverses them and initiates a process of government change.

Once a policy change has been effected, the same factors that hindered change in the past can now operate to consolidate it as the new **status quo**. Succeeding governments find the new **policy regime** difficult to change. Citizens – if they have lived with the new policy regime for a while and found it tolerable – start to defend it against any proposed change, just as they did with the old one.

This process fits with the observation that **budgetary allocations** are marked by long periods of stability interspersed with occasional 'punctuations', where relatively rapid and complete change occurs in the allocations to different policy areas. This reflects the changed priorities which a government in its second term can now substantially enforce – and thoroughly consolidate if it manages a third term.

How can governments stay in office that long, given the difficulties we have noted in the way of doing so? However hard a government party tries to maximize its vote, too many things are happening to give it much control over events. Its best chance is that some kind of structural change occurs – either in the world at large with wars or crises, which make it prudent not to change government, or among the opposition parties.

The best thing that can happen for a governing party is if a new party even more opposed to it than the others splits their votes. In a constituency-based electoral system, this could result in delivering many of them – with their legislative seats – to the government. At any rate, it will result in fragmenting and weakening the opposition. This gives the incumbent parties (and particularly the plurality party) more chance to continue in the government and push on with their policy targets.

It is therefore largely chance factors which facilitate policy change. But these give democracies a certain flexibility in adapting to new conditions, which is perhaps necessary to confront a changing world. Parties with their relatively extreme policy targets are really the dynamic forces in this necessary adaptation. Although policy change may be imposed by them at first, it does not necessarily widen the gap between popular preferences and enacted policy for long. Popular preferences are framed in relation to specific contexts, with current policy as a major criterion in evaluating new proposals. The popular tendency to favour the known status quo against unknown consequences of change means that newly effected proposals – if they survive initial opposition – stand a good chance of becoming the eventual popular preferences. The formation of a popular preference is not a wholly independent process but a dynamic interaction which mostly requires parties and governments to take initiatives to which electors and voters can respond. In turn, this means that policies and preferences can mutually adapt rather than one always determining the other. Although policies will ultimately be judged on whether they are tolerable to the majority, the majority forms in reaction to proposed or existing policy and to that extent is influenced by it. In the next chapters, we will examine these interactions more closely by representing them in terms of a **policy space**.

Policy space
One of more lines or 'dimensions' representing policy positions.

End-summary

This chapter has focused on the way electors and voters translate their personal preferences into public ones, and on the role played by opinion polls, parties and governments in providing a context within which they can be framed and developed. In particular, the chapter has emphasized the following:

- We should always consider electors and voters as separate groups. Not only do they consist of different though overlapping bodies of citizens, but they also find themselves in different choice situations when they come to formulate their policy preferences.
- This is partly due to the fact that general elections offer a choice only between party 'bundles' of policies.
- It is also due to voters having to choose between parties in terms of many non-policy criteria – candidates, competence, historical record, crises and scandals.

- This makes it difficult to interpret general-election results as a pure policy mandate. However, the fact that policymaking is an important aspect of government activity means that the party (or parties) given a government mandate can interpret that as a popular authorization to pursue their own policies in government as well.
- The party with the clearest mandate to govern is the one with most votes, the plurality party. In rare cases, the plurality party is the majority party with 50% + 1 of the vote. Where it gets a clear majority, the plurality party can govern on its own and pursue its own policy targets. Where it has a clear lead over rivals, the plurality party can act like the majority. Otherwise, it will go into coalition and modify its own policy targets in line with those of its government partners.
- Whatever targets the government adopts, they will likely encounter strong initial opposition, which contributes to policy inertia in the sense of government 'targets' being translated into effected policy at only a speed of 10%–15% of the current distance between them each year.
- This usually means that parties in government are only about halfway through implementing their policy when they are replaced by another party after a general election. This will reverse targets back to where they were before.
- Citizens are generally happier with compromises which do not change existing policies much. So this alternation of parties in government helps bring policy into line with 'centrist' citizen preferences.
- More radical change can take place, however, when a party dominates or runs government for two or three terms. Over that time period, it can bring policy in any area totally into line with its targets. Both change and stability are thus possible under democratic party government, though relative stability tends to be the norm over time.

Systematic working assumptions coming into this discussion

Following our general practice, we list the general measurement and other assumptions in this chapter, which enter into the overall propositional summary in Chapters 8 and 19. The propositions below are numbered as they are in the overall summary in Chapters 8 and 19.

10 The most extensive sharing (of decisions about policy and who makes it) occurs in democracies, since by definition these have to guarantee that public policies necessarily reflect the preferences of citizens for them.

11 This guarantee is provided by regular and competitive elections of governments and/or policies open to all groups and individuals, where votes reveal citizen preferences and authorize them either indirectly as policymaking governments or directly as state policy.

Empirical

Describing and
explaining how
things are rather
than how they
ought to be.

14 The unifying focus of **empirical** theory and research – extending
from preference formation and expression to policymaking and
implementation – is thus on the extent of policy-preference correspondence and how it is achieved.

15 Popular policy preferences do not usually emerge spontaneously but
rather are formed as reactions to policy proposals put forward by
governments, parties or other political actors.

17 The popular preferences with which public policy must necessarily
correspond in a democracy can be specified sufficiently to form a
basis for public decision-making only if estimated from voting outcomes in free and open elections (or from election-like formatting of
questions in well-conducted surveys).

Sources and resources

Ian Budge, Hans Keman, Michael D. McDonald, and Paul Pennings (2012) *Organizing Democratic Choice* (Oxford, Oxford University Press) Chapter 4 'The
Dynamics of Divergence' pp. 91–110.

Michael D. McDonald, and Ian Budge (2005) *Elections Parties Democracy*
(Oxford, Oxford University Press) Chapter 2 'Mandate Theories' pp. 19–27.

Russell J. Dalton, and Christopher J. Anderson (2011) *Citizens, Context and
Choice: How Context Shapes Citizens' Electoral Choices* (Oxford, Oxford
University Press).

Stuart N. Soroka, and Christopher Wlezien (2010) *Degrees of Democracy* (Cambridge, Cambridge University Press) Chapter 2 'The Thermostatic Model'
pp. 22–42.

Suggestions for class papers

1 What is the 'paradox of democracy'? Can it be solved? How?

2 Could electors ever frame their own preferences? How?

3 Why do electors usually react negatively to government policy proposals? Are there exceptions to this?

Suggestions for class projects

1 Using polling data over an extended time period, check out the
assertion that electors are usually negative about government policy
proposals.

2 How far do governments fulfil their election commitments? Check
this out with manifesto and expenditure statistics (cf. Briefing 16.1).

3 Compare the relative success of long-lived governments compared to
one-term governments in changing policy in line with their targets for it.

Chapter 4

Measuring electoral preferences

Chapter overview

This chapter builds on the general picture of the democratic process presented in Chapter 3, whereby party alternation in government keeps enacted policy relatively close to popular preferences in the centre. Here we go on to look more closely at how issue preferences can be expressed and measured. Together with the measures of party policy discussed in Chapter 6, this look at issue preferences enables us to translate general ideas about their relationship into more exact quantitative and predictive explanations, which we do in Chapter 7.

Polls usually ask how far electors 'strongly agree', 'agree', 'disagree' or 'strongly disagree' with a policy proposal. Such preferences can be represented as a line which records the percentages of electors endorsing the various alternatives. This line (or 'scale' or 'dimension') gives the positions of electors in only 'more' or 'less' terms. However, if respondents are asked to place themselves on a 'ladder' between strongly agree (10) and strongly disagree (1), we can estimate the exact distances between preferences.

Using such distances, we can see if electors put themselves at almost identical positions in replying to questions about different policies. If they do, and these also seem similar in terms of their content (dealing with higher unemployment benefits *and* retirement pensions, for example), then they are probably both reflecting preferences on the same underlying issue of 'social care' and answers can be combined into one 'scale' or 'dimension' which measures overall preferences on 'welfare'.

This idea can be extended to combine large numbers of separate policy proposals into one general policy stance. This is useful in giving an overall summary of individual or party policy positions, even though it misses out on detail as compared to more specific policy measures. It also helps us estimate how voter, elector, party and government policy positions relate to each other and how their relationships change over time.

The most general and useful summary measure is between 'left' and 'right' positions on issues. This distinction has been a central reference point for political analysis and discussion over 200 years. The chapter shows how this great divide of modern policies can be measured and used to trace the government and party alternation which eventually brings public policy into line with popular preferences for it.

The specific topics covered in this chapter are as follows:

- Representing policy preferences 'spatially' along a line.
- Combining preferences in specific policy areas into one overall policy preference.
- Framing policy preferences in left-right terms along a straight line.
- Locating preferences on such a line.
- The importance of the median (middle) position on this line and also more generally.

Locating policy preferences along a line

Surveys (polls)

Where a sample of electors are asked various questions, some on politics.

Framing

Defining the possible actions to be considered on an issue.

The commonest way of getting electors to state their preferences is to ask in a **survey** if they agree or disagree with a policy proposal, thus **framing** the issue for them, which is what happens in real life with government policy proposals. Electors are generally asked if they agree or disagree with a statement such as 'The government should do more to help the unemployed'. In addition, they might be given the option of expressing no opinion. When all the responses have been collected, the percentages endorsing each alternative can be calculated – for example, 15% saying they strongly agree; 20% saying they agree; 15% saying they have no opinion; 30% saying they disagree; and 20% saying that they strongly disagree. These percentages have an 'ordered' relationship with each other, going from strong support for government aid to the unemployed to strong opposition to such a policy – with varying degrees of support and opposition in between. Because positions are fixed in this way, they can be represented on a line going from strong support to strong opposition, shown in Figure 4.1.

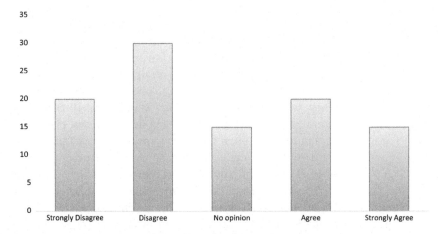

FIGURE 4.1 Representing support or opposition to a policy proposal along a straight line, e.g. 'The government should do more to help the unemployed'

This 'spatial representation' of reactions to the proposal presents them more concisely than if they are just reported in words. It has the disadvantage that we don't know if the distances between positions on the line are all the same or if 'strongly agreeing' and 'agreeing', for example, come closer to each than 'disagreeing' and 'disagreeing strongly'. They are conventionally shown as equal in Figure 4.1, for convenience. But we don't know, in fact, what the distances are, because the way the question has been worded doesn't tell us.

We can get more information about the exact distances separating the various groups of individuals along the line by asking electors where they would put themselves on a 'ladder' divided into 11 equally spaced positions between strongly agree and strongly disagree (Figure 4.2).

When we do this, we can represent the various groupings of electors as being at different positions along the line shown in Figure 4.2. Having interviewed a number of respondents selected as representative of a larger population (e.g. the national electorate), we can then aggregate their expressed preferences (i.e. put them all together) and represent them on the kind of line shown in Figure 4.2. For convenience in comparing these preferences on the proposal with those of other groups of electors, we change the original numbers into percentages so that all add up to a base of 100 (including non-respondents). These percentages can be represented along a line which relates them to each other (people neither agreeing nor disagreeing or giving no opinion are put in the middle). By glancing along the line (the spatial representation), you can see what the balance of opinion is: more people (48%) oppose the idea of government giving more help than support it, and roughly similar numbers (13% at positions

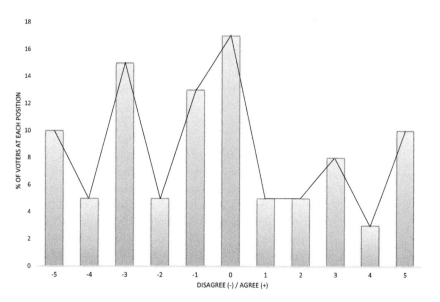

FIGURE 4.2 Representing and measuring preferences on a policy proposal 'spatially' by asking electors to place themselves on a ladder between agree and disagree

Briefing 4.1

From statements of preferences to policy placements

Figures 4.1 and 4.2 show how you can get from a simple survey question about interviewees' feelings of support for or opposition to government policy proposals in various areas to a spatial representation of general preferences on the proposal. The first step shown in Figure 4.1 is to put the government proposal in simple terms and ask the person being interviewed how far they agree with it. Presenting the proposal in this way and offering the interviewee the possibility of expressing strong or moderate agreement with or strong or moderate opposition to it gives people a concrete policy proposal to react to. This provides a context within which they can orientate themselves. In technical language, the question frames the response. So if it had been worded differently, the answer might have been a bit different. In assessing survey and polling data, one always has to be aware that answers to different questions on the proposal could be affected by different wordings rather than the fact that interviewees have different opinions or have changed their minds about them. This is just one source of error in the estimates for which some allowance has to be made, statistically or otherwise.

Counteracting such 'error variation' is the fact that questions about policy are pretty much standardized, and over large numbers of individuals and surveys the opposing biases introduced by different wordings tend to cancel each other out. (See the discussion of error and measures of error in Chapter 16.)

+4 and +5) agree strongly with it as disagree strongly (15%) at -4 and -5. If people were only placed (rank ordered) in terms of strong agreement or disagreement, we would not know, from the way the question was put, whether all these expressions of opinion are equally distanced from each other or not. This could be important, because groups feeling more intensely about their preference could be more active in support or opposition to it.

Self-placements along an actual 'ladder', as shown in Figure 4.2, do reveal the actual distance between groupings, however, and also allow them to express their preferences more exactly. The 'ladder' on which interviewees place themselves is already a 'spatial representation' of their opinions. It is more standardized and suited for general comparisons than simple expressions of agreement/disagreement, as in Figure 4.1. Putting all the individual positions together and changing them into percentages, as in Figure 4.2, also allows us to use real numbers to estimate how distant preferences on different issues are from each other, as we show immediately below.

Since we know that the various points on the ladder are now the same distance from their neighbours, we can give them scores which reflect this, from +5 for strong agreement to -5 for strong disagreement. 'No opinion' comes at 0, in the middle. Because the respondents have all voluntarily placed themselves at these points, we know we are not mis-representing their positions too much in the 'policy space' constituted by the line.

Presenting opinions as numbers in this way is just as concise as rank ordering them in Figure 4.1 but provides more information. For example, we know that the distance between electors placing themselves at the two most positive points on the line (+5 and +4) is half the distance between the most positive (+5) and the third most positive (+3). We can go on to make statements of this kind for all positions. Even more informative, if we knew what party positions on this proposal were (e.g. Party A at +1 and Party B at -1), we could say which was closest to the position taken by most electors. We can be even more precise and say what preference the 'middle' or 'average' elector takes up. This is the neutral position at 0. The middle elector position is the median preference – the median being a Latin word signifying 'middle'. In order to form a majority to support more government help, you need their support. In order to oppose it suc-cessfully, you also need the 17% at 0 on the scale to get majority support. This gives the electors at the middle or median position considerable influ-ence in moving policy towards their own position, as we shall see. For many purposes, it is useful to represent the policy positions in Figure 4.2 by a continuous line rather than by blocks. We can get to a continuous line by joining up the midpoint at the top of the block, as also shown in the figure. This zigzag line can then be smoothed out to form a continu-ous distribution, which is the kind of special representation postulated in many theories. An example of a continuous distribution is given in Fig-ure 12.2 – which also illustrates how party positions can be represented by a vertical line and related to electoral ones.

Relating two 'preference lines' on different policy proposals

Having precise measurements rather than rank orderings also allows us to examine the relationship between different policy proposals. We can do this by using one to define the horizontal side of a graph and the other the vertical, then by representing individual electors as points in the two-di-mensional space created in this way by using joint scores on the lines representing the two original proposals.

In this example, electors' preferences on the two policy proposals are closely related to each other (Figure 4.3). For example, if they strongly disagree with one proposal, they will with some exceptions strongly dis-agree with the other. As both proposals relate to government aid to the disadvantaged groups in society *and* they **correlate** so strongly with each other, one can ask if they are not really both measuring the same underly-ing general preference about government intervention on welfare. In this case, we might put the two measures together to create one unified spatial measure which is easier to use (one measure and line instead of two) and

Correlate

Go up and down together.

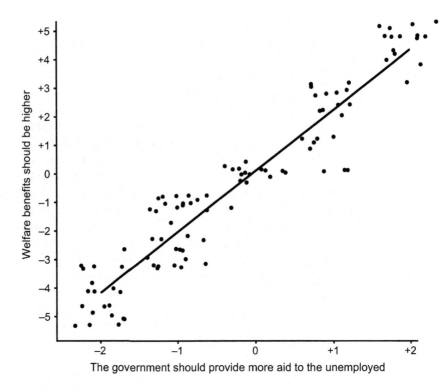

FIGURE 4.3 Relating preferences on two policy proposals to each other

a bit more general – relating to general preferences about government help rather than just the unemployed or benefits. We can see how the two original scales can be put together in Figure 4.4, where the two original dimensions are combined into the best-fitting line between them, on which all electors who responded to the original questions can now be placed because of the correspondence between their positions. In Figure 4.5, the combined scale is shown on its own, with a distribution of preferences in the same form as the one on the original welfare proposal in Figure 4.2. The figure illustrates how the percentages of electors endorsing each position can be represented as a 'distribution' along the new preference line, by vertical 'lines' or 'bars' of various heights corresponding to percentage endorsements of each position. Another alternative is a line joining the top of each bar, from which the percentage at each point can be read off.

This way of representing preferences can also be useful in another way – by relating party proposals on the issue to electors' preferences about it. Thus, if we knew that Party L, for example, placed itself at +4 on the question of government aid (strong support) and Party R placed itself at -3 (quite strong opposition), we can see which would be supported by a majority of electors (Party R). We could also see how support would shift if they made their positions more extreme or more moderate. We shall elaborate on these relationshipswhen we go more deeply into the question of how far policy supply (in terms of party positions on policy proposals) matches demand (expressed by citizen preferences on the proposals). (See

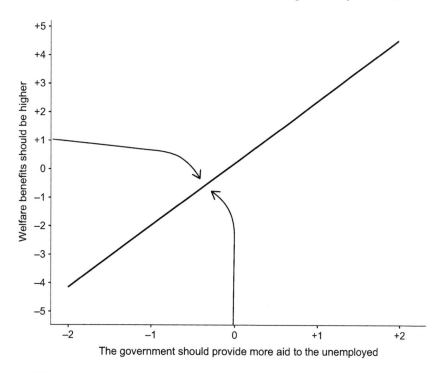

FIGURE 4.4 Collapsing two related scales into a single combined dimension

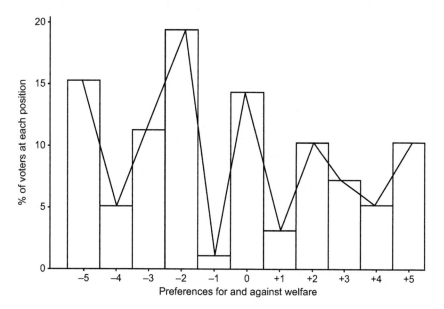

FIGURE 4.5 Distributing electors along a new measure of preferences for and against government extension of welfare provisions

Figure 12.2 for an example of how such 'spatial representations' can be used to relate theoretical ideas to data.)

In practical terms, the two original proposals on welfare and unemployment could be combined by substituting one question for the other or adopting a more general question: how far do you think the government should help groups like old people and the unemployed? It is of course possible to think of even more general questions tapping into even more general preferences about government intervention – for example, how far do you think the government should act directly to help people whenever there is a problem in society? Answers to such a proposal should relate to the more specific ones about helping out on welfare and unemployment. But they cover a range of other topics as well. It is also likely that such preferences would extend out beyond one's own country across the world – for example, how far do you think our government should help out when there is a crisis in some other country? Such preferences might even go beyond concrete aid by one's own government to co-operation between governments – for example, how far do you think our government should get together with others to tackle world problems?

Preferences on specific proposals for the government to help groups at home and abroad might all relate to (correlate with) each other and tap into a general preference for (or opposition to) active and interventionist government. Of course, some people who support welfare at home might not support it abroad. So raising the level of generality of the question and the corresponding line, scale or 'dimension' which represents it will probably result in it being less accurate in characterizing each individual's exact opinions.

However, some loss of detailed accuracy is tolerable as long as it is limited, particularly as it confers other advantages of generalizability and comparability. Instead of asking electors a string of questions about specific policies, we can get their general reaction on government activity as such, which anticipates much of what they would state as a preference on specific areas of action, like welfare.

People do not necessarily conceptualize their preferences in the agree/disagree form favoured by pollsters and surveys. They also think in terms of action priorities. For example, if there is high unemployment, they may consider this is the most important problem facing the country, on which any government should take action. But if there is a huge natural disaster at home or abroad – fire, flood or a power plant explosion – they then substitute these as priorities to be tackled first. In doing so, they are also expressing preferences for action, a bit more indirectly than with direct agree/disagree responses, but probably just as strongly. Framing issues in terms of such priorities for action at a general level is the way political parties typically present their policies to voters at election time (see Chapters 6 and 11).

This is important in influencing popular thinking, because citizens often find it hard to translate their private preferences into stands on current issues (Figure 3.1). They depend on proposals being set out for them by pollsters, governments and parties. Electors' and voters' expressions of preferences are thus rarely spontaneous individual ones. They are the product of an interaction with proposals or priorities set out publicly by parties, pollsters and governments – a process generally referred to as framing preferences. Most citizens need to have concrete possibilities to react to rather than provide their own frame of reference. So political intermediaries perform a necessary task in facilitating popular expressions of opinion – though they may also try to bias them in their own favour, as we shall see.

Citizen self-placements as left or right

To get a general idea of where citizens stand on government policy, pollsters and political parties often find it useful to frame policy opinions in left-right terms and to ask electors in their surveys to place themselves on a ten-point 'ladder' between a strong left position at 1 and a strong right position at 10. Generally the interviewees are simply invited to place themselves at some point between left and right without such positions being explicitly defined for them; it is assumed that the terms are so well known to everybody that electors can make an informed judgement of where they stand between them.

This leaves open the possibility that different individuals may base their self-placements on different conceptions of what left and right are. For many, the left position may be associated with government intervention and high spending on public services and the right with limited government and low taxes. For others, it may be peace and international co-operation

---

Briefing 4.2

Left-right divisions over policy

We will encounter the idea of a general left-right division over policy at many points in this book, as it is used so often at all levels – media, party, pollsters and electors themselves – as a shorthand term for political divisions in all sorts of policy areas. The terms 'left' and 'right' themselves derive from the tendency of radical party representatives wanting social reforms to place themselves on the left side of the legislative chamber and the parties resisting them to place themselves on the right (with the centre in between!). Their physical positioning was then transferred as a descriptive term to the policies they advocated. At the core of those on the 'left' side is faith in the possibility of government intervention making social and economic conditions better. On the right, there is scepticism about this and a corresponding desire to limit intervention and support free enterprise and free choice. The centre also believes in maximizing these but also in government intervention where such freedoms have left families in crisis. Freedom is seen as one of the traditional values which centre parties and (particularly) the right defend and which needs to be safeguarded by force if necessary, at home and abroad. The left believes more strongly in international peace and co-operation. Most (but not all) political party policies (Figure 6.1) can be classified as left, centre or right in these terms and the parties grouped accordingly.

Briefing 4.3

The Eurobarometer series of left-right self-placements

Many surveys from all over the world invite respondents to place themselves along a left-right scale or ladder of the type described in this text. Earlier on, in the 1970s and 1980s, there were many differences in the way the question was framed in different surveys, making comparisons across countries and time difficult and prone to **statistical error**. A growing consciousness of potential error has led to much greater standardization in 'self-placement' questions in recent years.

One annual series has, however, been presented in almost the same format to respondents in many countries over an extended time period. This is based on a question in the annual surveys conducted by the **European Commission** over all member states. It has been consistently asked (every year since 1972) in the context of other, varying questions on administrative, social and economic matters. The question itself has been in almost the same format from year to year. It invites those interviewed to place themselves on a ten-point scale between left (1) and right (10). From 1989 the wording and measure have remained relatively consistent. The question in the 1989 Eurobarometer (31A) is as follows:

In political matters, people talk of 'the left' and 'the right'. How would you place your views on this scale?

[This survey asked the same question for parties]

And, where would you place the political parties (of your country)?

The responses were framed in terms of positions on a 1–10 left-right scale, laid out along the lines of Figure 4.2 (though with slightly different scorings). For the nine countries which made up the European Economic Community in 1973, when the series started, we have self-placements from 1973 to 2018. For later members, the series goes from the date they joined the EU (or slightly before) to the present.

The continuity and uniformity of its format, along with its wide extension over time and space, render the Eurobarometer series the most widely used measure of left-right popular preferences. However, results from using it do not differ much from other series that have been constructed for the US and countries outside Europe. All show a strong tendency for the majority national preferences to fall in the centre of the scale, broadly between 5 and 6.

For more information on accessing the Eurobarometer data sets, refer to www.gesis.org/eurobarometer-data-service/search-data-access/eb-trends-trend-files/. For more general information, refer to http://ec.europa.eu/commfrontoffice/publicopinion/index.cfm.

Statistical error
The probability of being wrong.

European Commission
The bureaucracy of the European Union (EU).

---

versus military alliances and nuclear deterrent. Or it may be some combination of these as represented by the election programmes of the different political parties. Certainly, the parties play an important role in framing these choices for electors. In Chapter 6, we look at how they do this.

No general policy measure, however, is going to fit how all individuals think about policies and choose between the political parties' offerings. We will examine some of the problems that this creates. However, there is no doubt that the left-right division is the best overall summary of people's policy views that we can get, over time and over different countries and political parties. Inside each country it also emerges as the main political division. Other policy divisions or 'cleavages' which emerge are peculiar to each country, rendering comparisons of them difficult or impossible to make.

It is also true that the overwhelming majority of electors in every country are able to place themselves in left-right terms on the numerical 'ladders' or scales provided in surveys. This indicates that this particular characterization of policy choices must enter into their thinking at some points – either during general elections, when it is a guide to choosing between competing **political parties**; perhaps when particularly important issues like government spending or war and peace come up; or possibly as a way of cutting through the array of specific policies to be decided when these become too complex and confusing.

It is likely, therefore, that (almost) all the people use the left-right characterization to think about policy some of the time, and some of the people use it all the time. It is unlikely, however, that all of the people use it all of the time. Evidence for this comes from surveys across nine countries asking electors both about their left-right position and their choice of party in the latest national election. Only about a third overall voted for the party closest to them in left-right terms. In some countries, one-half to two-thirds did, but in most only one-fifth to one-third! Of course, as we have noted, voting choices in general elections are affected by many other factors than policy, such as candidates, competence, immediate crises and so on. So a complete equivalence between vote and policy preferences is rarely achieved. Nevertheless, these percentages suggest that the party left-right placements shown in Figure 6.1 are not the whole of the policy story. More precisely put, left-right characterizations may not cover all the ways electors think about policy.

This creates problems for having an overall measure of the popular preference since it cannot be summarized simply as some point between left and right. In turn, this means that there are additional problems for parties and governments in responding to popular preferences if these cannot be concisely and generally characterized in the first place.

Left-right does not therefore capture the whole of electoral policy thinking, as has been heroically assumed for purposes of theorizing and **model building**. But it captures a good deal of it and must always be considered, along with more specific policy measures, in analysing citizen preferences and responses.

The major evidence for the general usefulness of left-right in thinking about policy is the willingness of almost all citizen electors interviewed across the world to place themselves at some point between left and right when confronted by a spatial representation of it as a ladder, scale or '**dimension**' of some kind. They are also willing to locate the national political parties in the same way, at a particular 'left' or 'right' position. Such locations cannot be taken at face value, as the parties' 'true' positions, since there is a tendency for electors to see the party they support (possibly on non-policy grounds) as standing close to their own preferred

Political parties

Organizations which run blocs of candidates for election to public office based on a policy programme and organize them to continuously support it.

Model building

Theories expressed in a form (spatial or numeric) which will allow them to be checked against data.

Dimensions

Lines running between total support for and opposition to a policy on which governments, parties and electors can be placed.

Briefing 4.4

Comparative survey data

For 20 years after survey-based research really got going in the 1950s, projects tended to be conducted by individual researchers in their own countries with only limited reference to each other and often at subnational level. Gradually a common point of reference emerged in the shape of the American National Election Studies and leading questions were taken from these and used in a variety of countries. The increasing importance of cross-national and over-time research (tracing developments over long periods of time) has led to collections of all existing political survey data wherever and whenever obtained and to the standardization of the responses as much as possible, so that they can be used in comparative investigations to generalize about political relationships across time and space. The major collections are:

- CSES (Comparative Study of Election Systems): www.cses.org/
- EES (European Election Studies): http://eeshomepage.net/
- ISSP (Initiative for Science, Society and Policy): www.issp.center/

position. But it does again argue for a widespread popular willingness and ability to use left-right in characterizing policy and party preferences for it.

As we shall see in Chapter 6, these measures of general preference make it possible to assess the extent to which party policy positions (measured independently from their '**manifestos**') reflect elector and voter preferences as measured generally by surveys. Other comparisons also need to be brought in to round out the picture, but correspondence between the left-right positions taken by citizens and parties is certainly the most important one.

Manifestos

The published policy programme of a political party in a general election.

Looking at popular left-right preferences on their own also provides a crucial bit of information. They are predominately centrist: the majority of electors in all the countries place themselves between 4.1 and 6.50 on the Eurobarometer 'ladder' – that is, about halfway between totally left (at 1.0) and totally right (at 10.0). These locations are confirmed when we look at a wider series of self-placements collected from various national surveys by the CSES around 2000.

The distribution of preferences spreads out more towards the left and right extremes in some countries compared with others (Figure 4.6). But the centre position of 5.0 is always the most populous one, where the middle or 'median' elector is found. As noted, the median elector's preference must always be adopted if you want to build up a policy majority for any proposal. So the fact that it is always found around the centre is important as a moderating influence on the policies adopted by governments.

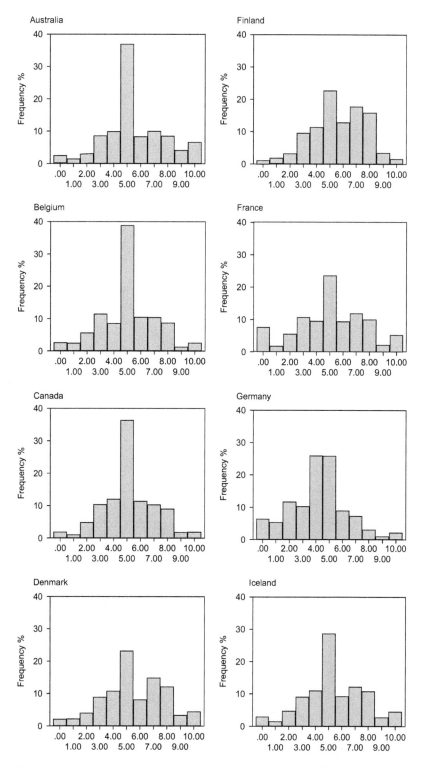

FIGURE 4.6 Distribution of citizen self-placements on a left-right 'ladder', showing their concentration at the centre

Source: Calculated from CSES 2001–2006 Module 2 and EES 2004 (cf. Briefing 4.4)

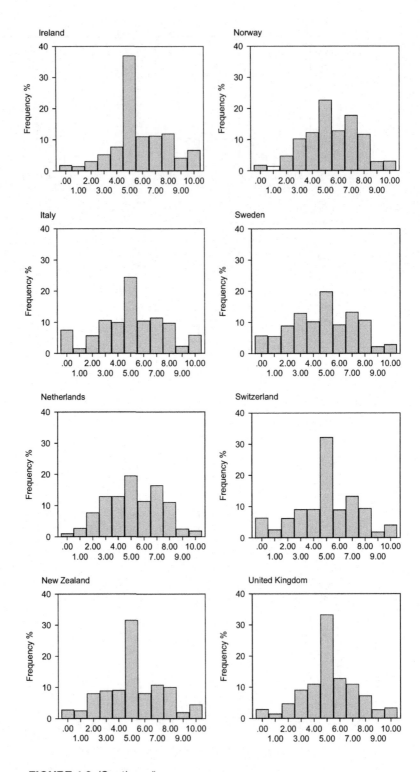

FIGURE 4.6 (Continued)

Briefing 4.5

Policy mood

The evidence for electoral centrism between left and right does not come solely from self-placements. A measure of 'policy mood' has been constructed from all the specific issue questions put more than once to electors in a country over the post–Second World War period (1952–2015). Over four countries, including the US, this puts the median (middle or average) policy position of citizens between 50 and 60 on a left-right scale of 0–100 – again close to the centre.

For this measure, see James A. Stimson (1999) *Public Opinion in America* (Boulder CO, Westview Press).

Briefing 4.6

Is popular centrism guaranteed by free party formation over time?

When we talk about a 'centre' or even about 'moderate' policy views as compared to 'extreme' ones, we are implying that they lie in some space, with a central point and more 'extreme' positions as you move away from it. This is most obvious when policies are represented by a (left-right) line of the type we have been discussing. However, a 'policy space' with a centre area could also be two dimensional, as in Figure 4.3. It could even be multidimensional, with the many lines defining it composed of separate issues. Parties position themselves in such 'policy spaces' by taking up positions on issues that define them, thus in combination marking off a particular area or 'policy segment' of the overall space.

Electors are also positioned in the same general policy space in terms of their issue preferences. However, over the long term, elector preferences also drive the formation of the political parties. In democracies the freedom of all significant opinion groups to form new political parties if established ones do not back their views, means that all preferences are represented in some party's 'bundle' of policies (or in several of them). This implies that electors' choices and preferences between the alternatives on offer are not 'forced' choices in the sense of some alternatives they might prefer being arbitrarily excluded.

Many electors – probably a majority – are members of more than one social group which has given birth to a current party: labour unions, churches, minority ethnic groups, ecologists, environmental movements and so on. They thus find some of their views – not necessarily the same ones – represented by several parties. In spatial representations of their preferences, they thus locate themselves in the central area between the party policy positions. Even some of the committed party supporters may be moderates, sympathetic to other parties whose views they see as overlapping with theirs. This too pulls them towards the centre of the overall 'policy space'.

In this way, democratic party formation, with all views represented by at least one party and most finding some resonance in several, guarantees and explains the finding that most electors are centrist – a finding which extends to the specific issues we examine in the next chapter.

Because political analysts usually concentrate on a single election or a short series of elections, the long-term process of new party formation has generally been overlooked. Electors and voters have usually been seen as simply reacting to the party choices available. In fact, their role is more dynamic than this, extending available choices by creating new political movements and alternatives and in the process guaranteeing a genuine majority centrist preference on most policies.

End-summary

If democracies aim to match policy outcomes to popular preferences for them, we need to establish what these preferences are and how they can be ascertained and if possible measured.

The chapter has focused on these questions, starting from how you can measure individual preferences through survey questions and put them together to decide what the majority preference really is. The way which solves most conceptual and theoretical problems in deciding what the majority supports, and putting its preferences into effect, is to see all policy issues as lying along a left-right line on which the political parties also take up positions. Doing so gives us an important analytic tool with which to sum up the correspondence between policy and preferences. It also reveals how moderate and centrist electoral preferences are in general and where the popular policy median – the middle elector position – is located – in the centre.

Key points to take from the discussion are thus:

- How individual preferences can be measured through responses to survey questions.
- How these can be arranged 'spatially' to identify the majority preference on a policy.
- How policy preferences on related issues can be combined to estimate the overall majority preference in a policy area.
- The general left-right division as a way of summarizing overall preferences for policy.
- The median elector position as a way of representing the majority preference.

Systematic working assumptions coming into this discussion

The discussion here links up most closely with the measurement assumptions in the general overview of systematic political science in Chapters 8 and 19. They are numbered as in the overview, in the order to which they appear among the other systematic assumptions:

6   Policy preferences and their implementation can be classified and measured for over-time and comparative analysis, based on textual, survey, expenditure and other statistical evidence.

7   This allows them to be represented as points in spaces constructed on various measurement assumptions, with a centre and extremes, which can also relate the policy positions of political actors (citizens, voters, governments, parties, etc.) as specified from either data or theory.

8   Such spaces can have varying 'dimensions' and measurements, the most common of which is a straight line running between left and right.

15   Popular policy preferences do not usually emerge spontaneously but rather are formed as reactions to policy proposals put forward by governments, parties or other political actors.

16   The free formation and functioning of such actors is thus essential to the process of estimating the full range of popular preferences.

Sources and resources

David Butler (1996) 'Polls and Elections in Lawrence' Le Duc, Richard G. Niemi, Pippa Norris (eds) *Comparing Democracies: Elections and Voting in Global Perspective* (Thousand Oaks, CA, Sage) Chapter 9 pp. 236–253.

Michael D. McDonald (2012) 'The Nature of Citizen Preferences: Meaningful and Stable?!' in Ian Budge, Hans Keman, Michael D McDonald and Paul Pennings *Organizing Democratic Choice* (Oxford, Oxford University Press) Chapter 8.

Shanto Iyengar (1993) 'Agenda Setting and Beyond: Television News and the Strength of Political Issues' in William H. Riker (ed) *Agenda Formation* (Ann Arbor, University of Michigan Press) pp. 211–226.

Stuart N. Soroka, and Christopher Wlezien (2010) *Degrees of Democracy* (Cambridge, Cambridge University Press) pp. 26–28: 65–78.

Suggestions for class papers

1   Which best reflects the way electors think about policy: specific issue preferences or a general left-right evaluation?

2   Can you really measure issue preferences? Why or why not?

3   What are the general consequences of electors being more moderate than party politicians?

Suggestions for class projects

1   Examine one or more historical accounts of political situations or events, to determine how far they rely on spatial assumptions (e.g. by talking about 'extremes', 'moderates' and 'centrists').

2   Use a country-based series of poll responses (e.g. the Gallup Political Index) to estimate how far preferences on the same political issues vary with question wording (i.e. the framing of the question).

3   How far do measures of 'average' opinion on an issue (i.e. the mean or median preference) remain stable across time while individual responses vary?

Chapter 5

Electors' policy thinking

From a joined-up left-right perspective to issue-by-issue reactions

Chapter overview

In this chapter, we move from the technical details of measuring citizen preferences to a more general assessment of how they think about politics. This affects the kind of policy preferences they have, particularly whether they generate a clear and stable majority preference.

This is not a problem if people think in general left-right terms, as the median position can always be located on the straight line going from left to right and the majority preference has to settle at or near it. (Without the support of the median voter(s), it would not *be* a majority.) As the political parties frame many issues in left-right terms, it is likely that most electors also view politics in this way much of the time, particularly during elections. Equally, however, many will break away at times from the general perspective this provides on politics and think in terms of separate issues and areas – sometimes though not always linking some together. To represent the position of two or three such issues in policy spaces, these must have two or more 'dimensions', which makes for difficulties in finding a median from which to estimate a clear and stable majority preference.

All this makes it difficult for electors to vote on policy and get an unambiguous message through to parties and governments about what they want. In addressing these questions, the following key points emerge:

- Why we can't assume that everyone thinks in left-right terms all the time.
- The consequences of thinking about policy in terms of different issue clusters.
- How this requires a space of two or more 'dimensions' to represent electors' preferences.

- The probability of this generating unclear and shifting majorities on the clusters of issues involved, rendering it unclear how party and government policies can respond to majority preferences.
- The similar consequences of thinking about issues separately, one by one, so that preferences on one issue (e.g. spending on services) may not be consistent with preferences on another (e.g. overall spending).
- A common solution where there are sharp inconsistencies and disagreements of this kind about policies is to stick with current practice (the status quo), which offers a compromise position.
- Getting a clear expression of popular preferences thus depends a great deal on the way preferences are framed and put to citizens and also on what type of policy space we choose to represent them in.

Why we can't rely on left-right as the sole measure of policy preferences

Left-right

Welfare, state intervention and peaceful internationalism on the left and traditional morality, freedom, and internal and external security on the right.

If everyone viewed policy in **left-right** terms all the time, all the problems of matching policy supply to demand could be reduced to the question of whether the government and the popular majority take up the same left-right position. As we have seen, this would be a centrist position around 5.00–6.00 on a 10-point line running from left to right.

Unfortunately, however, such a general matching leaves out of consideration the preferences of those electors who do not think in left-right terms. They may think in them only sometimes and in certain contexts but at other times separate out policy into different issue areas like welfare or defence without linking them up at all. If we ignored such preferences, we would not accurately measure public policy demands, since we might be leaving out sizeable groups of electors. So we have to take such other ways of policy thinking into account even though the problems this creates in the measurement of preferences – and even more in responding to them – are so grave. This rules out voting solely on policy as a way of enforcing popular preferences on government or even as an entirely accurate way of determining what they really are.

Multidimensionality

A policy space that has to be formed by putting together two or more numerical dimensions or lines.

Some of electors' policy thinking is **multidimensional**. Different groupings in the population put together their policy thinking in different ways. The 'left' and 'right' bundles put forward by most parties do not wholly coincide with these, as we shall see. Nor do 'green' policies coincide wholly with left-right preferences or with those of other parties like those focused on regional devolution. The free formation of parties means that all significant opinion groupings have their aspirations met in some party's policy agenda. But the way they are put together by an elector may not be matched in any one party's agenda. Thus, electors may well think their viewpoint is not properly reflected in the choices they get to make or that the parties they vote for do not properly represent them.

A second complicating factor is combinations of issues that can be contradictory and do not fit easily into a simplifying general framework such as left-right. In particular, electors often react to individual policy proposals one by one so a majority may want more generous state benefits combined with less government spending and lower taxes. So who is going to pay for expanded services? We consider both of these problems, along with their consequences for matching policy supply and demand, in this section.

Multidimensionality: clustered preferences may fail to produce a stable majority

Of course, where there is an overwhelming popular agreement on what the government should do on the most important problems facing it, matching policy targets to preferences is relatively easy. Overwhelming agreement on all policy areas is relatively rare, however. Particularly when issue areas are thought about separately and not linked together in the sense of wanting to cut spending on one line of policy to spend more on another, you can get potentially contradictory results (e.g. increasing spending and cutting taxes). Even where some issues are linked up but no overall view is taken of them, popular preferences may take on the shape of those shown in Table 5.1.

In Table 5.1, four clusters of policy thinking characterize an electorate. People who want governments to be proactive, at least on defence and welfare, the two issues shown, constitute 15% of the electorate. This cluster's first preference is for big government all around, with spending high on both defence (D) and social (S) programmes. If they can't get that, they would settle reluctantly for more spending on one of the areas while tolerating cuts in the other. They would least prefer cuts in both.

A more socially progressive grouping (40% of electors) prefer cuts in defence and more spending on social programmes. However, increases

TABLE 5.1 Preference clustering produced by considering two issues together which do not produce a clear or stable majority view

Preference clusters	Preference order			
	1st	*2nd*	*3rd*	*4th*
big government (15%)	↑D ↑S	↑D ↓S	↓D ↑S	↓D ↓S
liberal progressive (40%)	↓D ↑S	↑D ↑S	↓D ↓S	↑D ↓S
conservative (30%)	↑D ↓S	↑D ↑S	↓D ↓S	↓D ↑S
small government (15%)	↓D ↓S	↑D ↓S	↓D ↑S	↑D ↑S

Notes: ↑ D is increasing defence spending. ↓ D is decreasing defence spending. ↑ S is increasing spending on social and welfare programmes. ↓ S is decreasing spending on social and welfare programmes. Combinations of these courses of action are ranked 1st, 2nd, 3rd, 4th in terms of the order in which they are preferred by each cluster of electors.

in both would be an acceptable compromise. If social spending is to be cut, they would prefer defence to be cut too. Least preferred is increasing defence and cutting social spending.

Following classical conservative thinking about security being the most important priority, another group of electors (30% of the total) want increased defence and reduced social spending – but might agree

---

Briefing 5.1

How the different framing of policy issues by parties and governments at different times 'joins up' or 'separates out' policy issues from each other

We shouldn't think that citizens' tendencies to move away from a 'joined up' left-right perspective on policies to thinking about each separately constitute a fault in their political capability. They stem rather from the parties and governments themselves framing issues in different ways at different times. In election campaigns, they tend to link up issues in left-right terms because it is easier to talk in broad and simple terms, to communicate a clear message to electors. In the period between elections, however, specific policies get discussed and reviewed by separate legislative committees ('finance', 'home security' or 'social'). Such policy areas are also handled by separate 'ministries', 'departments' or 'agencies'. In both cases, the focus is shifted from a general perspective on the overall party or government programme to the particular aspects of each policy. Figure 5.1 illustrates how policy discussions shift from being 'linked up' (in spatial terms 'unidimensional') to being considered separately, between the election and inter-election periods.

In considering either clusters of issues or single issues separately, and not linking them up within a unified, probably left-right framework, electors are thus not demonstrating political naivety but following the lead set by parties and governments themselves.

This creates problems in terms of identifying a clear popular majority preference on policy, since there may be different majorities on different issues (e.g. for more social spending but also for cutting the taxes which might be necessary to pay for them). However, we should note the following:

a) Such inconsistencies occur among parties and politicians as well as citizens.
b) They depend very much on the way the question is put and the policy issue framed, which may vary with time or be open to change from the way we choose to present it, both as spatial analysts (cf. Chapter 17) or as practising politicians. A specific example of this is the possibility of improving services without raising individuals' taxes, by tackling tax avoidance by multinational corporations (Chapter 15).

We should bear this in mind as a caution both in this chapter and at many points in this discussion: preferences are to a considerable extent shaped by how we frame and interpret them, which is in itself a matter of technical and political debate.

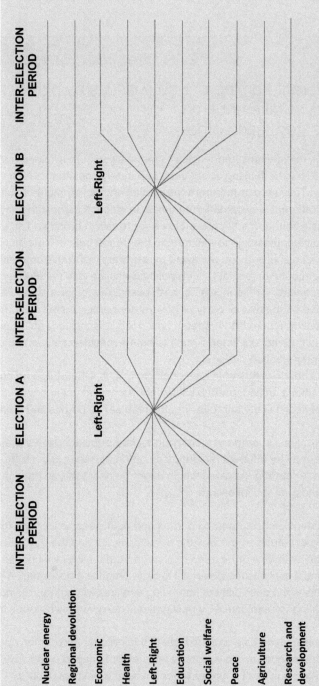

FIGURE 5.1 The dynamics of dimensionality: a (mostly) joined-up view of policies as linked together in an overall programme along one (left-right) dimension is split up into separate areas between elections

to increasing both since that protects defence. Least preferred is cutting defence while increasing social spending.

A last group of electors might pick up another element in current conservative thinking and want to cut the size of government (and its potentiality for interference) by reducing all spending. If pressed, they would prefer to cut social spending rather than defence and least of all want more spending on both.

These are perfectly reasonable policy positions to take. But they do create problems for parties trying to accommodate policies to majority preferences. The basic problem is the absence of any recognizable and stable overall majority, so any policy decision government makes on the interrelated issues is bound to displease some popular majority.

If we (and the government) were able to tackle each policy separately, there would be no problem about meeting majority preferences on each: 55% of the electors want more social spending (liberals and big government), and 55% want lower defence spending (liberals and small government).

However, these electors all think about these two policies together. When they do, no clear majority emerges. The overall preferences are for reduced defence and increased social spending. But this can be beaten by the conservative alternative of more defence and less social spending. The big government grouping cannot have their first preference, so they accept a second best and opt for the conservative line – as does the small government group. So 60% could choose this way.

Furthermore, despite the existence of these two majority positions, there is no stable majority for any of the policy profiles in Table 5.1. All four can be substituted by at least one alternative majority:

- Big government by the liberal alternative.
- Liberals by the conservative alternative.
- Conservatives by the big and small government alternative.
- Small government by big government and liberal.

This helps explain why many electors who think this way feel their preferences are not being wholly met, since their policy cluster loses out as a whole even if many get one of their preferences enacted. The situation might be exacerbated if the issue clustering brings together three or four policy areas, as some electors may do in their thinking. The underlying problem is that no stable clear majority preference emerges from the population. So in trying to match preferences to policies, parties and governments lack even a firm starting point and have to work on a shifting foundation.

Of course, to the extent that electors *do* think in left-right terms, seeing more social spending as necessarily involving cuts in defence (or vice versa), a clear majority can emerge for one of these alternatives ($\downarrow$D$\uparrow$S versus $\uparrow$D$\downarrow$S) over the other. With electors ordering their preferences within these different frameworks, parties might well be inclined to privilege the grouping that thinks like they do, in strict left-right terms. There is little

Briefing 5.2

Representing the majority by the median

The median preference has a special position in policymaking. This is summarized in a well-established theorem (mathematical proof) on the *Power of the Median*. It can be illustrated from Figure 5.2, where policy-motivated electors or politicians prefer any position closer to their own over any position further away, on a left-right or any other one-dimensional line. This puts C – at the middle position in Figure 5.2 – in the most powerful position. Actors on both sides need C in order to form a majority. C (whether individual or party) can thus bargain for a public policy close to their preferred position at the middle – by threatening to join the alternative majority if it is not adopted. Compared to the policy positions of voters on one wing, C's position will be preferred by the people on the other wing. Thus, majority preferences (under the conditions specified) must be at or near the median position at the centre. Unfortunately, as we see from Table 5.1, the existence of a median as a foundation for a stable centrist majority is only guaranteed when preferences spread out along a single line, such as between left and right or on a single issue taken by itself. In a policy space of two or more dimensions, it is not guaranteed. It may in many cases prove to be there, but its presence as the basis for a stable majority cannot be taken for granted.

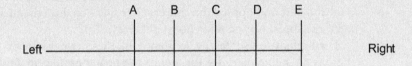

FIGURE 5.2 The dominant position of the median actor, C, in a one-dimensional policy space

Notes: Assuming an even distribution of support for all the positions – which must also in this situation rank policy positions nearer to them over ones further away – C is dominant because it can decide between joining a winning coalition with either AB or with DE. Given this, it can bargain successfully for a policy position close to its own preference to be adopted by any coalition.

evidence, however, for such thinking always being prevalent among all the electorate, as we now show.

Contradictory preferences

Given the problems just described, when some issues are linked together outside a unifying overall framework such as left-right, could the solution lie in electors considering them separately, one by one – as many electors probably do? In Table 5.1 there are clear overall majorities for cutting defence and increasing social spending when each is considered on its own. Separating them out thus reveals a clear majority preference on defence and social spending respectively.

It is likely that quite a lot of electors do think in this way, confronting issues one by one as they attract media attention and are emphasized by the political parties and governments. The advantage is that they each form a single dimension which can run, for example, from strongly favouring spending cuts in a certain policy area to strongly favouring increases, with intermediary points in between. With citizens spread along these ordered alternatives as in Figure 4.2, there is a position at or near to the middle (the 'median') around which a majority can form. This is because all the electors at both extremes of the line will prefer a middle position to the alternatives further out in the other direction and therefore support the median preference, even if it is more moderate than their own preferences would be. Taking issues one by one can therefore produce a series of clear majorities for preferred courses of action. Electors separating out issues in this way would thus add to the stabilizing effects of those thinking in overall left-right terms to give a decisive and clear indication of the majority view.

The snag comes, however, when governments have to put these single-issue expressions of preferences into effect – which they have to do under general constraints, notably within their overall budget. However much revenue they may take in, there are limits to overall spending. Electors who think in terms of separate issues, however, are not worried about long-term co-ordination but react in terms of immediate effects.

This is dramatically illustrated by Table 5.2, which reports citizen preferences – aggregated across 16 democracies around the year 2000, over a range of separate policy areas – for government spending on them (on a line scored from 1 (strongly favour increased spending) to 5 (strongly favour cuts in spending)). Table 5.2 reports the position that the median citizen will take, since that is the position the majority will tend towards. The table shows that the median (majority) position is to favour increases in immediate personal services (health, education, etc.); to favour the existing spending levels in more general services such as defence and culture; but to have overall government spending reduced. This general pattern is found within almost all individual countries.

These majority reactions are of course entirely rational when you separate out the issues and express your immediate preferences on each. They are not necessarily inconsistent from an overall point of view either. You could, for example, cut government spending *and* taxes by borrowing to finance spending in specific areas – or you could print more money or

TABLE 5.2 Median citizen preferences for increased or reduced spending in various policy areas

Environment	Health	Police	Education	Retirement	Defence	Culture and arts	Unemployment benefits	Overall government spending
2	2	2	2	2	3	3	3	4

1 = Strongly favour increase, 2 = Favour increase, 3 = Same level as now, 4 = Favour cuts and 5 = Strongly favour cuts

Source: Calculated from 2006 ISSP survey data from 16 democracies in approximately 2000 (see Briefing 4.4)

benefit from oil discoveries in your territory – or, as Chapter 15 points out, you could tax multinational companies effectively (but not individual citizens). Governments have done all of these things. But such manoeuvres have often worsened the financial situation in the long term, resulting in tax rises and cuts in spending on the very services electors want strengthened.

We can therefore say that the citizen electors approaching policy questions in this way are not inherently irrational – no more at any rate than their parties and governments. But single-issue reactions do create potential contradictions and problems in putting them all into effect together. It is clear that the majority preference on most of the issues, as measured by the median position, is strongly centrist – 2 or 3 on the 5-point scale. Only on cutting overall government spending does it tend to the extreme, at 4. Since that position has such widespread effects on all government programmes, the strong feelings expressed here are influential and have potentially derailing effects on the other issues.

Measuring policy demand from inconsistent and unstable majority preferences

It is only realistic to take into account the different ways democratic citizens react to policy issues rather than arbitrarily assuming they all must think in left-right terms all the time. The more they do that, of course, the more a consistent and stable majority preference will emerge for increased spending balanced by increased taxes or service cuts combined with lower taxes. As we have repeatedly noted, popular preferences do not emerge spontaneously or form in a vacuum. They are reactions to questions set by pollsters or to targets and priorities emanating from governments and parties. So before we can reach final conclusions about their nature and stability, we need to look at how political parties in particular seek to present policy issues, shortcutting some of the difficulties we have examined by presenting them in terms of priorities between left and right. We do this in Chapter 6.

Meanwhile, some important points emerge from this discussion. The first is that there is a lot of 'noise' and potential error involved in measuring popular preferences. Given the problems of '**cycling**' identified in Table 5.1, where a majority for one double-issue alternative can be replaced by another in a repeated vote or where policy contradictions may arise from a focus on single issues such as those in Table 5.2, it is obviously sensible to check out whether popular polls or votes are actually revealing settled preferences for a particular course of action. There might be doubts about this if opinion was divided fairly evenly on questions, with narrow majorities going one way or another. A sensible precaution here would be to require repeated polling or voting to establish whether we had a true majority for a proposal or simply a shifting one. It might also provide a middle ground even for the shifting double-issue clusters of Table 5.1, if one allowed the 'status quo', the current levels of spending, to be included as a possible option as that might be a tolerable compromise for all groupings.

Cycling

Every potential policy majority can be beaten by another.

Problems of this kind are particularly associated with voting on policy in referendums or initiatives when a particular policy proposal is put to the population to be decided. This avoids problems of preference instability in two ways:

a   Restricting choice to two alternatives – leaving things as they are, as opposed to changing them as proposed. This certainly simplifies choices for voters, though in an arbitrary way (ruling out other proposals for change, for example). However, where later popular initiatives are allowed to call for a vote on another form of the proposal, the whole range of alternatives can be considered over time.

b   Holding a *series* of votes on various proposals within the policy area may also allow for change in the majority preferences over time. We need not take preferences as necessarily fixed but as dynamic and changing. This also allows for them adapting to experience and changed circumstances, which would possibly resolve some of the contradictions identified in Table 5.2. Sometimes cuts in government spending might be indicated by, for example, a current financial crisis; sometimes an extension in personal services might take priority. Political parties may take the lead here by emphasizing some priorities and putting them first in electors' minds at a particular point in time.

It must never be forgotten, however, that the way almost all democracies handle decisions over policy is not by voting on them directly but indirectly through a general election where the choices lie between political parties and alternative governments rather than different policies. It is true that policies enter into the choice and may even dominate it in some cases. But they have to compete with other party attractions, such as candidates, record and competence, as well as temporary scandals and crises.

Deciding on policy through party choices in general elections, indirect approach though it is, may counterbalance some of the destabilizing factors inherent in pure policy voting, which we have already considered. A clear majority may emerge for what a party offers, including its policy programme (among other things). Over time, shifting policy majorities may even play a positive role in alternating governments to produce the centrist policies which the electorate favours on a variety of issues. These are all possibilities we consider in the following chapters.

End-summary

If democracies aim to match policy outcomes to popular preferences for them, we have to establish what these are and how they can be ascertained and if possible measured. Chapter 4 considered the technical aspects of constructing scales on which citizens could place themselves in terms of their policy preferences – notably on a left-right scale summarizing a general policy stand over a wide range of issues.

This chapter has demonstrated, however, that when electors think of policies in terms of narrower clusters, or of single-issue proposals, there is no guarantee of finding a settled policy majority for parties and governments to respond to. This makes it difficult to rely on pure policy voting, either on single proposals (**referendums** and initiatives) or as a way of choosing a party government, to link up popular preferences and government policy. By wording proposals appropriately to restrict the courses of action on offer, one could get clear majority decisions. But this might prevent many citizens from expressing their own preferences in the way they actually think about them.

Referendums

Popular votes called by governments or courts to decide a policy proposal (as distinct from an initiative called by a popular petition).

What this discussion has emphasized above all is the importance of the way preference questions or proposals are worded and – following in part from this – the fact that all measurements of preference (including votes) are likely to contain some error, which needs to be estimated and compensated for. We do this in Chapter 6.

The important points to take away from this chapter are thus:

- You must bear in mind the possibility that varying but substantial numbers of electors may think about policies in ways which are outside the unifying left-right framework.
- This may undermine the possibility of finding a stable and clear majority to which governments may respond to in terms of public policy.
- Questions and proposals about policy should therefore be worded in ways which facilitate clear-cut answers and allow a stable majority preference to emerge.
- Even so, you should always be conscious of the possibility of error and make allowances for it (e.g. by estimating its extent).
- The possibility of error in all measures of policy preference ought also to be allowed for in election results.
- Certain forms of policy thinking by electors produce unstable or inconsistent majority preferences over a range of issues.
- However, the tendency of majorities is to endorse a centrist policy position both overall and on separate issue areas.
- Direct popular voting to decide on policy (in referendums and initiatives) generally restricts the alternatives on offer to two so as to eliminate unstable majorities (but restricting or excluding some preferences in the process).
- Most policy choices are settled indirectly, by voting for parties in general elections, where other factors than simply policy influence the outcome. This is a process considered in the next two chapters (Chapters 6 and 7).

Systematic working assumptions coming into this discussion

Following our general practice, we list the general measurement and other assumptions in this chapter which enter into the overall propositional

Proposition

Concise statements of some part of a chain of reasoning.

summary in Chapters 8 and 19. The **propositions** are numbered as they appear there, making it easy to see how the topics covered in the chapter fit into the general political science context:

10   Democracies by definition have to guarantee that public policies necessarily reflect citizen preferences.

15   Popular policy preferences do not usually emerge spontaneously but are formed as reactions to policy proposals put forward by governments, parties or other political actors.

17   The popular preferences with which public policy must necessarily correspond in a democracy can be specified sufficiently to form a basis for public decision-making only if estimated from voting outcomes in free and open elections (or from election-like formatting of questions in well-conducted surveys).

18   However, all political – like other – measurements contain errors (which can nevertheless be estimated and corrected on the basis of various assumptions).

19   This is necessarily true of election votes in their role as measures of popular preferences. The rules and procedures which structure votes (e.g. the order and wording of alternatives being voted on and methods of aggregating individual votes to produce a collective decision) can all distort the final outcomes and have to be allowed for in estimating settled preferences.

Sources and resources

Benjamin Page and Robert Y. Shapiro (1992) *The Rational Public: Fifty Years of Trends in Americans' Policy Preferences* (Chicago, University of Chicago Press).

Ian Budge, Hans Keman, Michael D. McDonald, and Paul Pennings (2012) *Organizing Democratic Choice* (Oxford, Oxford University Press) Chapter 5 pp 113–136.

Stuart N. Soroka and Christopher Wlezien (2010) 'Public Opinion and Policy in Representative Democracy' in *Degrees of Democracy* (Cambridge, Cambridge University Press) Chapter 1 pp. 1–21.

Suggestions for class papers

1   Why is the way citizens think about policy questions important?

2   Why have left-right divisions over general government policy lasted so long?

3   How does bringing time into consideration solve some of the problems of finding a true majority preference on policies?

Suggestions for class projects

1   Analyse post-war polling and survey data to check out the idea that electors see issues in 'joined-up' left-right terms more during election periods than in inter-election periods (cf. Figure 5.1).

2   Use 'open-ended' questions in polls and survey data to see how often electors do consider two or more issues together, as suggested in Table 5.1. When they do, does this produce unstable majorities as indicated?

3   Analyse survey and poll data to determine whether most electors think in 'joined-up' terms most of the time or in terms of separate issue-by-issue proposals.

Chapter 6

Party policy thinking

Framing policy targets and election-based estimates of majority preferences

Chapter overview

Framing
Defining the possible actions to be considered on an issue.

Political parties are central both for focusing and **framing** popular policy preferences and for implementing them in government. To understand these processes better, we have to see how parties present their policies. Understanding this then enables us to measure these in a way which can be related to measures of electoral preferences. This in turn is crucial for estimating how far they match up with each other, as they must do if democratic processes are working – a question we investigate directly, in Chapter 7.

The specific questions we cover in this chapter are thus:

- How parties present their policies – in terms of priorities more than specific proposals for action.
- How this shapes the writing of their election programme (their 'platform' or 'manifesto').
- 'Ideology' and its role in distinguishing parties from each other: grouping them into international 'families' and influencing the policy issues that they take up, particularly in terms of left-right positions.
- Party positions along the left-right 'continuum' and how these can be estimated from emphases in their election programmes.
- 'Mapping' party differences and their movements over time.
- Estimating voter (as distinct from elector) policy preferences from left-right party positions and their votes.
- Limitations of left-right as a complete summary of party and voter policy preferences.

Party priorities: 'framing' policy choices in election campaigns

As noted in Chapter 3, governments often make specific policy proposals (capping certain benefit payments, sending troops to intervene abroad,

Thermostatic reaction

An expression of popular support for or (more often) hostility to government policy proposals.

Parties (political)

Organizations which run blocs of candidates for election to public office based on a policy programme and organize them to continuously support it.

selling off property). As a rule, these provoke immediate, usually hostile, reactions from affected groups. Such a **'thermostatic' reaction** often prompts the government to modify or withdraw the proposal. Wise governments try to anticipate opposition by negotiating an acceptable proposal in advance. In either case, the policy concessions made by government become less disruptive of current arrangements and hence closer to popular preferences for limited change.

Governments have to proceed in this way, setting targets for action, if they are to govern at all. The situation for **parties** fighting an election campaign is different. It is true that the election results will set a general direction for public policy, depending on which party or parties gain votes and form a government. In the election itself, however, the last thing parties want to do is to alienate voters, particularly affected groups who could mobilize their supporters against the party.

One way to avoid such reactions is to concentrate the campaign on candidates and competence to govern. However, parties cannot avoid talking about policy to some extent. Policy is an important aspect of governing, so all parties have to issue written statements ('manifestos', 'platforms') to give some indication of what they will do in government. These constitute guidelines issued in advance of the campaign itself. Parties and their candidates have to stick to them during the election or risk accusations of inconsistency and internal party splits. Programmes also form one of the bases for negotiating with other parties to form a government coalition after the election. Such a government often negotiates a 'coalition agreement' on the various policy targets it agrees to pursue, which is influenced by the various partners' election programmes (see Chapter 13). Even in the case of a single-party government, its manifesto still comes in useful as a policy programme which the party can claim was endorsed by voters. In any case, party leaders are so taken up with all the details of policy and administration that they have no time to draw up alternative plans for governing. So their manifesto with its 'policy targets' forms the only basis they have for co-ordinating the activities of the various ministers and ministries which compose the government.

The various roles that the election programme fulfils require it to be stated at a fairly general level. But there is another consideration to bear in mind. Specific proposals for action (to cap welfare benefits, raise taxes, send troops abroad) are all more likely to provoke opposition than to gain support. This may be unavoidable when parties are in government. But there is no need to stir up feeling on them when seeking to gain, or hold, votes in an election.

How can you say anything significant about policy without tying yourself down to specific proposals? The answer is easy: talk – or better still, hint – at priorities for action without saying too much about what exactly you propose to do about them. Thus, you can talk about the waste of human and other resources involved in unemployment: focus particularly on the personal tragedy of unemployment; recount what your party has done in the past in terms of combating unemployment; and promise to make it a first priority if the party participates in government.

Briefing 6.1

The saliency theory of elections: a predictive success – but only under particular conditions?

In the early 1980s, researchers used ideas about parties stressing the different issue priorities on which voters saw them as better, to make predictions about the overall vote that each would get when 'their' issues were prominent in the election. This involved generalizing about issue effects across the 23 democracies for which there was data. So the research had to make national election issues comparable by classifying them into general 'types', as shown in the first column (Type of Issue) in Table 6.1. Each 'type' was then characterized as favouring/disfavouring left- and right-wing parties (typically socialist, labour, or (social) democrat on the left and conservative, republican and some Christian democrats and (neo-)liberal parties on the right). Statistical analysis showed that a large impact issue produced gains or losses for a party of 3% of the national vote, medium 2% and small 1%. These are shown in Table 6.1.

By seeing what vote parties would get on these assumptions if issue effects were held at zero, a stable basic vote due to non-policy effects could also be estimated for each party. This was (for the first post-war period 1950–1980) much larger than issue effects – typically around 35%–40% of the national vote compared to 1%–5% from issues. However, the issue vote added to or subtracted from the basic vote usually made the crucial difference in terms of legislative seats gained or lost in the election.

TABLE 6.1 Expected magnitude and direction of percentage changes in support associated with each type of election issue, for left-right party competition

Type of issue	Magnitude of changes produced	Direction of net changes in support
1 civil order	large (3%)	+right party – left party
2 constitutional	medium (2%)	+right party – left party
3 foreign relationships	small (1%)	+right party – left party
4 defence	small (1%)	+right party – left party
5 candidate reactions	erratic (1, 2 or 3%)	can favour either right or left dependent on circumstances
6 government record and prospects	erratic (1, 2 or 3%)	can favour either right or left dependent on circumstances
7 moral-religious	large (3%)	+right party – left party
8 ethnic	large (3%)	+right party – left party
9 regional	large (3%)	+right party – left party
10 urban-rural	small (1%)	+right party – left party
11 socioeconomic redistribution	large (3%)	-right party + left party
12 government control and planning	small (1%)	+right party – left party
13 government regulation in favour of individual	small (1%)	+right party – left party
14 initiative and freedom	small (1%)	+right party – left party

The anticipated vote derived from this application of 'saliency theory' could then be compared with actual vote over post-war elections to determine whether it characterized them better than naive predictions (such as saying the votes in the current election would be the same as those in the preceding one). They *were* more successful. More interestingly, in light of what we have been saying about prediction as a way of picking out the best explanations, Table 6.1 was used as a basis for predicting ten elections – usually about three months ahead. In nine out of ten of these cases, the overall outcome was correctly predicted, with the naive predictions correct in seven or eight cases – a narrow lead for the theoretical prediction.

Unfortunately, the increasing **volatility** of voting in most democracies from the 1980s onwards made basic vote more unstable and difficult to separate out from issue effects themselves. So saliency theory, while still influential in interpreting election results and voting patterns, has not been much used subsequently to predict election outcomes in the way described.

For further detail, see Ian Budge and Dennis J. Farlie, *Explaining and Predicting Elections* (London: George Allen and Unwin 1983) http://amzn.eu/gTdPmRk

---

Volatility

instability or changes, usually in voting.

Putting things this way is particularly effective if the party has a good record of tackling unemployment in the past. This lends support to its assurances that it will do something about it, even if it does not say quite what.

Rival parties may not have such a good record in combating unemployment. But they may be renowned for their competence in running past governments and keeping taxes low. They thus have a considerable incentive to emphasize these topics and downplay unemployment as the main problem and priority. Addressing the unemployment question directly, or emphasizing it unduly, really promotes the other party rather than themselves, since it is the one with the positive reputation for getting things done in this area.

Of course, if there is massive unemployment at the time of the election, even the rival parties cannot help mentioning it in their campaign. However, they will still try to frame the debate in terms of their own areas of strength, perhaps by stressing the importance of lower taxation to get the economy going, again emphasizing their party's good record in doing so.

Issue ownership and saliency theory

Because most parties have a history of the policies they have targeted in the past and what they have done in government (see Box 5 in Figure 3.1), they cannot just repudiate it. Instead they build on it, emphasizing past achievements and hinting at what they will do in the future in their area of strength. At the same time, they avoid talking too much about their areas of weakness, where they might have been associated with hard times and policy failures.

Other parties are of course doing the same thing. Each party bases itself on somewhat different social groups to whom its policies and priorities are tailored (see Table 6.2 and Chapter 12). Their talk of successes and failures, policies and priorities is geared to group members and designed to appeal to them. Hence, parties tend to stress different problems and priorities even when they are involved in the same election campaign. Reading through a set of party manifestos, you often feel that they must relate to elections in different years, so radically does their description of the situation and analysis of current problems and priorities differ even when they are competing in the same election!

This situation stems in the first place from the fact that parties feel they 'own' certain issues, in the sense that a majority of electors see the party as best able to tackle them in government. Hence, if these issues become the most important in the current election, the party associated with them is likely to gain votes. It thus tries to emphasize them in its appeals to the electorate – above all in its election programme, the manifesto or platform.

As other parties are emphasizing 'their' issues in *their* manifestos, and doing their best to downplay rival issues, the parties often seem to be talking past one another. But in fact, what they are doing is trying to convince voters that *their* priorities are the important ones – by emphasizing them a lot. Parties therefore compete in policy terms on relative priorities, rather than 'agreeing' and 'disagreeing' on the same issue proposal. The 'saliency theory of elections' states that parties seek to emphasize their own issues as much as possible while playing down their rivals' issues. Other things being equal, the party that succeeds in doing so will gain votes and get into government – though of course many other factors shape voting in general elections, notably candidate appeals, the general state of the economy, foreign wars and scandals, which all the parties have to talk about at some point.

Party campaigning thus tries to simplify general-election decision-making for voters, so they do not have to decide on the merits of each and every specific policy proposal that might be made by a future government. Rather they have the simpler task, based on personal experience, of deciding what problem weighs most heavily on them now – and then choosing the party (or parties) with the best record in tackling it. Between general elections, electors may react to the specific proposals made by the government. But in determining the general policy targets of the next four to five years, voters can make their decision based on problem priorities – which they are better equipped to evaluate from their own experience anyway.

Issue priorities and ideology

Parties do not get associated with particular issues by chance. Priorities are not a haphazard bundle of associations a party has acquired over time. They are usually related to each other in terms of a particular analysis of societal problems and appropriate political remedies for them which

Ideology

A set of assumptions about the world leading to certain kinds of political action.

Ethnic groups

Culturally distinct groups.

Bourgeoisie

A group of financially better-off people.

Middle class

Generally the small employers and professionals.

Working class

Employees and manual workers.

brought groups together to start up their party in the first place. This is illustrated by the fact that most parties are members of some kind of **ideological** family or grouping reflected in its name. Parties term themselves socialist, (social) democrat, liberal, republican, Christian or conservative – all of which signify connections with a particular social group and their needs and view of the world. So parties may have started off by basing themselves on the Catholic Church or other churches (Christian democrats), farmers (agrarians), minority **ethnic** groups (from which a party may take its name – Scottish national party, for example), industrial workers (communists, socialists), the 'middle class' or **'bourgeoisie'** (liberals or conservatives) and so on.

Parties associate themselves with such groups to get their support – and originally to get going as a political organization. During 1850–1950, when most modern parties emerged, their first priority was to organize and secure candidates and finance. These were most easily recruited from an already established group like a workers' or farmers' union or a church. In turn, these groups wanted to influence public policy in favour of their members – often to the extent of founding a party themselves, to make and promote their particular proposals.

A first priority in many cases was getting the right to vote (the 'franchise') for members of their support group. They in turn helped their party get elected into the legislature. To achieve this, the party had to expand beyond its initial base to appeal to broader sections of the population. An important element in doing so was the production of a programme which would attract voters outside the core group. It thus had to base itself on a general analysis of societal problems ending up with general policies for the whole country while still stressing the centrality and importance of its core group concerns to the national well-being.

A good example of this process is the evolution of Catholic parties – concerned at first with the recognition and support of church schools. However, they soon began to call themselves Christian democrats with a comprehensive national programme based on the social encyclicals (theological statements about social problems and how to tackle them) which the popes issued at the end of the nineteenth century. These took as their fundamental principle the support of the Christian family. To survive and flourish, the family had to have its (often small) property respected. At the same time, state intervention and support was necessary in times of hardship, and such measures might override the property rights of richer people. Christian workers too might well have to organize unions and co-operatives to secure a living wage from their employers to support their families.

In many ways, therefore, this message cuts across oppositions between the **middle class** and the **working class** by stressing rights to property, but relative to social needs rather than in absolute terms. In the language of priorities used in Christian parties' manifestos and electoral programmes, they stressed family and traditional values, education within religious traditions, social justice and welfare – all going back to the reasoned arguments and social analysis of the papal encyclicals of the 1890s.

Other parties followed the same general path, as other social groups or opinion groupings recognized that they needed to organize themselves politically to get their opinions and preferences recognized. In the case of the liberal middle class and conservative landowners who already had political representation in parliament, they recognized the need to organize themselves outside parliament to gain support from the new mass electorates. Previously unrepresented groupings also had to do this to get representation and to finance themselves from subscriptions from the membership in return for promoting their interests and opinions. A membership party of this kind was formed by all groups once one of the groupings in society had done so. Others then had to do the same or lose out in the shaping and distribution of **public goods**.

Public good

A service or benefit which has to be provided for everyone.

These developments and their consequences are summarized in Table 6.2 as a predictive theory. It consists of a series of numbered statements or **propositions**.

Proposition 1 summarizes the process we have just been describing, where all significant groupings in a democracy have to either find or create a party to promote their interests in its programme and, through the efforts of its members, get it accepted and implemented. Otherwise, they will lose out or even, in the case of linguistic minorities seeking to have schooling in their own language, disappear altogether.

Propositions

Concise statements of some parts of a chain of reasoning.

Proposition 2 of the theory concerns a main strategy parties employ to promote their supporters' concerns – that is, developing a general ideology to show how these advance the general interest of at least large sections of the society. For example, respecting the rights of the ethnic or religious minority represented by the party can be presented as contributing to more general satisfaction, support and stability of existing states and to a wider and more varied culture within them.

Since most democracies contain groupings divided by class, ethnicity, religion or residence (urban versus rural), the parties that form on each of these social bases are broadly similar; they borrow ideas from each other; and they can thus be grouped cross-nationally into families with similar

---

TABLE 6.2 Developmental-family theory of parties and policy

1. All significant socioeconomic and opinion groupings in society either find an existing party to promote their concerns or develop a new one to do so.
2. Parties develop these core concerns into a general ideology showing how they advance the general interest and their group interest.
3. On this basis, national parties can be grouped cross-nationally into ideological families that can mostly (but not always) be arranged along a left-right line.
4. Party election programmes can be distinguished according to the core concerns they uniquely and continually emphasize, even though they may – in common with other parties – stress other issues more than these in any one election.
5. Party policy is thus generally more extreme than the popular majority would prefer; it reflects the views of its minority core supporters and their policy concerns rather than adapting to the preferences of the overall majority of citizen electors.

names, ideologies and support bases. This is noted in Proposition 3 of the developmental party-family theory.

A consequence of this – which is often overlooked or ignored in political discussions and analyses – is that parties, embedded in a particular ideological family, cannot just abandon it in pursuit of election votes. To do so would endanger both its long-term support and identity. They must in their programmes and proposals always stick to their core concerns, even though they may emphasize other issues more at any one election because of their immediate importance. It follows from Proposition 4, which makes this point, that parties can almost always be placed in a family in terms of the issues which they (in common with other family members in other countries) uniquely emphasize in their programmes.

Another consequence of such an emphasis is noted in Proposition 5 of the predictive theory. Party preferences on 'its' issues will always be more extreme than those of the overall majority in a democracy, which is partly formed by supporters of opposed parties. Median or 'average' citizens are thus likely to find themselves between the parties, near the centre of any section of a **policy space** marked out by their positions.

Policy space

One or more measured lines or 'dimensions' which allow governments, parties and electors to be located in terms of their policy preferences.

This is a long-term consequence of the way parties develop and of their ties with particular groupings in the population, which we build into the alternation theory presented in Chapter 7. A more immediate prediction from the developmental-family theory which can be used to check its validity against actual evidence, is found in Proposition 4. That specifically expects party programmes to be distinguishable in terms of their particular issue concerns – which should in turn permit people to clearly identify their family affiliation. We check this prediction directly in Table 6.6. As it turns out, 80% of individual parties across Europe can be successfully assigned to ideological families based on their characteristic issue concerns.

As a successfully validated predictive theory, this explanation of party development and continuing 'family' concerns – marking off a relatively extreme policy position in respect to other parties and the general population – creates the 'paradox of democracy'. The paradox is that relatively extreme parties are supposed to make policy in line with relatively centrist popular preferences. This paradox forms one of the starting points for the alternation account of democratic representation in Chapter 7. A further contribution which developmental theory makes to explaining democratic representation is stated in Proposition 1. All significant opinion groupings in a democracy have their concerns catered to in some (or several) parties' programmes for action. In spatial terms, this implies that the centrist position taken up by the popular majority vis-à-vis the parties is a genuine reflection of their policy preferences and does not result artificially from excluding some of them from political debate. This is obviously an important consideration in assessing the quality of democratic representation.

On the way to building a full account of democratic processes, we shall examine other contributing theories stated in propositional form, like this one. Meanwhile, we have more to say about parties and their ideological and policy concerns, in the next sections of this chapter.

The ideology of 'left' and 'right'

Karl Marx

Major theorist who saw class conflict as driving politics.

Lenin

A Marxist who created the Soviet Union in Russia.

Capitalists

Employers and others who benefit from an unregulated economy.

Policy dimensions

Lines running between total support for and opposition to a policy proposal.

The best example of a general ideological analysis of national and world problems is to be found in the work of **Karl Marx** and his successors, particularly the updated analysis produced by **Lenin** in his book on *Imperialism* (1916). Following on other progressive writers of around 1900, Lenin saw the nineteenth century system of industrial production as falling into crisis as a result of working-class resistance to wage-cutting and exploitation of labour in the factories. Having successfully ensured that the newly democratic Western states regulated working conditions and provided rudimentary welfare, trade unions and their allied socialist parties had driven up manufacturing costs to the extent that **capitalists** could no longer extract enough profit from them to keep going. Their solution had been increasingly to conquer territories in Africa, America and Asia, where they could successfully exploit the population and bolster their own financial returns.

Socialist and labour parties followed through this analysis in their programmes by stressing the need for social welfare – *and* state intervention to secure it – while extolling peaceful internationalism and respect for the rights of all peoples. These policy positions all had a general appeal, extending beyond the working class as such to underprivileged citizens and altruists throughout the whole population. Their opponents in the so-called bourgeois parties did not directly oppose such appealing priorities. They put their emphases instead on safeguarding freedom – which could be extended from the preservation of individual rights to business privileges. This also implied protecting property and the promotion of traditional values such as hard work and social order.

Such contrasting 'left' and 'right' priorities, and the analyses on which they are based, formed the main democratic division or 'cleavage' of the twentieth century that continues to dominate present-day politics. It connects with so many issues of large-scale social and economic management that it continues to be relevant. This is partly because the problems involved in this confrontation are ones which large-scale industrialized societies continue to face today, particularly the extent of government intervention and taxation in the economy and society.

As a result, much political comment at election time is about the extent to which the parties are 'moderates' or 'extremists' – will move to 'left' or 'right' or 'capture the centre ground' (already occupied by such parties as the Christian democrats with a mix of 'left' and 'right' priorities and some of their own religious traditions). It is as if political parties in stating their priorities took up some position on a line between a pure left and a pure right position and moved from side to side along this at different elections. As we saw in Chapters 3 and 4, electors and voters often describe themselves (or others!) as left or right, and on this basis, they choose to support one party rather than another.

This left-right 'line' or '**policy dimension**' thus forms a concise and useful way for both parties and electors to summarize political discussion and usefully cut through details and complications. It is a common 'spatial' language they can use to communicate with each other and to analyse and describe politics. It bundles together so many issues in the way described above that it gives a general overview of the whole of politics – not just party politics but all the social and economic problems which citizens and governments have to confront as well. It is indeed such a convenient way of describing and representing political reality that analysts use it in all these contexts, as we shall see. Its power as an analytic tool is even greater because most of the main participants in democratic politics – parties, media and citizens – all use it to orientate themselves to what is going on. In the next sections, we shall see how we can use it descriptively, to map popular and party policy positions. Later on, we will draw on it at a theoretical level, to explain relationships between parties, electors, voters and governments.

'Mapping' policies and preferences along the left-right dimension

We have seen how electors, governments and parties can initiate and react to policy at several levels – making specific proposals like increasing benefits, which, however, taps into more general predispositions about the need for government intervention to improve social conditions. We have also seen how even more general predispositions towards privileging certain kinds of social and economic priorities link up targets and preferences across otherwise diverse policy areas. At first sight, these might not seem connected at all. But **ideological** writings have linked them up in convincing ways, using arguments which still resonate – some of which we have summarized.

Ideology
A set of assumptions about the world supporting various kinds of political action.

This is partly because they are embedded in the structure of contemporary parties and **party systems**. To gain political influence, the emerging parties of the late nineteenth century had to justify the claims of their supporting groups – workers, Catholics, farmers, minorities of all kinds – to a wider public. The best way they could do this was to show that they met general needs and were the best way to organize the economy and society. Christian doctrine already did this, but reasoned arguments could also be made by socialists, along the Marxist-Leninist lines that we have indicated (and also by nationalists, liberals, greens and others).

Party system
The number and types of parties operating in a state.

Some existing groups and parties seized on these ideologies to justify their own claims. In other cases, parties were unresponsive to new demands. So adherents convinced by these arguments founded their own party to propagate and effect their priorities (e.g. environmentalists created the greens). Having once built the ideology into the party structure, by officially incorporating it into the party constitution and writing their manifestos and other programmes on its basis, the party could not repudiate it without calling into question its own existence and relevance. Of course, ideologies often rest on long and complicated reasoning, so parties could emphasize and de-emphasize various bits, depending on what best fitted the current situation and their own electoral needs. We trace out such ideological 'movements' in Chapter 12.

The isms of around 1900 – socialism, liberalism, conservatism, nationalism – thus shaped the main modern parties, who in turn provide the main reference points for contemporary political debate. This has framed general issues for voters and electors up to the present day. The ideologies themselves constitute a continuum from left (socialism) through centre (Catholicism and 'social Christianity') to right (conservatism and 'state' nationalism). This can be represented as a line running from left to right along which almost all parties can be placed. Figure 6.1 illustrates how this can be done – more easily for some parties than others, though.

Locating parties from left to right along a line

The line here looks a bit like Figure 4.6 and other figures in Chapter 4 where electors were distributed along a left-right line. There is an important difference, however. The earlier figures are based on the way electors respond to various issue proposals and group those issue proposals together. They are accordingly inductive in nature – that is, inferred from the way people put things together at the time their responses were recorded. Figure 6.1, in contrast, lines up the parties as they relate to the political ideologies they adopted a century ago. In this sense, their positions are said to be a priori or deductively derived, independently of whether people see them that way today.

Of course, it is important whether or not they *do* continue to see them that way; otherwise, their left-right positioning would not be relevant to current politics. That is something we check out below. It is an open or 'empirical' question, however, which we can check with evidence – principally on whether being 'left' or 'right' pushes parties into different kinds of policy decisions in the ways we would expect. The fact that this left-right classification was developed by theorists a century ago does have advantages since it provides a stable context for looking at party policy. We can also use it to provide a fixed framework within which to measure party changes over time. If we simply depended on left-right positions emerging from the groupings that people make now in response to survey questions about how they

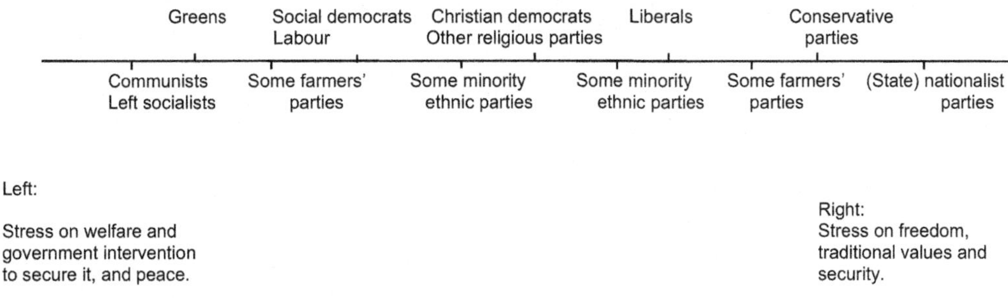

FIGURE 6.1 Locating political parties from left to right along a line

see the parties, there would be no guarantee that it will stay the same. The meaning of left and right would itself change over time (as new issues like climate change got added in to the left) or others fell out from the right (traditional values, for example). Comparing parties in 1950 and 2015, we would then never be sure if we were comparing the same left and right positions.

In contrast, if we base ourselves on the way discussion went in 1900 – and only then – we know, if we compare party positions on this basis, that the measure is the same. Are the arguments of 1900 still relevant to politics in the second millennium, though? There might be some doubt about that since some parties do not fit as neatly within the left-right classification in Figure 6.1 as others. This is the case with farmers' and peasants' (agrarian) parties and particularly with minority ethnic parties. These have a common ideology which stresses the importance of their group's distinctiveness and interests – sometimes to the extent of demanding a state for their own territory independent of the one they are currently in. However, some are passionate about having government intervention to help their group, while others want economic as well as ethnic freedom. The first is a leftist position, while the other is a rightist position. To reflect this difference, minority ethnic parties have been placed at two different points along the line from left to right in Figure 6.1.

However, this failure to uniquely characterize some party families should not be taken as evidence that the left-right classification is less relevant today than it was one hundred years ago. Minority ethnic parties are one of the oldest types of party which exist. Their priorities for autonomy and/or the independence of part of the existing state territory were just as incompatible with a left-right summary of policy one hundred years ago as they are now. It is just that any general classification of policy positions and preferences will not fit with every detailed nuance in electoral and party positions. Nevertheless, if it fits most of them, it can be useful, as we will see. And the ability to place almost all current party families at a definite point on the left-right dimension demonstrates that it is still an illuminating way to characterize parties, even if not entirely perfect. We shall pursue these points below. First, however, we need to see how – and from what – we can measure left-right positions more exactly, across time and across countries, rather than just draw up a general classification, as in Figure 6.1.

Measuring policy priorities from manifestos

Manifestos or platforms

Published policy programmes of a political party in a general election.

We have seen how voter preferences are framed by the policy choices that parties offer in elections. These are set out in their election programmes (often termed '**manifestos**' or '**platforms**'). Few ordinary citizens read these or even see them. However, their contents get reported and endlessly discussed in tweets, on websites, in newspaper articles and on radio and television programmes. These then offer voters a chance to react to the important problems that parties identify and to decide what their own priorities for action are.

As the manifesto texts are the agenda setters which define policy priorities for each election, any 'mapping' of where the parties and voters position themselves has to start with them. We cannot just take them as they stand but rather try to relate and compare them in some way. This involves measuring their policy statements more precisely in terms of exactly scored positions. How do we get from words to numbers in order to do so? It can be done simply by counting the sentences and phrases that the text is made up of and attributing them to one of 56 policy categories which cover the range of possible election topics. These are listed in Table 6.3 under the seven broad headings: External; Freedom and Democracy; Political;

TABLE 6.3 The comprehensive range of policy categories into which manifesto sentences can be assigned and counted

Domain 1: External Relations

101	Foreign Special Relationships: Positive
102	Foreign Special Relationships: Negative
103	Anti-imperialism: Negative
104	Military: Positive
105	Military: Negative
106	Peace: Positive
107	Internationalism: Positive
108	European Community: Positive
109	Internationalism: Negative
110	European Community: Negative

Domain 2: Freedom and Democracy

201	Freedom and Human Rights: Positive
202	Democracy: Positive
203	Constitutionalism: Positive
204	Constitutionalism: Negative

Domain 3: Political System

301	Decentralization: Positive
302	Centralization: Positive
303	Governmental and Administrative Efficiency: Positive
304	Political Corruption
305	Political Authority: Positive

Domain 4: Economy

401	Free Enterprise: Positive
402	Incentives: Positive
403	Market Regulation: Positive
404	Economic Planning: Positive
405	Corporatism: Positive
406	Protectionism: Positive
407	Protectionism: Negative
408	Economic Goals: Positive
409	Keynesian Demand Management: Positive
410	Productivity: Positive
411	Technology and Infrastructure: Positive
412	Controlled Economy: Positive

(*Continued*)

TABLE 6.3 (Continued)

413	Nationalization: Positive
414	Economic Orthodoxy: Positive
415	Marxist Analysis: Positive
416	Anti-growth Economy: Positive
Domain 5: Welfare and Quality of Life	
501	Environmental Protection: Positive
502	Culture: Positive
503	Social Justice: Positive
504	Welfare State: Positive
505	Welfare State: Negative
506	Education: Positive
507	Education: Negative
Domain 6: Fabric of Society	
601	National Way of Life: Positive
602	National Way of Life: Negative
603	Traditional Morality: Positive
604	Traditional Morality: Negative
605	Law and Order: Positive
606	Social Harmony: Positive
607	Multiculturalism: Positive
608	Multiculturalism: Negative
Domain 7: Social Groups	
701	Labour Groups: Positive
702	Labour Groups: Negative
703	Agriculture: Positive
704	Middle-Class and Professional Groups: Positive
705	Minority Groups: Positive
706	Non-Economic Demographic Groups: Positive

Economic; Welfare and Quality of Life; Society; and Social Groups. After counting the number of references made to each in the manifesto, we can compare parties in terms of the extent to which they emphasize each topic – seeing in this way how distinct their policy stands are from each other.

With such a broad range, it is clear that the topics listed in Table 6.3 and the party election programmes whose content they reflect cover most of national and indeed international life. They are indeed like 'five-year plans' for the country involved – the only comprehensive review of the national situation and of what priorities need to be tackled. Only the political parties produce such documents because they are the only bodies whose job it is to form future governments and formulate an appropriate plan of action of what to do nationally over the next four to five years.

Of course, such plans are far from perfect, detailed or comprehensive. Each party takes a highly selective view of the national situation based on its own ideology and is designed to rally its own supporters while putting the blame for problems on the others. It mostly emphasizes those issue areas in which it has an advantage – that is, has a good record and commitments favourably viewed by a majority of potential voters.

Five-year plans

Development programmes listing priorities for the economy and society under a 'controlled' or 'command' economy.

The tendency of parties to emphasize their 'own' issues is illustrated in Table 6.4 which provides a first example of how you can use these measurements to see more exactly how parties behave.

In Table 6.4, parties are grouped into four ideological 'families', including communists and left (or extreme) socialists; more moderate socialists, commonly called social democratic or labour parties; Christian democrats, usually Catholic but sometimes fundamental Protestant; and liberal-conservatives on the right wing. We can check the average percentage of

TABLE 6.4 Mean percentage distribution of manifesto sentences over 56 policy categories within various party families in 24 OECD (the Organization for Economic Cooperation and Development) countries 1945–1998

Party families/categories	Communist/left socialist	Labour/social dem	Christian democrat	Liberal-conservative
Foreign Special Relations +	0.984	1.020	1.295	1.609
Foreign Special Relations -	0.989	0.422	0.208	0.196
Anti-imperialism	1.046	0.375	0.464	0.198
Military +	0.190	1.235	1.478	2.631
Military -	3.375	1.292	0.363	0.273
Peace	2.829	1.499	0.771	0.931
Internationalism +	1.819	2.868	2.439	2.089
European Community +	0.252	1.188	2.636	0.904
Internationalism −	0.890	0.321	0.194	0.402
European Community -	1.166	0.118	0.041	0.081
Freedom and Human Rights	2.184	2.275	3.049	2.614
Democracy	6.024	3.727	3.877	2.445
Constitutionalism +	0.821	0.752	1.275	0.758
Constitutionalism -	0.622	0.404	0.161	0.563
Decentralization	1.153	1.617	3.071	1.978
Centralization	0.089	0.203	0.218	0.226
Gov't-Admin Efficiency	1.292	2.794	3.704	3.583
Political Corruption	5.282	1.100	0.373	1.070
Political Authority	5.282	3.266	1.949	4.335
Free Enterprise	0.124	0.696	2.956	4.556
Incentives	0.953	2.034	3.157	3.991
Market Regulation	2.338	2.402	1.805	1.165
Economic Planning	1.758	1.760	0.975	0.987
Corporatism	0.201	0.439	0.588	0.261
Protectionism +	0.399	0.422	0.106	0.481
Protectionism -	0.092	0.197	0.122	0.458
Economic Goals	2.438	3.876	2.668	3.430
Keynesian Demand	0.230	0.369	0.307	0.296
Productivity	1.657	2.537	1.973	3.312
Infrastructure	2.206	4.432	4.821	4.691
Controlled Economy	2.169	1.532	0.513	0.410
Nationalization	1.894	0.825	0.101	0.096
Economic Orthodoxy	1.017	1.893	2.342	5.391
Marxist Analysis	0.523	0.071	0.001	0.009
Anti-growth Economy	0.182	0.176	0.116	0.029

(*Continued*)

TABLE 6.4 (Continued)

Party families/categories	Communist/left socialist	Labour/social dem	Christian democrat	Liberal-conservative
Environment	2.820	2.745	2.940	2.087
Culture	1.708	2.103	2.871	1.614
Social Justice	6.251	5.716	3.826	2.597
Welfare +	6.556	7.994	6.610	5.428
Welfare -	0.033	0.140	0.382	0.620
Education +	2.880	4.207	3.684	3.438
Education –	0.009	0.038	0.100	0.117
National Way of Life +	0.325	0.661	1.093	1.592
National Way of Life -	0.359	0.072	0.095	0.045
Traditional Morality +	0.330	0.628	4.221	1.454
Traditional Morality -	0.215	0.222	0.106	0.052
Law and Order	0.600	1.130	1.778	2.345
Social Harmony	1.119	1.845	2.105	1.838
Multiculturalism +	0.238	0.384	1.675	0.405
Multiculturalism -	0.075	0.194	0.067	0.133
Labour +	5.744	3.931	1.997	1.830
Labour -	0.058	0.083	0.070	0.472
Agriculture	1.970	3.658	3.396	4.003
Middle Class	0.762	1.102	1.492	1.911
Minority Groups	0.832	0.948	1.090	0.689
Non-economic Groups	3.454	4.224	4.617	3.753
N	182	441	159	249

Notes:

Communist/left socialist parties were drawn from Denmark, Finland, France, Germany, Greece, Iceland, Ireland, Italy, Luxembourg, Japan, Norway, Portugal, Spain and Sweden (14 countries).

Social democratic parties were drawn from all OECD countries with the exception of the US (23 countries).

Christian democratic parties were drawn from Austria, Belgium, France, Germany, Italy, Luxembourg, the Netherlands and Switzerland (eight countries).

Liberal-conservative parties were drawn from Australia, Canada, Denmark, Finland, France, Greece, Iceland, Ireland, Italy, Japan, New Zealand, Norway, Spain, Sweden, the UK and the US (16 countries).

references that these make to the various policy areas over time. The table shows that references to these do vary systematically, with socialists and Christian democrats emphasizing welfare and social justice more than liberal-conservatives and the latter's references concentrating more on freedom, tradition and financial orthodoxy.

Of course, we are not saying that any party can totally ignore the others' issues, since these are also important items on the political agenda often set by external events beyond any single party's control. Parties have to address such issues to some extent to establish their own credibility as a party able to participate in government. However, what saliency theory indicates is that disadvantaged parties will stress such issue areas less while emphasizing 'their' issues more – as in fact does appear in the table.

Summarizing party differences in left-right terms

Keeping track of issues in 56 separate areas – or even seven broad ones – is still a hard task for most ordinary people. Even politicians and commentators find it difficult not to get bogged down in details. One solution suggested earlier is to see the opposing stands and emphases as manifestations of one major underlying division between left and right. Seeing all the specific problems as related in some way forms a shortcut to deciding on all of them at the same time – if only one can place them easily to the left or right along a line like the one shown in Figure 4.5. For both parties and voters, such a framework is provided by the overall narrative deriving ultimately from the writings of Karl Marx, which understand modern developments as driven by the desire of capitalists – industrialists and bankers with their political allies – to find profitable investments. Doing so requires building factories to maximize production and reduce costs. Industrialization of this kind creates an industrial working class whose wages are one of the main costs which need – from the point of view of increasing profits – to be kept down. Concurrent costs such as health, housing and environment are to be off-loaded as far as possible onto the workers themselves, other taxpayers and/or the state. At the same time, taxes are to be kept low because these also take away money from direct investment.

Capitalism is a dynamic system constantly creating new technologies and management systems to drive down costs and maximize returns. So individual factories and firms are combined into ever larger conglomerates which grow into multinational corporations closely linked to banks, which operate at an increasing remove from individuals and even smaller governments – one aspect of a process we now term globalization (see Chapter 15). The main contours of Marx's nineteenth century analyses are still recognizable.

At the same time, concurrent developments have taken place, partly as a consequence of the Marxist analyses linking most social problems to capitalism. These stimulated the formation of mass parties – socialist, communist, social democrat and even greens – to resist capitalist exploitation; and the creation of unions, popular movements and linked parties to take over state control. In government decision-making such parties pushed through policies which improved working conditions, instituted health and welfare schemes of various kinds and incidentally raised taxes and costs on businesses.

As a result, investment at home became less attractive. So to maintain profits, businesses looked abroad for fresh natural resources to exploit, where native populations were less able to protect themselves against exploitation. Where they resisted, they could generally be subdued and taken over by a technologically superior military force, turned into colonies or have compliant governments installed.

In Marxism and its modified variants, like social democracy, we have a comprehensive analysis of domestic and international problems, together with policy proposals for their solution: state intervention to secure welfare and decent living standards at home and support for popular movements, peace and co-operation abroad. This 'leftist' ideology provides a framework and a perspective on practically everything that comes up in politics and the appropriate action to take on all of them.

'Leftist' ideology

An ideology which sees most problems as caused by social inequality and seeks to reduce them by democratic state action.

Of course, the interpretation Marxism provides is not accepted by everyone and is indeed actively opposed by many on the right. They start off by presenting capitalism (or as they would term it, free enterprise) not as a threat but as the route to a better society for all. Its capacity to produce goods and services ever more cheaply benefits consumers, providing expanding employment for everyone and generating the wealth which supports public services. Thus, the whole of the nation benefits from the dynamic economy powered by the entrepreneurs, who should not be hampered by excessive state regulation or taxation. Apart from radicals who want to change the traditional moral values of freedom and opportunity, the main threat to national prosperity is from foreign competitors and subversive elements at home. National unity and internal and external security are essential in confronting these and maintaining everyone's well-being.

Not all parties on the right emphasize these themes equally – liberals generally stress freedom more than security. Christian parties, basing themselves on religious values, place themselves more in the centre, with a focus on the family, the need to give it a firm basis in property rights and a decent standard of living. These may have to be secured by state intervention.

Right, centre and left are thus defined ideologically more by a stress on different desirable goals rather than by a direct confrontation. Even when arguing about the desirability of state intervention, the most obvious point of contrast between them, they are liable to talk in terms of specific interventions in pursuit of desirable ends, like regular inspections to prevent child abuse. Few would oppose this where there have been scandals. Arguments against government intervention often cite businesses having to leave the country because planning regulations stop their expansion. This shapes the way parties write their manifestos. As we have seen, they stress different priorities rather than argue about the same issues – for example, preventing abuses on the one hand and freeing up business initiatives on the other. Electors and voters in turn tend to think in terms of what are the important issues to confront rather than of opposing courses of action on them.

Measuring left-right differences along a single line

Participants in the political debate – media commentators, journalists, politicians and the political parties themselves – all summarize politics in left-right terms, which then frame general perceptions and preferences, as we saw in Chapter 4. By emphasizing different clusters of 'left' and 'right' priorities in their public utterances, all effectively place themselves on a line between the two extremes, depending on how far they stress leftist as opposed to rightist priorities ('welfare' as opposed to 'freedom', for example).

Having already identified the major topics of political debate (Table 6.3) and measured the emphases that parties give them by classifying manifesto sentences into the relevant categories, we can build on these to create a numerical left-right scale – analogous to but more exactly measured than the one in Figure 6.1. All we need to know is which of the topics identified in Table 6.3 belong on the left and which on the right. Once we have identified the relevant clusters, we can add up the percentages of individual manifesto sentences belonging to the clusters on each side. By subtracting the aggregated 'left' percentage from the aggregated 'right' percentage we can get an overall left-right score for each party manifesto. This would run from +100 (all sentences and phrases in a manifesto are right) to –100 (all sentences and phrases are left).

To identify which topics belong on the left and which on the right, we can draw on the narratives reported above, grouping categories like social service expansion, controlled economy and decolonization on the left and support for the military, freedom and traditional morality on the right. The exact range of topics on each side are shown in Table 6.5.

The topics on each side are the ones highlighted in terms of the contrasting ideological narratives given above. Note that the topics *not* listed in Table 6.5 still contribute to the overall left-right score since the percentages added and subtracted are *total* percentages calculated on all the sentences in each manifesto. So if a topic which is neither left nor right is stressed, it pushes the position of the party in that manifesto towards the centre. This seems appropriate as the party is taking up neither extreme left nor extreme right positions.

Another way parties could end up in the centre is by stressing a mixture of left and right topics. There is no reason why parties shouldn't do

TABLE 6.5 Scoring left-right positions on the emphases that party manifestos give to the topic

Right emphases: sum of percentages for		Left emphases: sum of percentages for
Military: positive		Decolonization
Freedom, human rights		Military: negative
Constitutionalism: positive		Peace
Effective authority		Internationalism: positive
Free enterprise		Democracy
Economic incentives	*minus*	Regulate capitalism
Protectionism: negative		Economic planning
Economic orthodoxy		Protectionism: positive
Social services limitation		Controlled economy
National way of life: positive		Nationalization
Traditional morality: positive		Social services: expansion
Law and order		Education: expansion
Social harmony		Labour groups: positive

so. And Christian democrats, as we mentioned, are prone to put together social well-being, public services, *and* traditional values – all to preserve family stability. However, the parties on the left and right founded on and defined by these pure ideologies tend in practice to keep themselves quite distinct from each other by emphasizing their different priorities.

Mean position

The sum of right or left scores that a party has divided by its total number of manifestos.

We can see this by looking at the average or **mean position** that parties have taken up over the post-war period. This distinguishes the parties fairly clearly from each other in terms of a left-right ordering rather similar to the general one in Figure 6.1. The difference here, however, is that we can now measure the precise differences separating parties because each has an exactly measured left-right position.

Using left-right to describe parties and governments more exactly

We can see from Figure 6.2 how different countries differ from each other in terms of their overall ideological leanings. Norway, for example, with practically all its parties left of centre, contrasts with Australia, where two out of three are firmly to the right.

Perhaps an even more interesting use is to trace left-right variations (i.e. movements) over time, within a country. This is important in analysing democratic representation, because it will let us see how far the left-right targets which parties and governments adopt correspond to public preferences as measured by surveys; these can be estimated by electors' left-right self-placements done at the time of the election or more elaborately by their 'policy mood'. However, it is also instructive to see how the parties themselves become more or less ideological over time and how far they agree or disagree at any one time about what the general policy targets should be.

Figure 6.3 shows how the two major American parties have changed positions over the post-war period. The Republicans have always been more to the right than the Democrats but came close to them on the left in the late 1950s. In the 1970s, they made a decisive move to a very right-wing position, which they have more or less held since. The Democrats were consistently on the left until 1992, when they followed the Republicans to the right. They have oscillated more since then between left and right and are often in the centre.

The US's two-party system can be contrasted with Norway's – with the latter generally more to the left and with five to seven parties at various times. This gives the parties more of an opportunity to 'leapfrog' each other at particular elections. However, they still remain fairly distinctive ideologically, as Figure 6.4 shows.

Leapfrog

Changing policy positions with another party.

Not only party positions can be read off from these figures. Provided we know the votes the parties obtained in each election – actually an accessible bit of information – we can say in the case of the US what the policy position of the next government will be. The election winner's candidate

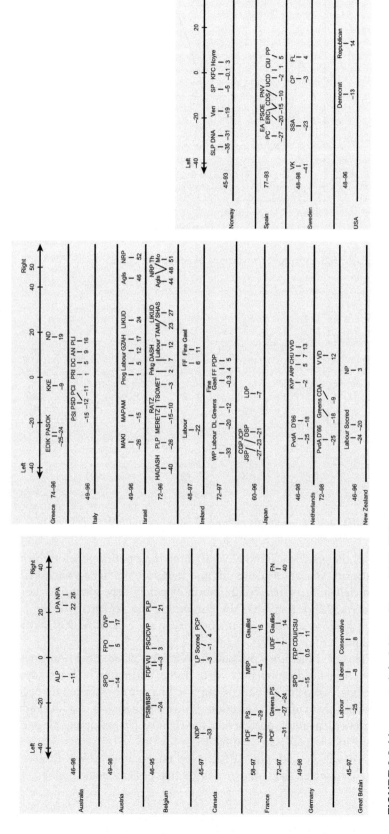

FIGURE 6.2 Mean party left–right positions 1945–1998

Notes:

Full names of all parties shown in Figures 6.2 and 6.4 are given in Appendix I (pp. 193–213) of Ian Budge, H.-D. Klingemann, Andrea Volkens, Judith Bara and Eric Tannenbaum (2000) *Mapping Policy Preferences* (Oxford, OUP).

Left–right placements on the line reflect the relevant parties' emphasis on right- or left-wing topics, as shown in Table 6.5.

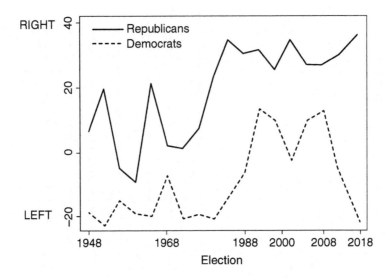

FIGURE 6.3 Left-right movement of American parties 1945–2016

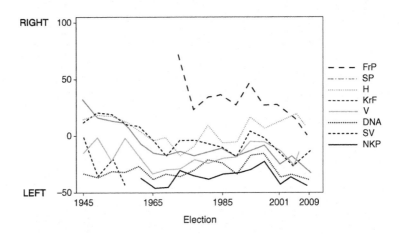

FIGURE 6.4 Left-right movement of Norwegian parties 1945–2017

holds the presidency and have declared their policy position through their platform. We can measure this and therefore predict a switch between left and right targets or a continuation of policy depending on who wins the election. More than that, by comparing the present with the prior left-right position of the government, we can say exactly how great the change will be.

This is a bit more difficult in Norway, where coalition governments (governments formed by two or more parties or at least governments needing two or more parties' support) have to be formed by negotiations between them after the election. However, there is a certain predictability to these depending on whether the right or left groupings of parties get a majority of votes (see Chapter 13).

We will go into the question of government policy targets and the extent to which they influence the actual policies being applied. The party

Briefing 6.2

Expert judgements of party positions on left-right and other issues

An alternative way to measure party policy preferences is to conduct a survey of political experts and/or country specialists and ask them to place political parties on a 10- or 12-point line between left and right or between opposed positions on specific issues (welfare, defence and so on). This is a similar approach to asking for electors' self-placements, as described in Chapter 4. As with electors locating themselves on a scale, it may not always be clear what criteria experts use in assigning parties to positions between left and right. Are they judging party behaviour in both elections and coalition governments? Or are they concentrating only on recent elections? Latterly, they may have been influenced by the placing of parties as revealed by themselves in manifestos and other texts.

Whatever the basis of the expert judgements may be, there is generally quite a high agreement, over 80%, between the manifesto-based left-right scale and the expert ones. Over time, expert judgements have become more detailed and exact, moving from general characterizations of party left-right positions to answers to specific questions about what the party position was on particular issues at a specified point in time or in a named election. This allows analysts to trace party policy movement on them over time. A useful feature of such expert surveys of party positions is that they allow them to be compared with electors' own reported preferences on specific issues. These comparisons form part of our discussion in Chapter 7.

policy positions, such as those mapped in Figures 6.3 and 6.4, also provide information about another measure of political opinion, however – the plurality voter preference as represented by the left-right position of the **plurality party**.

Plurality party

The party that got the most votes in the last election.

As pointed out in Chapter 3, individuals may vote for parties for a variety of reasons other than their policy programme. These could be their past record, candidates, presumed competence in running the government, freedom from scandals and so on. So it is difficult to say categorically that voters who have chosen the plurality party totally endorse its policies. No doubt some do. But we never know how many. The most we can say is that those who voted for it were not put off by its policies. They can thus be said in this weak sense to have endorsed them under the circumstances existing at the time of the election.

This is important because a party's general-election vote is taken as an endorsement (or non-endorsement) of its policies as well as of its eligibility for government. As we shall see in Chapter 10, general elections lump all sorts of decisions together in one vote. This is then set in stone as authorizing the party both to carry through its programmes and to participate in government for the whole of the inter-election period.

Briefing 6.3

Election rules and voting paradoxes

Difficulties in the way of finding the true majority preference on any issue – even through direct voting on it – are raised by the fact that even if electors voted solely on policy grounds, certain distributions of opinion are subject to 'cycling' effects – that is, no stable majority can be found. So if the issues are voted on in a different way or at a different time, another majority may form different from the last. We have already seen an example of this in Table 5.1, stemming from the absence of any overall median position over the two issues (defence and social welfare), which some electors may link up. This means that there is no fixed position around which to build a stable majority.

Preference distributions of this kind may be rare, but there is no guarantee that they may not occur where there are no constraints put on preferences (like being able to vote on issues only one by one). Part II is devoted to discussing such problems, inherent in free votes where each counts as one. It reviews possible solutions to them – all of which, however, raise problems of their own.

Parties, political commentators and population all take a vote for a party as a public endorsement of its policy. The aggregate public vote thus constitutes an overall expression of political preference, whatever motives individuals cast it with. Under a system of general elections – such as almost all contemporary democracies have – this is necessary and inevitable. The aggregate votes are the only authoritative expression of popular opinion we have, so we must use them as such, whatever their imperfections. Things would be different if we had direct popular votes on each policy (Chapter 9). But few contemporary democracies do, even to a limited extent.

If we do take the vote share of each party as a general endorsement of its policy targets, a majority vote can be taken as an expression of popular preference for the policy position of the party which obtained it. In a two-party system like the US, one party will generally get a majority, take the presidency, form the government and take its policy targets from the platform it put forward in the election. These have popular endorsement in the shape of the majority who voted for the party.

However, the US is almost unique in having only two effective parties at national level. Most countries have three or more, which generally split the vote between them without getting a clear majority. One party will, however, get more votes than any rival: a plurality.

The question then arises of whether its plurality gives one party so much of a lead over its competitors that it can be treated as almost a majority party (and awarded a majority of legislative seats – for example, as single-member district plurality (SMDP) systems tend to do – see Briefing 10.1). Or is the plurality party's vote not so different from that of the other parties so that it has to go into coalition with them to form a government?

Election-based measures of popular policy preferences

These are questions which we consider in detail in Chapter 13. Besides affecting government formation, however, they also touch on the extent to which preferences as expressed through votes provide a way of estimating popular policy choices. If the plurality is (almost) a majority, it has a stronger claim to represent the popular will than if the plurality vote is larger but not much larger than the other parties in terms of votes and parliamentary seats.

The plurality vote

In any case, the plurality voter position must always be regarded as one indicator of the popular preference. It is the largest group which has emerged spontaneously from the population to publicly endorse a particular policy position. If public policy is to meet popular preferences, it must therefore respond in some way to the expressed preference of the plurality voter.

The left-right dimension and the median voter

Being able to measure the left-right dimension of politics enables us to determine exactly what the policy position of the plurality voter is and to compare it with the government position. In combination with the distribution of votes, left-right party placements also let us identify another carrier of the popular preference – the middle or median voter. That is the first voter's position after 50% of voters have been counted going either from left or right. As we are dealing with groups of party voters rather than individuals, we have to assume that the voters in the middle grouping are evenly spread around the party position and that the one in the middle is the median.

The median position has two important properties. First, if preferences are spread along a line, as with left-right, it will always form part of any policy majority that can be formed – you have to include the median to form a majority in the first place. Second, the position on the distribution minimizes the distance between it and all the other positions. In other words, if you adopt the position occupied by the median voter as public policy, you minimize the disappointment suffered by all the other voters as a result of not adopting their exact preference.

Policy space

One or more measured lines or 'dimensions' which allow governments, parties and electors to be located in terms of their policy preferences.

These characteristics qualify the median to act as another measure of popular preferences besides the plurality position. It lacks the spontaneous endorsement which the latter has received. On the other hand, the plurality is often to be found at one extreme or another of **policy space**. So even though it has more fervent endorsement, it tends also to be more strongly opposed by other voters. Minimizing disappointment and representing an 'average' of preferences the median is a less controversial and divisive position to identify as the majority one – and better than the average or

Briefing 6.4

Calculating the median voter left-right preference

A slight complication in measuring the median voter position as one indicator of majority preference is having an even rather than uneven number of voters overall, so a gap exists between 50% of voters on one side and 50% on the other. In that case, it probably makes most sense to see the median preference as being in the middle of the gap.

When we want to identify the median left-right position for millions of voters in a general election, we can calculate it in three steps:

1 For each election, we score each party in terms of their left-right position.
2 For each party, we need to find an interval on this dimension where its supporters are located. For each party, we calculate the midpoint on the left-right dimension between this party and the one immediately left of it and another midpoint between this party and the one immediately right of it. We assume that those who vote for this party fall into this interval between these two midpoints on the left-right ideological dimension. This is a simple application of the preference relations. Simply put, voters are assumed to choose the candidates/parties that are closest to them in left/right terms. Voters beyond the left side of this interval will vote for the party on the left of this party and the ones beyond the right side will vote for the party on the right of it.
3 For each election, we find the percentage of the vote received by each party. At this point, we now have the percentage of the electorate that falls into the policy interval around each party that we have created. Having now transformed the data to what is called technically a 'grouped frequency distribution', we estimate the median position by using the following mathematical formula:

$$M = L + \left\{ (50 - C) / F \right\} * W$$

M = the median voter position (ideological score).
L = the lower end (ideological score) of the interval containing the median.
C = the cumulative frequency (vote share) up to but not including the interval containing the median.
F = the frequency (vote share) in the interval containing the median.
W = the width of the interval containing the median.

The formula indicates that the median position is found by adding up the percentage votes of the parties to left or right of the interval containing the voters who will push the count over 50%. We assume that voters are evenly distributed over this central interval and identify the one in the middle of the interval, who must on this assumption be the median voter. This procedure yields an exact left-right score for their position, which we take as the median.

Calculating this from votes and party left-right scores for each election then enables us to trace the movement of voter majority preferences from left to right over time and compare this with the positions taken by parties and governments over time, to see how well they correspond.

Source: Hee-Min Kim and Richard C. Fording (1998) 'Voter Ideology in Western Democracies 1964–1989' *European Journal of Political Research* (33) 73–97.

Mean

The sum of all scores divided by the number of cases on which the scoring is based.

mean position, which can be unduly pulled to one side or the other by a cluster of voters with extreme right or left views.

Both the median and plurality vote measures of the majority preference have their own particular merits, so the choice between them is difficult and perhaps impossible to resolve. This means that both plurality parties and parties supported by median voters have something of a mandate to participate in coalition governments and effect some of their policies (and usually do – see Chapter 13).

The median elector

Voters, however, may express support for a party policy position for all sorts of non-policy reasons. To measure popular policy preferences more directly, we have to ask what the public would want if it could choose on pure policy grounds. Here the left-right dimension also helps in defining their position. As we saw in Chapter 4, many surveys now ask electors to place themselves at some point on a ladder between left and right, usually of ten units. From the overall distribution, the median can easily be picked out – all the more so as the majority of electors generally place themselves at the middle of the scale, favouring a moderate or centrist position in between the ones generally taken up by the political parties (Figure 4.6).

This preference for a middle course between more extreme party targets confirms the general characterization of electors in Chapters 4 and 5 as favouring the current state of affairs against radical changes. It helps explain why there is a generally negative reaction against government proposals for change in between elections and why these generally need to be modified or abandoned in face of popular resistance. This is one factor which, together with the institutional and legal difficulties of changing policy, contributes to the more general phenomenon of policy inertia, which plays a central part in our discussion of government alternation and its effects in the next chapter.

Left-right as an overall characterization of parties and policies: a general assessment

It is not only suspicion and fear of uncertainty which produces negative reactions to most changes proposed by governments. General elections

Briefing 6.5

Three measures of majority policy preferences for comparing with government policy to estimate policy-preference correspondence

Most democracies do not regularly hold popular votes directly on policy in the shape of referendums or initiatives. This makes it more difficult to measure the extent to which public policy reflects popular preferences for it, as it should in a democracy. As noted in the text, general elections record party voting support, which may in part be based on support for their policy programme. At least this has not put electors off voting for them. The distribution of votes allows us to see immediately which party has the most votes. Where we have knowledge of the plurality party's position on issues, we can say what policy the voters for that party endorse, if only by default. That gives us the plurality voter preference – a first indicator of the majority preference. The median voter preference can also be calculated from the vote distribution and knowledge of the party policy position, as described in Briefing 6.4.

That gives us two estimates of majority policy preferences, both of which must be taken into account in estimates of policy-preference correspondence. Both are authoritative because they are based directly on the only expression of popular opinion allowed for under representative democracy – the general election.

On the other hand, voters are not the whole of the body of citizens and are also constrained in their choice of policies by what the parties put on offer. Opinion polls and surveys at least try to measure the preferences of *all* elector citizens, even if they do not altogether succeed. They also try to get directly at policy preferences and constrain them less than in election choices. A democracy ideally aims at matching policies to all citizen preferences rather than just those of voters. Estimates of correspondence should thus match public policy to the median *elector* preference as well as to those of the median and the plurality voters in the last election. ('Policy mood', used in Figure 7.3, is an alternative measure of the median elector position over large numbers of issues.) In assessing the correspondence between public policies and popular preferences for them, we must therefore check out alternation theory against all these measures, as all give some indication of what the majority feeling might be. This was in fact allowed for in testing the theory, as reported in Chapter 7, all measures providing essentially the same positive results.

may be an effective way to cut through the instability and inconsistencies which affect direct voting on policies in referendums and initiatives (see Chapter 9). Instead, general elections focus on the choice of parties to form a government both on non-policy and policy grounds. For that reason many electors – up to 30% of them – abstain from voting at all, since they feel little personal involvement in the outcome. So, a party may get a majority in the election and an even bigger majority in the legislature, conferring an official mandate to implement its policies, with only a quarter to a third of citizens actually having voted for it. The people who actually vote do not therefore necessarily represent the views of the whole electorate. Across countries and over time, there is an average 12-unit difference in left-right terms between the median elector and median voter preferences. So citizens in general may well feel they have little say in the outcomes of elections decided by only three-quarters or two-thirds of their number, who are themselves not well represented over all their issue concerns by the parties they elect.

Besides this, the left-right ordering, which mainstream parties like socialists, liberals and conservatives adopt to differentiate themselves from each other, does not necessarily coincide with electors' own political thinking (as we saw in Chapter 4). Most electors probably use left-right much of the time as a way of making sense of politics. But at other times, they latch onto individual issues or 'bundles' of issues that may not correspond precisely to the policy bundles offered by the parties. All of electors' concerns are to be found in some party's 'bundle'. But the individual party bundles may not fit well with many electors' own 'bundling' of issues.

Parties favour a left-right ordering of their own positions and of overall policy in order to impose consistency on their programmes and on what they do in government (balancing the level of services with level of tax, for example). However, the ordering does not necessarily fit with all party positions and the policy concerns which characterize them. As noted in our discussion of Figure 6.1 (the left-right ordering of parties), both minority nationalist parties and agrarians (farmers' and peasant's parties) may in individual cases be either far to the left or to the right. So these party families are not well characterized by a left-right placement. Christian and religious parties mix right-wing and left-wing appeals. Thus, in terms of their overall 'bundle' of policies, they end up in the centre. Yet they clearly have other concerns about moral issues such as abortion, which are often more important to them and may well need another dimension of politics to represent them properly. This is well illustrated by Table 6.6, which shows the characteristic issues which each grouping of parties emphasize in their manifestos and which are most important in distinguishing them as a party 'family'.

Only some of the parties (often the largest ones – conservatives, liberals, socialist and labour) find their differences well described by mainstream left-right issues. Even the Christians are imperfectly fitted. Other defining differences, such as environment for the greens, agriculture for agrarians and decentralization for minority ethnic/nationalist parties, have little relationship with left-right differences – though they characterize the 'family' that relevant parties belong to well (see the scores in the last column of Table 6.6). And even some conservative parties have varying policy concerns (military versus market economy).

With inconsistencies on the party side as well as in electors' thinking (Chapter 4) we cannot therefore resolve the difficulties of policy representation by simply matching up overall left-right positions on both sides and seeing what correspondence there is between them. Both electors and (particularly) parties think in left-right terms a lot. That means we always have to consider the left-right correspondence in assessing how far policy

Briefing 6.6

Party 'families'

Party 'families' are the groupings of parties commonly used in comparative research with ideological positions held in common across countries. Mostly these are 'left-right' positions from 'socialist' on the left to 'neo-liberal' or conservative on the right. As noted in our earlier discussion, however, other groupings may have moral-religious or regional minority concerns at their core, so they have to be recognized as separate 'families'.

We need to group national parties in this or similar ways to do systematic comparative research at all. Otherwise, we could not put parties together across country boundaries and would be confined to studying individual national parties on their own (describing their history and current situation – but probably making implicit references to 'similar' or 'different' parties elsewhere, based on unclear criteria). Grouping them into cross-national 'families' is one way of making such criteria clear; distinguishing like parties from unlike ones; and generalizing about what parties of a similar type will do in any country where they are found.

Individual parties make it easier for political scientists to place them in families by choosing to call themselves 'socialist' or 'Christian democrat' or 'liberal' and joining international 'liberal', 'socialist' or other federations. We can also identify the characteristic issues each family stresses in their manifestos and assign national parties to a 'family' based on these. Table 6.6 shows which issues each party family uniquely stresses in its programme and the extent (in the last column) to which individual party members can be clearly identified by these, with scores running from 0.00 to 1.00. Mostly, individual parties can be identified clearly as belonging to an

TABLE 6.6 Distinguishing issues which each party family uniquely emphasizes in their manifestos and the extent to which they can be clearly identified by them

	Characteristic issues	Predictive efficiency
sociocultural parties		
ecologists	environmental protection	0.938
agrarian	agriculture	0.898
ethnic	decentralization	0.835
religious-social parties		
Christian democrats	traditional morality: law and order	0.854
mainstream (left-right) parties		
left socialists	peace and détente	0.482
social democrats	welfare state: expansion	0.516
liberals	market economy	0.638
conservatives		
(left) conservatives	market economy	0.631
(right) conservatives	military strength	0.511
state nationalists	military strength	0.543

Notes: The table reports those issues which each party family uniquely stresses. The third column reports on how well such emphases enable individual national parties to be placed in the appropriate family, on a scale from 1.00 to 0.00.

international family. However, the bigger mainstream 'parties of government' usually have to stress other issues which come up as well (scandals, crises, etc.), so they tend to be less clearly identified by their characteristic issues than smaller party families. This shows up in the distribution of scores in the last column of the table.

Source: H. D. Klingemann and Ian Budge (2013) 'Using the Manifesto Estimates to Refine Party Family Placements' pp. 49–65 of *Mapping Policy Preferences from Texts* ed. A. Volkens et al. (Oxford, OUP).

supply meets policy demand. But we also have to base comparisons on other criteria too, particularly agreement on single issues – which, as we saw in Chapter 4, may introduce complications and contradictions into government responses to policy demands. These would not be there if we could simply describe everything in general left-right terms.

End-summary

Chapters 4 and 5 examined the way electoral preferences form. In this chapter, we looked at the other side of the policy supply and demand relationship, in the shape of party policy offerings. As stressed throughout, citizen preferences are not independent of party and government policy proposals. Electors need both a stimulus to form their public preferences in the first place and a context to put them in or frame them. Both are provided by the proposals governments and parties put forward. It is thus the parties who take the initiative in policy supply and demand, being more or less forced to set out their stall and see how electors respond to their offerings, since there are few spontaneous demands to respond to. Party policies thus tend to be driven by their own ideologically based judgements rather than being just a response to the popular preferences which they set off in the first place (see Chapter 11).

Party proposals tend to be vaguer and more general than government ones, being less tied to immediate action. Priorities for action rather than specific lines of action tend to be stressed. This helps us to analyse the policy programmes (manifestos, platforms) that parties put forward in elections by counting their sentences into a set of categories covering the whole range of conceivable policies (Table 6.3).

To get an overall picture of the way parties distinguish themselves from each other and how they change in policy terms over time, we can combine their policy emphases into a left-right scale, contrasting government intervention, welfare and peace on the left with support for traditional values, freedom and military security on the right. Parties can be arranged in terms of these contrasts along a line between left, centre and right. This can also be used to map their general policy changes over time (Figures 6.2 and 6.3).

While this lineup fits most larger parties well, it fails to characterize others in terms of their central and distinguishing policy concerns. Taken together with the failure of left-right to completely characterize electors' policy thinking, this suggests that the policy-preference correspondence must be examined in issue-by-issue terms as well as left-right ones. We shall do this in the next chapter.

Specific points to take away from this discussion are thus:

- How to turn words into numbers on the basis of party election programmes (a technique which can be applied to all sorts of documents and texts – cf. Chapter 16).
- The creation and uses of a left-right scale in classifying and comparing political parties and their policy changes.
- Ideology as a basis for doing so and giving parties a basic and continuing identity.
- Limitations of left-right in classifying all parties and describing their behaviour.
- How parties' characteristic policies continue to mark them out as a 'party family', relative to other parties.
- Using a predictive theory (developmental party-family theory) to clarify and specify this process.
- How popular policy preferences can be estimated from party policy positions and votes, as well as from surveys and opinion polls.

Systematic working assumptions coming into this discussion

Our discussion in this chapter brings in several of the assumptions which combine with those in other chapters to provide a basis for political explanation (Chapters 8 and 19). The ones which come up here are:

6   Policy preferences and their implementation can be classified and measured for over-time and comparative analysis, on the basis of textual, survey, expenditure and other statistical evidence.

7   This allows them to be represented as points in spaces constructed on various measurement assumptions, with a centre and extremes, which can also relate the policy positions of political actors (citizens, voters, governments, parties, etc.) as specified from either data or theory.

8   Such spaces can have varying dimensions, the most common being a straight line running between left and right.

18   However, all political – like other – measurements contain error (which can nevertheless be estimated and corrected on various assumptions).

Sources and resources

Anke Tresch, Jonas Lefevere, and Stefan Walgrave (eds 2015) Issue Ownership: How the Public Links Parties to Issues and Why It Matters. *Special Issue of West European Politics* 38(4).

Ian Budge, H. D. Klingemann, Andrea Volkens, Judith Bara, and Eric Tanenbaum (2001) *Mapping Policy Preferences* (Oxford, Oxford University Press).

Manifesto Project (MARPOR) www.manifesto-project.wzb.eu/

Suggestions for class papers

1   How would you decide which party suited you best? Specify and justify the considerations which influence your choice.
2   Do we really need to have political ideologies? Why or why not?
3   Which international party families do you think the US Democrats and Republicans belong to (if any?) Why?

Suggestions for class projects

1   What could be done to improve the coding suggested for manifestos/platforms in Table 6.3? Apply your new scheme to the party programmes produced for the last national election and assess how well it works.
2   Improving on the ideas of basic vote and election-specific efforts in Briefing 6.1, predict party votes in some coming national election(s), basing yourself on media and other reports of the campaign.
3   Devise a winning election strategy for leftist parties in the face of globalization and rightist parties' stance against immigration. Write it up in a platform. Why would your suggested strategy succeed?

Chapter 7

Matching public policy to popular preferences

Chapter overview

Having seen how popular preferences and party policy can both be measured, this chapter puts them together to tackle the central supply and demand problem of democratic politics – how do its processes ensure a *necessary* connection between public policy and popular preferences? Such a connection has to cope with the fact that parties have their own aims and purposes, which do not necessarily match up with those of electors.

First, we consider how the connection can be 'mapped' and measured in the kind of policy spaces we have been discussing. Next, we go on to the election process itself and its major paradox: how can competing parties with their own relatively extreme policy agendas bring policies close to centrist preferences as they alternate in government, especially when voters' and electors' preferences seem to lie between the party policy extremes and parties mostly position themselves towards the extremes? This chapter shows how the slow rate of conversion from government policy targets into actually implemented policy means that the alternating targets of changing party governments keep actual policy zigzagging around the centre of the policy space, where most voters and electors locate themselves. At the same time, this process is responsive to changing popular priorities, expressed in the preference of plurality voters, in the sense of actual policy moving towards (though rarely reaching) their more extreme position.

This dynamic equilibrium created by policy inertia and government alternation makes the necessary 'democratic' connection between policy supply and demand and is illustrated for left-right policy space (Figure 7.1). It also works for other policy spaces and specific issues, however, under the same conditions.

The main points covered by our discussion are thus:

- How thinking of policy in terms of straight lines and other kinds of spaces helps us measure the correspondence between party and government policies on the one hand and popular preferences for them on the other.

- Distinguishing policy proposals and targets from actual implemented policy.
- How thinking of policymaking and elections as dynamic processes over time rather than as unique and separate events makes it easier to see how preferences and policy can be brought together by parties alternating in government.
- 'Thermostatic' reactions to government policy.
- The crucial conditions for policy-preference correspondence – party 'bracketing' of majority preferences: the distance between their policy positions; their alternation in government; and the slow rate of policy target implementation.
- Putting these together to form a predictive explanation of policy-preference correspondence.
- How the extent of correspondence can be predicted from this and checked against actual practice in various countries.

The spatial analysis of political relationships

Chapters 4–6 show how general ideas about the way voters, electors and parties interact, discussed in Chapter 3, can be made more precise by representing them as spatial relationships – that is, as distances between points in a space. Such 'spaces' can be formed in a straight line, like the left-right line from the last chapter (Figure 6.1). With only the one line or dimension, this is referred to as a single-dimensional (unidimensional) space because it has only the one, horizontal dimension – a straight line running between a pure left and a pure right position.

Support for or opposition to party or governmental initiatives in some areas seems also to form on separate issues, not necessarily adding up to an overall left-right position. These have to be analysed on their own, not just in terms of left-right, if we are to get a complete picture of how preferences are met. There are quite a lot of 'separable issues' of this kind. They are not just considered on a one-by-one basis by electors but are also handled and discussed separately by different government departments (Chapter 14) or specialized legislative committees so that decisions on one do not depend on another. Each issue can be represented along a different straight line, with different median positions, and parties possibly ordering themselves along it in a different way from the positions they take on other issues.

Frame

A frame defines the possible actions to be considered on an issue.

The left-right division we have been examining is used generally by parties to **frame** electoral responses and covers most issues in most countries. So we shall focus on it in the following discussion. But our reasoning can also be applied to other issues – even clusters which link up with each other in ways other than in left-right terms [cf. Table 5.1].

Measuring similarities between popular policy preferences and implemented policy

Estimating the extent to which policies reflect preferences is simplified by being able to measure the distance between them when both are represented as points in the kinds of **policy space** we have been discussing. What we are essentially interested in comparing is the extent to which the median elector or voter preference for policy is matched by the actual policy being implemented in each country.

It is easy to identify the actual present-day policy with the current government's stated policy, but to do so would be a mistake. As shown in Figure 7.1 and discussed in the next section, they are two different things. Especially with a new government, its aspirations for policy are simply words. The actual policy being applied by the state administration has been shaped by the last government (and even the one before that and the one before that). Until the new government has had time to change things, its own aspirations are not being fully implemented, and if it loses the next election after a short time in office, those aspirations will be delayed indefinitely. This means that the actual policy being implemented will be pulled one way and then the other over time – a process which generally keeps it close to centrist popular preferences.

What we focus on here, therefore, is the distance separating currently applied policy from the median position over time as measured within appropriate policy spaces. There is no point looking at only one election to see how this works out. At any one point (again as shown in Figure 7.1), the distance separating policy from median preference might be exceptionally large or exceptionally small, depending on chance events. To make sure that the relationship is stable and can be attributed to the operation of democratic processes over time, we need to look at relationships over a number of elections, as illustrated in Figure 7.1.

What the idealized illustration in Figure 7.1 mainly shows is that there is a close relationship between implemented policy and popular preferences over time. They are close in three senses. In each year, actual policy is quite close to citizen preferences for it. So, if we average the differences between preference and policy in each year (i.e. the absolute difference, not taking account of whether the difference for each is positive or negative), we can get a measure of year-by-year 'congruence' between them.

However, in looking at the long-term correspondence between the two lines, we might also be interested in how far leftward differences are balanced by rightward differences. This would mean that on balance, while policy does not match preference exactly in any one year, it does so in the long term, as deviations in one direction cancel out differences in the other direction over time. So there is no consistent representational bias in the long term, even when there is not an exact policy match in each year. We could not really expect the democracy to get an exact match every time, because unexpected developments pull policy off course. But

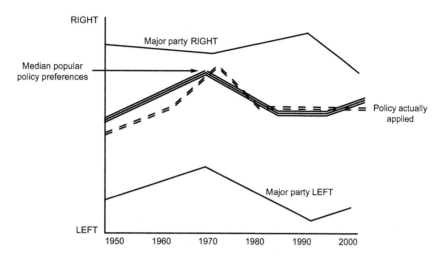

FIGURE 7.1 Relating public policy to citizens' left-right preferences for it over time

Notes: The figure shows parties 'bracketing' the median preference over time (the horizontal dimension), in the sense that their policy positions consistently fall right or left of the median policy line. As the parties alternate in government, policy targets veer slowly to the left or right. Actual policy remains, as a result, quite close to the median position.

if its general processes get the balance fairly right over a period of time, it would still be performing pretty well in matching policy supply to policy demand. This long-term correspondence or lack of bias is therefore a second way we could look at the required connection between preference and policy.

We can also see from Figure 7.1 that the policy being applied generally follows preferences, particularly in the early and later years of the period – that is, it moves left when preferences move left and moves right when preferences move right. Responsiveness of this kind is the traditional way of looking at supply and demand: when demand for goods increases, does the supply of goods also increase? So we can also consider the dynamic interaction between *policy* supply and demand here.

Of course, if preferences and policy are congruent in every year, we would also expect to see long-term correspondence and responsiveness as well. So congruence is the measure we mostly focus on in our analyses. However, long-term correspondence and responsiveness could exist even when year-to-year congruence did not. As we have seen from Figure 7.1, positive and negative deviations in different years will cancel each other out over time. So all is not lost for democracy's 'necessary connection' between preferences and policy even when year-by-year congruence is not found. As we will demonstrate, however, democratic processes *do* foster congruence – which means that they also produce long-term correspondence and responsiveness, as we shall see.

Policy inertia – the effects of a slow translation of government targets into actual policy

As we have stressed, government policy targets are not the same as the actual policy being applied by the bureaucracy and administrative apparatus. This difference is because each new government, formed as a result of an election ousting some or all of the parties previously in control, comes in with different policy targets. Because of the serious legal, financial and administrative obstacles in the way, however – not to mention popular 'thermostatic' reactions – the conversion of targets into practice is generally slow. On the face of it, this must surely weaken democracy. If a popularly elected government cannot easily effect the programme it was elected with, surely that must be a bad thing.

As the last chapter pointed out, however, the government, even if it has a majority of votes, has not necessarily had its programme endorsed by a majority of citizens. Voters may have chosen the party for largely non-policy reasons. **Plurality parties** – the largest parties but without even a non-policy majority – often have relatively extreme policies which are not necessarily ones approved by the majority of citizens with centrist preferences. So it actually strengthens democracy to have targets implemented rather slowly, giving everybody time to consider if this is what they really want and to react to policy changes at the next election (or even before, by reacting 'thermostatically' against government proposals as they are made).

The overall relationship between policy targets and applied policy is shown here in a general formula derived from data analyses over many countries:

Current Applied Policy = 0.15 Target + 0.85 Applied Policy in Previous Year

This **equation** says that current policy mostly carries on with the policies that were being applied in the previous year. Government efforts to modify it in their preferred direction do have a certain effect, however, so that the policy being applied each year of their term of office slowly moves towards their target for it. However, only 15% of the distance between the actual policy being applied and their target policy is being covered each year. Governments last three to five years on average, so they are likely to achieve only half their desired policy modifications before they face another election. Only if they succeed in forming the same government after the election do they have more of a chance to make applied current policy conform to their ideal for it.

However, as we saw from Table 3.1, there is a good chance of any government being replaced by one with opposed targets at the next general election – to the left rather than right, or right rather than left – for or against types of spending. The new government will then try to swing policy back in its preferred direction. But it can do so only slowly. The bulk of the policy being applied will be the one partially modified under its predecessor. Only by the end of its term will the new government get

Thermostatic reactions

Expressions of popular support for or (more often) hostility to government policy proposals.

Plurality parties

Parties with the most votes or seats.

Equation

States a numeric relationship between processes.

Policy inertia: difficulties in actually implementing government targets

Once a new government has been formed (often with a delay if it is a coalition of two or more parties), most commentators focus their attention on the policy targets set out in its manifesto (if it is a single-party government) or on the coalition agreement made between the parties composing it. Such documents, however, outline only the general policy *targets* that the government aims to achieve, not the actual policies being implemented and enforced during its term of office. The longer the government is in power, the more it will be able to bring targets and currently implemented policy together. But even after a normal term of four to five years, it will have got only halfway there.

The following are the reasons for such policy inertia – so often overlooked even by experienced analysts and communicators:

1   Constitutional constraints. Any important policy change probably needs legislation to put it into effect. This has to be prepared and drafted in detail taking four to six months at a minimum. It then has to be slotted into the legislative process, which itself requires not just general debate and vote approval but probably committee hearings as well. Legislative hearings and votes on any one policy proposal can be crowded out by others as government ministries compete to get their proposals through. Objections by affected interests and popular 'thermostatic' reactions against the proposal may cause the government to withdraw or amend it.

2   Legal challenges. Even if passed by the legislature, the law or resolution in which the new proposal is embodied may well be challenged in various courts, going right up through several tiers to the top and involving numerous court hearings and delays if not the outright annulment of the legislation.

3   Previous contracts and commitments. The outgoing government may have made long-term contracts to build roads, hospitals, barracks or ships or to have services of different types supplied by national or foreign firms. Either the other bodies involved have to be compensated and paid off or their contracts left to run till the date previously agreed.

4   Administrative changes. A new bureaucracy grouped into a new or existing ministry or agency may have to be created to supervise and push the new changes. This takes money and time and is liable to be restricted by other ministries defending their own policy objectives and budgets. Under a coalition, with different parties controlling different ministries (see Chapter 14), such bureaucratic quarrels may be carried up to cabinet level. Even under a single-party government, different factions (see Chapter 12) controlling different ministries may well conflict.

With all these difficulties in the way, it is a wonder that established policies ever get changed! And indeed, few are changed substantially. Most policies and the institutions which administer them carry on in much the same way regardless of changes of government. It is only the five to six at the top of the incoming government's agenda that will be changed significantly – out of the many hundreds of policies at all levels being applied. 'Policy inertia' – that is, unchanging or partially changing policies – is the general rule for governments and bureaucracies, only partially overcome by party initiatives.

halfway to where it wants to go. But then it faces an election, which it is quite likely to lose, so policy targets will again be reversed by the following government.

Slow policy change and reversal over a sequence of elections and governments

This process of slow policy change and reversal has been illustrated graphically in Figure 7.1. Targets change much more completely and radically between successive party governments than the actual policy being applied, which largely stays in the middle. This is true even when strongly opposed single parties alternate in government. In multiparty coalitions – the norm in most democracies – the more extreme parties usually have to compromise with their partners. Even the government targets then come closer to the middle, as does actual policy, of course – particularly as past policy is also likely to have been inherited from previous centrist coalitions.

The exception to all this is when a single-party government of relatively extreme views manages to get re-elected, perhaps even three or four times. If it then consistently sticks to its initial targets, it can change the policy actually being applied to conform to these. Eventually, however, it will lose an election, and its successor government will again have a chance to pull policy back in its own direction across the centre.

Policy supply and demand – the full picture

Slow change in actual policy and frequent alternation between governments with different policy targets thus keeps current applied policy broadly in the centre of the policy space, where most citizens prefer it to be. Of course, this requires too that there are alternating parties at both sides of the centre, 'bracketing' the mass of electors. By 'pulling' policy to one side, then the other, these ensure that it zigzags across the centre reasonably close to most electors' preferences.

The only alternative arrangement for satisfying centrist policy demands would be to have a permanent centre government itself located in the middle. Some coalition governments do have a centrist party carrying on as a more or less permanent partner. But even centrist-dominated governments change their policy targets from left to right as other parties with their own policy targets join the centre party in government and pull its targets more towards their own extreme.

The full supply and demand process is illustrated in Figure 7.1. As the two major parties (i.e. the only two capable of getting a majority or a dominating plurality in the legislature) alternate in government, they try to impose their targets, slowly, on actual current policy. This moves it from a previous position on the opposite side of the median position, across the centre, towards the current government's preferred direction. Before it can get far, however, the other major party takes over government after another election and starts to move policy in its own direction. Things get a bit confused when two major parties participate in a coalition government together. Any single-party government following on from this succeeds better in pulling actual policy over to its own side but still leaves it close to the centre. We can see how this process will continue indefinitely in the presence of competing parties with opposed policy agendas alternating in government as they gain or lose votes in recurrent elections. As a result, the actually applied policy supply will always – more or less – meet policy demand in the centre of the space.

Of course, it will (as pointed out above) match it less at one time compared to another. Policy and preference tend to meet at the centre but do not at all times exactly match up. The democratic process thus produces a dynamic rather than a completely stable policy **equilibrium**. The end product is an approximate matching of applied policies and popular preferences, which varies in exactness over time. This process is summarized in Table 7.1 in the shape of ten detailed propositions (numbered statements) which spell out the conditions and processes presented spatially in Figure 7.1.

Propositions 1, 2 and 7 make the point that general elections, with so many factors entering in to influence the vote, produce rather random and unpredictable effects so far as policy is concerned. The main one from our point of view is government alternation between parties with fairly inflexible policy targets. Individual party policy mostly reflects the concerns of their support groups and sympathizers, which are extreme from the viewpoint of most electors. In aggregate, however, all views find an echo in some party programme (Proposition 4), leaving the median (majority) elector in the middle between the individual party policy positions (Proposition 5), where enacted public policy also needs to be to correspond with the popular preference (Proposition 6).

Party alternation in government provides the mechanism for doing so by pulling policy repeatedly back towards the middle (Propositions 7 and 8) and keeping it around there. We can see how this process will continue indefinitely in the presence of competing parties with opposed policy agendas alternating in government as they gain or lose votes in recurrent elections, slowly making adjustments to existing policy (Proposition 9). As a result, the actually applied policy will always – more or less – meet policy demand in the centre of the space.

Of course, it will match it less at one time compared to another. Policy and preference tend to meet at the centre but do not at all times exactly match up. The democratic process thus produces a dynamic rather than a completely stable policy equilibrium. The end product is an approximate matching of applied policies and preferences, which varies in exactness all the time (Proposition 10).

Equilibrium

A political process that tends towards the same outcome over time.

TABLE 7.1 The alternation theory of policy-preference correspondence

1. General elections, with political parties competing for votes and defining the alternatives to be voted on, bring in other considerations bearing on voting choice than pure policy ones.
2. This is because at any one time, political parties – running blocs of candidates in the election and organizing them afterwards – may attract votes based on candidates, record and various short-term factors as well as the policy bundles they put in their programme, rendering election outcomes unpredictable except in the short term.
3. Over time, however, the characteristic policies of parties continue to distinguish them relative to other parties, while their other appeals show no such continuity.
4. The free formation of new political parties – as guaranteed in democracies – ensures that at any one time the policy preferences of all significant opinion groupings are contained in one or several existing parties' programmes.
5. This implies that the majority policy preference must always be centrist relative to those of the parties: the preferred policy position of most electors must either coincide with one party position or lie between two or more of them, therefore on the boundary or within the boundary of the most concise segment of any policy space which can be defined by the party positions within it.
6. Ensuring a correspondence between centrist popular preferences and enacted public policy thus requires that enacted public policy should also be centrist most of the time.
7. Unpredictable (i.e. random) election outcomes alternate parties and their extreme (relative to electors) policy targets in government over time.
8. Alternations of parties in government pull previously enacted policies, tending to one extreme, across the centre of the party-defined policy segment towards another extreme, in the current inter-election period.
9. Policy change is, however, usually incremental and slow, so enacted policy tends to be only part way to an extreme target before another government alternation takes place, when the process repeats itself in reverse, again pulling enacted policy across the centre.
10. Correspondence between popular policy preferences and public policy, the ultimate guarantee and justification of democracy, is thus mostly produced through its institutional mechanisms of party competition in general elections, which regularly alternate different party policy carriers in government. This combined with slow incremental change in enacted policy, keeps it near the centre. This process applies equally to overall policy (e.g. left vs right) or specific policies, provided that parties are differentiated on them and bracket the majority preference, as measured by the median position.

Briefing 7.2

Political equilibriums

In general terms, an equilibrium exists when a process always produces the same result (e.g. a centrist policy). In spatial terms, this would mean that actual policy always remains at the same point in (the middle of) the space. A 'dynamic' equilibrium is one in which policy outcomes do not always land at the same point but tend to move back towards it over time (even if they never or infrequently reach it, being diverted by influences from other forces or processes than the one under consideration). Both the 'party alternation' and 'thermostatic' processes considered in this chapter will tend towards a centrist outcome in terms of actual policy if the majority popular opinion is centrist.

These points can be put together systematically to form the predictive explanation of policy-preference correspondence, which we have referred to as alternation theory. This has the same format as the predictive theory already encountered in Chapter 6 and set out there – (developmental party-family theory). That is, it consists of an interconnected set of numbered statements about the nature of party election competition and its effects in changing governments and their policy targets. Most of these statements can be checked against independent evidence on how these processes work out in practice – some more easily than others. The main interest, however, lies in how they add up in combination to explain (and predict) policy-preference correspondence, in the same way as Figure 7.1 does spatially. They are in fact the verbal equivalent of the figure's spatial representation of alternation and its effects, but they add a bit more detail about the assumptions involved in getting there.

Explaining negative thermostatic reactions to specific policy proposals

Not only do alternation ideas show how, overall, actually implemented policies meet popular preferences for them, creating an overall equilibrium between public policy supply and demand. They also help to explain why the specific policy moves that governments make to translate their policies into action during the inter-election period generally encounter strong opposition, slowing down implementation and thus reinforcing their centrist tendencies. Figure 7.2 shows government alternating between parties which support more and less spending on a specific policy (e.g. support for the unemployed). The continuous line showing where the government starts to get actual policy in line with its policy targets each year runs from the top of the figure (1950) right up to 2020. The percentages at the base of the figure show the distribution of electors in terms of support for more or less spending on the unemployed. As the 'peak' at the middle of the distribution of opinion shows, most are centrist in the sense of favouring current levels of spending in the area. However, there are sizeable but opposed minorities favouring less or more spending.

We can see this situation working out in Figure 7.2 over the lifetime of several governments. Starting from 1950 at the top, we see a more restrictive government inheriting an expansionist policy and starting to decrease spending. This initial move provokes opposition from supporters and beneficiaries of the previous policy but little support from the centrist majority, as it is still quite distant from their position. This is even truer of the party's own supporters, who see their own ideal, restrictive policies reflected in little of what their party and government are actually doing (as opposed to their stated targets).

As actual policy moves closer to the majority of citizens at the centre, it gets more support from them. But it only coincides briefly with their ideal position before moving back towards increased spending under the next

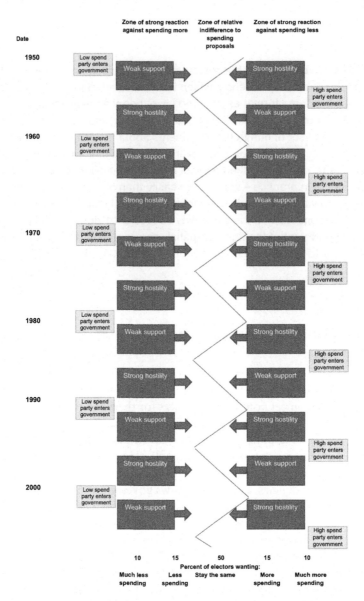

FIGURE 7.2 Relating policy alternation in government (zigzag line) to negative 'thermostatic' reactions to government policy proposals – losers are more strongly against than gainers are for

Notes: Figure 7.2 shows how, as governments change over time, their policy targets and individual policy proposals for a policy area move from spending more to spending less and vice versa. Actual policy cuts and increases are represented by the zigzag line running down the middle of the figure, between spending more and spending less. Electors' preferences on spending are shown as stable and fairly balanced over the time period, about 25% wanting more and 25% less, both sides feeling fairly strongly about the decision. The plurality of electors would prefer things to stay as they are but are not strongly concerned. As spending changes with governments, those who have enjoyed the immediate effects from the policy react strongly against the change; the electors in the middle are indifferent; and those who would ultimately benefit don't feel any immediate benefit so give only weak support. This explains why 'thermostatic' reactions to policy proposals for change are generally negative. On balance, only towards the end of each government do the gainers begin to show strong support for the new policy. But then the government changes; policy moves away from their preferred position again; and they react with hostility to the new proposals – a process which then repeats itself in reverse in the next phase and so on recurrently.

Source: Adapted from the thermostatic theory of Stuart N. Soroka and Christopher Wlezien (2010) *Degrees of Democracy* (Cambridge, CUP).

government. This provokes increasing opposition from the centrist major-ity and from those who support less spending. Because it is still relatively distant from those who believe in drastic increases, however, it gets only lukewarm support from them.

This process repeats itself in reverse as a restrictive government again takes over and unveils its proposals to move actual policy over towards its targets. Again, opposition makes itself felt much more strongly than support. Policy proposals always fall short, to a greater or lesser extent, of most citizens' ideal position. So they generally see 'too much' or 'too little' as being done and either oppose it or at least do not offer support. In aggregate, therefore, inter-election policy proposals trigger a negative 'thermostatic' reaction not just on their own demerits but also as part of the government's general programme for change. Its inevitably slow prog-ress under constraints leaves moves towards its targets (whether in gen-eralist left-right terms or specific proposals) relatively distant from most citizens' preferences most of the time.

This thermostatic process is vital from a representational point of view because here we have a process which operates at the level of separate individual issues as well in a general left-right 'linked-up' perspective. Election-based alternations in policy targets can of course keep actual policy on specific issues centred over the long term and at the general left-right level. But 'thermostatic' interactions during the inter-election period strongly supplement general alternation effects. They might even be seen as the major representational process for fine-tuning the correspondence between policy and preferences for those electors who think on an issue-by-issue basis rather than taking a general linked-up view of policy.

Table 7.2 sets out the thermostatic theory in five numbered proposi-tions, which explain how and why more react negatively to government policy initiatives than support them. These encourage issue-by-issue thinking among electors, as they come out one by one and have attention focused on them without much discussion of side effects on other policy

TABLE 7.2 The thermostatic theory of government – electoral interactions

1. Between elections individual government policy initiatives frame most electors' thinking about policy.
2. On issues separated out this way, more people generally oppose government policy than support it.
3. This is largely because the beneficiaries of existing policy are immediately and negatively affected by changes and oppose them strongly, whereas potential beneficiaries of the change will only gain in the medium to long term, so they give it only weak support.
4. Faced with strong opposition, governments generally compromise and/or slow down the policy change.
5. This contributes (a) to a slow rate of policy change in general (policy inertia) and (b) to a closer correspondence between public policy and popular preferences for it, particularly in terms of responsiveness.

Notes: For a complete exposition and a successful predictive testing of the 'thermostatic' theory, see Stuart N. Soroka and Christopher Wlezien *Degrees of Democracy* Cambridge University Press, 2010. The formulation here presents the theory in spatial terms to link up with the general alternation theory presented in Table 7.1.

Briefing 7.3

Representing popular preferences issue by issue over time

Thermostatic interactions are vital not only because they show how governments can respond more sensitively to popular demand than if only alternation were at work but also because they suggest how potential inconsistencies among issue-by-issue preferences can be resolved – *if* we look at thermostatic processes at work over time.

As we saw in Chapter 5, electors thinking in single-issue terms want services to be left as they are or enhanced but also taxes to be reduced. This raises the problem of how to pay for services (welfare, health, roads, etc.) if governments simultaneously cut their financial basis for paying for them.

In the short term, governments could find the money by borrowing, printing more money, 'growing' the economy (if they can), cutting services like the military or benefiting from windfalls such as mineral discoveries on their territory. None of these is likely to be a permanent solution, however. Thermostatic theory suggests that over a longer time, there is another process going on which does balance out potentially inconsistent single-issue preferences. These as we have noted are not static but change in response to the current situation. That is, as governments reduce taxes and cut services, a demand arises for more services. When governments respond to this thermostatically, by increasing services and taxes, popular demand for services lessens and attention focuses on reducing taxes. When taxes and services are cut, demands focus on services again.

Viewing decisions on taxes versus services as made sequentially over time in response to changing popular demand enables us to view issue-by-issue decision-making as a process of incremental trade-offs and adjustments rather than as a massive inconsistency in popular policy thinking or in government decision-making. This is a temptation if they are considered only at one time-point. In a parallel process, party alternation at the government level ensures that actually implemented policy does not go too far in the direction of either providing services or cutting taxes.

---

areas. For the reasons graphed in Figure 7.2, more people oppose the initiative than support it. Proposition 3 fills in the detail of why this should be so by noting that these adversely affected by changes are keenly aware of them and react strongly, whereas potential beneficiaries do not. All this helps make policy implementation slower (Proposition 5a) so that it remains closer to centrist preferences (but still shifts responsively in line with majority opinion).

Extremist parties and centrist citizens – the paradox of policy supply and demand

Electors are mostly moderate, centrist and opposed to major changes either to the left or to the right. This reinforces the spatial mechanisms described above in provoking opposition to specific policy moves towards more extreme targets during the inter-election period. Such opposition is part of the 'costs of governing' which government parties incur. This contributes to an average 2.25% loss of their vote from one election to another, favouring party alternation in government.

In general elections, however, citizens have to frame their choices less freely, as a vote for a relatively extreme party – more extreme at any rate than most would prefer. On the face of it, this seems an odd way of matching popular demand with a supply of preferred policies. It is particularly paradoxical as parties may get votes in general elections from candidate appeals and general competence and not on policy grounds at all.

The key to getting a satisfactory, self-adjusting match between popular preferences and public policy is the slow pace of real change, which stops policy adjustments from exactly matching government targets and keeps them near the political centre, populated by a majority with relatively moderate views (Figure 4.6). As pointed out in Chapter 2, governing requires governments to make policies to deliver public goods. Parties must have policies which they can apply in government and are characterized by the 'family' of policies that they uniquely emphasize (Christian, nationalist, left or right, etc.). But they are not necessarily *elected* on that policy. This selection of governments almost by chance limits their life and favours party alternation in office.

It also ensures that the process of policy change, illustrated in Figure 7.1, applies to all policy spaces. We have pointed out that some issues (environment, the EU, wider trade deals, decentralization or secession) may not fit within the broader left-right framework but be 'separable' within their own one-dimensional issue space. Some interdependent issues may even form 'multidimensional' spaces in conjunction with each other, if electors tend to think of them as linked together in other ways than left-right. So long as parties have different policy views on the issue or issues involved and **bracket** the electoral majority, supply and demand will operate as in Figure 7.1.

Bracket

Party positions lying on both sides of electors' positions.

From ideal to actual: *does* party alternation match policy to preferences in practice?

This is the theory. How far, however, does party alternation really produce correspondence when we look at what goes on in actual post-war democracies? We can run a first check by creating graphs like Figure 7.1 for contemporary democracies. The difference is that these graphs are now based on actual measurements of where the parties stand in left and right terms for each year; what electors' left-right preference is; and where actual policy is (with spending in the area converted into left-right units as described in the notes to Figure 7.3).

Figure 7.3 shows how party left-right positionings, popular preferences and actual applied policy for the US relate to each other year by year, over

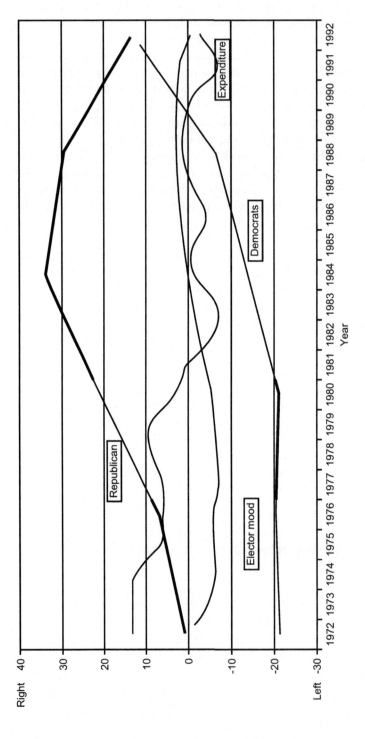

FIGURE 7.3 US relationship between elector preferences, party positions and total government spending 1972–1992

Notes: The figure traces out changes in party left-right positions (representing their policy targets): total government spending, representing more government activity (supported by Democrats on the left – at the bottom of the graph) or less (supported by Republicans on the right – at the top of the graph). So reduced expenditure is represented by an upward movement in the graph and increased spending by a downward movement. Expenditure was originally measured in percentages of GNP. Here each percentage is taken as equivalent to four left-right units, as indicated by comparative analyses of their relationship. The line is 'anchored' in the graph by making left-right zero equivalent to mean expenditure over this period. 'Policy mood' is an aggregate measure of left-right preferences among the electorate, which in effect measures their median position. It is 'anchored' in the graph by making its mean of 60% equivalent to left-right zero. For more detail on these points, see the discussion in Budge et al. *Organizing Democratic Choice* (OUP, 2012) pp. 160–164. For other findings cited in the text see the same source pp. 226–247.

the 20 years for which information was available (1972–1992). Because the US is clearly a functioning democracy, we would expect relationships to closely resemble the idealized ones we have postulated in Figure 7.1 in line with alternation ideas. That is, we expect the plurality party positions not to be too far away from each other on average and at roughly equal distances from the policy position preferred by electors as a whole, though on either side of it. We also expect governments to change in terms of which party controls the presidency (shown by their thicker lines in the graph for the party period in office). And we expect expenditures to change slowly from year to year. The expenditure line should not shift abruptly all over the place – as indeed it does not. On the graph, each year's expenditure is mostly like the previous year's, resulting in a line that mostly stays steady near the middle, most of the time.

Reasonably symmetrical distancing of plurality parties from each other on each side of the median elector ('bracketing'), their alternation in government and the slow rate of actual policy change are the main conditions that we expect to bring policy outcomes close to the general preference for them, as shown in Figure 7.1. This is what generally happens in Figure 7.3 (with one or two blips). The line which traces out overall government spending from year to year is mostly close to the one representing the popular majority preference. There is an average distance between them of only seven units in left-right terms. When we take into account the extent to which deviations to the right are balanced by deviations to the left over the entire period, the difference between preferences and actual policy is reduced to four units. It is also clear that, over time, implemented policy falls into line with popular preferences for it. Thus, on all three measures of representation (election-by-election congruence, lack of long-term bias to one side or the other, responsiveness), the theoretical expectations represented spatially in Figure 7.1 are borne out in practice here. Not shown, to avoid overcrowding the figure, is the fact that the median voter position, another measure of majority preferences, also shows a close connection with implemented policy – which also changes broadly in line with plurality preferences. The only aspect of the figure which goes against expectations is that the two parties are quite distant from each other ('polarized') most of the time. We pick up on this anomaly in Chapter 18.

Confirmation for alternation theory as a whole is even stronger than this, as Figure 7.3 is only one of nine similar graphs prepared for nine democracies (eight in Europe) over the same time period. Six out of eight produce much the same 'pictures' as in Figure 7.3 – that is, with relationships which do not differ too much from the ideal ones in Figure 7.1. This is what we would expect in most clearly working democracies.

The two other country cases which deviated from the ideal set of relationships upheld the theory in another way. 'Bracketing' of elector by party target positions was absent – and so too was any close correspondence between popular preferences and policy output. This is just as the theory predicts, of course, but the reverse of what one expects in democracies and shows that these ones may be in some trouble.

Conditions for policy-preference correspondence across countries and issues

The important remaining question is, how far do the conditions for producing a policy-preference correspondence exist across countries on political issues which may be viewed by some electors one by one and in their own terms rather than as part of a general left-right cleavage? Because of limitations on the data available, we cannot directly check out the theoretical ideas put forward in Figure 7.1 and Table 7.1 against actual observations on single issues as has been done with left-right policy moves across democracies. However, given the validation left-right policy moves provide for alternation theory, we can determine whether the conditions that it specifies for preference-policy agreement are in place for producing a correspondence between preferences and enacted policy on specific issues. This is a less severe check on the theory than the direct one just applied in Figure 7.3. However, if the conditions specified for policy supply matching demand on single issues were not in place in most of the functioning democracies we examine here, this would raise doubts about their plausibility and general applicability.

The conditions necessary for policy-preference correspondence are thus:

1   Reasonably symmetrical plurality party bracketing of the middle electoral preference. This ensures that as the major parties alternate in government, they will repeatedly pull enacted policy across the middle elector position to roughly the same extent, thus guaranteeing the general policy-preference correspondence that democracy requires.
2   We may also need parties that are not too 'polarized' – that is, stand at too much of a distance from each other, thus keeping enacted policy too much at one side or another of the centre.
3   Given that actual applied policy is close to the centre, we don't want it to move away from there too quickly and therefore require a slow rate of change in enacted policy – the 10%–15% annual change of implementation towards the target which we have already identified as being present on left-right issues.
4   For these conditions to work, we also of course need reasonable alternation of the opposing plurality parties in government.

We know from Table 3.1 that all the democracies examined here do have reasonable government alternation. We have no evidence about the rate of policy change as it affects single issues rather than general left-right expenditure movements. What we do have is survey-based evidence on symmetrical bracketing and distancing by the plurality parties across 15 countries, together with self-placements by their electors, which show whether they are in fact located at or near the centre on most political issues.

Evidence on these points comes from **ISSP** comparative surveys of electors' self-placements on a ten-point scale, from 'fully in favour' of various

ISSP

Initiative for Science, Society and Policy (see Sources and Resources).

issue proposals (0) to 'fully opposed' (10). Experts located party positions on the same type of scale for the same issues, so we can see whether the two major parties in each country stand on each side of the median elector on various specific issues. Many of these, such as state intervention and redistribution, are closely linked to the general left-right conflicts that we have examined.

As we have seen in Chapter 4, however, many electors think in terms of separate issue proposals without linking them up overall. So rather than looking at left-right positions in general, we can look at the extent to which the major parties bracket the position of the median elector on each specific issue on which we have comparative evidence. On five issues, which are broadly about government intervention into economic and social life, 75 comparisons of party and median positions can be made with evidence on five issues across 15 democracies. Specifically, 55 of the 75 comparisons show the two potential plurality parties bracketing the median elector – whose preference is the best measure of the majority position. So party bracketing, a major condition for policy-preference correspondence in the alternation model, is widespread but not universal over these issues.

In their case, the failure to find bracketing everywhere is, however, mitigated by the fact that 12 of the cases of no bracketing show one party as being only half a point on the wrong side of the median position. So 55 out of 75 cases show bracketing, and 67 show either full bracketing or something close to bracketing, where the misplacement might be due to measurement error.

There is, however, a general failure of the parties to bracket the majority position on two of the examined issues. These concern the question whether the EU should be given more or less authority to intervene in the member country concerned and whether economic growth should take priority over the environment. Citizens predominantly favour fewer EU powers and more priority for the environment than experts judge the major parties as favouring. Parties in almost all countries therefore generally fail to bracket majority positions on these two issues. As a result, we should expect enacted policy to be out of sync with popular preferences there.

We lack comparative evidence about enacted policy on all these issues. So we cannot check in detail whether the presence of party bracketing on most of the first five issues produced more of a correspondence on them than on the EU and the environment. There has, however, been an unusually high number of popular **referendums** held on whether or not to grant more powers to the EU. Not leaving this decision to be made by the normal process of parties seeking votes and support in general elections is itself an indicator of tensions on the issue. Of the referendums held on the EU in member countries, almost all had initial majorities against government proposals for more EU powers (one in fact voted for the country to leave the EU). These results provide a general indication of an unusual level of popular disagreement with enacted or proposed policy, which is in line with expectations where bracketing does not occur.

Referendum

A popular vote called by governments or courts to decide on some policy proposal.

Looking over the issues and countries as a whole, however, party bracketing of the majority elector position occurs on 60 out of 105 comparisons. If we add to this 60 the 12 cases of near-bracketing already mentioned, we have 72 'bracketings' in all – almost three-quarters of the comparisons that can be made.

Alternation theory does not depend on bracketing being present in all cases. Rather, it expects bracketing to produce more policy-preference correspondence and non-bracketing less. These are the expectations it should really be tested on. However, if we did not find extensive bracketing in functioning democracies, all of which claim to be responsive to the popular will, we would certainly begin to doubt this theory. The prevalence of bracketing thus helps to bolster confidence in it.

As well as bracketing of the issue median itself, long-term representation would be facilitated by it being symmetric, in the sense of each plurality party standing at a roughly equal distance from the median. If it were not, party alternation would produce policy outputs with a distinct bias in one direction or another.

Again, what we see is broad, if imperfect, support for the symmetry of bracketing. Broadly, if one major party stands to one side of the median elector position on an issue, the other stands to roughly the same extent to

---

Briefing 7.4

Why parties should generally bracket the majority policy position

Propositions 4 and 5 in Table 7.1 suggest that the free formation of political parties under democracy allows all significant opinion groupings either to find representation of their preferences in an existing party or to found a new one to represent them. We can assume that party supporters are fairly evenly distributed around the party's general position on any issue (otherwise, it would move its position to reflect the internal majority one). Half of its supporters are thus positioned towards the centre of the policy space defined by the party positions around it. This will be true of all the parties opposing each other, so at least half of electors will find themselves between the party positions. If we add to such committed party supporters, electors who find themselves in partial agreement with several parties, and average out the positions of all the more extreme and opposed party supporters, the majority position will generally be between the parties and usually bracketed by them, even if preferences are not able to be represented along one line as they are on left-right or, usually, on single issues.

Of course, there may be reasons for this process of centre majority formation not working out (e.g. the state may not be fully democratic or external influences may be at work). So we would not expect to find party bracketing of the majority in all the cases we observe, quite apart from observational error. However, if we did not find majority bracketing in most political units accepted as democratic, we would begin to doubt our theory of how policy-preference correspondence comes about.

the other. The balance is rarely perfect but reassuringly approximate. We have to take into account that the positions and distances are affected by sampling and measurement error. Given these, this is probably as good a result as we can get with the evidence available at the present time, and it is one which facilitates the workings of party alternation from a representational point of view.

If we take centrism as indicated by a score of 2–3 on the five-point scale, we can also see from Table 5.2 that the mass of elector preferences falls within that interval. Centrism is a facilitating condition for alternation theory rather than essential, of course. But its prevalence does lend further support to the conclusion that the theory's working conditions are in place for specific issues as well as general left-right differences.

Determinants of public policy supply and demand: an equilibrium analysis

In classical economics, the supply of goods and services stably matches demand when the price is right – that is, when consumers can afford to buy the good and what they pay covers the cost of production and distribution, plus a reasonable profit for the producer. Supply and demand are then said to be in 'equilibrium'. Enough goods are produced to meet demand so that there is no temptation to either cut or increase production – that is, to move away from the equilibrium that has been established. Rather than taking up a fixed position, the equilibrium point might of course oscillate within a limited range, as factors like the weather increase demand for a service temporarily, and supply rises within certain limits to meet it but reverts back once external conditions change to what they were.

With the aid of alternation theory, we can look at public policy supply and demand in much the same way, seeing how particular conjunctions of the conditions we have identified as affecting correspondence produce different – but predictable – ranges of correspondence between preferences and policies. Doing so gives us a concrete example of how alternation theory provides us with a basis for predicting and assessing the quality of democracy within a particular country.

From Figure 7.1 we can see that the extent to which enacted policy stays close to the centre on any issue or set of issues depends primarily on (1) party bracketing of the median; (2) the extent to which party governments alternate; and (3) the pace of policy change. To put together all the conditions which maximize correspondence between the possible positions which actual government policy will take up and the centrist preferences of citizens, we need to calculate the policy equilibrium interval (i.e. the range of possible values which actual implemented policy could take up) as a proportion of the left and right scores of the major parties. On average and over a large number of countries, the major parties on each side stand at +13 (to the right) and −13 (to the left), as shown in Figure 7.4.

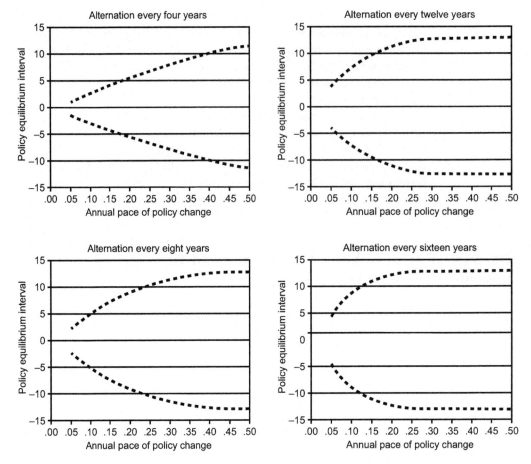

FIGURE 7.4 Theoretical expectations for the size of policy equilibrium intervals under varying conditions of speed of policy change and frequency of alternation in government

Notes: The policy equilibrium interval – the distance between the dotted lines in the figures – represents the range of left-right positions which enacted policy could take on under varying rates of government change and the pace of enacted policy change towards the government target. As median citizens are located at the centre (zero) on the vertical dimension, the wider the interval, the more chance there is of enacted policy departing from their preference.

If we assume (unrealistically) that a new government can enact its targeted policy positions within one year, then the possible range of positions which actual policy could take up stretches all the way to +13 when one party is in power and -13 when the other party displaces them. That means that actual policy might then be a long way out from what is demanded by citizens at the centre (where the left-right score is 0).

Suppose, however, that the pace of change is much slower. Only 15% of the distance to the target value can actually be achieved in a year. Then the equilibrium interval – the range of positions that actual policy could take up in the time likely to be available to the government – is reduced to ±4.33 from 0 (one-third of the distance to either of the two major parties).

Briefing 7.5

Formalizing alternation theory in spatial and predictive terms

The range of correspondence between actual policy and (centrist) popular preferences can be specified in terms of a dynamic equilibrium analysis similar to those applied to supply and demand in economics. Alternation ideas provide a clear structure for this, focusing attention on the policy positions taken up by the two leading political parties. These have to meet four conditions for good correspondence:

1   Symmetrical bracketing of the median citizen-elector.
2   Moderate policy distancing between the plurality parties on the right and left (i.e. limited polarization).
3   Regular alternation of these parties in government.
4   Slow policy change.

In this analysis, the focus is on the pace of change, the frequency of party alternation in government and a set of positive and negative target values for government policy. We designate the current policy actually being implemented as G; the targets as T; and the pace of policy as β – inertia being the converse of the pace of change (so 1 - β). For simplicity, the time interval between government alternations (k) is set initially to one year (so k = 1). A simple formal equation shows that the policy equilibrium interval (i.e. the range of values which actually applied current policy could settle at) is a proportion of the magnitude of the target values.

We start from

$$1. \quad G_t = \left(1 - \beta^{k-1}\right)T_t + \beta^{k-1}\, G_{t-1}.$$

This simply states that actual policy (G_t) in any year is equal to the proportion of the target that has been implemented, plus the proportion of previous policy which continues to be implemented.

At the time of alternation *across* the position of the median (where italicizing 'across' reminds us of the bracketing condition we take for granted), a positive G_t follows a negative G_{t-1}, or vice versa. Thus, for example,

$$2. \quad G_t = \left(1 - \beta\right)T_t + \beta\left(-G_t - 1\right).$$

Rearranging it,

$$3. \quad G_t - \beta\left(-G_{t-1}\right) = \left(1 - \beta\right)T_t.$$

Or

$$4. \quad G_t - \beta\left(G_{t-1}\right) = \left(1 - \beta\right)T_t.$$

And because $+T_t$ and $-T_t$ have the same magnitude (both plurality parties being at the same distance from 0),

$$5. \quad (1+\beta)\pm G_t = (1-\beta)\pm T_t.$$

Therefore,

$$6. \quad -G_t = \left[(1-\beta)/(1+\beta)\right]+T_t$$

Or

$$7. \quad +G_t = \left[(1-\beta)/(1+\beta)\right]-T_t.$$

All this is saying that the size of the equilibrium interval within which enacted policy will settle (i.e. the range of values it will take on) is a proportion of the positive and negative values set as targets by the plurality parties and that proportion is determined by the inertia of policy change.

If there is no carry-forward of the governing position from the previous governing position, $\beta = 0$. Then, continuing to assume k = 1 (the target value is reached in one year), the equilibrium interval reaches all the way to the positions of the plurality parties on the left and right – since [1–0)/(1 + 0)] = 1. If, however, the 'stickiness' of change is 0.5, then the equilibrium interval is one-third of the distance to each of the target values – since [(1–0.5)/(1 + 0.5)] = 0.333. Therefore, the more polarized the major parties on the left and right *or* the faster the pace of change, the wider the policy equilibrium interval.

The role of party polarization is intuitive as the party positions set the limits to which changes can go. But the less obvious pace of change can play the same role. A fast-paced system, such as $\beta = 0.2$, with parties standing at ±12, has a policy equilibrium interval of ±8. A slower-paced system, such as $\beta = 0.6$, with parties in the much more divergent positions of ±32, has the same equilibrium interval – that is,

$$8. \quad (0.4/1.6)(\pm 32) = \pm 8.$$

Most governments in Western democracies last more than a year, and when short-lived governments change, they do not often alternate from left to right. To account for longer time intervals between alternations, a per-year pace of change needs to be added, as do durations of more than one year between alternations – that is, for k > 1. We choose values for the slowness of annual policy change between 0.50 and 0.95 – that is, 0.50 < 0.95. We set the frequency of alternation between plurality parties on the left and right at 4, 8, 12 and 16 years. And we again set the major parties at ±13. The four graphs in Figure 7.4 show how wide the policy equilibrium interval would be under these various conditions.

This is obviously much better from the point of view of policy representing popular preferences for it.

Both the distance between the major parties (their 'policy polarization') *and* the rate of change from policy target to policy practice thus play a part in determining the interval. A fast rate of change such as 0.8, with parties taking up positions of +13 to the right and -13 to the left, has a policy equilibrium interval of ±8 from the centre. A slower rate of 0.6, with parties really far apart at ±32, has the same Policy Equilibrium Interval (PEI) of ±8.

The other factor to take into the calculation is the alternation of the parties in government. Most governments in Western democracies last more than a year. Even when short-lived governments succeed each other without an election, they usually all remain either on the right or left. We also need to allow for the exceptional cases where governments (or much the same governments) succeed in staying in office for as long as 8, 12 or 16 years.

Figure 7.4 keeps constant the extent of polarization or distance between the major parties but varies their alternation in government and the speed of policy change to examine the joint effects of all three in matching policy supply and demand. The calculations set speed at values between 0.00 and 0.50; polarization of the major parties around the centre at ±13; and government alternation at 4, 8, 12 and 16 years.

The policy equilibrium interval – the distance between the dotted lines in the figures – represents the range of left-right positions which enacted policy could take on under varying rates of government change and varying paces of enacted policy change towards the government target. As median citizens are located at the centre (0) on the vertical dimension, the wider the interval, the more chance there is of enacted policy departing from their preference.

Under alternation every four years, a slow pace of change, in the neighbourhood of 0.05 per year, creates a narrow and centrist equilibrium interval, between ±2. This enhances the possibility of congruence between currently enacted policy and centrist popular preferences. How large the interval is with faster-paced change depends on the frequency of alternation in government. With frequent alternations, say every four to eight years, an annual pace of change up to 0.15 creates an interval between centre-right and centre-left (i.e. ±7.5) in the range which covers the observed centrist positions of most Christian democratic and liberal parties. The combination of less frequent party alternation in government and any moderately fast-paced change, however, pushes the equilibrium interval to include policy alternations that swing to and from the major party positions on the right and left, relatively distant from centrist preferences as represented by median electors at 0 on the left-right scale.

This quite precise specification powerfully operationalizes our leading theoretical ideas in a measurable form. All you need to judge this aspect of public policy supply relative to demand is the average frequency of government alternation; the average left-right scores of the leading parties on left and right; and the pace of policy change. Then you can place the democracy in question at a point on the appropriate graph in Figure 7.4 and see how wide its range of possible policy outcomes is about the centre. For example, taking a democracy with a 0.15 rate of policy change and government alternation every four years and the major left and right parties at ±13 from the centre would produce a policy equilibrium range of ±5 from 0. This means that policy would probably never be further than five left-right units from the median elector position (the best estimate of the popular preference) – and might of course be considerably less.

Compare this with another democracy, where governments alternate every eight years and the rate of policy change is 0.20, with parties still ±13 from the centre. We can see the range of possible outcomes has doubled to ±10 from the centre (0), where median citizens (representing the majority) are likely to be. In turn, this means that policy could end up, on average, double the distance from the popular preference than in the first case.

Formalizing and quantifying the way in which parties, governments, elections and electors interact in democracies thus expands our ability to identify the necessary conditions making for a close connection between popular preferences for policy and public policy itself. In economic terms, this constitutes the dynamic equilibrium range for optimal public policy supply and demand, matching the efficiencies of the ideal free market in supplying private goods and services.

End-summary

This chapter has built on the general discussion of democratic processes in Chapter 3 to put numbers on them, using the estimates of popular preferences presented in Chapters 4 and 5 and of party policy in Chapter 6. These enable us to specify more precisely some of the relationships involved in making a 'necessary connection' between popular preferences and public policy. They also let us quantify theoretical expectations about supply and demand equilibriums similar to those made in economics for private goods.

Specifically the chapter has discussed the following:

- The different measures of correspondence between popular preferences and actual policy are election-by-election congruence; long-term correspondence and non-bias (averaging out deviations to left and right); and responsiveness, in the sense of public policy changing in line with changes in popular preference.
- Because election-by-election congruence guarantees long-term correspondence and responsiveness, the chapter has concentrated on congruence between the median citizen/elector preference and actual implemented policy.

- The median elector preference is the best measure of what citizens want because (a) the median position is the unique point which most minimizes the distance to all individual citizen preferences and (b) has to be included within any majority to make it a majority.
- The policy actually being followed by bureaucracies and other administrative bodies has to be distinguished from stated government policy (targets).
- This is because it takes time to change the existing policies inherited from previous governments (policy inertia).
- As parties gain or lose control of the government based on general-election success, they pull actual policy left or right by changing it in line with their targets.
- Because governments change relatively rapidly and the pace of change in actually implemented policy is slow, actual policy zigzags across the centre to produce public policy positions reasonably congruent with the centrist positions taken by the median elector.
- The balance between public policy supply and demand as measured by such congruence is determined by government alternation, the policy distance between major parties, their 'bracketing' of the median elector and the speed of real policy change. These can be combined and measured in policy equilibrium diagrams, corresponding to supply and demand curves in economics (Figure 7.4).
- 'Thermostatic' reactions to specific, inter-election policy proposals (Figure 7.2) generally provoke more popular opposition than support, contributing both to party alternation in government and slow policy change.
- Parties are 'carriers' of many policies. All the conclusions reached in regard to left-right policy space therefore also apply to other issues. As parties alternate in government, they try to pull actual policy into line with their own (differing) priorities, thus producing a zigzag across the centre which ensures congruence: a matching of policy supply and citizen demand on single issues most of the time.
- Government alternation and the slow rate of actual policy change thus resolve the central paradox of democracy – how relatively extreme parties can supply policies which match relatively moderate majority preferences.
- Both the conditions for such a result and an actual matching of policy outcomes to citizen preferences are found in most post-war democracies. Where the conditions are missing, there is no close match between policy and preferences.
- The alternation theory of democracy (Table 7.1) is the most comprehensive and extensively validated explanation of democratic processes up to now – unless and until it fails further checks. (For further discussion on this, see Chapter 18.)

Systematic working assumptions coming into this discussion

The next chapter will put together all the working assumptions coming into the discussion so far, to provide an overall context for the ideas put forward in the individual chapters. The assumptions underpinning discussion here are numbered as they will appear in Chapter 8:

6   Policy preferences and their implementation can be classified and measured for over-time and comparative analysis on the basis of textual, survey, expenditure and other statistical evidence.

7   This allows them to be represented as points in spaces constructed on various measurement assumptions, with a centre and extremes, which can also represent and relate the policy positions of political actors (citizens, voters, governments, parties, etc.) as specified from either data or theory.

The chapter has used these assumptions to develop a specific predictive theory of the democratic process – namely alternation theory, which can be summarized as saying that correspondence between popular policy preferences and public policy, the ultimate guarantee and justification of democracy, is mostly produced through its institutional mechanisms of party competition in general elections – which regularly alternate different party policy carriers in government – together with slow incremental change in enacted policy. This process applies equally to overall policy (e.g. left-right policy) and specific policies, provided that parties are differentiated on them and 'bracket' the majority preference.

Readers who are still curious about how alternation theory, with its supporting assumptions, fits into the general argument of this book can see how in Chapter 8. This puts them all together to provide a context, and theoretical and methodological support, for the predictive theory of democracy presented here.

Sources and resources

Ian Budge, Hans Keman, Michael D. McDonald and Paul Pennings (2012) *Organizing Democratic Choice* (Oxford, Oxford University Press) pp. 91–290.
Initiative for Science, Society and Policy (ISSP) www.issp/center/
G. Bingham Powell Jr. (2000) *Elections as Instruments of Democracy* (New Haven, CT, Yale University Press).
Stuart Soroka and Christopher Wlezien (2010) *Degrees of Democracy* (Cambridge, Cambridge University Press).

Suggestions for class papers

1   What is the paradox of democracy? How far do you think the alternation and/or thermostatic theories overcome it?

2   Do you think the alternation and thermostatic theories give a complete account of how democracy works? If not, what is missing?

3   What policy proposals might produce positive rather than negative 'thermostatic' reactions? How might they fit into the general theory?

4   Would institutional differences (e.g. between presidential and parliamentary organizations of governments) require modifications in alternation theory for it to apply under the different systems?

Suggestions for class projects

1   Suggest and apply other checks on alternation theory by updating previous data or assembling new data.

2   Compare the various indicators of majority policy preferences (median and plurality voters and the median elector) to see how far these agree with each other across time and countries.

3   Generate other predictions from alternation theory and/or thermostatic theory, and check them out to further test the credibility of the theory or theories.

Chapter 8

The 'web of explanation'

Relating process theories to each other within a general political science context

Chapter overview

Predictive explanations, and even the evidence used to check them out, are never complete in themselves. They depend on a web of supporting explanations to supplement and support them. These are of two kinds, both of which enter into discussion here.

First, there are the predictive explanations dealing with other political processes than the one immediately under consideration – in this case, the alternation theory of how a policy-preference correspondence is brought about. Its main assumptions are that parties alternate in government, bracket the majority popular preference with their relatively extreme policy targets, 'differentiate' themselves through these and can implement policies only slowly. In the context of alternation theory, these conditions have to be simply assumed to occur rather than explained and investigated. Other theories, however, predict that such conditions will generally emerge in democracies and explain why this should be. Their success lends more plausibility to the explanation of correspondence that alternation theory gives. Several such theories are discussed in the book. We have already encountered two – the thermostatic theory and the developmental party-family theory – while referring forward to incrementalism (Chapter 14) and party factionalism (Chapter 12). We link all these up in the 'web of (supporting) explanation' in Figure 8.1.

All these **substantive explanations** of how politics works, including alternation theory, rest in turn on a set of working assumptions about what political explanation should focus on and how it should be done. We cannot check out such assumptions directly, because many are **definitions**, such as the idea that public goods are characterized by having to

Substantive explanation

An explanation of some actual process or behaviour.

Definitions

Statements of what something is within the relevant context.

be provided universally. However, they can be justified indirectly if the theories they support 'work' in the sense of providing good explanations and predictions of political processes.

These background assumptions are common to many political science theories and explanations, including those examined here. In this chapter, we explore both the general working assumptions and definitions which underpin systematic political science and the specific predictive theories which within this overall context constitute a 'web of explanation' around the alternation theory of democracy.

Specific features of this discussion are thus:

- The predictive explanations which feed into the alternation theory of policy supply and demand.
- The ways in which these interact with each other and generally support alternation theory.
- How these emerge from the working assumptions of systematic political science – of which an overview is provided at the end of the chapter.

The web of explanation

It follows from what has been said that no one theory is totally free-standing. It is formulated within the context of the widely accepted working assumptions examined later. And it gains more immediate credibility from its compatibility with other specific, substantive theories of political processes which feed into it. Showing that its starting assumptions emerge as implications from another validated theory immediately renders any explanation more plausible. A specific example is the alternation theory's assumption that parties have their own internal policy agenda, which leads them to adopt more extreme targets than most electors and voters are entirely comfortable with. The developmental party-family theory (Table 6.2) and the factional theory of party policymaking (Chapter 12) explain how parties' identity and ideology shape their choice of policy targets and make them generally unresponsive to other considerations. In the absence of a supporting explanation, theorists are often forced to make a priori assumptions such as these about the ideological rigidity of party behaviour. Where these emerge as predictions from another explanatory theory, the whole explanation is extended and strengthened.

This 'web of explanation' of mutually supporting theories is illustrated in Figure 8.1. This notes the specific support the other theories give to the main assumptions of the alternation model (e.g. 'incremental' budgeting which limits ministries' ability to expand and contract their activity and 'thermostatic' and negative popular reactions to government policy initiatives in the inter-election period). Both contribute powerfully to slowing down policy change – a key assumption of the

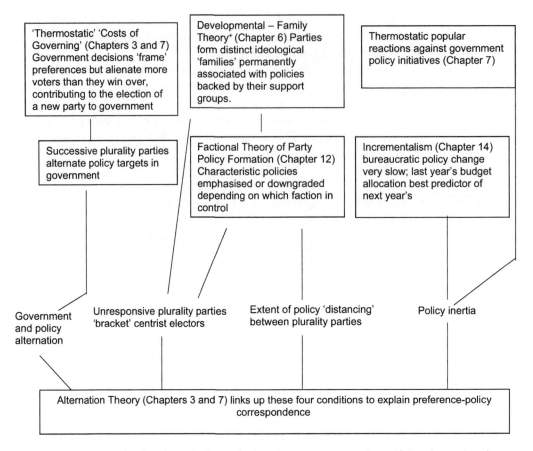

FIGURE 8.1 The 'web of explanation' supporting the main assumptions of the alternation theory of policy-preference correspondence in democracies

Notes: The figure summarizes the way in which four free-standing theories about political processes explain why party alternation in government takes place and why bracketing, distancing and a slow rate of policy target conversion into policy application exist as conditions which can then facilitate policy-preference correspondence. The free-standing theories are thermostatic reactions (Chapter 7), incrementalism (Chapter 14), factional policymaking inside parties (Chapter 12) and developmental party-family theory (Chapter 6). Each can stand on its own as an explanation of why these particular processes and behaviour occur. When brought together with alternation ideas, they provide a unified account of how democracy works.

alternation model. Other theories' contributions to the overall reasoning are also noted. Taken together, they provide a more extensive insight into the full range of democratic processes than any one theory can. Figure 8.1 shows that such processes are not only compatible with but also highly relevant to each other, their interactions helping to match policy outcomes to majority preferences within the general context of alternation. These other theories frame most of the chapters of Part III, dealing with the behaviour of key actors like parties and governments in the democratic process and fleshing out the explanatory links summarized in Figure 8.1.

Briefing 8.1

An integrated account of democracy? The wider 'web of explanation'

Besides theories explicitly related to alternation in Figure 8.1, other theories of processes and institutions discussed in Parts II and III provide a supporting context which adds up to a general account of how democracy and its constituent institutions work, with political parties as the key actors. In Part II we see that the way in which party votes are aggregated to produce majorities have their own effects on outcomes – each procedure having its own biases which can, however, be allowed for in interpreting the popular will. The effects of parties and governments in stimulating and framing – and sometimes biasing – popular preferences is revisited at the beginning of Part III. Mostly, however, Part III looks at political processes at the top levels, which are more influenced by pure policy considerations. The theory of government formation (Chapter 13) interprets party behaviour as driven primarily by ideological and policy concerns rather than seeking office. These also push parties into getting and holding relevant ministries, which in turn focuses these on certain policy objectives to the exclusion of others. This push contributes to policy continuity and inertia, reinforced by incremental budgeting, which leaves only a limited scope for new initiatives.

Taken separately, each of these theories is free-standing and predictively successful in anticipating the political outcomes it focuses on. When put together, they support conceptions of democracy as a set of slow-moving centrist policy programmes which are, however, capable of adapting to new conditions, particularly through the emergence of new parties with novel policy concerns and targets, which alternation then gives them some chance to effect.

The methodological context for predictive theorizing: systematic political science

We have just seen how predictive explanations support each other and provide an overall context for the behaviours and processes they explain. If every explanation went back to its starting point and covered all the basic assumptions necessary to generate it, however, it would be as long as a book. An example of this is the idea that policy positions can be located in a space of some kind. This makes so many assumptions about measurement and the properties of the space, which would need to be repeated for every new theory and tests basing themselves on it, that they would overwhelm its unique contribution to the specific problem it confronts. Normally, therefore, basic assumptions about measurement and other supporting features of the theory are taken for granted (unless in seeking to diagnose faults or achieve a deeper understanding of what it is telling us, we need to rethink these).

All this is true of the alternation theory of democracy, which we have been discussing. For most purposes, it can be quite adequately stated in terms of the four conditions for policy correspondence which it lays down: alternation, bracketing, differentiation and rate of policy change. As this chapter will illustrate, however, such a summary statement bypasses questions of why we should concern ourselves with democratic policy-preference correspondence in the first place and how we should conceptualize and measure it.

At some point, we need to consider these supporting assumptions to fully understand how we arrive at the predictive explanations and what they add up to. The appropriate place to do so is in a textbook like this with its focus on 'doing political science'. That is why we provide a comprehensive overview of these assumptions. In theory, we could go back from many of these to *their* supporting assumptions and so on ad infinitum, in a near endless chain. What we have tried to do is state working assumptions at a reasonable level of generality – as far back in the chain of reasoning as political analysts themselves are ever likely to want to go.

All these assumptions are stated as numbered prepositions, in the shape you have already encountered at the end of earlier chapters which have based their discussions upon them. A proposition is a succinct statement of some point in a chain of reasoning sequentially numbered so you can refer back to it easily. Our summary of the working assumptions behind the body of political research which generates and supports predictive explanations contains 20 of them. A few might be added, subtracted or amalgamated. The summary does not claim to be a conclusive statement of 'systematic political science'. It is rather a first stab at defining its content and scope as succinctly as possible.

After this, we comment briefly on the assumptions themselves. Readers are probably best advised to first go through the propositional summary to get the full picture. But where they really need elucidation, they can go on to the comments or even to the concluding chapter (Chapter 19) of this book, where there is a detailed discussion of each proposition.

Systematic political science – a propositional overview

Definition Systematic political science integrates the working assumptions of that body of political theorizing and research on the basis of which a set of interrelated predictive theories of political processes can be generated and tested, particularly of democratic processes.

General working assumptions

1 States form the basic unit or context for political research.
2 States are governments with supporting (quasi-)military, administrative and other institutions, recognized by other governments as

providing public goods and services (including the regulation of non-state activities) within specified territorial boundaries.

3   Public goods and services are those provided universally so that no one can be individually charged for them or excluded from benefiting.

4   Only states can guarantee the provision of public goods and services through their unique ability to finance them by taxes and other means.

5   Government decisions about what public goods and services to provide and how to provide them are recorded as state laws and policies to guide the actions of state and other bodies and the behaviour of individual citizens.

6   Policy preferences and their implementation can be classified and measured for over-time and comparative analysis, on the basis of textual, survey, expenditure and other statistical evidence.

7   This allows them to be represented as points in spaces constructed on various measurement assumptions, with a centre and extremes, which can also relate the policy positions of political actors (citizens, voters, governments, parties, etc.) as specified from either data or theory.

8   Such spaces can have varying dimensions and measurements, the most common being a straight line running between left and right.

9   States vary in the extent to which decisions about policy and who is to make it are shared widely among citizens.

10   The most extensive sharing occurs in democracies, since by definition, these have to guarantee that public policies necessarily reflect the preferences of citizens for them.

11   This guarantee is provided by free, regular and competitive elections of governments and/or policies open to all groups and individuals, where votes reveal citizen preferences and authorize them as either policymaking governments or directly as state policy.

12   Democracies are the only states with such key political procedures in common across the world. Hence, they are the only states whose policymaking processes can be analysed and explained at a general level by political science.

13   Ideally explanations should take the form of predictive theories consisting of propositions or equations which can be checked for predictive success against independently observed outcomes or behaviour.

14   The unifying focus of such theories – extending from preference formation and expression to policymaking and implementation – is on the extent of policy-preference correspondence and how it is achieved.

15   Popular policy preferences do not usually emerge spontaneously but rather are formed as reactions to policy proposals put forward by governments, parties or other political actors.

16   The free formation and functioning of such actors are thus essential to the process of estimating the full range of true popular preferences.

17   The popular preferences with which public policy must necessarily correspond in a democracy can be specified sufficiently to form a

basis for public decision-making only if estimated from voting outcomes in free and open elections (or from election-like formatting of questions in well-conducted surveys).

18 However, all political – like other – measurements contain error (which can nevertheless be estimated and corrected on various assumptions).

19 This is necessarily true of election votes in their role as measures of popular preferences. The rules and procedures which structure votes (e.g. the order and wording of alternatives being voted on and methods of aggregating individual votes to produce a collective decision) can all distort the final outcomes and have to be allowed for in estimating settled preferences.

20 Alternative ways (among others) in which public policy can be studied are:

a Normative political theory, which focuses on the extent to which the democratic policy-preference correspondence can produce good public policy, as judged by independent criteria of its quality which it develops.

b Policy analysis, which assesses policies in terms of whether they achieve their own stated goals.

c Class-elite analysis, which investigates who benefits from adopted policies.

Discussion

Actually, the propositions making up this overview of systematic political science do not need much justification and comment since they have emerged naturally from each chapter discussion (and have been reported as doing so at the chapter end). It is indeed instructive to see how far a fairly conventional overview of the contextual and historical developments affecting modern politics, such as that contained in the Introduction, makes the powerful assertions of Propositions 1 and 2, which put states and their governments at the focus of investigation.

Similarly, Propositions 3–5 about public goods and policies and problems of collective action (Chapter 2) are prominent both in modern political theory and in welfare economics. They are particularly relevant and challenging at a time when climate change and terrorism require collective interstate action in the absence of an overriding political authority.

What we concentrate on here is of course collective action within states and particularly democracies (Propositions 9–12). Current political research and quantitative analysis is overwhelmingly focused on democratic politics. These propositions simply state what is generally accepted in practice. The same is true of the measurement assumptions of Propositions 6–8 and 14–19. Most political analysis takes on an explicit or implicit spatial form (regression analysis in Chapter 18, for example). This is so much taken for granted that it is rarely explicitly stated. But in a systematic overview of the operating assumptions of political science it needs to be. Of course, policy can be examined in other ways and on other criteria than correspondence with popular preferences. Proposition 20 explicitly recognizes the different concerns of political philosophy and traditional, normative political theory, as well as the evaluative and technical concern of many analysts with effective policy implementation rather than its correspondence with popular preferences. The question of who ultimately benefits from policy decisions also comes in.

However, the policy-preference correspondence enters as either a major or a dominating concern for most political research conducted in democracies. It is, however, an interactive process in which preferences are framed by policy proposals and then influence them (Propositions 15 and 16). With globalization, research on democracy is increasingly comparative and seeks to validate general hypotheses against a growing mass of quantitative evidence from many countries (Big Data). This constitutes a basis for validation through prediction (Proposition 13), though surprisingly few analyses take on an explicitly predictive form. The logic of explanation does push it this way, however, as argued in the Preface and Part V of this book.

Most of the points made in the propositions of this overview are thus found in the working assumptions of mainstream political science today. It is, however, unusual to state them so explicitly and put them together as an integrated summary. Doing so fosters an intelligent understanding of what they add up to and where they lead us. That is the main use of an introduction to the study of politics, such as this book aims to be.

This propositional overview of its systematic working assumptions therefore stands at the centre of our discussion, being repeated and commented in more detail in the concluding chapter (Chapter 19) of Part V (Explanation). Readers who wish to go into the propositional summary in more detail could skip to that chapter at this point, before continuing with the discussion of democratic rules and procedures in Part II.

End-summary

This chapter has finished with the working assumptions and research underpinning the specific predictive theories contributing to the 'web of explanation' discussed in its first half. These assumptions do not need to be restated every time a specific predictive theory is presented. However, they do form the generally accepted methodological and theoretical context within which most specific theories are developed, as emphasized by the general propositions at the end of each chapter discussion. Major points arising from the propositional overview are thus:

- The focus of most political science research and theorizing on democracy and its processes of policy supply and demand.
- The emphasis on explanations capable of predicting political outcomes as the major way of assessing their usefulness.

- Their potential for being modified by new evidence, so their acceptance as true is always provisional.
- However, a replacement theory must also be plausible in itself, generate clear predictions and be open to testing in its turn.
- Potential error is always present in this process, including the measurements and evidence used to evaluate explanations. So its presence should always be checked and guarded against.
- Error extends to establishing what actually is the majority preference, since nearly all procedures for aggregating individual opinions into collective decisions are subject to arbitrary constraints, paradoxes and flaws. We examine these in Part II.

Suggestions for class papers

1   Why do we have to link up all the theories in Figure 8.1 rather than just considering them separately (e.g. as explanations of party or voter behaviour)?

2   Could we not just get down to explaining politics without bothering about the assumptions stated in the propositional summary? Why or why not?

3   Are there any points made in the propositional summary that you strongly disagree with? Pick them out and argue your case.

Suggestions for class projects

1   Identify the working assumptions in the propositional summary which each of the theories in Figure 8.1 (the 'web of explanation') makes. Do they use them all? If not, does this render unnecessary the ones they don't use?

2   Analyse some newspaper accounts of political events and identify and propositionalize their working assumptions for comparison with the ones in this chapter.

3   Develop an alternative account of political research to the one given in the propositional summary, expressed in the same propositional form.

Part II

Rules

Rules designate – but may misrepresent – majority preferences, thus biasing policy outcomes

All human encounters and interactions are shaped by rules – even seemingly unstructured ones such as passing on the pavement. Do we acknowledge each other explicitly (say 'hello' or 'good morning') or pass by in silence? Which side do we use when heading in different directions? When it comes to road traffic, such rules are more formalized, since the consequences of a collision are much more serious. As football has evolved from a battle between two village teams, where the object was to place the ball in the middle of the other side's territory, to scoring a goal at the rival end of the field, it has required ever more elaborate rules, such as how many should be in each team, how they should behave (no kicking at each other's shins or shoving), what constitutes a real goal as opposed to offside and how a team wins the game.

Rules are thus necessary both to characterize and order events: are we voting in an election or betting within the context of a sporting contest? Both have common elements, so we need rules to sort out which is which and characterize the outcome. Under different rules, outcomes might differ: do you win simply by scoring more goals, or is their quality also assessed? Is the election winner the one with most votes or most legislative seats?

Rules influence but do not wholly determine specific outcomes, such as the winner of an election. Depending on whether votes are added up inside constituencies – and additionally whether you need an overall majority to win the seat or simply more votes than any other candidate – or whether parties get legislative seats in proportion to their national vote, different parties will get different shares of seats, different governments will form and different policies will be pursued. On the other hand, the number of votes also count: no set of democratic rules is going to make a clear minority the winner.

We comment on all of these points in the next two chapters (Chapters 9 and 10). But we have already said enough to indicate the importance of the rules by which elections are run and the majority preference designated – particularly where opinion is closely divided. Nowhere is this more evident than in the contrast between general elections and elections which decide on specific policies (i.e. referendums and initiatives). Policy elections such as these record popular support for a policy more directly. But would the decision be the same if the election were held another day? We consider that possibility – a common criticism of democratic votes – along with other problems of aggregating individual preferences into a collective choice, in the next two chapters.

Chapter 9

Majority choice of policies

Voting paradoxes and attempted solutions

Chapter overview

The simplest way of ensuring that public policies match popular preferences for them – as democracy requires – is to let citizens vote directly on the relevant alternatives. The policy most favoured by the vote would then be implemented by government. This is indeed what happens in some democracies, which have referendums and popular initiatives. However, these are not generally held over the whole range of policies, nor in most democracies. More often than not, citizens are allowed policy votes only when governments decide to hold them and then only in a form which the government lays down. These restrictions are often justified by the alleged difficulties in identifying the true majority preference from a popular vote. This then supports the argument that it is better identified indirectly, through party votes in general elections and deliberation by those elected in a representative assembly (i.e. a legislature or parliament).

We have already discussed such indirect processes of representation in Part I and will consider them further in Chapter 10. Here we focus on the question of whether popular 'policy elections' could provide an alternative or supplementary way of discovering the popular preference. A major problem stems from inherent features of voting processes, which make it difficult to guarantee that a stable popular preference will be clearly expressed. This chapter discusses voting problems and paradoxes first, before considering possible solutions. Though none are perfect, they might clear the way for purposive policy voting and popular initiatives to supplement the alternation of parties in government as another mechanism rendering public policy responsive to popular preferences. This is a possibility we consider in conclusion.

Key points in this discussion are thus:

- The different kinds of policy elections – referendums, often called by governments when they find it convenient to do so, and 'initiatives' called by citizens themselves (often prompted by political parties).

- Counting votes equally as expressions of preferences or 'weighting' them by strength of feeling about the alternatives on offer.
- Bias in voting procedures, which may misrepresent real citizen preferences.
- The median (middle citizen position) as the best indicator of the majority preference.
- Problems with shifting majorities where there is no guaranteed median position – can any settled popular preference then be identified?

Ways of making collective choices

Democracy guarantees that public policy will match popular preferences for it. As we have seen, however, there are various ways of doing this. The most obvious contrast is between representative democracy and direct voting by citizens on policy proposals – termed 'direct democracy'. This chapter focuses on the procedures which the latter might adopt to get a true reflection of popular preferences on policy – though as we shall see, there are inherent problems in such votes which are not obvious at first sight. One point which needs to be strongly emphasized is that these problems are associated with any kind of policy voting – by legislatures as well as by electorates. So they should not be taken as reflecting uniquely on *citizens'* decision-making capacity.

Purposive policy voting is given its freest rein in referendums and initiatives, which by definition focus solely on policy. This renders problems about aggregating votes to identify a majority even more pressing, since these directly affect the choices to be made, rather than combining with non-policy factors to produce programmatic alternation over time in the wider context of general elections.

Where there is a strong majority favouring a particular policy, it is likely to get its way under any voting procedure. In any collection of individuals, however, there is likely to be some disagreement about the actions they should take as a group. Some of these can be resolved by deliberation – intensive discussion and debate among citizens. Proponents of 'deliberative democracy' point out that discussion has a great potentiality for resolving disagreements by ensuring that all aspects of the situation are properly considered (including facts which may previously have been ignored by some) and thus promoting compromises and agreement. These are even more likely to emerge from a long process of discussion based on trials of alternative policies to see what their advantages or disadvantages are in practice.

To save on the commitment of time which all this would involve, one might delegate discussion to a representative sample of citizens to see what they decide to do after debates and briefings by experts. Improvements in modern information and communications technology render extended discussion through blogs and tweets, not to mention TV and radio, more feasible and possibly better informed. So traditional objections to

Briefing 9.1

Referendums and initiatives

There are many ways in which direct policy voting by citizens might be organized – all having a potential effect on which policy gets majority support. The most general and far-reaching contrast is between votes which are initiated by the current government or required by the constitution before certain types of decision can be made ('referendums' or 'plebiscites') and 'initiatives' whereby a vote can be called by (a certain number of) citizens themselves, often prompted by opposition parties.

Clearly where citizens prompted by non-government parties can take the initiative in setting the timing and terms of the vote, they have more influence over policy outcomes than where a government determines timing (often when they think they can get a majority for their own preferred policy) and sets the question to be voted on – often biased towards their own preference.

Legally required referendums fall between these extremes (e.g. stipulations in the constitution that popular approval is required for certain kinds of foreign treaties). However, they still depend on how judges and courts interpret these requirements, so they are to that extent independent of popular demand for them. Other kinds of rules (e.g. is a majority to be defined as a majority of those actually voting or as 50% +1 of all citizen electors?) may also produce varying outcomes from referendums and initiatives.

deliberation in terms of the colossal time and effort involved in prolonged debate have become less relevant than before, where discussion always had to be face to face.

However, it is unrealistic to think that all differences can be resolved by discussion, thus producing unanimous agreement. Individuals may have quite different values and preferences – religious, moral and cultural – or quite opposed economic interests (cheap prices versus high wages) which cannot all be settled by debate. In the end, a vote will need to be taken to decide on a preferred course of action, and a majority and minority will emerge – or perhaps a **plurality** and several minorities.

Plurality

The largest number of votes.

If there is near unanimity and a strong majority for a particular policy alternative, there will be little disagreement about this representing the collective view. Not only is it shared by most citizens now, but it is also likely to remain so for the foreseeable future and so represent a settled popular preference over time.

Problems of interpretation, however, arise in the more usual cases where there is not a strong majority or its members are a bit uncertain and qualified in their opinions – especially if it confronts a cohesive minority who feel strongly that another alternative is better and should be adopted as public policy. One solution in such a case is to require a 'qualified' majority – more than simply 50% x 1 of the voting body – perhaps 60% or even two-thirds (66%) of voters or electors. If one emerged, we could be pretty sure that this was the settled popular preference.

Briefing 9.2

Deliberative polling

As we have seen in Chapters 3 and 4, voters, electors and citizens often find it hard to form a spontaneous opinion on public policy proposals and rely on having it framed by political parties, governments or pollsters so that they can react to their specified alternatives. One problem with these is that framing the proposal differently at different times results in respondents changing their preference. So it is often hard to say what citizens' *settled* preference really is. The majority could shift from one policy to another as the individuals comprising it shifted positions. More extended discussions of the question could help fix opinions so that a settled majority emerges. The trouble is that most people do not have the time or energy for extended political discussions.

One way of getting around this is to bring together two or three hundred people selected randomly from the population so that they form a representative sample of it. They can then have discussions among themselves and with experts about the question and cast a vote on the proposals under consideration based on much more information about them. This could then either be taken as authoritative or at least indicative of what the general public would want if they had had full information and discussions. Deliberative polling of this kind could then offer a less biased guide on how to vote in the referendum or initiative than that provided by parties, governments or special interests, which stand to benefit or lose by the result.

Republic

A republic, as opposed to a democracy, makes procedures and a balance of powers between institutions rather than a popular majority determining of policy.

Such a rule would certainly ensure that policy changes could be effected only if they were backed by a strong majority likely to endure over time. However, this comes at the cost of transforming the minority into the majority. It is hard to get a super majority for any proposal, so in most cases, a minority needs only to stick together to block proposals. This gives it a decisive veto in adopting a policy (unless indeed that has nearly unanimous support). This may be a **republican** solution to deciding on collective action in the sense of enshrining minority rights. But it can hardly be taken as an unbiased reflection of popular opinion in a democracy.

If the answer does not lie in making strong minorities rather than majorities decisive in enunciating the popular preference, perhaps it lies in going beyond mere numbers by considering the degree of commitment each grouping has to their opinions. This is often measured as the 'intensity' with which individuals hold an opinion – 'very strongly' or 'not very strongly' in the words of many poll questions. If 40% of citizens strongly oppose nuclear power while 60% support it weakly and with some doubts, there might be grounds for at least postponing a decision until more evidence is available.

There is also a time factor involved. The people who feel intensely about the policy are more likely to have already gone into it and hence to stick to their opinion than the more apathetic and dubious majority, which might change over time.

We will consider a procedure for voting on policy options which does take intensity of feeling into account. Objections to such intensity-weighted voting often rest on the assertion that we cannot compare the exact intensity of preferences between individuals. I, for example, may be the kind of person who feels strongly about everything, while you may be shy, diffident and doubting in all your opinions. In balancing expressions of intensity between us, a good committee chair would probably take account of this difference and weight opinions accordingly. But it is hard to do this in a mass poll or in popular voting.

For this reason, democratic theorists have usually argued for each individual vote to count only as one and no more than one. One has to recognize, however, that this takes an equally strong position on the interpersonal comparison of preferences. By counting them equally, it assumes that they are all the same! The basic point is that we cannot simply get away from the question of relative intensity just by ignoring it. Doing so is to take one particular position (they all equal 1), just as explicitly weighting intense preferences means that some votes count more than others. In face-to-face interactions, we probably use both intensity-weighted and equally weighted voting at different times and in different situations, time being an important factor. Having to make an immediate decision probably favours majority rule on a one-to-one basis in order to get things done quickly. But in long-term decision-making, we might wish for prolonged discussion where the intensity and stability of opinions might be more important.

Briefing 9.3

Non-voting as a (rough) way of allowing for the (non-)intensity of preferences

There is one way of letting intensity count in voting procedures which is in widespread use in almost all democracies. That is, in making no effort to get people who are uninterested or apathetic about proposals to vote in policy elections (or for that matter in general elections). The obvious way to do this would be to make voting compulsory so that everyone has to vote or be fined, or face further sanctions. But this is actually done in only a few cases.

The result is that only preferences held with high and medium intensity get represented in the vote, since the voters holding them are more likely to turn out. This may affect outcomes where a majority of all electors (rather than just of those voting) is required to pass a proposal. In practice this means that abstentions are counted as votes against proposals for change. Where only a majority of active voters is required, this privileges those who feel strongly enough to go and vote. In the case of non-voting, preferences held with higher intensity score 1, and those of lower intensity are scored 0 in the vote – thus running counter to the democratic requirement that everyone's votes should be scored equally. Since the disadvantaged groups in society vote less, such an intensity weighting tends to bias policy outcomes against them, as we shall see (Table 10.2).

We shall consider ways of registering preferences where only numbers are considered and also where intensity is explicitly brought in as well. Each have their problems. This emphasizes one fundamental and basic point: there is no perfect rule which takes care of all potential misreadings of underlying preferences. This indeed is true of measurement in general. In seeking to assign numbers to preferences, whether by voting or in responses to polling or opinion surveys, we always risk being in error. We could always be wrong in reading the popular preference either from a majority vote or from one weighted by intensity – or indeed from one taken at one particular time as opposed to another.

But this is no more than to say we could be wrong about measurement in any context – in the extent to which expenditures accurately reflect policy outputs, for example. (Spending more on policing does not necessarily mean there is better policing – just as in medicine, a high temperature does not always indicate disease).

Looking at various voting and election rules as different measures of popular preference, each with their own strengths and weaknesses, is a useful way of approaching our discussions about finding a majority through the alternative procedures we discuss. We will then see how they

Briefing 9.4

Voting and measurement error

As we shall see (Chapters 16 and 17), practically all numeric estimates and the techniques used to present and analyse them are prone to error. This is a fact often ignored in political debate, where statistics are often taken at face value even by those whose arguments they discredit.

In fact, however, error creeps in at all levels of estimation, even where the best procedures are followed closely. We know mathematically, for example, that even random samples taken from a population independently of each other will give different estimates of what they are thinking – quite apart from errors which may have crept in counting answers or in framing questions. Even in vote counts, electors may pull the wrong levers in voting machines, or humans counting ballot papers may assign them to the wrong piles. And the impact of a dramatic event may switch votes from what they would be at another time even if it is quite irrelevant to the subject being voted on.

None of these problems discredit voting counts or statistics in general. But they do mean that allowance must be made for votes or other estimates not exactly reflecting popular views. This is usually done by placing an error band or 'confidence interval' around the estimate which recognizes that the true value may be higher or lower than the one we have. In close votes, this would imply that a 51%–49% outcome probably means opinion is evenly divided rather than that there is a settled majority on one side and that we ought to rerun the vote after some time to see if it produces the same result.

are applied in practice to referendums and initiatives – the main forms which popular policy voting takes on in democracies today.

Estimating majority preferences

As we will rarely if ever get 100% support for any proposal, an obvious compromise in estimating preferences is to go for the policy alternative supported by the greatest number. This could either be a plurality – the alternative which gets the greatest single number of votes – or a majority – the alternative which gets more than half (50%) of the votes. A majority clearly has more claims to represent the popular preference than a mere plurality.

Most of the population might be said to have voted against the winning proposal rather than for it when the plurality is in the 30% range or lower (as it might be where several alternatives were being voted on). With a majority of 54% or 55%, there can be no doubt that most people have supported it (beyond the possibility of measurement error).

A majority must by definition include the median or middle voter. We can see why from Figure 5.2, where voters prefer any policy closer to their own preference on spending. This puts the median voter, C, who favours moderate spending, in the pivotal position. Supporters both of less spending and more need C to form a majority. The closer the potential majority position comes to the position of Cs (moderate spending), the more likely a policy will get their support and form a definite majority. C's position will always be preferred by voters on one wing of the policy **continuum** to positions on the other wing. So although C's position may not be ideal from their point of view, it is preferable to the other feasible alternatives, so they will back it. Thus, C's position will always constitute the point to which majority-backed policy tends, where voting is motivated solely by relevant policy preferences. In technical terms, this is known as an equilibrium point: collective policy preferences will tend to shift towards it, and once there, will have no reason to move away from it.

Two consequences follow. One is that the median position is the best general estimate of the preferred majority position and hence of the popular policy preference, within a policy voting context. In practical terms, when we want to analyse how far public policy corresponds to the popular (majority) preference, we can compare actual outputs to the median preference for them and estimate their congruence. It is useful for such measurements to have a single position representing the popular (majority) preference and we find this in the median.

The other desirable property that the median has – lying as it does at the centre of the distribution of preferences – is to be the single point on the distribution of preferences which is closest, on average, to all the other positions held by individual voters. It will have to be the position adopted by the majority in order for them to be a majority in the first place. But at least it is the policy preference which causes least dissatisfaction by being adopted. Any alternative position would be further away from at least one

Continuum

A line running between opposed alternatives at each end.

Briefing 9.5

Does the majority (or plurality) always get it right? Condorcet's jury theorem

At the end of the eighteenth century, the Marquis de Condorcet, a French mathematician, demonstrated that if every individual in a group had even a slightly higher probability (say 0.51) at arriving at a correct judgement rather than a wrong one, then the majority would always arrive at it too. This conclusion depends on there being only two alternatives to choose between. However, the proof has been extended to situations of three or more cases where a plurality is involved rather than an absolute majority (see Christian Best and Robert E. Goodin (2001) Epistemic Democracy: Generalizing the Condorcet Jury Theorem. *Journal of Political Philosophy*, 9, 276–306). This is reassuring if you are undergoing a trial by jury! – but also for democratic processes which rely on it for majority or plurality decision-making.

---

individual preference and so cause more dissatisfaction when adopted as the general preference.

The median and the majority are thus closely associated with each other. The majority policy position claims to be the best measure of the popular preference, and the median position is the best estimate of what the majority preference would be if it were influenced solely by policy considerations.

In practical terms, we find out what the majority preference is by looking at the distribution of votes over policy alternatives. For example, if we were trying to discover what popular preferences were about using nuclear power to generate electricity, we could put the question to a vote for or against doing so. If the agree option got 53% of votes and disagree got 47%, we would say that the popular preference was to go ahead with using nuclear power.

There are qualifications on this, however. The two sides are very close, numerically. If quite a large number (say 20%) had abstained from voting, we might well have doubts about whether the majority would continue to be a majority if another vote were to be held later. Moreover, older people continually leave the electorate and younger folk come in. Would they vote differently, thus changing the result over time?

The larger the majority lead, therefore, the surer we would be that this was a true and settled majority preference. Doubts about this might also be a reason for bringing intensity back into the measure of 'settled preferences' as we shall see: intense voters are less likely to change opinions.

Framing

Defining the possible actions to be considered on an issue.

There are also other considerations linked to our earlier discussion of **framing** votes and opinions (Chapters 3 and 4). We pointed out there that the expression of preferences depends not only on the way people feel about the proposal under consideration but also on how it is put to them or framed. People may well answer differently depending what questions are asked or what alternatives are offered for voting on.

We can see this in the context of voting on policy proposals. To get at the full range of opinions on methods of electricity generation, we might not wish to restrict opinions to being for or against nuclear generation. Instead, we could list the full range of generating methods, asking individuals to rank order them according to their own preferences and then to vote on them. We could hope from this to get a preferred option, such as gas-fired generation, which would beat all the others and thus emerge clearly as the generally preferred option. That would also reassure us about the stability of the preference. After going into the matter in this relatively detailed way, individuals would be more likely to stick to their preference if the matter came up again.

A policy alternative which beats all the others in a series of paired votes is termed a 'Condorcet winner' after the mathematician who proposed the procedure in the eighteenth century. Its great advantage is that it is explicitly preferred by a majority to all other proposals.

Unfortunately, Condorcet also pointed out there are voting situations in which no such winner emerges. We have already illustrated this with the preferences in Table 5.1, over defence and social spending. There was in this case a perfectly clear majority median position on each of these issues taken separately – for cutting defence spending on the one hand and raising social spending on the other. However, when the alternatives are voted on together, there is no 'all-round median' (i.e. on both issues put together), and any majority that can be formed can always be beaten by another combined option. It is not clear how many citizens put two or more issues together like this; they are more likely to be considered separately, one by one, or aggregated on the left-right continuum. But to the extent that they do think along the lines pictured in Table 5.1, this approach would undermine prospects of finding a clear and stable majority preference.

The possibility of such a situation emerging is a real problem in aggregating the equally weighted votes of all citizens to define a clear majority preference. It could be overcome, however, by changing the rules and weighting votes by the strength of the preference for each option, as indicated by its rank order. A procedure for doing so was suggested by another late eighteenth-century mathematician, Borda.

Borda's procedure was for each voter to rank the policy options being voted on in their order of preference for them, the most preferred being given the highest rank (with four alternatives, the highest would be 3; the second highest 2; the third highest 1; and the least preferred 0). These numbers would be multiplied by the size of the group to produce a weighted vote for the policy option (e.g. the big government voters in Table 5.1 would contribute (15 × 3) to increasing both defence and social spending). All the weighted votes for each option would then be added up. The option obtaining the highest score would win, as it would be most intensely preferred by most voters. (In the case of a tied vote, with two policy options receiving the same aggregate score, the two could be rerun against each other.)

This procedure is illustrated in Table 9.1. For example, the option of increasing both defence and social spending (↑D↑S) gets 45 from big government voters (3 × 15), 80 from liberal ones (40 × 2) and 60 from

TABLE 9.1 Preference profiles not yielding a stable majority under equally weighted vote procedures but producing one with a Borda count

Voter profile	Preference order			
	1st (3)	2nd (2)	3rd (1)	4th (0)
Big government (15%)	↑D↑S	↑D↓S	↓D↑S	↓D↓S
Liberal (40%)	↓D↑S	↑D↑S	↓D↓S	↑D↓S
Conservative (30%)	↑D↓S	↑D↑S	↓D↓S	↓D↑S
Small government (15%)	↓D↓S	↑D↓S	↓D↑S	↑D↑S

Notes: Compare this table with Table 5.1. Bracketed numbers are weights given to first-, second-, third- and fourth-ranked options under the Borda count procedure. This in turn depends on the assumption of equal intervals between rank numbers (i.e. $2 - 1 = 3 - 2$).

conservatives (30×2). This adds up to 185, which is the highest score that any option gets. Under the Borda procedure, this is taken as the winning option. This is a stable outcome with some claim to represent popular preferences where paired voting does not work. However, not everyone would agree with its definition of a majority based not just on counting votes but also on rank ordering of preferences.

What this example illustrates again is that any estimate of the majority preference is strongly affected by the way the initial question or proposal put to electors is framed and by the way their votes are aggregated afterwards. For example, if the alternatives included keeping spending on both defence and social welfare at current levels, it is likely that that would be adopted by a majority as a compromise position. Such a majority would probably win under pairwise voting procedures. But it might well not attract the highest Borda count. On the other hand, if Borda was used only where pairwise voting failed to produce a stable majority, there could be agreement on it as an acceptable substitute.

Another point to take from this discussion is thus that the same procedures and rules might not apply under all circumstances. The intensity of the preferences might be important under some circumstances, such as a minority's cultural rights to have education provided in its own language – where the majority is indifferent or only slightly opposed – but not where general state policy was concerned.

Unbiased estimations of majority preferences

Preference profiles

Sets of preferences organized in a particular way.

Many of the estimation problems discussed above derive from attempts to reflect true majority preferences in the rules and procedures adopted rather than imposing arbitrary shortcuts and solutions biased against certain **preference profiles**. As we shall see, such restrictions are imposed on how popular policy voting is actually conducted in contemporary democracies, rendering the alternation between party governments discussed in

Part I a more attractive alternative for producing majority-supported outcomes over the long term.

Some minimal and eminently democratic conditions for fairness in rules for estimating majority preferences in policy votes are:

1   The procedure must cope with every possible individual ordering of preferences. This is very democratic because everyone's preferences then have equal weight in determining outcomes. As we have seen, some combinations of individual orderings will not produce an unbeatable winner, so the procedure will always break down and produce unstable majorities at some point. This is not to say, of course, that in many circumstances it will not actually produce a **Condorcet winner** – only that it cannot guarantee one.

2   If every individual prefers a given alternative (w) to another (z), the majority should prefer w to z.

3   The overall ranking of any two alternatives should depend only on individual rankings of the two and is unaffected by 'irrelevant' third alternatives being either inserted or withdrawn or more generally by voting manipulation of any kind which would get in the way of discovering the true, sincere majority preference.

Condorcet winner

The one that beats all the others in a series of paired contests.

Taken together, these conditions have posed a dilemma for democratic theorists over the past hundred years. They seem essential to finding the real majority preference – but they also offer a sharp and unpalatable choice: either abandon democracy (as defined by the three conditions outlined above) or give up the idea of always achieving non-arbitrary and stable collective choices. One crucial question here is how often, using fully democratic Condorcet procedures, we could expect to end up without an unbeatable winner. Assuming that all individual preference orderings are equally probable, the probability that there is no such winner varies strongly with the number of options being voted on and more weakly with the number of voters. With three alternatives in play and a large number of voters, one might expect to get a Condorcet winner in over 90% of votes. This might be reasonable; after all, we expect a certain level of error in all measurements, including strictly scientific ones where this would be an acceptable level of accuracy. With eight alternatives and large numbers of voters, however, a winner would emerge in just under 60% of cases. That would hardly be acceptable. On the other hand, eight alternatives are rarely on offer anyway, and choices are much more likely to be made between three or four alternatives. In fact, the rules could reasonably require this limit on the number of alternatives being voted on.

Cycles

A cycle is where different majorities might emerge, depending on the order in which policy alternatives are voted on.

The reason why some individual elections and policy votes would produce a Condorcet winner, and others not, lies in the fact that the array of individual preference orderings would differ in each case. Either naturally or artificially, preference orderings might not include those which give rise to **cycles**. The commonest example is where alternatives can be arrayed along a single dimension (e.g. from left to right) and diminish in attractiveness to voters the further they are distant (in either direction)

Briefing 9.6

Strengthening Borda procedures for estimating the majority preference

To use Borda procedures at all, you must accept that votes should be weighted by how strongly those casting them feel about the policy alternatives on offer rather than by each person having one vote and thus counting equally. Once this is accepted, however, the other problems about the procedure stem from the Borda count using rank orderings rather than real numbers. Thus, we know that a person who ranks an alternative at 3 favours it more strongly than someone who ranks it at 2. But we do not know if the difference between them is the same as that between two other persons ranking it at 2 and 1. Rank orders are not real numbers which are guaranteed to measure distances and intensities in the same way. This also leaves them subject to manipulation, such as when an irrelevant alternative is introduced or withdrawn simply to change the rankings to favour or disfavour the other more serious alternatives being voted on.

Both these problems can, however, be overcome by asking voters to place alternatives on a ten-point ladder (or a ladder with another number of points) between 'strongly favour' and 'strongly oppose'. We discussed this in Chapter 4, where we gave examples of survey questions measuring preferences on 'ladders' with equal intervals measuring actual distances between preferences rather than just rank ordering them.

Putting yourself at some point on the ladder for each alternative being voted on produces a true numeric score not dependent on the scores given to other alternatives and therefore unaffected by variation or withdrawal of other alternatives. Moreover, the same metric is being used throughout, so all distances are comparable (4 to 3 is the same distance as 2 to 1 or as 10 to 9, for that matter). With these two major weaknesses addressed, the Borda count is available for voting purposes, perhaps as a supplement to Condorcet pairwise contests when these produce cycling – always provided of course that the relative intensity of preferences is accepted as one factor in identifying majorities.

from them (the condition known technically as single-peaked preference orderings). In such a situation, the alternative supported by the median elector at the middle of the distribution will always be the Condorcet winner. If those to the left of this position try to vote it down, it will be supported by all those to the right of it, as it is closer to these voters than is any alternative supported against it by the left. And for the same reason, it will be supported by those on its left whenever attacked by those to its right. We have already illustrated the power of the median (Figure 5.2) in this context. It will always attract 50% of the vote, plus 1 voter. No other alternative can beat it, and the median position will always emerge as the majority choice with a guaranteed winner.

Such convergence on the median can be generalized. Suppose that there are a number of issues to be voted on but that each is decided separately. This is what happens in practice with initiatives and referendums because courts have ruled that each proposal must be voted on separately. It may often make sense to do things in this way because, for example, decisions about river quality have no discernible connection with prison-sentencing policy. On the other hand, spending decisions may affect both of these, as we saw in Chapter 5, leading to difficulties in producing a coherent and consistent overall plan. Such difficulties, however, could be resolved by popular subsequent votes. No one outcome need be set in stone. Current practice is certainly on the side of voting on proposals one by one and adjusting overall expenditure later. Elected representatives follow this practice in legislatures and parliaments so that there is no obstacle to making such adjustments in the case of popular policy votes as well.

Policy voting in contemporary practice – initiatives and referendums

This leads to the question of how popular policy voting can be organized in practice to provide a reasonably accurate representation of citizen preferences even if it falls short of ideal criteria. Most democracies do hold policy elections at the present time, but only sporadically and on issues outside mainstream politics. These usually involve constitutional or moral questions – often issues on which governments and parties have internal disagreements on which they might split. A convenient solution to such internal divisions is to agree to put the issue to a popular vote and abide by the outcome.

The form such consultations take is commonly called a referendum. That is a popular vote called for a certain date by the government on a question that it has formulated (though sometimes it is subject to review and rephrasing by the courts). Such sporadic popular consultations are clearly not a regular feature of national decision-making, but they are held only on particular kinds of issues outside the main concerns of the parties – usually moral issues, such as abortion or divorce, or constitutional issues.

Occasional referendums are thus held at the convenience of the government or parties, usually on matters that they do not want to decide themselves. This renders them unsatisfactory as a way of discovering settled popular preferences. The referendum may be held at a time which favours one option over another, and the question may be worded so as to elicit one kind of response rather than another.

Other types of referendum are less subject to this kind of manipulation. These are ones which are held retrospectively on certain kinds of legislation or government decisions because doing so is required by the state constitution (see Briefing 9.7). The kinds of decision on which a popular consultation is required can vary widely. They will, however, be held on certain proposals regardless of whether they are convenient or inconvenient for the government or any other political actor. Thus, they do provide for more spontaneous expressions of popular preferences than where timing and wording

Briefing 9.7

Constitutions and constitutional law

The 'public goods' discussed in Chapter 2 include decisions about individual and collective rights and ways of deciding on these. Such decisions are usually made as laws passed by parliaments and legislatures. The body of laws relating to rights (and procedures for making decisions on these as well as other matters) is termed the 'constitution' of a state, and in some democracies it has to be referred to in calling referendums and initiatives. Where there are disputes about what such laws mean or about how they should be applied to specific cases, these are generally settled by judges and courts rather than directly political bodies like legislatures.

are controlled by government. Where the range of matters covered by a popular vote is also wide, and the wording of the question is decided by an independent body or by a state's supreme court, even less scope is left for manipulation. In such cases, the winning preference is more likely to correctly reflect popular wishes.

Initiatives fulfil this potential to an even greater extent. As the name implies this type of popular vote can be prompted by popular action. Usually a petition carrying 50,000–100,000 signatures putting forward a proposal to be voted on by electors is enough to trigger the procedure. Collecting so many signatures requires a degree of organization and co-ordination, particularly if they have to be obtained from all over the country. This gives a certain advantage to political parties who already have the organization and supporters to do so. Parties not in government often find this a useful tactic in modifying government proposals or building up party morale before a general election. In this way, initiatives form a more potent vehicle for challenging government decisions in the inter-election period than **thermostatic reactions** or opinion polls.

Thermostatic reactions

Expressions of popular support for or (more often) hostility to government policy proposals.

Popular votes can thus be classified as in Figure 9.1 according to the freedom of expression granted to citizens, from the occasional referendums called by governments for their own purposes (which may of course include a genuine desire to know what the public is thinking), through constitutionally required referendums to get popular approval on certain matters, to initiatives which can be called on any subject by large enough numbers of citizens.

Popular policy votes as they are conducted now in contemporary democracies thus vary considerably depending on their spontaneity of expression. In other respects, however, they show strong similarities:

1   They cover only a limited range of topics, usually 'moral issues' like abortion: constitutional issues, such as the franchise and voting arrangements, and territorial issues (whether to have a nuclear

Referendum called when and how government wants	Referendum required by constitution but subject to government interpretation	Referendum strictly mandated by constitution, requirement interpreted by courts	Initiative promoted by citizens' petition stimulated by some parties	Initiative prompted by citizen petition, minimum control by parties
HIGH				**MINIMUM**
CONTROL				**CONTROL**
(e.g. UK referendum on membership of EU 2016)	(e.g. French referendum on direct election of President 1962)	(e.g. Irish referendum on single European Act 1987)	(e.g. Italian referendum on divorce 1974)	(e.g. Californian Proposition 13 putting a cap on taxes)

FIGURE 9.1 Referendums and initiatives contrasted according to government control

power station or incinerator built nearby). In contrast, there has rarely been a popular vote on economic policy, such as 'should we cut public services or raise taxes to eliminate the budget deficit?' This is partly because these wider questions have already entered into the general-election campaign.

2 Proposals being voted on are thus specific and narrow rather than general and broad. The form they take is generally a choice between two alternatives: whether to adopt a particular proposal (e.g. for nuclear power generation) or stick with current arrangements, the **status quo**.

Status quo

The situation as it exists now.

Note that this two-option choice is also the form which legislative voting generally takes – for or against a 'motion' (i.e. a policy proposal). The fallback position is always the status quo.

By having only two options, the theoretical difficulties already discussed – which all derive from voting on three or more options – are avoided. This comes at the cost of ignoring relative intensity on both sides (only the number of votes counts). Impacts on other issues are also not considered. It is true, however, as we saw in Chapter 4, that there is only a loose relationship between the various issues covered in party programmes. Treating issues as separable thus may not carry great costs for the coherence and consistency of public policy.

A final point to note about popular policy voting is that the outcome usually favours the status quo in the standard two-option choice, between change and the status quo. Contrary to the fears commonly expressed by political theorists and established politicians, the majority of citizens display a healthy scepticism about proposals for change, which is well summed up in a famous proverbial saying: 'Better the devil you know than the devil you don't know'. The existing situation may be seen as having many imperfections, but at least they are known, and the majority can cope with them. Change will undoubtedly bring new problems as well as benefits. So voters, who will bear the brunt of them, must be convinced before they will support them. Enthusiasts for direct democracy often support radical changes which they see as being blocked by the current political setup. Their new proposals are so obviously beneficial, they feel, that if only they could be put directly to the people they would be approved. The actual experience of popular policy voting goes against this: current arrangements, if not obviously problematic, will generally be favoured.

This finding concurs with the public's 'thermostatic' reactions to government policy proposals, generally favouring 'less' or 'more' of a policy than the government wants to provide. It also chimes with citizens' settled preferences being generally 'centrist' and against extreme policies on either side. This is vital as we have seen, in estimating how far actual policy comes close to people's preferences for it (Chapter 7).

Policy elections and general elections complement each other in translating popular preferences into public policy

Parties play a reduced role in direct policy voting than compared to in general elections. But parties are nevertheless important in framing opinions and policy options – and in prompting a popular vote in the first place. And of course, they are central to general elections – clarifying the programmatic alternatives (often linked to left and right) on the one hand and carrying them into government on the other.

There is indeed a sense in which parties can be seen as having extended popular influence over policy in a way which has also strengthened their own hold on democratic politics. This derives from how, in the nineteenth century, they transformed what had been a series of separate contests between individuals for legislative seats (or in presidential regimes, for executive office). By grouping potential MPs (members of parliament) or deputies as teams, running under one party label and pledged to support the party and its programme, parties introduced policy voting into general elections. As we have pointed out, policy is not everything considered when voting for a particular party in general elections, nor is it even dominant in many voting decisions. But nowadays, voters do decide on policy – among other things, like candidates' competence, past record and so on.

Moreover, the policy debated in general elections does not just focus on a single issue but consists of a loosely linked set of policy proposals put forward in a common programme (a manifesto or platform). To the extent that a decision on one issue has implications for another, the parties bring these out, often in terms of the general left-right contrasts discussed in Chapters 4 and 6.

In modern democracies, therefore, policy elections and general elections have come to resemble each other more – through the pervasiveness of policy voting in both and the political parties' role in organizing it. As between the two kinds of democracy, direct and representative, the latter has come further, no longer based on individual representation but rather allowing for policy voting (among other considerations) with the successful party as the guarantor of the programme being effected in government. Direct democracy has continued to differentiate itself as direct popular voting on individual policies, most often policies not central to ongoing party politics.

We can see this better by examining actual practice in contemporary democracies. Popular policy votes tend to be held disproportionately in five areas: (1) changes in the constitution; (2) territorial questions covering secessions or extensions of the national territory, devolution and autonomy; (3) foreign policy; (4) moral matters, such as divorce, abortion and gay rights; and (5) ecology and the environment (including local campaigns for protecting particular features or in opposition to the siting of a power plant). Fiscal matters are increasingly voted on, usually involving tax limitation and restrictions on the size of government.

Policy voting thus tends to take place either on issues of a certain level of generality – constitutions or foreign policy measures like membership in the EU or trade liberalization that will have a long-term effect – or in areas that fit uneasily into the general left-right division of party politics and that might indeed provoke internal party splits, like moral and ecological matters. The closest that policy votes come to influencing the current political agenda is on fiscal matters. Even tax limitation has a long-term effect rather than an immediate effect, however. Almost never is a vote held, for example, to 'prioritise unemployment now', 'stop inflation', 'end the war' or 'reduce the prison population'.

Several factors contribute to this pattern of policy consultation. First and perhaps most importantly, governments do not want to put their central policies to a referendum. So, where they have control over their timing and initiation, voting will not cover issues central to the main party conflicts – only off-issues that might split the party. New and opposition parties have generally also mobilized to put such issues on the agenda and not to refight continuing party battles.

A party-based explanation is only one part of the answer, however. The same pattern occurs also in fairly unregulated popular initiatives, where parties have less control. It is probable that electors themselves, and even interest groups, are less focused on medium-term policy plans which have largely been decided by the general election. So it is natural that parties should be left to get on with these at least in their first years in office (and it often takes time to organize a referendum or an initiative).

In this way, a certain division of labour seems to be emerging in contemporary democracies between general, programmatic – but also non-policy-influenced – general elections and direct policy voting on individual issues. Where issues are linked together and form an integral part of the activity of governments, usually within the traditional left-right framework, the parties in power are left to get on with them. Where individual issues have long-term implications and do not fit so easily into a unifying framework, they tend disproportionately to be the subject of special popular votes. The overall mix does not seem a bad way of translating popular preferences into public policy, with more fine-tuning possible than with general elections alone.

This all fits into a general pattern of democratic politics. General elections and the party alternation they produce set the broad targets which pull actual policies across the centre, where popular preferences lie. This secures a rough long-term correspondence between actual policy and (centrist) citizen preferences for it. Fine-tuning in the inter-election period, however, is provided by votes on specific policies – probably ones not covered in general party programmes published in the general election. These bring preferences and opinions more immediately together on issues outside the inter-party debate.

The most recent development is continuous detailed polling on current issues, often concerned with popular reactions to recent government policy proposals. Having such a detailed information stream enables governments to adapt 'thermostatically' to public opinion, often changing and shaping their proposals to counter and anticipate hostile reactions. This in turn improves their proposals' congruence with current preferences and at the same time slows down the implementation of ultimate policy targets. Such inertia is a crucial element in promoting the correspondence between preferences and actually implemented policy (Chapters 3 and 7), in the context of general elections and party alternation in government.

Direct policy voting and programmatic alternation in government can therefore be seen as jointly bringing together popular preferences and implemented policy – the first in the short term and the second in the long term. In that sense, direct and representative democracy feed into each other, partly owing to pervasive party influence on the political scene. Direct policy voting could – and probably will – play a larger and more active role in this process in the future. Modern developments, such as interactive instantaneous communication and an increasingly educated and informed electorate, will drive it on. It is unlikely ever to completely replace general elections and government alternation, however. Democracy will probably always involve several concurrent processes adjusting policy to preferences – which is not a bad thing, because the weaknesses in one, such as the voting paradoxes that we have considered, can be corrected and balanced by the others.

End-summary

This chapter has carried on the discussion in Part I about how popular preferences can be framed and expressed. Where Part I concentrated on the way parties operate in general elections, this chapter has looked at possibilities and practice in situations where electors vote directly on the policy proposals to be adopted.

What seems at first sight to be a fairly simple procedure of identifying popular support for specified policy options turns out to be much more complicated than you would think, especially if everyone's wishes – including the idiosyncratic ones – are given equal freedom to be expressed. This can lead to the problems of 'cycling' and unstable majorities, examined in the first part of the chapter. Another problem is how far to accommodate intense feelings – especially among some minorities – on matters where the numerical majority does not feel so strongly involved.

These problems have often been raised as objections to any form of 'direct democracy', understood as a setup where citizens vote directly on policy. But they arise wherever policy is voted on, in legislatures and parliaments as well as among the body of citizens. And errors occur whenever we try to measure things, be they physical, social or political. Votes are our most authoritative measure of what popular preferences are. But that does not mean they are a perfect measure. We should be satisfied if they provide good estimates of popular feelings most of the time. Being correct in 90% of cases is an acceptable level in scientific investigations, so we shouldn't be too worried about it in democratic politics.

One thing we should do, however, is *allow* for error – hence the importance of procedures such as voting more than once on a proposal to see if the results come out the same way. Such procedures are usually followed in legislative voting, so there is no reason for them not to apply to popular voting on policy as well. More restrictive procedures involve separating out issue areas to vote on them one at a time, thus ensuring that there is always a median preference around which a stable majority can form. This is common practice both in legislative voting and in referendums and initiatives at the present time. It is often supplemented by framing the proposals being voted on as a choice between a change of policy and keeping things as they are. Such a dichotomous choice also eliminates voting cycles and ensures a majority. Both procedures, however, infringe democratic guarantees of giving equal weight to all citizen preferences, by eliminating ones which might be expressed in more unusual ways.

Particularly where there are strong differences of opinion, all this might point to different voting rules being applied at different times and places, to ensure that popular preferences are being properly reflected. Popular policy voting can also be supplemented by opinion polls, as a check on its accuracy. And ongoing processes of electing and alternating governments also have a potential for translating popular preferences accurately into actual policy, at least in the long term.

We should therefore regard democracy as being tied not simply to one kind of political process but several, each of which complements and strengthens the others and balances their faults, within general guarantees of transparency and freedom of expression. A final lesson is that no one voting rule or procedure is ever completely neutral. It will always tend to favour one type of outcome rather than another – though never, in a democracy, completely determining it. Popular preferences, if strong, should always get through. But in marginal cases, where they are diffuse and less intense, they may be diverted in one direction rather than another by the way they are channelled by the rules. Having examined the effects of these on direct policy voting, we go on in Chapter 10 to investigate the way they shape policy indirectly through general elections and the kind of party governments they produce.

Key points following from this discussion are thus:

- The increasing role of direct popular voting on policies (along with opinion polls) in establishing majority preferences.
- The importance of establishing procedures (including repeated votes) to ensure that outcomes reflect settled majority preferences.

- Avoiding bias in the rules for calling popular votes and shaping the options on offer.
- Noting once again the 'centrist' and moderate nature of popular majority preferences in terms of support for current arrangements (the status quo) in most post-war referendums and initiatives.

Systematic working assumptions coming into this discussion

9   States vary in the extent to which decisions about policy and who is to make it are shared widely among citizens.

10   The most extensive sharing occurs in democracies, since by definition, these have to guarantee that public policies necessarily reflect the citizen preferences for them.

11   This guarantee is provided by free, regular and competitive elections of governments and/or policies open to all groups and individuals, where votes reveal citizen preferences and authorize them as either policymaking governments or directly as state policy.

17   The popular preferences with which public policy must necessarily correspond in a democracy can be specified sufficiently to form a basis for public decision-making only if estimated from voting outcomes in free and open elections (or from election-like formatting of questions in well-conducted surveys).

18   However, all political – like other – measurements contain error (which can nevertheless be estimated and corrected on various assumptions).

19   This is necessarily true of election votes taken as measures of popular preferences. The rules and procedures which structure votes (e.g. the order and wording of alternatives being voted on and procedures for aggregating individual votes to produce a collective decision) can all distort the final outcomes and have to be allowed for in estimating settled preferences.

Sources and resources

Ian Budge (1996) *The New Challenge of Direct Democracy* (Cambridge, Polity Press).
James Fishkin (2018) *Democracy When the People are Thinking* (Oxford, Oxford University Press).
Lawrence Le Duc (2003) *The Politics of Direct Democracy: Referendums in Global Perspective* (Peterborough, ON, Broadview).

Suggestions for class papers

1   How far does letting the whole population vote directly on policy solve the problem of matching policies to popular preferences?
2   Should we weight votes by intensity of feeling about the alternatives being voted on? Why or why not?
3   Does deliberative polling meet all the criticisms usually made about citizens' competence to vote directly on policies?

Suggestions for class projects

1   Compare the actual outcomes from referendums with those from initiatives to determine whether there are systematic differences between them.
2   To what extent do popular votes on policy systematically favour left-wing as opposed to right-wing policies?
3   Organize a deliberative poll to decide some policy proposal and evaluate the improvements it brings to the quality of decision-making compared with non-deliberative polling.

Chapter 10

General elections and election systems

Finalizing the collective choice of policies

Chapter overview

The dynamics driving the processes examined in Part I are elections – general elections, in which at regular intervals parties try to secure votes based on their candidates, record and policy programme. With sufficient votes, they can either form a government or participate in one and claim a 'mandate' for getting at least part of their policy through.

The next election, however, may well put them out of government before they have had much of a chance to get their policy effected and put in another government with different policies. In this sense, general elections are the central institutions in the democratic process, since their results determine the overall direction of policy (even though voting in them is not wholly based on policy). Other arrangements may supplement these, and we have just considered the main alternatives: referendums and initiatives, elections which decide policy directly. Public opinion polls also provide governments with continuing feedback on popular reactions to their policy proposals, which they may modify 'thermostatically' for fear of general election consequences.

We already discussed voting in general elections in Chapter 3 (cf. Figure 3.1). There we showed that it is multi-motivated, based to varying degrees on party candidates, record in government and policies. Voting may also be affected by concurrent scandals and events which may occur by chance but might well favour one party over another.

Voting may also be affected by strategic considerations. Voters might decide that some parties which they would prefer on other grounds, such as their policies, just would not stand a chance in their district or constituency and so vote for second best or even to keep the least preferred candidate out. This situation is more likely to arise in small territorial constituencies than in larger units.

Hence, election systems – the rules by which votes are assigned to parties and then translated into legislative seats – are crucially important

Mandate

An authorization and a requirement for the government to see something gets done.

in influencing outcomes in general elections, just as they are in the pure policy-voting situations examined in Chapter 9. First in this chapter, we consider general-election rules. Next, we look at their political consequences, primarily in terms of the number of parties they encourage and how easy they make it for new parties to start up and gain significant numbers of votes.

This raises important questions about the long-term effects of election systems on parties. There are also questions – carrying on from the last chapter – about the short-term election results and their ability to properly characterize the majority and their policy preferences. Would the same party majority or plurality emerge under another set of rules – for example, if parties were compared with each other in turn and voters were invited to choose between them in a series of paired contests? We consider which party is most likely to emerge as the majority or plurality winner under pairwise voting and whether this is the same as the one identified by the actual general election. This is important in ensuring that the majority preference does get correctly reflected in the votes.

By choosing governments, voters also choose policies, albeit rather indirectly. Do the various kinds of election rules have implications for what kind of policy gets adopted either in the short or long term? As with policy elections (referendums and initiatives), the rules under which general elections are held have important consequences for all the participants involved, primarily the political parties, which we go on to examine in Part III.

Only in the cases where candidates in a two-party democracy are contesting a nationwide office such as the presidency does the overall percentage of votes determine directly who forms the government (and not always then, depending on institutional arrangements). Major points made in the discussion here are thus:

- What is the real majority and the party favoured by it?
- Effects of election rules ('election systems') on the party system (i.e. numbers and types of parties).
- In particular the contrast between rules which award a seat to the largest party in each constituency (SMDP), as opposed to rules which seek to reflect national vote shares in the legislature (PR).
- The policy differences associated with these.

Rules and (missing) majorities

Even in the case of presidential elections where there are three or more serious candidates, it is unlikely that any one of them will get an absolute majority – over 50% of the vote. If candidates get 40%, 31% and 29% respectively, who is the winner? Do we go for a plurality – more votes than anyone else? Or do we eliminate the weakest candidate with 29% (but only 2% less than the next strongest) and have a second 'run off' election between the two leaders?

There is no conclusive yardstick to tell us which alternative will best reflect the majority preference. If the third candidate's vote split evenly, the leading candidate would clearly win and could even be declared the winner without further ado. But there are no guarantees of this. And one cannot vary the rules to fit different situations; otherwise, there would be too much opportunity for manipulation in a particular party's interests. Rules have to be relatively stable to maintain a minimal respect for them.

Most general elections are more complicated than the presidential case. They are held to decide what share of seats political parties should have in the legislature. In legislative elections, there are almost bound to be three to five **effective parties** contesting the election. So it is unlikely that any of them will get an absolute majority of the vote (50% + 1). This creates difficulties in translating vote shares into seat shares.

The obvious solution is to make them equivalent. So if a party gets say 10% of the vote, it gets 10% of the legislative seats, thus satisfying the requirements of accurate representation. The largest party (the plurality) would then have considerable influence the closer it approached 50% of the vote (thus getting nearly 50% of the seats). The 'centre' party, occupying something like the middle position on the main dimension(s) of conflict, would be able to use its indispensability to most majorities formed in the legislature to bargain with potential partners – most importantly the plurality party – to moderate their policies in return for its support (see Chapter 13).

The most important legislative majority to be formed is the one supporting the government. Under **parliamentary government**, it is usually a requirement that the government can depend on a legislative majority. Under a presidential system, the government is appointed by the president under their own authority. But a presidential government must have substantial if not majority support in the legislature simply to get laws and other measures passed. So the role of the legislative parties is still crucial, even under separately elected presidents.

The need for legislative support to make governments effective – or even to form a government in the first place – forms an argument for moving away from proportional representation (PR) of votes by seats, as described above, to a biased system of translation which favours the largest (plurality) party. The justification is that the largest party is clearly the one most favoured by the electorate and should therefore be given both the power and opportunity to govern and carry through its policies. With a single-party majority government, it is also clear who is accountable for what goes right or wrong during its period of office. So it is easier for electors to confirm it or dismiss it at the next election and substitute another clear (legislative) majority and government if they dislike what it has done.

The electoral system which most effectively privileges the popular plurality party and transforms it into the legislative majority party is the SMDP system (sometimes reduced to simply SMD) – Single Member District Plurality. Here voting takes place in small territorial constituencies, each of which elects one member to the legislature. The party candidate who wins more votes than any competitor (the plurality of the vote) wins the seat. So

---

Effective parties

Parties with enough votes or seats to get into government or to influence policymaking.

Parliamentary government

Whereas a presidential government is one where a directly elected chief executive forms the government, a parliamentary one is where the government has to have majority support in parliament.

---

if the percentage distribution of votes between the three leading candidates is 34, 33 and 32, the first wins the seat, even though two-thirds of the votes might be said to have been cast against that candidate. If the main leading party had fairly uniform national support, it can repeat that result in most constituencies and thus get a strong majority of seats with slightly above one-third of the national vote. Conversely, an uneven distribution of votes

Briefing 10.1

The main electoral systems: plurality and proportional representation

Free elections are the backbone of modern democracy, and although at first sight they may appear to be a simple matter – expressing a preference for one party over others – they turn out to be complex affairs. There are two main types of electoral systems in modern democracies: simple plurality voting in small electoral districts (SMDP) and proportional representation (PR).

Simple plurality

Sometimes called the first-past-the-post system, this only requires the winning candidate to get more votes than any other candidate, no matter how many candidates there may be and no matter how small the winning percentage of the vote may be. In a three-way contest, the winner may get little more than a third of the total, and in a four-way contest, little more than a quarter. Simple plurality voting is usually linked with single-member constituencies, and the whole package is called SMDP. In Europe, it is used at present in the UK, and outside Europe, in the US and Canada. The advantage of the system is simplicity. The disadvantage is that it is likely to produce disproportionate election results in that the distribution of votes between parties does not closely match their proportion of seats in the legislature. The simple plurality system also means that minor party supporters may 'waste' their vote.

Second ballot

The second ballot system tries to avoid the worst disadvantages of the simple plurality system, by requiring winning candidates to get an absolute majority (50% +1) of the votes cast in the first around. Failing this, a second (run-off) ballot is held for the two strongest of the first-round candidates.

Alternative vote

Another variation on simple plurality voting is to allow voters to indicate their first and subsequent preferences among candidates, so that if no candidate receives a majority of first preferences in the first count, second (and subsequent) preferences may be brought into play in second and subsequent counts.

PR

PR is an allocation formula which tries to distribute seats among parties in proportion to their votes. In other words, PR tries to ensure that minorities and majorities are represented in proportion to their voting strength. The three main ways of doing this are the party list system, the single transferable vote (STV) and the additional member system.

Party list

One of the simplest ways of ensuring that seats are proportional to votes is to distribute the seats on a national basis or in large regions. Parties draw up a list of candidates in order of preference, and they are elected in proportion to the number of votes their party receives, starting from the top of party lists. This gives a lot of power to the party leaders, who decide where candidates are ranked in the list.

STV

Under this system, voters may rank order their preference for candidates, so that their second, third or subsequent preferences can be taken into account. If their first-choice candidate achieves the desired quota before the other seats have been filled, then their lower preference(s) may come into play. Or if their first-choice candidate is eliminated, then their second or subsequent preference can be taken into account. In this way, those casting a first choice for a minor party can choose to cast a second choice for another party, thereby reducing the chances of a 'wasted' vote and making electoral alliances important. There are many different variations on STV and many different ways of calculating the final result, such as where voters can order their preferences within and across parties, thus ensuring the closest possible relationship between voter preferences and candidates elected. STV must be used in conjunction with multimember districts.

Additional member systems

These are ways of trying to keep personal links between elected representatives and voters while still making the end result more proportional. Two election systems are used: single-member districts elect representatives by simple plurality, second ballot or the alternative vote, and additional seats are allocated in such a way as to achieve overall proportionality between each party's percentage of votes and its percentage of legislative seats.

across constituencies may mean that a party with strong support nationally may still end up with a much weaker legislative position.

The great contrast to SMDP is PR (Proportional Representation). This aims to make the parties' shares of legislative seats the same as their share of the national vote. PR does this by making the constituencies as large as possible – ideally the country as a whole – and running party lists of candidates voted for as a block. Seats for the constituency are then given to the highest-ranking candidates on each list in proportion to the votes their party received.

There are of course many variants on the 'pure' versions of SMDP and PR described so far. Mathematicians and statisticians have devised rules for linking seats to votes in the most proportional way. They have shown, for example, how candidates can be elected by bringing in voters' second and third choices to ensure that their votes are not wholly 'wasted' or their preferences ignored.

Underlying the bewildering diversity of detailed rules is the major contrast between SMDP with relatively small territorial constituencies and PR, which depends on having much larger constituencies to function properly. Indeed, where you have party lists competing within small constituencies, the overall national results are not so different from those you would get from plurality rules in the same constituencies (where the five or seven party candidates who get the most votes are awarded the seats).

Trying to estimate the effects of election rules in isolation is difficult, however, because political outcomes are not simply the result of the rules in and of themselves. They are instead shaped by interactions between the rules and the types of political party which make up the national party system.

The political consequences of different election rules

Because electoral systems do not wholly determine outcomes, there are exceptions to their general effects, both for SMDP and PR. SMDP exerts its effects at constituency level. So if a small party has strong enough support in certain constituencies, it will emerge as the plurality winner in these and gain a bloc of seats in parliament – larger or smaller depending on the number of small constituencies it is stronger in. A small party of this type – often minority **ethnic parties** popular in a particular region – may thus survive and flourish under SMDP. It may even hold the balance of power in parliament by choosing one of the two larger parties to form a coalition government with. It is freer to choose between them because smaller parties of this type often pursue policies and attract support on issues outside the main left-right division on which the two major parties differentiate themselves. This is valuable in democratic terms by matching policies to preferences in specialized areas of politics which the major parties would otherwise neglect. As a coalition partner, the minor party is able to bargain to get policy concessions on issues important to it, to which its larger partner is largely indifferent (see Chapter 13).

Ethnic parties

Parties representing a culturally distinct minority.

Government coalitions involving minor parties and policy bargaining are more usually associated with PR than SMDP. By matching vote shares to seat shares in the legislature, PR encourages a multiparty situation there. This means that governments have to bring two or more parties together to get a parliamentary majority. However, PR encourages rather than guarantees multipartyism since again the extent and nature of party divisions play a part. If, for example, two large parties confront each on left-right issues and mobilize votes on that basis across the country, they can monopolize representation in parliament and produce a series of alternating single-party governments, even though a fairly pure system of PR with large constituencies is in place.

There are thus exceptions to the general 'law' that SMDP produces single-party legislative majorities by privileging the plurality party and that PR produces multiparty legislatures with no clear majority. However, the exceptions *are* exceptional and the bias of the electoral rules towards producing such outcomes is clear. The next question to ask concerns the stability of the resulting setup. Clearly under SMDP, the plurality party in one election does not hang onto power forever. Indeed, it will be lucky to hang on to its position beyond the next election given the 'costs of governing' identified in Part I. Enough voters will switch at the next election to make its leading rival the plurality choice and give it all the advantages over the seat-vote translation which its rival enjoyed before. It will then form a new single-party government and set about changing previous policies in the way described in Part I (Figure 7.1).

SMDP thus tends to produce a limited form of short-term political instability involving alternation of the two major parties in the plurality and governing positions. From a longer-term perspective, this process can be interrupted in two ways:

a   A challenger to one of the major parties can appear – usually at a more extreme position to left or right – taking away part of its vote. This puts it at a permanent disadvantage relative to its main rival given SMDP's bias towards rewarding the plurality party disproportionately with seats. The smaller, more extreme challenger will win few seats and probably fade away after one or two elections. Paradoxically, however, it will while it lasts give power to the party on the other wing, more ideologically distant from it, by splitting the vote on its own wing. In turn, the electorally favoured party can use its unusually long stay in government to move actual policy more in its favoured direction than it usually can. This then becomes the new **status quo**, with all the inertia and popular resistance to subsequent policy change that this entails.

Status quo

The situation as it is now.

In contrast to SMDP, PR makes it easier for new parties to establish themselves both at the electoral and legislative levels. Though the new party may make a quick impact and enter coalition governments, it cannot hope to gain more than 10%–15% of votes and seats, given the competition offered by the variety of other parties. To get any of its policies through, it has to compromise and collaborate with them or remain substantially ineffective. Superficially more susceptible to the impact of new parties, therefore, PR limits

Briefing 10.2

Creating a new issue to destabilize current political arrangements

Political alliances, like coalition governments, usually form based on simplified representations of politics, notably left-right differences. So left-wing parties tend to go into (or support) governments formed by other left-wing parties, and right-wing parties go with other right-wing parties (or even might ally with a centre party but rarely with the parties on the other ideological wing).

As we have seen, however, such ideological coherence is usually achieved by ignoring other issues, such as devolution (independence of parts of the state territory) or moral or religious questions. For this reason, such issues are often handled by holding a separate 'policy election' (referendum or initiative) which limits its impact on mainstream coalition politics.

Suppose, however, an opposition or new party managed to make one of these other issues vital nationally (perhaps by holding a referendum on it). Then two government parties which had joined together to support more social welfare might find themselves strongly and publicly opposed on, for example, allowing same-sex relationships or intervening in a foreign war. This would split the coalition apart and possibly let the opposition parties take over government and win the next election.

Manipulating issues in this way is termed 'heresthetics' and rests on the view that politics is inherently multidimensional. That is, many issues are involved, most of which can be made more salient at some point to destabilize existing political alignments. This introduces more difficulties in identifying the 'real' majority and further destabilizes governments.

and absorbs their influences. Like the other smaller parties already represented in the legislature, a new party may well represent special interests and minorities off the main dimension of political conflict. Its legislative bargaining position in coalition government formation (Chapter 13) may give it opportunities to advance these, which are lacking under SMDP. This in turn may account for some of the striking differences in policy outcomes which appear between the two kinds of electoral systems (reviewed in the last section of this chapter in Table 10.2).

b   The second source of long-term instability under SMDP comes from the very plurality bias which normally confines competition to the two major parties. These can squeeze out or limit other party contenders so long as their own national vote stays around 35% or above – enough to emerge in many constituencies as the plurality winner and thus dominate parliament.

However, if a new party manages to reach this level of support, it will rapidly benefit from all the advantages that a plurality confers and displace one of the established parties. Such a wholesale reorientation of politics is unlikely under PR, which instead encourages frequent but limited change in the party system.

To sum up, SMDP opens up the possibility of extensive party and policy change, focused on the major dimension of party competition (usually left-right). Change outside the regular alternation of the two main parties in government is limited. But when it comes, it can be significant. PR, on the other hand, opens the way to new small parties, which generally exert policy influence off the main dimension of politics. PR is unlikely, however, to encourage the wholesale replacement of one large party by another – which is always a possibility under SMDP.

Who really represents the majority view under different electoral systems?

Framing

Defining the possible courses of action to be considered on an issue.

Ideology

A set of assumptions about the world which support certain kinds of political action.

The general political effects produced by the election rules are important. Given the 'necessary connection' that democracy seeks to establish between public policy and popular preferences, their role in **framing** the latter is absolutely crucial. Whatever policy-preference polls elicit from the public, the vote distribution at the general election remains the only fully authoritative statement of public opinion till the next election (unless there is an intervening policy vote on an issue – see Chapter 9).

The question is, what do the party votes in the general election really tell us about majority policy preferences? We know in the first place that parties often attract votes on non-policy grounds (or rather, grounds not based on current policy) – past policy stands, record, candidates, perceived governing potential and so on. Current policy must always be an element in the party 'bundle' of election offerings. But it will not always be the major element in the frame that they provide for voting choice and quite often it is a minor one.

On the other hand, parties, through their **ideologies** and the contrasting election programmes derived from them, always provide some policy alternatives for voters to react to. Even where these are not the major basis for voting choices, we can at least say they have not put voters off voting for the party. So it does obtain some kind of mild policy endorsement with even non-policy orientated votes.

Party policy endorsements have to be seen within the institutional context of the general election, which deliberately concentrates all the main political decisions by citizens for the next three to five years into one general vote to decide what party or party grouping is to govern, who will lead it and what policy programme is to be followed. It is inevitable within this kind of frame that some – even many – votes will be cast on non-policy grounds. But this is not a failing of individual citizens or a reflection on their political capacity. It is rather a consequence of the way existing democracies choose to organize popular decision-making. The party vote distribution emerging from general elections is at one and the same time a mandate to govern *and* to pursue certain policies in government. It thus paradoxically produces decisive policy outcomes which pure voting on the policy itself might fudge.

This means that the party percentage votes in the last general election, and the resulting distribution of seats in the legislature (and/or control of the presidency) become the determining political influences till the next election regardless of how the preferences of the wider electorate, as reflected in opinion polls, may change during that period. As we have seen (in Chapters 3 and 7), governments more often than not encounter opposition on the specific policy proposals they make in the process of effecting their programme. Its endorsement in the previous election, however, and the party's 'mandate' to govern, means that it can go on trying to modify existing policy in its preferred direction throughout its term of office – though slowly. In the long term, the alternation of parties and the contrasting government targets they try to effect will bring enacted policy closer to centrist citizen preferences for it, as shown in Part I.

The immediate question in the short term, after party votes in the general election have been declared, is which party can be taken as representing the majority preference and given the right and responsibility (the 'mandate') to pursue its policy targets in government.

In the case of presidential elections, this will be clear at the end of the electoral process. Whatever the arrangements for a majority or plurality endorsement or for **run-off** arrangements between the leading candidates, only one of them can occupy the office in the end and go on to appoint a government and pursue a programme. Generally, the winning candidate will have the best claim to be the majority choice.

In the case of parliamentary governments and elections, the party which represents the majority may be less clearly identifiable. Obviously, any party or electoral alliance of parties which gets a majority (50% +1) of votes has an undisputable claim to form a government. However, true electoral majorities are rare; they emerge in only 12% of parliamentary elections in the world.

If a majority is lacking, why not settle for the next best thing – a plurality party, especially if it approaches 50% of the vote and gets substantially more support than its nearest rival? SMDP works to transform the plurality party electorally into the parliamentary majority party. Under PR, election outcomes are more complicated since the plurality party is less likely to get votes in the 40%–50% range and less likely to stand out from its rivals. Nevertheless, the plurality party is still privileged. It is usually asked to take the first turn in forming a coalition government and is almost certain to be a member of it and provide the prime minister.

There is, however, another claimant with a case for representing the majority preference in a multiparty situation. This is the party endorsed by the median voter in the declared distribution of votes. We discussed the claim of the median preference to be the majority preference in Chapter 4. As the median is by definition the middle voter (50% + 1) in any distribution of votes on policy, it is crucial to forming any majority and

Run-off

A second general election usually to decide which of the leading candidates from the first will win office.

Briefing 10.3

The 'double complement' rule for deciding when a plurality party is really a majority

The 'double complement' rule says there is probably no need for a second election to determine the election winner if one party's vote percentage in the first election is closer to 50% than it is to the vote percentage of the second-placed party. A party with 45% of the vote (five percentage points from 50%) is the winner if no other party reaches 40% because it would almost certainly beat all other parties in pairwise voting. This result then justifies the plurality party acting as the majority party (e.g. getting the presidency or a majority of legislative seats and/or forming a single-party government – cf. Matthew S. Shugart and Rein Taagepera (1994) 'Plurality Versus Majority Election of Presidents: a Double Complement Rule' *Comparative Political Studies* 27: 323–348).

can change majorities by switching between them. Therefore, in any bargaining situation, potential majorities have to woo the party or person at the median by shifting their policy position closer to theirs. There is thus a strong dynamic at work pushing any majority policy position closer to the median one.

That is one reason for considering the median position the best indicator of the majority preference. The other is that the median position – located at the centre of any preference or vote distribution – is the one which most minimizes the distance between it and all other individual positions. It is therefore the preference which best gives voters what they want in policy and most minimizes dissatisfaction if it is adopted by government.

Of course, all this assumes that a general median policy position and median voter *can* be identified. Finding it is helped if there is a central underlying policy dimension along which voters and parties can be lined up and ordered. We have seen in Chapters 5 and 6 that parties' organization of issues along a left-right dimension achieves this, even though it provides only a rough and ready approximation to the full complexity of policies and issues and does not comprehend all of them entirely.

Table 10.1 sums up the rival claims of the median-supported party and the plurality party to 'carry' the majority voter preference. Both have strong claims which cannot be easily refuted on one side or the other. Where the plurality party is also supported by the median voter, there is of course no problem: it is the clear majority representative and almost always leads the government. Where the plurality and median-supported parties are different the solution to the representational impasse is to include both in governments. And in fact, most coalition governments do, whether formed under PR or SMDP (see Chapter 13). As we have noted, however, SMPD operates mostly to give the plurality party a majority in parliament with which it can form a single-party government with more extreme policy

TABLE 10.1 Arguments for the median or plurality positions to be taken as representing the majority preference

Median voter	Plurality voter
1. Power of the median: the median voter is essential to creating a majority under pure policy voting, so the policy majority has to settle near its position.	1. The plurality grouping failed to become the majority only by accident, possibly owing to non-policy-based factors affecting voting. A rerun of the election might make it the majority while changing the current median position.
2. The median position is defined by the voting preferences of all voters, not an extreme group, as could be the case with plurality.	2. The plurality emerges spontaneously as a result of voting. It is not artificially calculated on dubious policy grounds from the final distribution of votes, like the median.
3. The median minimizes the overall distance between individual voter preferences and the election party outcome, while the 'plurality position' gives no guarantee of this.	3. The 'plurality position' is the single revealed preference most representative of majority opinion, particularly if it clearly had more support than the next largest party grouping.

targets than those supported by most voters or citizens. We have seen in Part I how this arrangement operates in the long term to bring the public policy that is actually being implemented closer to the centre and thus to citizen preferences. This is also true for changing multiparty governments containing both plurality and median or centre parties. But although their policies also zigzag (though moderately) in line with plurality preference as centrist parties ally with left or right parties in turn, they tend to come closer to citizen and voter preferences in the short term as well, because of necessary compromises with the median and centre parties in the coalition.

The real test of which party best 'carries' the majority's policy preferences is whether it would get more votes than other parties in a series of paired contests with them. That is, with three parties – A, B and C – running in an election, would A win when it competed separately against B and then against C? If it did, it would clearly be the majority preference to form the government and pursue its policy targets there. There is considerable evidence to show that the plurality party is in this position, particularly if it has above 40% of the vote and a clear lead over its main competitor. To prevent it winning in pairwise contests, all the votes for the least popular parties would have to go to its rival in the pairwise contest. Unless there is clear evidence for this being likely, the plurality party can be taken as the majority choice from general elections.

Of course, as we have pointed out, this will never be a choice based purely on policy. General elections are institutionally designed to let other influences on the vote come in. This is the major reason why voters and their choices differ from electors' preferences as expressed in responses to questions in opinion polls or election surveys. The questions these put forward can concentrate on pure policy or get electors to locate themselves in their preferred position on a left-right scale. Electoral preferences, as expressed in this way, do not have to compromise by lining themselves up with parties which may be relatively far from them in policy terms.

It is these 'pure' electoral preferences which democratic processes are ultimately supposed to translate into public policy, through general elections and governments based on the party vote distributions they produce. So the question has to be asked, how far do voters' policy preferences correspond to those of electors?

We have already looked into this question in Chapter 4. There we discovered that electors' preferences at least on the dominant left-right cleavage, generally lie in the centre (Figure 4.6). This is also true of median voter, who by definition must occupy a position in the middle of the vote distribution. In the short term, however, the policy targets endorsed by the *plurality* party voter are likely to veer more to the extremes of the left-right dimension (unless the plurality party is centrist). After any one election, there is likely to be some discrepancy between the target endorsed by the main representative of the voting majority and the one preferred by the body of citizens.

However, if we average out plurality preferences over a series of elections, as the election pendulum swings between parties on the left and parties on the right, we find that the long-term preference of the plurality voter also lies in the middle, close to that of the median voter and the median elector. This is also where the actual policy being implemented by the administration lies, as a result of governments on one side and the other pulling it towards their own position. Thus, we may say that in the long term, over most issues, both indicators of voter preference (median and plurality) coincide with electoral centrist preferences – and that actual public policy, as it should, also ends up close to them.

A particular point to add here is that this matching process also occurs with single issues and policies, which do not fit into the left-right dimension. Parties are 'carriers' of many issues on which they have opposing priorities and proposals. As they implement differing issue-specific targets over time, they pull actual policy over and around the middle, so that most of the time it stands close to most electors' preferences on these issues as well.

Policy consequences of SMDP and PR

Fiscal orthodoxy

Balancing budgets and paying off debts.

Free enterprise

Policies which give private businesses as much freedom as possible.

Apart from their varying efficiency in matching public policies to preferences, different election rules are also associated with different kinds of policy targets and outcomes. Countries that organize their elections under PR generally pursue more leftist policies than countries operating under SMDP. This is true both of the policy targets adopted by their governments and of the policies actually enacted. With regard to policy targets, SMDP governments tend to cut both taxes and services as elections or economic crises occur, acting within the 'fiscal orthodoxy' and free enterprise theories of the economy, which partly define right-wing positions. PR governments, in contrast, increase welfare and other spending before elections and in recessions. On other policies more marginal to the left-right divide, there are also differences: under PR, there are more liberal abortion policies, more pollution control, gentler criminal justice (a

TABLE 10.2 Implemented policies in a number of areas under PR compared to those under single-member district plurality voting (SMDP), over 21 countries round about the year 2000

	PR		SMDP		Average PR-SMDP difference
	Average (mean)	Overlap (standard deviation)	Average (mean)	Overlap (standard deviation)	
Social security support payments as % of GDP	15.0	(2.2)	12.2	(3.1)	+2.8
Extent to which social benefits are provided as a right	31.1	(5.3)	19.5	(5.8)	+11.6
Total public social expenditure as % of GDP	23.5	(4.4)	19.9	(4.8)	+3.6
Total government expenditure as % of GDP	46.4	(6.9)	41.4	(6.6)	+5.5
Wage inequality (ratio of lowest paid workers' earnings to median workers')	1.62	(0.6)	1.86	(.15)	−0.24
Average real individual income	9092	(1598)	10999	(1784)	−1947
Carbon dioxide emission as a ratio of GDP	.39	(.13)	.55	(.20)	−.16

Notes:

Social security support: social security transfers to individuals as percentage of GDP, 2004 (National Accounts of OECD Countries, 2005)

Social benefits as a right: Esping Andersen's 1980 decommodification score (Esping Andersen, 1990, 52)

Total public social expenditure: total public social expenditure as percentage of GDP, 2001 (OECD Social Expenditure Database, 2004)

Total government expenditure: total government expenditure as percentage of GDP, 2004 (National Accounts of OECD Countries, 2005)

Wage inequality: ratio of earnings of worker in 90th percentile to median wage earnings (Iversen and Soskice, 2006)

Average real individual income: real per capita income, 1950–1996 average, constant 1985 USD (Iversen and Soskice, 2006)

Carbon dioxide emission as a ratio of GDP: kilograms of CO_2 per 2000 USD (Fuel Combustion, IEA/OECD, 2005)

Source: Adapted from Michael D. McDonald (2007) 'Policy Consequences of SMD Versus PR', Centre for Democratic Performance (Binghamton University, NY) *mdmcd@binghamton.com*

Full published sources for indices in table are: Gosta Esping Andersen (1990) *The Three Worlds of Welfare Capitalism* (Princeton, NJ, Princeton University Press).

Torben Iversen and David Soskice (2006) Electoral Institutions Parties and the Politics of Class: Why Some Democracies Redistribute More than Others. *American Political Science Review*, (100), pp. 432–446.

notable feature being the absence of the death penalty) and less inequality. On the other hand, there are generally higher prices for consumer goods – possibly because of more as opposed to less economic regulation. This is all compactly illustrated in Table 10.2.

The table presents measures of the varying policies actually being implemented in reasonably developed countries around the world with either PR or SMDP methods of aggregating votes into legislative seats. The table compares the mean for PR countries and SMDP countries, obtained by adding all the individual figures for the countries in each grouping and dividing by the number of countries. An error check is included in the shape of the standard deviation (the bracketed figures). The larger this is relative to the main figure, the more countries in each grouping spread out and overlap and the less reliable contrasts between overall means become when applied to individual countries. The table shows that overlapping is fairly limited so that the contrasts between the mean or average estimates for each grouping also apply to most individual country-by-country comparisons.

Table 10.2 makes a direct comparison between the policy outcomes actually implemented under the two kinds of electoral systems. Social security transfers as a percentage of GDP are almost three points higher in PR systems compared to SMDP systems. A similar difference exists on the welfare index, a summary indicator of the extent to which social services are provided as a right so that maintenance of citizens' living standard is possible without relying exclusively on being able to buy them. General social spending and total government spending are higher, on average, among countries with PR as opposed to SMDP systems. Wage inequality, per capita income and CO_2 emissions as a ratio of GDP also differ in ways one would expect as a result of more government action in these areas (PR) or less (SMDP). Again, these social and environmental consequences are associated with the political differences between left and right. Inequality is uniformly higher under SMDP than under PR. However, income is generally higher under SMDP systems. And the CO_2 emissions associated with climate change (standardized by output), are generally lower under PR. All these differences are upheld under various tests for error.

Such systematic policy divergences between the two types of election system can hardly be accidental. How can we explain it? The most likely possibility is that effects are channelled through the **party systems** which the different sets of rules encourage. The ability of small parties to get support and representation under PR allows voters more choice between varying party 'bundles' of policy and other attributes. They can vote for a wider range of parties along the left-right dimension, including ones at the centre. Voters can also favour parties whose policy concerns lie off the main axis of conflict – such as Christian parties, whose concern is with the preservation of traditional and religious values through education and support for the family. This has led them to advocate many of the welfare schemes and extended social provisions favoured by the left.

Another consequence of differing election systems is the greater fragmentation of rightist parties under PR as compared with those on the centre and left. Both Christians and socialists have organizational bases in churches and unions in the first case and co-operatives and unions in the second. Of course, such support bases are also available under SMDP. There, however, the premium on having large parties to compete effectively has prompted the centre-right to unite against the potentially dominant left, using bases such as churches which under PR have supported centrist religious parties. Under PR, the potential rightist

Party system

The number and types of parties operating in a state.

coalition has fragmented around a number of causes, such as freedom in the case of liberals and enterprise in the case of conservatives – along with more off-beat issues like agriculture in the case of agrarians and devolution for ethnic and regional nationalist parties. All can hope to get some representation under PR and hold a crucial place at some point in negotiations to form a coalition government. They can then hold out for concessions on their special concerns, such as civil liberties in the case of liberals.

With a more cohesive and disciplined support base, the Christians and/or social democrats thus tend to emerge as the largest parties under PR. Large is of course a relative term in this context. However, a vote of around 30%–40% may be enough to give a party the advantages associated with a plurality even under multiparty coalition systems. Having these parties as the largest ones also means that more votes are cast for parties of the centre and the left, giving expressed popular preferences more of a leftwards cast and adding the impetus of a mandate to centre-left policy targets.

We can therefore see that although election rules do not produce direct policy effects of their own, they create conditions where different kinds of voter preferences can be expressed in their party choices, and different kinds of parties can pursue their policy targets more effectively. Over time, this all contributes to creating the policy differences between the electoral systems listed in Table 10.2.

End-summary

Governance

What party (or parties) form the government and what they do there.

Initiative

An initiative is a popular vote on a policy proposal called by petition.

Referendums

A popular vote called by governments or courts to decide some policy proposal.

This chapter has reviewed the workings of the main decision-making institution in modern democracies, the general election. Although this decides the main lines of policy for the next three to five years, voting choices are not exclusively or even wholly made on policy grounds. Most democracies concentrate all their decisions about **governance** into the one general election. So which party's policy targets get adopted depends partly on its other attractions, particularly candidates and perceived competence. However, the general-election vote is also the authoritative basis on which a party gets to pursue its policy targets in government (whether alone or in combination). Its policy programme has not put its supporters off voting for it. One cannot say that such a policy mandate is a strong one compared to voting directly on each proposal in **initiatives** and **referendums** (Chapter 9). Where these are absent, however, the general election becomes decisive even on specific policy matters, and in any case, it sets the direction of general policy for the medium term.

General elections create a need to aggregate party votes into presidential majorities or shares of legislative seats. Here a variety of rules can be applied. The main distinction lies between PR and the SMDP systems, whose main effect is to empower the largest single party (the plurality party) in both legislature and government. The potential of the plurality party to beat all other parties in pairwise contests if there were a rerun of the election makes it the most likely representative of majority opinion even under PR. However, the party in the middle (the median party) also has standing there, especially given the centrist views of most electors. Both the plurality and median parties tend to participate in government under PR. The resulting policy compromises bring government targets closer to voters' and electors' centrist preferences even in the short term. Under single-party plurality government, targets are further from popular preferences in the short term, though brought closer in the long term through government alternation and policy zigzags across the centre.

All this illustrates the political consequences which different ways of conducting general elections have. By empowering more, and different types of, parties, PR also helps produce more left-wing policies than SMDP. In Part III, we look more closely at political parties and other participants in the democratic process to see how they adapt to the varying election and post-election contexts that constitutional rules create. Our first concern is with how different election rules and party systems help to frame the electoral preferences which then become part of the input for government policymaking.

The main points to take from this discussion are thus:

- The strong contrasts between rules for allocating legislative seats (or presidential office) in terms of party votes.
- In particular the effects this has on the numbers of parties represented and how they form governments.
- Resulting differences in the kinds of policies produced by PR and plurality rules.

Systematic working assumptions coming into this discussion

9 States vary in the extent to which decisions about policy and who is to make it are shared widely among citizens.

10 The most extensive sharing occurs in democracies, since by definition, these have to guarantee that public policies necessarily reflect the preferences of citizens for them.

11 This guarantee is provided by free, regular and competitive elections of governments and/or policies open to all groups and individuals, where votes reveal citizen preferences and authorize them as either policymaking governments or directly as state policy.

14 The unifying research focus is therefore on the extent of policy-preference correspondence and how it is achieved.

17 The popular preferences with which public policy must necessarily correspond in a democracy can be specified sufficiently to form a basis for public decision-making only if estimated from voting outcomes in free and open elections (or from election-like formatting of questions in well-conducted surveys).

18 However, all political – like other – measurements contain error (which can nevertheless be estimated and corrected on various assumptions).

19 This is necessarily true of election votes in their role as measures of popular preferences. The rules and procedures which structure votes (e.g. the order and wording of alternatives being voted on and methods of aggregating individual votes to produce a collective decision) can all distort the final outcomes and have to be allowed for in estimating settled preferences.

Sources and resources

Lawrence Le Duc, Richard D. Niemi, and Pippa Norris (eds) (2006) *Comparing Democracies 2: New Challenges in the Study of Elections and Voting* (Thousand Oaks, CA, Sage).

G. Bingham Powell Jr. (2000) *Elections as Instruments of Democracy: Majoritarian and Proportional Visions* (New Haven, CT, Yale University Press).

Russell J. Dalton, and Christopher J. Anderson (2011) 'Citizens, Context and Choice: How Context Shapes Citizens' Preferences in *Electoral Choices* (Oxford, Oxford University Press).

Suggestions for class papers

1 How far do general elections overcome problems associated with direct popular voting on policies?

2 What do you think is the best way to relate general-election votes to party participation in government? Give reasons for your answer.

3 Do presidential as opposed to parliamentary elections provide a better way to match public policy to popular preferences for it? Why?

Suggestions for class projects

1 Turn the explanation provided in the text for the different policy outcomes under SMDP and PR into a predictive theory, checking it against relevant data to determine whether its predictions stand up.

2   Compare rates of government alternation under SMDP and PR systems, and estimate the extent to which this improves policy-preference correspondence under the two different electoral systems.

3   Estimate the actual extent to which centrist parties have more power under PR compared to SMDP (note that this involves defining both the 'centre' and 'power' to measure them properly).

Part III

Protagonists

Parties and governments shape popular preferences and reflect them in public policies

The protagonists in the political processes described in Part I are the political parties and governments – and of course the electorate whose interactions have created them in the first place. Parties seek to form governments to implement their policies. Governments make policy proposals, which they try to implement and to which electors then react. An important fourth actor is the government's supporting – and unelected – bureaucracy, which often tries to modify what the government is doing, in light of its own ideas and administrative convenience.

Parties, governments and ministries are often termed 'institutions' or 'collective actors' because they bring together large numbers of people within an organization with common purposes and set rules and procedures for formulating and pursuing them. In many theories, they are also regarded as 'unitary actors' – that is, they are treated as if their shared purposes and ambitions made them act like a single individual with unquestioned goals and strategies and no difficulties in deciding on them.

This simplifies theory building but at the cost of rendering it unrealistic. Individuals within any organization tend to divide themselves up into different groupings (or are divided up inside the institutional structure itself into separate departments and agencies). Electorates divide between different parties; parties themselves have internal factions and factional conflicts; governments are often coalitions of parties with competing ideologies and policies; and bureaucracies divide most obviously into departments or ministries covering different areas – divisions exacerbated by the political parties which habitually take them over in any coalition bargaining necessary to form a parliamentary government.

Unless we take account of internal conflicts within these collectives of individuals, we are not going to characterize their behaviour properly.

Internal divisions can also be useful as a basis for theorizing about the dynamics of the processes that drive them, like the way electors formulate their preferences (Chapter 11) and parties approve policy (Chapter 12). Internal divisions should be focused on as an opportunity for theorizing about internal processes rather than being unrealistically ignored.

The 'collective protagonists' and 'collective actors' examined in this part (Part III) of the book have of course already figured prominently in the democratic processes described in Part I. The government alternation model makes various assumptions about their behaviour, which then produces the guaranteed correspondence between popular preferences and public policy that is its focus. We pointed out in Chapter 8, however, that these behavioural assumptions are themselves derived from theories about protagonists' behaviour which stand further back in the 'web of explanation' surrounding policy-preference correspondence (Figure. 8.1).

Alternation theory does not directly depend on these supporting theories being correct. So long as its assumptions are plausible in themselves and in combination predict policy correspondence successfully, we can accept them without having to provide other supporting explanations for assumptions such as parties forming policy autonomously of electorates' preferences.

However, if the theory leading to such a conclusion is itself upheld by available evidence, it does add more credence to the overall theory which draws on it. Similarly, if all of the theories in the 'web of explanation' supporting the alternation model are upheld, this adds considerably to its own credibility.

It is for that reason that we focus on theories of protagonists' behaviour here – also of course because they provide the best available explanations of why the central democratic institutions play the parts they do in democracy. The discussions may thus overlap with some of the points already introduced and discussed in Part I. However, the focus on protagonist behaviour itself rather than on the part it plays in the overall democratic process, introduces new points. These will emerge in the following chapters, which go on from citizens' and electors' preferences for policy (framed of course by the parties) to governments and ministries (collective actors themselves) and to the internal processes which shape their policy decisions. Each of these is the subject of a clear predictive explanation discussed and assessed in the corresponding chapter. As well as describing relevant aspects of policy, Part III thus shows how predictive explanations can be formulated and then applied to political realities to render these more understandable – another objective of this book.

Chapter 11

Citizens, parties and governments

Interactive preference formation

Chapter overview

The theories which explain how popular preferences are shaped and communicated are (1) the thermostatic model, which conceives of them in a short-term perspective as reactions to the policies made by parties and governments, and (2) the developmental-family approach, which sees particular groupings of electors forming new parties to represent their characteristic preferences if the existing ones do not do so. This creates a long-term link between party programmes and the policies advocated by their founding and support groups (Table 6.6). Before going into detail on these, we must explain how they interact to give the electorate an initiating as well as a reactive role in democratic policymaking.

Democracy defines itself by making public policy reflect citizen preferences. The difficulty is that these cannot express themselves unaided. The people must be helped to speak. Otherwise, we will either get silence or a babble of conflicting voices. Public opinion thus needs to be channelled in order to be clear. Most often, a structure is provided by government or party proposals, which individuals can react to, in the process aggregating opinions so they add up to a majority position on the proposal. The government can then itself react to how much support their original or modified proposals will get.

This process is given even more weight when it takes place in the context of a referendum or initiative – often promoted in opposition to current policy and framed by the questions put by its sponsors. The results may modify current policy and even affect subsequent voting in a general election.

Paradoxically, therefore, the processes which define public opinion and allow popular preferences to be expressed – at least in the short term – are mostly initiated and framed by other protagonists than electors themselves – parties, **interest groups**, polling agencies, media, even

Interest groups

Organizations which promote policies without running candidates in elections.

Political class

The social grouping from which most politicians and party activists come.

Frame

A proposal or preference, that defines the possible courses of action to be considered on it.

the government itself, which is also the ultimate recipient of the messages they send about popular preferences. Obviously, there is a lot of scope for distortion and disagreement here over what exactly is being communicated as the public preference. Over a longer time period, however, we can see that this process also works in reverse in a way which gives the public a big role. The major framers of popular opinion, the political parties, derive from popular movements with distinct interests and political preferences, which have not found an adequate expression within the existing political setup. Potential differences and grievances are often identified and built up by political leaders from outside the existing **political class**, who use them as a support basis for a new party. Through the entry of such new parties, this process extends the short-term **frame** within which popular preferences can be defined and expressed.

Briefing 11.1

(New?) Social movements

This is a term used to describe groupings in the population which arise spontaneously outside established institutions and processes. In the late eighteenth century and the nineteenth century, these were often evangelical churches like Methodism in the UK and the US. Later, working-class and farmer groups founded unions and co-operatives. These often developed or took over an ideology (Catholicism, Marxism) and recruited a mass following which contributed money and volunteers for further activities and expansion. In the twentieth century, women's and ecological movements developed similarly. To push their ideas, such movements often developed a political wing, which turned into a political party, running candidates for election or pushing for referendums to promote their causes. In the first part of the post-war period, such groups were often termed 'new social movements'. But they acted much like the older social movements of the nineteenth century, providing a continuing basis for the emergence of new political parties if the established ones did not support or respond adequately to the causes they had at heart.

Initiatives

An initiative is a popular vote on some policy proposal called by petition.

Constitution

A constitution is a set of laws laying down political rules and procedures.

The wider electorate are thus not simply bound to react to the frames and cues which existing processes and actors provide them with. Quite apart from the formal popular **initiatives** which can be organized where they are provided for by a **constitution**, or from their ability to pursue media campaigns or initiate polling on policies affected by government proposals, elector groupings can also intervene in the regular political process by founding new parties. These then change the existing party system and possibly alter its bias towards producing certain types of policy (as explored in the last chapter).

The processes shaping public preferences never go just one way, therefore, though they may seem to do so in the short term. The people rarely speak unaided. Nor do they just react to proposals set out from above.

The context which most resembles a top-to-bottom situation is the general election, where voters usually have to choose between existing parties and the policy alternatives they offer (Figure 3.1). These are generally more extreme than electors as a whole would ideally prefer. But in the long run, alternation between parties in government pulls enacted policy back towards the more moderate centre in the way described in Part I. Meanwhile, if a significant opinion grouping feels passed over by the existing party alternatives, it can always found a new party. If this strikes a chord with the electorate as a whole, it will permanently extend the range of choices available in elections.

The general-election campaign is the preference-defining process considered in the first, and immediately following, section of this chapter. More scope for autonomous preference formation is given by the policy elections and polling processes – though even here, public reactions are often framed by government policy proposals which heavily influence the kind of questions pollsters ask.

General elections, policy elections and polling all operate in short-term contexts. In the long run, the public can themselves intervene in opinion framing by creating new parties and political movements in the ways examined in detail towards the end of the chapter. We then go on in Chapter 12 to examine the parties themselves. Points to focus on in this chapter are thus:

- The interactive process by which popular preferences are formed and manifested at any one point in time – as reactions to proposals made by the other protagonists.
- The ways in which popular preferences emerge interactively within the democratic process rather than coming in independently from outside.
- If parties and governments change their policy positions, electoral preferences may change too within the new frame this provides for them.
- Electorates themselves can also produce such changes by generating new parties to 'carry' their preferences and offer new choices in general elections.

Expressing and empowering preferences through general elections

The major way in which popular preferences are shaped and expressed under democracy is through general elections. Electors are given a choice between competing parties and their policies and vote for the one(s) they prefer (subject as we have seen to other, non-policy influences). The distribution of votes between the parties then influences (but in the two-party case generally determines) which party will be in government. Examples of the kinds of vote distributions which emerge from general elections are displayed in Table 11.1. More immediately important in forming a

TABLE 11.1 Party distribution of votes and of legislative seats in comparable Dutch and British elections

The Netherlands, 3 May 1994	Party vote percentages	Legislative no. of seats held by parties	Party seat percentages
Labour Party (PvdA)	24.0	37	24.6
Christian Democratic Appeal (CDA)	22.2	34	22.6
People's Party for Freedom and Democracy (VVD)	19.9	31	20.72
Democrats 66 (D'66)	15.5	24	16.02
SGP/RPF/GVP*	4.8	7	4.6
General League of the Elderly (AOV)	3.6	6	4.0
Green Left	3.5	5	3.2
Centre Democrats (CD)	2.5	3	2.0
Socialist Party (SP)	1.3	2	1.2
55+ Union (Unie 55+)	0.9	1	0.6
Others	1.8	0	0.0
Total	100.0	150	100

The UK, 9 April 1992	Party vote percentages	Legislative no. of seats held by parties	Party seat percentages
Conservative Party	41.93	336	51.6
Labour Party	34.39	271	41.6
Liberal Democrats	17.85	20	3.0
Scottish National Party	1.87	3	0.3
Plaid Cymru	0.47	4	0.6
Official Ulster Unionists	0.81	9	1.6
Democratic Unionists	0.31	3	0.5
Ulster Popular Unionists	0.06	1	0.2
Social Democratic and Labour Party	0.55	4	0.6
Sein Féin	0.23	0	0.0
Others	1.43	0	0.0
Total	100	150	100

Notes:

*Political Reformed Party/Reformational Political Federation/Reformed Political Association (right-wing Protestant parties)

The notable point about these elections of the early nineties held in the Netherlands and the UK under fairly similar conditions, but with an extremely proportional form of PR in the Dutch case and small constituency-based SMDP in the UK, is the close correspondence between the party percentages of popular votes and legislative seats gained in the Dutch case and the notable discrepancy between them in the UK. In the Netherlands, votes are spread out over a large number of parties, with each receiving an almost equivalent percentage of legislative seats. With the largest party having only a quarter of these, multiparty governments are inevitable, often composed of three or four parties. Nevertheless, the new plurality party (Labour) was still able in 1994 to form a government excluding the former plurality party (CDA), which had formed part of all coalition governments of the previous 80 years!

In the UK, on the other hand, the largest party (Conservatives) with only 42% of votes got over 50% of the seats, enabling it to form a single-party majority government for the next five years. The third party, the Liberals, with nearly 20% of the vote got only 3% of seats, rendering it ineffective in influencing parliamentary voting or policy. Labour got more seats than its votes entitled it to but was a permanent minority in British Parliament, excluded from power under the 'elective dictatorship' sustained by SMDP.

government is the distribution of legislative seats that this gives rise to. These seats may or may not correspond closely to the popular vote proportions, depending on the type of electoral system in operation. The dramatic difference that this makes is shown by comparing results from two elections held in the 1990s in two neighbouring countries (Table 11.1). The negotiations which then take place to form a government are discussed in Chapter 13. A common feature is that any plurality party with a clear lead over the others dominates and thus sets the general direction of policy for the new government.

Party system

The number and type of parties operating in a state.

If the plurality party is at the centre of the prevailing **party system** – particularly if it held the plurality position in the previous government – little change in policy may actually take place. As we have seen, this may often be the case under PR (Proportional Representation), thus bringing both government targets and enacted policy closer to centrist electoral preferences in the short term.

Where fewer significant parties exist, and especially when there are tendencies to a two-party system, with two major parties competing to form single-party governments, the plurality party is likely to pursue policy preferences which are less close to centrist popular preferences in the short term. The attempt by the new government to pull existing policy towards its own position will often bring that back towards the centre in line with popular preferences if it follows an alternation of the major parties in office. In this way, it will promote both a short-term congruence and long-term correspondence between preferences and the public policy which actually gets implemented – even though, paradoxically, voters are forced in the election to choose between two relatively extreme parties (see Figures 7.1 and 7.3).

Though such a correspondence is guaranteed in the long term by party alternation, the short-term congruence between preferences and actual policy may actually decrease where two or three governments dominated by the same relatively extreme plurality party succeed each other and pull policy ever more to its side. It is only in the long term that alternation with a resulting policy correspondence can be fully guaranteed. Over a one- or two-election period, congruence may actually diminish. As noted, this is less likely to happen under PR than SMDP (Single Member District Plurality Voting).

Representative democracy may thus fail to provide immediate policy representation – at least in terms of its major mechanism, the general election. It is here that secondary inter-election processes such as referendums and initiatives or public opinion polling and 'thermostatic reactions' become more important as a way of formulating preferences and bringing immediate policy into line with them. We shall look at these in the next section.

It remains true, however, that it is the voting distribution from the general election, in conjunction with the party system, which determines the overall direction and shape of policy until the next election. Recorded party votes assume an almost independent existence, determining which party will be better able to push its own policies and giving it an authorization and justification for doing so. No matter how current opinion may change subsequently, the government can claim a popular mandate for its programme up until the next election. Only if policy elections are

Briefing 11.2

How elections and resulting party systems may influence popular preferences

'Duverger's law' states that where the party with the largest vote takes the seat in small constituencies (i.e. under SMDP rules) only the two largest parties will survive there as effective competitors in the long run. This is for a variety of reasons. Electors will shift their votes strategically to the one of the two likely winners which they prefer more, even if ideally they would prefer one of the smaller parties' policies. Otherwise, their vote will just be 'wasted' and not affect the outcome. Since the smaller parties are unlikely to win, they in turn may stop even running candidates. This does not of course guarantee that there will be a two-party system at national level, because strong locally based parties could be one of the main contenders for the constituency and because this might well generate a multiparty system over the country as a whole.

However, where the two main parties' support is spread fairly evenly over the country, a strong two-party system will emerge at national level. This in turn will affect media coverage and citizens' policy thinking. Both will tend to view policies in either-or terms rather than see possibilities of compromise at a centre position. If one of the main parties stays in power for a long time, the policies favoured by most citizens will shift towards its position. So what was previously regarded as extreme will become the new normal now supported rather than rejected by most citizens – at least until a new party and its policies manage to successfully compete with one of the old contenders. Thus, not only voting but also policy thinking may change as a result of the election system in operation, as Duverger's law implies.

authorized by the state constitution and thus have an autonomous role to play can the direction of policy at least in certain areas be altered – unless of course 'thermostatic' opposition to its proposals becomes so overwhelming that the government itself thinks it wise to moderate them. We now examine these possibilities.

Expressing popular preferences between general elections

**Mandate/
(Government)
Mandate**

Both an authorization and requirement for the government to do something.

Governments chosen on the basis of the general election results claim to have a general 'mandate' to make decisions on behalf of the country as a whole. They also claim to have a policy **mandate** to carry out the programme they have outlined in the election. This will most often involve alterations to existing policy targets, which will be more or less extreme depending on how far the new government differs ideologically from the previous governments.

The speed with which enacted policy changes in line with government targets also varies. Implementing policy more slowly produces a smaller and less immediate impact on the population.

As the major source of policy initiatives and primarily responsible for the political changes going on, the government and its proposals are naturally the focus of most comment and debate in the mass media. In turn, this shapes public opinion polling. Polling agencies wish to find out – either on behalf of specialized clients or for the media – how electors are reacting to government actions and how this might affect voting in the next general election.

The main short-term frame for popular expressions of preference thus becomes survey questions asking about reactions to what the government is proposing to do in different policy areas. As we have seen, this provokes a 'thermostatic reaction': the more the government pushes a policy, the more electors oppose it – or, conversely, the less it intends to provide, the more electors want (Figure 7.2).

Such reactions generally lead the government to slow down and negotiate compromises with affected groups, to limit possible losses of votes. Adverse popular reactions to policy change contribute to the '**costs of governing**', from which all incumbent parties suffer, and hence ultimately lead to some or all of the current opposition parties taking over the government. Resulting slowdowns as policy targets are then changed back also contribute to the relative stability and centrism of the policy actually being implemented.

Both government alternation and slow policy change are major factors keeping public policy closer to public preferences in the long term. So 'thermostatic' popular reactions of this kind, slowing down change and weakening current governments, have an important effect in making democracy work.

The same may be said of 'policy elections' such as initiatives (initiated by a certain number of supporting signatures often collected by opposition parties and groupings) and referendums. Referendums fall into two distinct groups. The first group includes ones triggered independently of the government, often because they are stipulated constitutionally as necessary in certain areas when legislation is proposed. Such referendums resemble initiatives in this respect, although they often relate to fairly technical and non-controversial matters which just happen to fall under relevant constitutional provisions. The other broad type of referendums includes ones initiated by the government itself, either when it thinks it can win greater support for some of its own proposals or in areas outside its main areas of concern where it disagrees internally and hopes to settle the matter by a popular vote.

Not unnaturally, given its technical or off-beat focus, popular voting in referendums often shows strong support for the government position and/ or the status quo. This is less true of initiatives, which tend to be promoted by the parties not in government because they think they can derail part of its programme – or at least embarrass the government by showing there is strong popular opposition to some of its policies.

Costs of governing

Government losing votes due to negative reactions to its decisions during its term of office.

What can be said of 'policy elections', whatever their nature and end results, is that they do allow groups other than governments to frame popular preferences. However, the question on which citizens are asked to vote usually lines them up 'for' or 'against' something the government is proposing to do, thus severely restricting the range of **preference profiles** that can be expressed by a vote (Chapter 5). Moreover, the government normally tries to strengthen its own position in the vote by making concessions on the policy in question. All of these moves (plus the official side's defeat in some cases) make for some adjustment of policy to popular preferences, bringing the two together in a useful way which supports the democratic goal of congruence between them – even if it does not guarantee it.

Preference profiles

Sets of political preferences organized in a particular way.

In this respect policy elections in representative democracies exercise effects similar to opinion polls. That is, they influence expectations about the next general election by convincing government parties that some of their policy stands are losing votes and need to be withdrawn or modified. In the absence of regular, independently called and constitutionally decisive policy voting, however, general elections, with the government alternations they produce, remain the major mechanism bringing public policy into line with popular preferences.

The way these preferences are allowed to be expressed in general elections is nonetheless unsatisfactory. Popular policy preferences may influence the overall outcome or even determine it on occasions. But there is no guarantee of either, and many other non-policy factors enter into the overall result. Moreover, preferences have to be expressed as a choice between parties. Parties are 'carriers' of many policies. But do they carry all of those desired by electors – allowing most if not all preference profiles to be used as the basis of choice?

In the context of any one election – or even the short time span covering two or three – the answer to this question must often be no. General elections with their party-defined choices often severely contract the range of preferences that the electorate can bring to their choices. Such restrictions can, however, be countered in the long term, through the freedom which democratic processes provide to initiate and build new parties with policy programmes which better fit the preferences of excluded sections of the electorate. This preference-expanding aspect of democracy is often overlooked in a single-election context where the set of existing parties tends to be taken as given. The centrality of political parties in shaping and channelling popular preferences renders the electorate's ability to form new ones quite crucial, however. So we examine it in the second half of this chapter before looking at the political parties themselves in Chapter 12.

Ideology

A set of assumptions about the world supporting certain kinds of political action.

Expanding popular choice: party origins and ideology

Political parties are distinguished from other organizations and groups operating among the population by the fact that they run candidates for elective public offices. Most commonly, these are seats in a legislature. But they also include the presidency and other executive offices whose holder is chosen by election.

Of course, political parties do many other things besides nominating and supporting candidates and their campaigns. They also put forward general-election programmes, presented as 'manifestos' or platforms – four- or five-year plans for running their countries. Parties are unique in publishing such plans on a regular basis. These form the basis on which voters can choose on policy grounds between parties. We discussed in Chapters 3 and 6 how these are presented. Party programmes seek to frame election discussion by focusing it on certain topics favourable to themselves and influencing the terms of reference within which they are discussed ('framing').

Parties, of course, campaign in ways other than by presenting candidates and policies during general elections. They draw attention to their record, competence in government, current events at home and abroad – anything in fact that might make them an attractive proposition to vote for. As a result, general elections, though they determine the course of government policy over the next four to five years, are not necessarily decided on policy alone – or even mainly on policy – as we have noted.

Parties also participate in various ways in pure policy elections, promoting one side or another in support of their own position. Such elections are far from generally determining policy, however, as they affect only specialized areas which governing parties may deliberately keep away from to avoid internal divisions. Other groups may, however, join in to encourage 'yes' or 'no' responses to the proposals – business organizations, other types of 'interest' or 'pressure' group, trade unions, social and cultural bodies, churches, social movements of various kinds and even individual businesses and firms.

The borderline between such groups and political parties is thin and permeable. Parties have often originated as the political wing of an overarching social movement, as we shall see below. Even business firms have on occasions morphed into parties as they already have a country-wide organization to use for political work. The same is true of churches, although they are more likely to develop a purely political wing. Simply by getting involved in general elections and then running candidates any group or organization qualifies as a political party.

With such diverse organizational origins, parties can take on a variety of forms and appeals. Their common focus on taking over the government and legislature does mean, however, that one can generalize about the needs which drive them into their political engagement and how they seek to channel these into their own purposes (a summary is provided in Table 6.2 – the developmental-family theory already discussed).

Political parties as we know them today emerged because of the growing democratization of most developed countries in the nineteenth century. This involved a growing empowerment of legislatures and the elected governments which emerged from them, on the one hand, and a steady expansion in the number of citizens allowed to vote for them, on the other. This created expectations on the part of so far unenfranchised groups – religious or ethnic minorities, workers, the poor, farmers – about getting the vote too. The wealthy, already allowed to vote, had generated loose groupings of 'liberals' or 'conservatives' with limited support organizations – what we might call proto-parties. Rather than choosing and promoting candidates systematically, self-selected candidates grouped together after their election to form loose groups of like-minded individuals who tended to vote together in legislatures and supported each other in newspaper and election campaigns.

Such proto-parties of local notables then formed a model for the leaders of excluded groups, which they could develop further as a means of providing a wider range of election options, more congenial to their own preferences and interests. The first step was to agitate for an extension of voting rights to their own supporters since this would provide them with a sufficiently strong legislative base to promote their own policies for government – or even to take it over. To mobilize their fellow workers or farmers, co-nationalists or co-believers who were likely to be isolated socially or geographically and ignorant of politics, they had to develop a mass membership with branches in every part of the land. These had a three-fold function: mobilize likely supporters; propagate the party messages often through their own newspapers; and collect money in the shape of small subscriptions and contributions from members.

The key to building an organization which could then conduct political campaigns was the realization that recruiting many supporters making small financial contributions could in aggregate raise more money than would come in from a few large donations made by wealthy individuals. Politics ceased to be reserved to those who could individually afford it and was opened up to choices made by the new mass electorate. Under universal suffrage, where everyone could vote, this now extended to minorities and, ultimately, women.

What were the social groupings which political parties emerged from and increasingly helped to define by promoting their consciousness of themselves as a separate group, having more in common with fellow group members than with the rest of the population?

The most obvious examples are manual workers, who were low paid, deprived and segregated geographically in inadequate housing. First of all, trade unions, then socialist and labour parties, sought to mobilize them behind demands for better pay and working conditions enforced by state inspection and legislation.

Those expected to pay for these public goods through higher taxation and lower profits reacted by rallying behind the older parties, conservatives and liberals, which had traditionally represented their interests. Religious and Christian parties, on the other hand, sought to bridge this class 'cleavage' by convincing both working-class and middle-class Catholics or Protestants that they had more in common with each other than with non-believers of the same class. They should therefore help each other out when there was obvious deprivation, particularly as it affected the family. The same cross-class appeal was made by minority ethnic and linguistic

Group consciousness and 'false' consciousness

There are two ways of belonging to a group. The first is in terms of your job or social position – you are a manual worker and so belong 'objectively' to the working class as opposed to the middle class. Or you can be a 'bourgeois' intellectual like Karl Marx who 'identifies' with the working class and so belongs 'subjectively' – that is, in terms of his own thinking – with the working class. To forge an effective political movement, the members must both belong to the working class objectively (i.e. be doing manual work) *and* feel that they *are* working class, having more in common with other working-class individuals than with anyone else. If certain workers, for example, felt that they had more in common with fellow Catholics or Protestants than other workers, regardless of their religion, then they would from this perspective be suffering from false consciousness, not recognizing that class shaped all their life chances and opportunities and should therefore be addressed by every means possible, above all by supporting class-based organizations like trade unions and socialist parties. One of *their* main tasks, indeed, should be to increase class consciousness among their supporters to mobilize them in support of class objectives like equalizing income and abolishing inequality.

While the idea of 'false consciousness' and group consciousness originated with class, it is of course a problem for all groups, social movements and parties. People who 'objectively' go to church or speak the same minority language have to be convinced that these social links are overwhelmingly more important than others – in other words, brought to a true rather than 'false' consciousness of their overwhelming importance. They can then be mobilized to support the appropriate political party.

Convincing potential supporters of their shared interests is indeed a major task of the political party – necessary for mobilizing a mass base which will make it a political force.

parties often with ambitions to take their own territory out of the state within which they were embedded. Large and small farmers often felt that food prices were artificially kept low at their expense while expanding towns and suburbs encroached on their land and changed their way of life. Agrarian parties thus formed to protect country dwellers against exploitation by people in towns.

The 'cleavages' produced by tensions between these groups and their growing self-awareness are summarized in Table 11.2, which shows which kinds of social and opinion groupings tend to support each type of party.

The core political demands made originally by each group and its party representatives rapidly expanded in the process of campaigning and debate. No party or group was large enough to generate a general-election majority on its own. It had to persuade undecided voters that its programme hung together as a consistent plan for running the country and providing desirable public goods for everyone. For example, ensuring a fair wage for workers and reasonable food prices for farmers both involve more government regulation and higher taxation to pay for it. Making a case for greater government regulation and intervention in society to improve life for the majority enabled socialist and agrarian parties to appeal beyond their own group supporters to sympathetic outsiders, thus giving them more votes, seats and influence after the next general election.

In this way, parties develop a general ideology – that is, a fixed set of assumptions about politics and society which provides an immediate framework for action, both in making election appeals and formulating government policy. Ideological assumptions about human nature and society then form a basis both for writing election programmes ('party manifestos' or platforms) and for representing party policy positions spatially, as discussed in Chapters 3 and 6.

The process of party formation still goes on today. With the loss of distinctiveness of older social groups under the pressures of social change (e.g. manual work is no longer so prevalent, segregated or distinctive and minority languages are disappearing), opportunities increasingly arise for new parties to appeal to wider opinion groupings with new ideological appeals – a prime example being green or environmental parties, concerned about the degradation of natural processes and about climate change.

Briefing 11.4

Ideology and ideologies

The term 'ideology' is used in many different ways, but essentially it is a system of ideas and assumptions which help us understand and interpret the world, so we can take appropriate political action when it is called for. It consists of a set of values and beliefs, factual assumptions and ideas which help us impose order on a complex world and which explain what is going on, why, and our place in this world. The term is often restricted to a fairly explicit, coherent and elaborate set of ideas – a real theory about society and politics. Marxism-Leninism is the best example. In this sense, relatively few people are ideologues. But many more subscribe to looser and less explicit ideologies such as socialism, liberalism or conservatism. Parties are built around those conflicting political principles ('principles' is a positive term which means the same as ideology in the broader sense).

Sometimes the term 'ideology' is used neutrally to describe any more or less worked out set of values and ideas about politics. But sometimes the term is used critically to imply dogmatism or blinkered vision. In a strict 'scientific' Marxist sense, ideology means a false view of the world – the 'false consciousness' created by capitalists in order to keep the workers happy. There is a sense in which ideology relieves us of the need to rethink and reanalyse every single new political event; we simply fit things into the old understanding. But there is also a sense in which everybody, not just those suffering from false consciousness, depend on an ideology to make sense of politics. In this sense, Marxism itself is an ideology but a highly developed, complex, subtle and general one.

TABLE 11.2 Social groupings and the parties representing them

Social groupings	Party families
students, radical intellectuals, social workers; reform and peace movements; some trade unions; feminists	socialist (left)
conservationists, nature trusts and their supporters and volunteers	'green' ecological
trade unions, co-operative movements, civil servants, teachers	labour, social democrats
churches, affiliated trade unions and co-operatives	Christian democrats
country dwellers, farmers, small holders	agrarian
linguistic and cultural minorities within the state; formerly independent regions	minority nationalist (ethnic, regional)
business interests and professionals, particularly lawyers	liberal
business (particularly small business); property owners; higher civil servants	conservative
veterans and patriotic associations	state nationalist

Notes: Political parties are listed from top to bottom in a generally left-centre-right ordering. As we have seen in Chapter 6 (Figure 6.1), however, not all parties fit equally well along this continuum, having other concerns which do not fit into general left-right differences. Notable examples would be minority nationalist parties, which aim at devolution or independence for their region but may be either left or right in socioeconomic matters, or agrarian parties, which may aim at land redistribution to small holders and peasants but in other cases want agricultural subsidies for property-owning farmers. Even Christian democrats, who do take a distinct genuinely centrist line on socioeconomic affairs have religious concerns quite separate from general left-right conflicts (state support for church schools, for example).

Social groups often split the support they give to parties. Manual and lower-middle-class unions, for example, might support both left socialists and social democrats or even be affiliated to Christian democrats in some cases. This tones down the impact of political divisions between groupings by creating 'cross-cutting' rather than sharply defined 'cleavages' between social groups (see Briefing 11.5).

Whereas older parties often emerged from a clear social support base for which they developed a matching ideology, new social movements and parties like the greens start with an ideology and develop a support basis of believers and supporters, reversing the older process; greens do, however, get more of a response from public service and voluntary workers than from business or private enterprise. In this way, greens and other new parties develop a distinct social profile in a way similar to older parties. Meanwhile, some of the latter – notably minority nationalist and ethnic parties – continue to define and mobilize a distinct social base.

All parties thus end up with both a social base and an ideology, reflecting one side of some 'cleavage' within their country. We shall go into these in more detail in the next chapter, focusing on parties as such. Here we are primarily concerned with the opportunities which the process of party formation offers to citizens to initiate and frame political preferences and choices for themselves. Any one general election seems to offer preset choices to voters which have been framed by party elites. That is, they have a choice only between existing parties and cannot express policy preferences or make voting choices other than between them.

Once we recognize, however, that in the medium and long term (sometimes even in the one-election context too) new party alternatives with distinctive policy positions can be set up, electors appear less as passive

Briefing 11.5

Social cleavages: does C = P + 1?

In theory there might be different social groupings in society which also live
harmoniously with each other. This is a vision shared by many idealists who believe that
conflicts will disappear once the root problems are dealt with in the way they advocate.

In practice, however, given limited resources and differences of race, language,
class and religion, which generate social tensions, there are always likely to be some
conflicts and disputes between them. These 'cleavages', as they are generally termed,
often spill over into politics, most obviously in the shape of political movements and
parties aimed at influencing the policies which distribute resources between groups or
which provide them with the public goods and regulations they want.

Viewed in this way, social and opinion cleavages explain the rise of parties, as
described in the text. Can the relationship be specified more exactly in such a way as
to predict the type and number of parties from the cleavages which exist in a state?
The equation in the title makes an effort to do this. Where C is the number of cleavages
in a society and P is the number of parties,

$$C = P + 1$$

The equation states that the number of parties will equal the number of cleavages
plus 1. Thus, if there is only a class cleavage (the most obvious one in modern
societies), then the number of parties will be two, with socialists and conservatives
forming up on each side of the political divide. If there is both a class and religious
divide, then the number of parties will increase to three (not to four because the upper
classes are likely to overlap with the established religious group while differing religious
affiliations will likely have split the workers into two different parties). This reasoning
can also be extended to the minority groups of all kinds: established groups will
probably cohere on languages to defend their majority language and religion and the
privileges these bring with them. Thus, they will cohere on one 'defence' party, and the
excluded groups will probably each have a party to represent their particular interests
and opinions.

This is an interesting idea, and it is nice to have it formalized in a neat little predictive
equation. There is a major problem in trying to apply it to explain party formation,
however. That stems from the problem of establishing the existence of politically
relevant cleavages (C) independently of the political parties associated with them.
How do we know if social differences are deep enough to constitute a politically
relevant cleavage? The obvious answer is that they have produced a political party
to push their interests! Thus, we know that a social cleavage is politically relevant if
it has a corresponding political party. But this means that C is made *equivalent* to P,
rather than functioning as an *explanation* of P. Until we can measure politically relevant
cleavages independently of the parties associated with them, we cannot use them as
building blocks of a predictive equation (which is not to say of course that independent
measures of sociopolitical cleavages could not be developed, perhaps as a class
project).

respondents in the voting process and much more as initiators. Popular preferences will always emerge from an interaction between framers (parties and governments) on the one hand and voters' predispositions on the other. This freedom to generate new parties, however, liberates popular preferences and choices from the criticism of being largely manipulated from above.

Freedom from manipulation is essential to the definition of democracy as a system which guarantees the translation of popular preferences into public policy. If such preferences were not autonomous and formed independently (at least in part) of the makers of public policy themselves (parties and governments), we could hardly see the causal influences as running from preferences to policy. Rather, it would be the other way around. The policymakers would simply be reflecting their own preferences for policy in the reactions they claimed to be getting from the public – rather like businesses shaping public demand by their advertising. This state of affairs would subvert any distinction between democracy and populist dictatorships, for example.

From the point of view of representing choices in a spatial and formal way (cf. Chapters 4 and 8), the fact that the existing set of parties can accommodate the full range of significant preference profiles among

---

Briefing 11.6

Democratic agenda setting? Decisions and non-decisions

Left-wing critics often complain that the fundamental causes of social and economic inequality never get discussed in democracies, because they are not raised by any of the parties and thus remain off the political agenda. Thus, property rights are never challenged, the question of an adequate minimum income for all is never raised and proposals to tax large international corporations to provide for this in the countries where they make their profits are held back until they get 'international agreement'.

There is a certain amount of truth in the criticism. Parties with any chance of winning power and joining governments tend to avoid controversial issues so as not to alienate potential voters or make it difficult to form a coalition with other parties after the election. Taking a long-term rather than a short-term perspective, however, we can see that the freedom to organize new movements and parties has led, for example, to restrictions on property rights and provisions for benefits such as free healthcare – though not yet to a guaranteed minimum income. It is not clear whether the popular majority actually want to go further than this (such topics have not been the subject of initiatives, for example). And the common outcome from both initiatives and referendums is support for the way things are. Radicals on both right and left are prone to think that their proposals are so obviously good that any failure to follow through on them is due to covert manipulation or conspiracy. With freedom to organize in support of such proposals if they want to, it is at least as likely that the proposed changes do not appeal to the majority of citizens.

electors is crucial. It means that party policy positions in the space usually cover all the policy options actually preferred by the population at that time. Individual elector preferences spill over all sides of each party position so that the popular majority lies in the central space. As a result, the median elector position can always be seen as located spontaneously within the policy segment the parties define. This is an aspect of the political and electoral situation that has been largely ignored in the social choice literature and that solves many of the problems that it has highlighted about identifying a stable majority policy preference (see Chapter 9).

As pointed out in Chapter 5 and illustrated in Table 4.1, we need to find such a position to demonstrate the very existence of a real and stable majority preference with which we can compare policy outcomes to determine whether they correspond – as democracy claims to guarantee. We also need to establish that it *is* at the centre, between the policy 'bundles' offered by the parties, as Chapters 4 and 5 have argued. Once this is accepted, we can as an additional check try to determine whether public policy also generally ends up there, in line with the popular will – and thus if democracy works in practice by bringing public policy into line with the popular preference for it.

Briefing 11.7

Pluralism, democracy and civil society

Allowing autonomous organizations and groups to form independently of the government is commonly taken as the identifying characteristic of pluralist democracy. The term 'pluralism' simply refers to the existence of a large number of groups with different interests, some overlapping, some conflicting, which can operate freely within laws which do not unduly restrict their political and other activities. As we have seen, this is crucial in making sure that all policy options have a party carrier and that the median position defined by party options is a genuine and not a manipulated one. The more traditional term '(strong) civil society', used extensively in classical political philosophy, is also used to describe such a situation.

Not just party formation but also party characteristics and functioning are crucial for democracy. That is why we consider these aspects of parties in detail in the next chapter (Chapter 12) before going on to the way they drive the process of governance itself (Chapter 13).

End-summary

Without freely formed and well-defined citizen preferences for policy, and ways of transmitting them to state decision makers, democracy could not work. The key political role of citizens and electors therefore lies in forming and expressing clear collective preferences which can then guide governments in making and enforcing the policies which produce public goods.

As previous chapters have shown, this is no easy task. No rule can guarantee an agreed and stable outcome from voting on a one-person, one-vote basis without arbitrarily excluding some spontaneously formed preferences. This goes hand in hand with shaping collective choices in ways which some individuals would not choose if left to their own devices. A prime example comes from general elections, the ultimate device in modern representative democracy for shaping governments and the policies they make. Electors can choose only between political parties and the policies that those parties offer rather than the policy combinations that electors might want to put together to vote on.

Seen from the context of any one election, electoral freedom of choice seems constrained. This is compounded by the fact that many non-policy considerations also influence party choice in general elections. So the major decision determining policy over three to five years may often be taken on non-policy grounds!

A common reaction to this situation, often seen among advocates of direct democracy, is to 'let the people speak' by excluding parties and other intermediaries and having direct voting on policy through initiatives. Given the **cycling** problems associated with various collective voting rules, there is no absolute guarantee, however, that the people *will* speak clearly.

Cycling
A situation where every potential policy majority can be beaten by another.

Some structure to allow the expression of clear popular preferences is necessary; otherwise, there is no way of determining what the popular preference is. Rules and institutions are clearly needed to focus and organize debate. With this consideration in mind, the chapter started off by examining general elections and the party choices they offer as a means of structuring policy-based voting. This is supplemented in the inter-election period by direct policy votes in referendums and initiatives and by continuous opinion polling, with accompanying 'thermostatic' interactions. Both popular votes and polls commonly ask citizens whether they agree or disagree with specified government policy proposals. Inviting yes-or-no responses avoids cycling but severely shapes and restricts the spontaneous preferences which electors might form, though certainly in different ways than general elections do. In both cases, however, parties in elections or parties in governments can be seen as equally important in defining popular preferences as citizens themselves. Yet democracy requires that popular preferences be reasonably autonomous and not manipulated by elites and decision makers.

The democratic mechanism which meets this requirement was examined in the last section of the chapter, in a predominantly long-term rather than short-term perspective. Parties are framers of popular preferences, providing them with the necessary structure and focus they need for clear expression. But parties themselves are formed spontaneously by citizens. Any group which feels that its preferences are not adequately expressed through the existing range of party choices can form another party to give them expression, using democratic freedoms and processes to do so. Eccentric individuals who do this will find that they lack support, so their new parties never get off the ground. Any significant grouping, however, will have its preferences reflected in a new party (or through policy adaptation by an older one) which becomes a more or less permanent carrier of the group-preferred policies.

Of course, general-election outcomes are not decided wholly on policy. Rather, we have to see them as mechanisms for the alternation of different party policy carriers in government, who by switching the preferred targets being enacted bring applied policy back to the centre of the party-defined policy space.

The important conclusion from this discussion is that this is where the popular policy preference will also lie *if* all significant preference groups find a representative in the party system. It is in establishing the centrist location, relative spontaneity and autonomy, and reasonable stability of aggregate popular preferences, that the significance of this discussion lies.

Political parties play an important part in all this by clarifying and expressing the preferences of significant groupings of the population. No more than citizens, however, can they be taken as unitary actors, where defining their policy position is unproblematic. In the next chapter, we look at how parties, made up of various distinct factions and interests, overcome this problem, again by a form of leadership alternation.

The main points to take from this discussion are thus:

- The interdependency of popular preferences and party policies, both of which shape the other but in different time-perspectives.
- In the long term, electoral groups form parties to represent their enduring interests and opinions.
- In the short term, parties frame choices for electors by putting proposals to them which they can either accept or reject.
- Electors' freedom to form new parties means that at any one time all electoral preferences are 'carried' by one or more parties.
- Thus, the majority preference, as represented by the median elector position must always end up at some point in the centre between the party policy positions.
- For public policy to correspond with the majority popular preference, therefore, it too must lie in the centre, between the party positions.

Systematic working assumptions coming into this discussion

10   The most extensive sharing (of decision-making about policies) occurs in democracies since by definition these have to guarantee that public policies necessarily reflect the preferences of citizens for them.

11 This guarantee is provided by free, regular and competitive elections of governments and/or policies open to all groups and individuals, where votes reveal citizen preferences and authorize them as either policymaking governments or directly as state policy.

15 Popular policy preferences do not usually emerge spontaneously but rather are formed as reactions to policy proposals put forward by governments, parties or other political actors.

16 The free formation and functioning of such actors is thus essential to the process of estimating the full range of true popular preferences.

17 The popular preferences with which public policy must necessarily correspond in a democracy can be specified sufficiently to form a basis for public decision-making only if estimated from voting outcomes in free and open elections (or from election-like formatting of questions in well-conducted surveys).

18 However, all political – like other – measurements contain error (which can nevertheless be estimated and corrected on various assumptions).

19 This is necessarily true of election votes, taken as measures of popular preferences. The rules and procedures which structure votes (e.g. the order and wording of alternatives being voted on and methods of aggregating votes to produce a collective decision) can all distort the final outcomes and have to be allowed for in estimating settled preferences.

Sources and resources

Russell J. Dalton (1996) 'Political Cleavages, Issues and Electoral Change' in Lawrence Le Duc, Richard G. Niemi and Pippa Norris (eds) *Comparing Democracies* (Thousand Oaks, CA, Sage), pp. 319–342.

Russell J. Dalton and Christopher J. Anderson (2011) *Citizens, Context and Choice: How Context Shapes Citizens' Electoral Choices* (Oxford, Oxford University Press).

Stuart N. Soroka and Christopher Wlezien (2010) *Degrees of Democracy* (Cambridge, Cambridge University Press).

Suggestions for class papers

1 Why can't electors just make up their own minds about political issues? Or can they? Make your case.

2 To what extent do referendums and initiatives free up citizens to exert a more direct influence on policy?

3 Why do electors generally have more moderate views than political parties do?

Suggestions for class projects

1   Devise a measure of social cleavages which is independent of the existence of an affiliated political party, and use it to check out the relationship between numbers of cleavages and number of parties $(C = P + 1)$.

2   Write a party manifesto for a minority ethnic party which presents both its core concerns and justifies them as good for the state as a whole.

3   Analyse the contemporary situation to identify the most promising basis on which to organize a new political party, and describe how you would put it into practice.

Chapter 12

Political parties

Ideological policy carriers

Chapter overview

Modern democracy is best described as party democracy, since parties do the crucial job of transmitting the preferences that they frame at the popular level into public policy at the governmental and state levels. They do not do this, however, by passively following public opinion. As Chapter 11 demonstrated, they play an important part in forming it, in the first place by presenting electors and voters with policy proposals they can react to.

Even so, it is often unclear what the popular preference really is. Parties are almost bound, therefore, to jump the gun and put forward their own policy preferences as the ones the public 'really' wants. If voted in at a general election, the successful party or parties then claims that the majority supports their policies and their implementation in government. This may or may not actually be the case, depending on the extent to which non-policy factors have entered into the election (candidate and government competence, crises, scandals, foreign threats, etc.). But in any event, the party (or parties) in government will plough on with changing policy targets to fit their own ideas. Such ideas stem from applying their own ideology to the current situation at home and abroad.

All parties have ideologies even if they claim to be non-ideological. Ideologies are theories about the way the world works, which point to particular strategies for dealing with it – even when information is scarce and results unclear. They often stem from and develop the outlook and interests of the group that the party originally sprang from (e.g. Catholic or Protestant churches or trade unions).

An ideology will often predispose a party to emphasize particular kinds of public goods more than others (e.g. welfare over security) and particular ways of providing them (state intervention rather than private enterprise). Ideologies thus generate policies, rendering them vital when we consider how these fit in with majority preferences of the population.

Against this general background, the chapter first considers parties as organizations and then goes on to look at them as members of international groupings centred on particular ideological beliefs, drawing on similar types of support groups, such as churches and their associated organizations; minority or majority ethnic groups, whether territorially or culturally based (or both); the working class and the middle class; conservationist and environmental organizations; and so on. All of these groups have different concerns. However, overlaps between them may promote temporary or permanent coalitions which then link up to form more heterogeneous political parties or party groupings. Of course, the wider a party can spread its network of support, the more votes it can hope to get at elections. Thus, many parties may 'carry' quite a range of policies into government even if their core ideology focuses on a narrower set of concerns.

After considering 'party families', their social characteristics and issue concerns, we will look at parties in a broader light as 'carriers' of a whole range of policies loosely related in an overall programme for government (election 'manifestos' or platforms). These can be regarded as general plans for how the state will develop and deal with current problems over three to five years (normally the period between elections). Parties are the only bodies which produce such general plans for the whole of their society on a regular basis, which again places them at the centre of the political and democratic process.

Plans are always strongly influenced by the assumptions they start off from, in this case the party ideology (cf. Chapter 6). That is not to say that parties always 'carry' the same policies and concerns equally over time. Crises and events require adjustments at certain points, though of course, these always take off from existing ideological assumptions. There is also disagreement within the party about what exactly the ideology indicates in the way of immediate action – and even sometimes on what it is really saying. There is usually a radical **faction** that wants a 'pure', uncompromising, ideological stand and a centrist faction that sees the best way forward as seeking agreement with other political forces. These compete for control of both the leadership and party policy. While one group pushes for more extreme measures, the other wants compromise – possibly with other parties to **the left and the right** of the general party position. Election reversals combined with increasing discontent within the party lead to the displacement of the current faction by the other on quite a regular basis and hence to switches of policy driven largely by internal considerations rather than direct responses to electors' wishes. Factional alternation within the party thus leads to change in policy targets just as alternation between parties in government leads to change in policy targets at state level.

There is a lot of scepticism about the extent to which election promises are really kept. But in fact, there is little doubt that parties try to effect their key policies when they can. So our discussions here form an essential background to considering party actions in government, which we do in Chapters 13 and 14. The predictive theories that the discussion rests on relate first of all to 'party families' – the idea that all parties belong to ideological groupings distinguished by characteristic policies. Since these are crucial to a party's identity and continuing existence, they are rarely

Faction

A grouping within a party with distinct views on policy and strategy.

Left-right

Welfare, state intervention and peaceful internationalism on the left and traditional morality, freedom and internal and national security on the right.

abandoned. However, they may be emphasized or de-emphasized, depending partly on past election performance but mostly on whether moderate or more extreme factions are in control internally. This theory of factional policy alternation is explored in detail at the end of the chapter.

Key points to note in the discussion are thus:

- Ideology as the key factor keeping parties together and maintaining their distinctiveness.
- The ideologically based 'families' to which individual parties belong.
- The contrast between more narrowly focused ('niche') parties and more general 'programmatic' parties.
- Policy continuity and change, as explained by the factional alternation theory.
- The role of computer simulations in developing and testing such predictive explanations.

We now revisit party families and their ideological differences.

Briefing 12.1

Inside political parties – structure, organization, factions

Political parties emerge from social and opinion groupings with a mission to promote their interests and beliefs. The most effective way to do this is through politics. This may in the end give them a part in making and implementing the policies which most affect their base group. Along the way, however, it also gives them opportunities to publicize their policy demands and convert others to the cause and stimulate group consciousness among members.

The party is therefore usually one among a number of organizations originating within some base grouping and pursuing its objectives. It may exist alongside co-operatives, unions, youth movements, newspapers and TV channels, sports clubs, churches and any number of other organizations operating alongside it. From these, it may hope to draw financial support, party workers and favourable publicity.

Electoral politics, however, require parties to develop a more specialized organization to run candidates for elective office (possibly at several levels: local, regional and national) and co-ordinate them if they do get elected. This is usually done by a central executive committee with a chair who takes the lead – or this role may be filled by a leader elected either by all the party members or by national and/or regional legislators and office holders.

Executive meetings are usually supplemented by a national convention or conference, with delegates from all levels of the party and affiliated organizations, which mostly debates policy with an eye to the writing of the party programme for the next general election (its 'manifesto' or platform). Regional, state and city

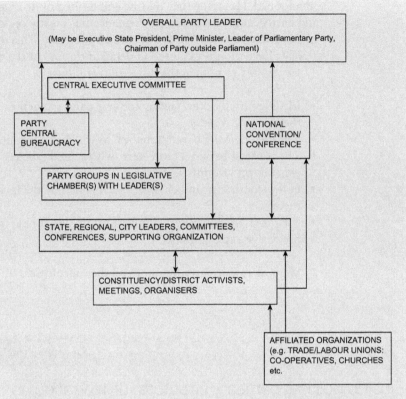

FIGURE 12.1 Party structure and organization: a general overview

Notes:
1 The party leader will always be the president under a presidential system
   of government. In that case, the party's legislators will have separate party
   leaders. In other systems the party leader will normally be chair of the central
   executive committee and lead the parliamentary parties as well.
2 The arrows in this figure indicate the following:
   a Who elects members of bodies like the central executive committee.
   b Who makes policy and other decisions which are binding on the body
      concerned. Double-headed arrows indicate a two-way flow of influence.
3 Regional, state and local parties have leaders, committees, conferences and
   organizations which generally mirror those at the national level.
4 The party leader can be elected by legislators, the national conference, party
   activists in the constituencies, members of affiliated organisations or many or
   all of these.

parties usually have their own chair or leader with a co-ordinating committee and
convention, and the parties have considerable autonomy in applying national policy
to their own area. All of these bodies will be supported by an office staffed by paid
professionals who collect debts and payments from members, keep records, do the
accounts and handle correspondence and publicity. Party candidates, particularly in
a constituency-based system, will have rooms where they can meet constituents and
conduct business.

This rather complex party structure can be viewed in two ways, vertically and horizontally, both giving rise to potential conflicts and divisions within the party. Horizontal divisions might stem from members organized in local and regional parties sticking closer to the pure ideology than national leaders do. This is because the latter are often forced to compromise with partners in a coalition government or not to appear too extreme in trying to attract centrist votes in a general election.

Lower down in the party, activists have less need to compromise and may do a great deal of unpaid work for the party because they believe in its cause. They often see this as being betrayed in the course of legislative or other manoeuvrings higher up and may well organize within the party to oppose the central leadership.

Such 'horizontal' confrontations between activist 'ideologues' and 'pragmatic' leaders may also feed into vertical divisions. Other organizations (e.g. trade unions) within the broader social movement behind the party may also oppose what they see as a betrayal of their interests by the political leadership. They may as a result criticize it internally or back an opposing faction within the party (pragmatists or purists, as the case may be).

Party factions are generally more vertical than horizontal in nature, usually led by disgruntled parliamentarians outside the core leadership group who try to gain support at all levels – base activists, affiliated organizations and local and regional politicians. Having organized some sort of mass support, they will keep up their criticisms and await an opportunity to overturn the existing leadership and take over – usually in the wake of bad polling or election results. Having done so, they will usually change party policy in the opposing direction to their predecessors. Factions within a party thus act rather like the parties do themselves within the wider political context, alternating policy without too much regard for popular preferences (cf. Table 12.2).

Figure 12.1 gives a schematic overview of party structure covering all the above points with notes explaining how to interpret it.

Ideology and 'party families'

A major characteristic of political parties as we have seen is their urge to push policymaking in their direction within their own state. To achieve this, they have mobilized support groups within the national territory through their political appeals. However, the ideas and strategies on which such appeals and strategies are based have rarely originated within their own country. They have travelled across national frontiers, spurred on by general developments in communication and technology which have been accelerating ever since the early nineteenth century. These have produced similar social developments everywhere, as peasants left the land to live in cities and work in factories and as universal compulsory education raised the question of what languages subjects should be taught in and whether churches should have control of schools or be subsidized to provide them. All this meant that governments became increasingly centralized rather than leaving most territorial administration to local elites.

Elites
A select group with more power and privileges than others.

These developments produced common problems – of finance; infrastructure, like roads and railways; public and private health within rapidly expanding cities; and so on. This raised questions on a state-wide scale about who was going to pay for it all and also concerns about immigration and territorial tensions as states competed for natural resources – all provoking political discussion and debate. These drew on experiences and thinking abroad to propose solutions to similar problems at home. Generalizing in this way across state boundaries led to similar action being undertaken, including the adoption of similar policies and programmes and the foundation of similar parties to publicize and effect them.

International
A cross-national grouping of parties.

Even in the nineteenth century, international meetings of parties were held under the sponsorship of trade unions or churches. These multiplied as communication and travel became easier. By belonging to the Socialist International, for example, political parties defined themselves as 'socialist' or at least 'leftist' within their own state. At the present time, there are also federations of liberal and Christian parties across countries. The proliferation of interstate groupings (see Part IV) also means that country parties can choose to affiliate themselves with green, liberal, socialist, conservative and (minority) nationalist groupings, which act as super parties, as in the European Parliament of the EU.

Briefing 12.2

The European Union (EU) and its parliament

The EU is a grouping of 27 states covering most of Europe outside Russia and the UK. The members are linked closely by a customs union (i.e. common taxes on imports of goods and services); a single market (free movement of finance, services, goods and people across countries); and increasingly a common currency, environmental and security arrangements and mutual recognition of professional and other qualifications. The ultimate aim is a federal union of states, as in Canada.

Managing all this requires common institutions like those of a traditional state. Alongside the executive institutions (commissions, councils of ministers), there is a parliament with wide-ranging powers of supervision and authorization, elected directly by PR across all member states. It has party groupings based on the traditional party families with which national parties can align themselves (almost all do). These groupings act like national parties do within individual state legislatures.

Parties thus identify themselves by names, both nationally and internationally, which refer to a common ideological heritage in the shape of doctrines like socialism (with its subdivisions into communists, social democrats and labour); liberalism (with its subdivisions into progressives and neo-liberals); and conservatism (with its subdivisions into neo-liberals and state nationalists).

We should note that these ideologies are broadly arranged along the left-right 'continuum' or 'dimension' which we have discussed at so many points before (notably in Chapter 6). Thus, socialist parties tend

---

Briefing 12.3

Socialist parties and tendencies

Socialist parties draw their ideology ultimately from the writings of Karl Marx, who in the third quarter of the nineteenth century produced a comprehensive analysis of modern developments based on the pervasiveness of class disparities. Industrialization had sharpened these, pushing the mass of people into a working class or proletariat exploited by property owners. The only way to remedy this situation was through political means, by founding trade unions to assert working-class interests and spread class consciousness and mass political parties to influence or take over governments in order to restructure society from top to bottom. Steps towards this would be payment of universal benefits and healthcare. But reform could not be fully achieved without a total takeover of the state and a subsequent restructuring of society.

It is on this point that the various segments of the socialist movement split. Labour and social, and other democrats settled for immediate political reforms like social welfare and a tax-funded health service, as well as political rights for trade unions. Left socialists and communists, on the other hand, wanted a complete takeover of the state with total direction of the economy and reform of society. They differed on whether this could be done democratically, by contesting and winning elections (left socialist) or by force if necessary (communists).

The socialist legacy is thus split into three major tendencies. Few communist parties remain after their general collapse of 1990. Left socialists, advocating radical reform within a democratic framework, have inherited many of their activists and supporters. Social democratic and other democrats and labour parties have generally accepted the case for a mixed economy, combining capitalist and state-run enterprises and services. As a result, they have become less distinguishable from bourgeois or capitalist parties.

Parties within the general socialist block are inclined to co-operate with each other in forming governments. Elements on both sides want to strengthen such co-operation. This contributes to the formation of factions of 'purists' and 'pragmatists' internally, with stricter and more relaxed interpretations of socialist ideology prevalent on each side – a situation made for the factional alternation of policy (Table 12.2). Such alternation is in fact common in all parties, whatever 'family' they belong to. For an up-to-the-minute analysis of socialist parties, see Hans Keman (2017) *Social Democracy* Abingdon, Routledge.

Briefing 12.4

Liberals, radicals, progressives and neo-liberals

In the nineteenth century, liberal parties emerged as representatives of the expanding urban middle class of factory owners and the professionals and managers associated with them. Their main demand was to get a share in policymaking, previously monopolized by landowners and bureaucrats associated with monarchies and courts. Liberal used their new powers to create a more efficient state structure which would improve communications and deal with security and planning in the new cities and which would free up trade within and across national frontiers.

To achieve these objectives, their political representatives often allied with wider popular movements – agrarians, minority ethnic parties and workers' movements – who also sought to get the vote and to expand infrastructure. However, as new socialist parties emerged, especially as they developed a mass organization, their demands for better working conditions and regulation of factories and other social improvements all brought them into increasing conflict with the industrial middle class who employed the workers – factory owners who would have to pay for improvements.

The mass parties which liberals increasingly formed to render themselves more effective politically thus had an ambiguous relationship with the other new parties, having some interests in common but others opposed. This situation produced diverging currents within liberalism itself. Having enfranchised the middle class and removed barriers to trade and manufacturing, some thought they had gone far enough. Equality and freedom were sufficient to give everyone the opportunities they needed to prosper. Other groupings, however, felt that poverty and bad social conditions threatened political and social stability, so they favoured alliances with working class and other new parties in order to get them. Political freedoms were not enough if the masses were too poor to exercise them.

Freedom is thus a unifying principle for liberals but different liberal parties (and factions within parties) interpreted it more narrowly or more broadly. Generally, these tendencies within liberalism could be distinguished by the names the parties gave themselves – progressives, radicals or democrats, as opposed to neo-liberals, who stressed the benefits of the free market and the dangers of interfering with it. In the twentieth century, neo-liberalism of the latter variety increasingly influenced the thinking of other parties like Christian democrats and conservatives. So as well as contributing to differences within the liberal party family, neo-liberalism also promoted factionalism within other parties, notably conservatives.

to emphasize social initiatives at home (and to favour state intervention as a way of carrying them through) and peaceful co-operation abroad. Progressive liberals tend to agree with these objectives but with less of an emphasis on state intervention as a way of achieving them. Neo-liberals, on the other hand, tend to see free enterprise as the way to resolve social problems and want the state's role reduced. Many conservatives agree with this. There are others, however, who are more focused on foreign

Briefing 12.5

Varieties of conservatism

Conservative parties, such as (American) Republicans and nationalists, are mostly descendants of the defenders and beneficiaries of the old regime, as it confronted the new popular movements of the mid nineteenth century. Originating in the loose groupings of notables elected to the new parliaments of the time with a restricted franchise, these quickly copied their opponents in creating a mass party organization and a new ideology to defend themselves better against the new ideas. The original conservatives were primarily concerned with maintaining the old state structures – army, bureaucracy, established church – and the old social hierarchies and traditional values. While they believed in maintaining existing inequalities of property and rank, conservatives often had a paternalistic attitude to those at the bottom, believing that they should be protected from the extremes of poverty so long as they recognized the dominance of their social superiors. Conservatives, who are often landowners and country dwellers, had common interests with large farmers when these formed agrarian parties to keep food prices high and restrict foreign imports. Where religious parties defended the interests of the established church (usually the Catholic Church), conservatives often allied with them or often took on the task of defending it themselves. However, as social Christianity came to the fore, with an emphasis on social justice and with associated trade unions and workers' movements, they increasingly parted company. More promising from a conservative point of view, given their traditional concern with internal and external security, was an appeal to the defence of their nation state against immigrants competing with natives and threatening the established culture and way of life. Such an appeal to state nationalism could lead to the foundation of a state nationalist party further to the right or to a faction within conservative parties who competed with those promoting neo-liberal and free market ideas as these became increasingly dominant in the late twentieth century (see Table 6.6 for evidence of this conservative split).

affairs and security threats and who would thus be prepared to give the state a greater role in promoting internal unity to make it stronger abroad.

In turn, these conservatives have something in common with state nationalists, who are particularly concerned with internal threats to the existing state and its national majority – often therefore opposing the dilution of its character by immigration or from integration into larger entities (the EU, the UN). Two consequences follow from the variety of outlooks within and across these parties:

1   There is obviously considerable scope for disagreement between the various groupings and tendencies which appear within parties. It is not that any of them want to break out of their overarching party ideology. Rather, they may interpret it differently or see it as suggesting different responses to the current political situation. The

most common disagreements are between revisionists, who see party doctrines as needing to be updated and modified to cope with modern changes, and hardliners, who want to stick to traditional 'pure' interpretations of the ideology. In spatial terms, these are often characterized as 'centrists' and 'extremists'.

2   Such disagreements often persist as the basis of factional disputes within the party. **Factions** try to get their own members into leadership positions and control statements of party policy. Changes in policy and in who the party co-operates with in government (Chapter 13) have more to do with which faction is in control internally than with responding to electors' wishes and preferences.

Faction

A grouping within a political party with distinct views on policy and strategy.

The fact that there is a range of opinion present within each party – often coming close at the extremes to members of another party – also means that party positions are best represented along a continuum or line, shading into each other rather than constituting tight and mutually exclusive groups. For the 'party families' we have been talking about, such a continuum takes the familiar form of the left-right dimension discussed in Chapters 4 and 6. This is not surprising, of course, because political parties largely shape or frame the political debate at the popular level too. If they organize discussion in terms of Marxist analyses of the situation as opposed to neo-liberal 'free enterprise', then electoral responses and preferences will generally spread out between these two alternatives.

As we have seen, left-right divisions of this kind do encapsulate many of the main issues of contemporary politics. So this is a useful way of representing them in most democracies. Characterizing them as 'left', 'centre' or 'right' helps both the parties and electors to organize the whole range of issues confronting them at home and abroad and to talk about it in a kind of spatial shorthand in terms of moving to the 'left' or 'right' or 'capturing the centre ground' – phrases often heard in the media and in general political discussion.

Table 6.5 explicitly contrasts the broad groupings of emphases and positions which characterize each end of the left-right continuum: welfare, government intervention and internationalism on the left, as opposed to security, order and freedom on the right. By giving more or less emphasis to these topics, parties can move themselves to the left and the right as shown in Figures 6.3 and 6.4. Electors can then place themselves at a position on the line, which reflects their own priorities. As we have seen, the majority of electors tend to take a centre position, reacting negatively to moves by parties and governments to the extremes (though parties may still make such moves for their own internal reasons).

Sharing such a centrist position with the majority of electors are the parties of another family not discussed so far: the Christian democratic parties. They are at the 'centre' in terms of left-right divisions because of their religious concerns with the traditional family and its security. This leads them to emphasize state support for welfare and health, like socialist and labour parties on the left, but also protection of its property and freedom to prosper, like the liberals and conservatives. Abroad, Christian parties tend to advocate peace and international co-operation but based on a strong defence, thus putting together elements of both left-wing and right-wing appeals.

However, the Christian democrats also have concerns which do not fit so easily into a left-right 'summary' of politics. With their roots and much of their support coming from the churches, they are concerned with

---

Briefing 12.6

Religious parties – Christian democrats

In the nineteenth century, religious parties in Europe and other parts of the West divided between Protestant fundamentalist and evangelical parties, often challenging the established state church with radical views which extended into the social sphere, and defenders of the state church (often the Catholic Church) who were associated with the old order. The new Protestant churches might support radical liberal parties, or they might form their own parties to promote their own views, such as on religious education. Catholics, Orthodox and Lutherans initially supported the conservative parties who defended their traditional privileges.

All this changed, however, as the nineteenth century merged into the twentieth, and churches became anxious to maintain and increase their following among the new urban working class. This led them to apply the potentially revolutionary doctrines of Christianity to the socioeconomic situation. Social Christianity developed among Protestants. In the 'social encyclicals' of the late nineteenth century, the popes encouraged reforming activities among Catholics. All churches reached out to the masses with Sunday schools, youth movements and social clubs, and the Catholics in particular founded Christian trade unions to fight for better working and social conditions. Churches all had an interest in educating children within a religious environment and therefore in founding church schools and getting the state to pay for them, now that there was universal compulsory education.

These were common interests shared by all churches across religious divides. As the latter became less salient during the twentieth century and politics increasingly focused on sociocultural matters, Protestant and Catholic parties drew closer together and increasingly amalgamated as Christian democrats. Catholic-Protestant differences still had the potential to generate factional conflicts within the broader parties, however.

Other religious parties (Jewish, Muslim, Sikh, Hindu) have followed the same path as the Christian ones in pressing for state recognition and support of religious schools and in concerning themselves with the social and economic well-being of their adherents. In the case of these groups as with the Protestants, many have joined reforming parties of the left, with their support of civil and religious freedoms, rather than forming their own parties. Fundamentalists tend to be more attracted to right-wing parties upholding traditional values or to religious parties themselves, where they exist. This makes them useful coalition parties with both centre-left and centre-right parties, as we shall see in Chapter 13.

Briefing 12.7

Niche versus mainstream parties: or should it be single-issue versus general catch-all parties?

The first distinction made in the title derived from research showing that larger, older parties generally gained votes when they modified their general policy stance while smaller, newer parties lost votes when they did so. Such niche parties generally focus on a single main issue (climate change, agriculture, a particular minority's rights) and tend to have supporters who are highly committed to that cause. They react negatively when it is toned down. Older, larger parties, on the other hand, carry a wider range of issues potentially appealing to the whole of society, so toning down more extreme policies attracts supporters and voters who have weaker commitments to any one issue and are fairly centrist in terms of overall policy preferences. The loss of supporters committed to their key defining issue can therefore be more than balanced by the gain in votes from 'floating' voters. Conversely, if and when these voters desert the party in a later election, it can get those core supporters back by re-emphasizing its defining issues. Niche parties – much more defined by their key issue – do not have that room to manoeuvre (however, see Briefing 12.10 on the greens).

preserving religious values and beliefs. This gives them strong moral concerns not shared to the same extent by any of the 'secular' parties (though with a fainter echo among conservatives and state nationalists).

Fitting their major concerns into a left-right framework is even harder in the case of the three remaining party families which we have not considered so far. These are agrarians, green or ecological parties and minority ethnic-regional ones. Agrarians are particularly concerned with defending farmers and peasants against regulation and exploitation by the central government. This last concern might line them up with green, environmental parties on some issues (preserving traditional ways of life and the countryside, for example). Representing peasants and small farmers, however, agrarian parties are more likely to focus on material improvements such as better rural infrastructure and higher subsidies and prices for the main crops.

Because minority ethnic or nationalist parties are often based on rural communities at the periphery of the state, where linguistic minorities have a better chance of surviving, their representatives have some concerns in common with both the agrarians and Christians. For one thing, ethnic minorities often deviate from the religious traditions of the majority in their state – or they may have preserved these more fervently than in the cities. The minority may also be predominantly rural and thus join with agrarians in pushing for material benefits for their region.

Despite some overlap, the core concerns of each of these party families do nevertheless differ sharply from each other and also from those of the 'programmatic', left-right families. This demonstrates the role of parties as

Briefing 12.8

Minority ethnic and regional parties

Though often referred to as nation states, most states in the modern world contain minorities who are different culturally and linguistically from the majority population. Recent immigrants who scatter over the national territory will mostly be assimilated to the majority by the second or third generation. Where there is a long-standing minority occupying a well-defined territory, however, and particularly where it had independence or its own political institutions at one time, a minority nationalism different from state-majority nationalism tends to develop, pressing for different cultural and particularly educational treatment and political devolution – or even secession to form an independent state on its own. The introduction of compulsory universal education in the state language was reacted against by minority ethnic parties which by their nature can hope to get support and legislative seats only in their own area. They may also espouse other causes and may be quite strongly 'left' or 'right'. But their basic constitutional and cultural concerns prevent any easy classification of the family on a left-right continuum on any state-wide appeal, making it a classic niche party where any change in its policies will lose rather than gain electoral support.

Briefing 12.9

Agrarian parties: origins and their modern development

While country-dwellers had concerns in common with other new parties, there was however an immediate source of conflict. Both the urban workers' movements and their employers wanted cheap food to counteract low industrial wages. This was most easily achieved by lowering barriers to cheap food imports from North and South America and from Australia. Lowering tariffs however hit the rural population at home who needed high food prices to offset their much higher costs of production. Cheap imports from overseas bankrupted landlords, farms and peasants alike and accelerated depopulation and the decline of rural communities. Landlords tended to join with other property owners in conservative and state nationalist parties to oppose the liberals and radicals. Farmers and particularly peasants banded together to protect themselves in rural co-operatives and agrarian parties. These often aimed at rural reform and land redistribution as well as protection for home food stuffs. They also agitated for improvements in rural infrastructure and the extension of public services there.

With continuing rural depopulation in the twentieth century and the expansion of city suburbs into the countryside, many agrarian parties lost their mass base, particularly the peasants. Those that remained either turned themselves into conservationist and ecological groupings close to green parties, or took the opposite road of pressing for subsidies for large scale agricultural production which changed traditional farming into industrial production. These two opposing standpoints formed a basis for internal factionalism as well as for divisions between different kinds of agrarian party.

Dimension

A line running between total support and total opposition to a policy.

Party system

The number and types of parties in a state.

carriers of a variety of issues, each of which may constitute a 'dimension' of politics on its own, if we think of them in spatial terms. However, our discussion also points out the need for established parties to take positions on the whole range of state policy in composing their election programme. Not doing so may lose them credibility even with their own supporters, since general state policy by its nature affects country dwellers and ethnic minorities, among others. These pressures help to position even parties of sociocultural defence (religious, ethnic, agrarian) on the left-right continuum. So this still retains its usefulness as an overall summary of the party position, even in the case of parties which started off by emphasizing other sets of issues. Indeed, the pressure on parties over time to take up concerns interpretable in left-right terms may render the latter even more relevant as a **party system** matures.

Briefing 12.10

Green parties – environmental, ecological, conservationist, yes – but also increasingly interventionist and leftist

Green parties emerged as serious political contenders in most states in the 1960s and 1970s, spurred on by increasing concerns about climate change and environmental degradation. Unlike older parties, which emerged as the political wing of an established social grouping (church, union, cultural ethnic organizations), green parties tended to emerge independently as the main representatives of environmentalism and to create their own support without having any clearly defined social base (see Table 11.2).

This gave such parties an unusually clear defining issue which has caused them to be classed as a niche or single-issue party. Potentially, however, measures to combat climate change constitute a complete general programme for society and economy. To be effective, such measures must involve major government interventions, both national and international. This brings the greens closer to the socialists and others on the extreme left, even leading to the formation of 'red-green' electoral alliances in some cases and allowing them to be located close to left socialists on the left-right dimension (cf. Figure 6.2).

Family issue concerns

Party ideologies – even their names – provide indicators of what common issue concerns mark them and their families out. As we have explained, these could possibly be modified or even displaced over time. So we need to have their continuing relevance confirmed by the party itself, using the main public document each national party issues at three- to five-year intervals, detailing its policy priorities for the country as a whole. These documents are the programmes ('manifestos', platforms) issued by parties at each general election and already discussed in Chapter 6. They may be regarded as summarizing the main policy targets the party would like governments to pursue. Many other factors shape the election campaign: party candidates, record in government, contemporary events. These may even be decisive in shaping the vote outcome. But policy is always a factor, and the party always states its policy targets as an integral part of its campaign. By analysing the platforms over time, we can see what these are and whether they change. We expect each national party to be distinguished from the others by the particular policy concerns characteristic of the 'family' to which it belongs.

Election programmes, commonly termed 'manifestos' or party platforms are booklets (occasionally books! – or sometimes just leaflets) issued by the leader or executive committee of a party and endorsed by its national party convention or general conference of members. They set out party policy systematically across the range of issues confronting the country at a particular time. Parties do not of course always deal with the same problems, since they have differing concerns, which lead to different views of the political situation. These stem from their underlying ideology, but they may also be influenced by strategic considerations about what is likely to appeal to voters. Physically, the programme is mostly composed of a number of sections dealing with different policy areas – youth, employment, defence and so on – with a general introduction and conclusion urging support for the party.

How can we analyse such a text systematically, to provide evidence on party issue concerns which can be reliably reproduced by other scholars if they wish to? The only way to do this is to convert the text through clear and specified procedures into numbers and then to analyse them by using a statistical procedure like spatial representations of party and voter positions or 'discriminant analysis' – to pick out those issue concerns which particularly distinguish each party (see Chapter 6, particularly Table 6.6).

The idea of turning a page of writing into a distribution of numbers sounds daunting but (as already demonstrated in Tables 6.2 and 6.5) can be done quite easily by counting sentences (the basic unit of meaning in most languages) into policy categories, which cover the whole range of concerns that the parties raise. Examples include military, freedom and domestic human rights, economic orthodoxy, social justice and agriculture. Such specific categories can be grouped into seven broad sectors, but statistical analyses are generally based on the number of sentences going into the more detailed categories (cf. Table 6.2).

Having got a comprehensive set of policy categories (56 in all), each sentence in the text can then be assigned to one of these. After this is done the whole document can be characterized according to the percentage of sentences it devotes to each policy. This quite simple approach directly measures party policy concerns and clearly distinguishes between parties in terms of these. Table 12.1 lists the outstanding issues associated with each party family in an analysis of all European election programmes (aka platforms) 1990–2002 (see also Table 6.6). Some of the parties in the analysis, largely in Western Europe, had been active in democratic elections for over 100 years. Other parties and the democracy they were active in had only recently been established (mainly in Eastern Europe). Even new parties, however, have grouped into established 'families' and adopted their ideology.

Table 12.1 demonstrates empirically how important their ideological concerns are in distinguishing one type of policy programme from the others. Being ideologically based, these policy concerns are also the ones you would expect from the name the party has adopted. Thus, green (ecological) parties put most emphasis on environmental protection; agrarian parties on agriculture; and ethnic and regional parties on decentralization of power to themselves (the regions). Christian parties uniquely support traditional morality. Extreme socialists go for world peace, while more moderate social democrats want more welfare. Liberals go for a free market economy – the neo-liberals inside these parties outweighing progressive liberals. Conservative parties divide between those giving the free market economy their support and those stressing foreign military alliances.

The numbers opposite each policy category measure the relative importance of that leading policy in picking out parties as family members (in technical terms, its correlation with the discriminant function putting

TABLE 12.1 Dominant policy characteristics discriminating election programmes of a particular party family from all others

Party family	Dominant party characteristics	Discrimination index for each issue
Left socialist	Planned Economy	0.3
	Welfare State Expansion	0.5
	Peace and Détente	0.5
Social democrat	Welfare State Expansion	0.5
	Economic Infrastructure	0.3
Liberal	Market Economy	0.5
	Welfare State Limitation	0.5
	Freedom and Human Rights	0.3
Conservatives	Market Economy	0.6
	Military Strength	0.5
	Economic Infrastructure	0.4
Christians	Traditional Morality and Order	0.9
Agrarians, ecologists	Agriculture	0.9
	Environmental Protection	0.9
	Peace and Détente	0.3
Minority ethnic/regional	Decentralization	0.8
	Social Groups	0.1
State nationalist	National Orientation	0.5
	Military Strength	0.5
	Centralization	0.2

Notes: The table identifies the issues in the published manifestos of each party family which best distinguishes it from the others. The last column shows how well it discriminates on a scale from 0 to 1.00.

Source: *Mapping Policy Preferences from Texts*, p. 64

together all the policy emphases distinguishing that family). This is not necessarily the policy that the party mentions most but the one that it stresses most uniquely – which of course is the one we would expect from its name, international affiliations and underlying ideology. It is the 'sociocultural' parties at the bottom, focused on a particular social group which are best picked out in terms of unique policy concerns. But these extend also to the Christians, with their characteristic religious concern with traditional morality. This does not distract these parties, however, from enunciating a broad centrist programme in left-right terms, as we have noted.

The classic left-right 'programmatic' parties, on the other hand, have policy concerns less clearly focused on one particular issue area. This is marked in Table 12.1 by the lower contribution which even their leading concerns make to distinguishing parties as members of a family. Conservatives even split on what should be their leading concern – internal or external, free market or international security. Of course, such parties can pursue both concerns, as these are not necessarily contradictory. However, there is a basis for internal disagreement and factionalism here, which we shall examine in more detail in the last section of the chapter. Before we go on to this, we want to know how relevant their traditional policy concerns are to parties today. Do they still influence their actions and strategies, in the ways you would expect from their ideological affiliations? A good test of this that uses available evidence is to try to predict what international groupings an individual party will join, based on what it says in the most important policy document it produces, its national election programme. If anything clearly shows off its ideology and traditional concerns, it is this. So we can test if they continue to influence important party discussions.

The most important decision most European parties had to make in the 1990s was which international grouping to join in the European Parliament. This had not only enhanced powers over discussions which crucially affected all the member states of the EU but also determined national parties' access to financial and other support which they could not get at home.

Based on the issues stressed in their national election programmes, 80% of 504 individual parties across Western and Eastern Europe were correctly predicted to be in the parliamentary 'family' grouping that they actually joined, convincingly demonstrating the relevance of their traditional preoccupations to their current decisions.

Parties as policy carriers

There is thus a remarkable continuity between the names that parties choose for themselves, the groupings they belong to, the interests and outlook of their core supporters and groups and the issues that they emphasize (as anticipated by the developmental-family theory, Table 6.2). This conjunction explains why some parties have carried on with broadly the same policies for over a hundred years and why newly founded parties in the same 'family' take up the same positions. Doing so plays an important part in distinguishing them from other parties and building up base support.

Briefing 12.11

Do vote-seeking parties converge on the median? – nice theory, pity about the evidence!

The obvious way to ensure a correspondence between government policy and popular preferences is letting citizens vote in the parties that most faithfully reflect the majority preference. This is the idea that has dominated general theorizing about democratic representation to date, and it has focused much empirical research on (often small) policy moves by parties in line with popular opinions. It finds its clearest expression in the spatial theory of two-party competition put forward by Anthony Downs in *An Economic Theory of Democracy* (New York, Harper, 1957), pp. 115–118.

This guarantees efficient representation by postulating that in a general election, vote-seeking parties will adopt more or less the same policies close to the median voter. This position maximizes their vote at least under two-party (or quasi-two-party) competition, as any majority vote has by definition to include the median voter (see Figure 5.2). The median preference is also the one at the least aggregate distance from all the others.

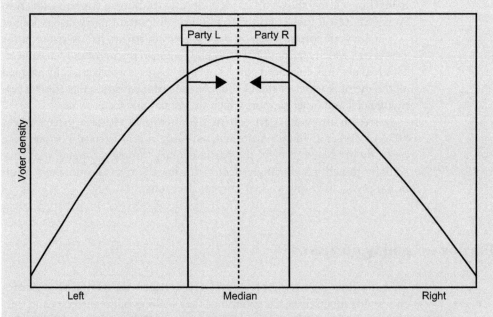

FIGURE 12.2 Schematic of hypothetical elector and party locations, for a normally distributed electorate in a two-party system: parties converge on the median position to maximize their vote

Downs explained these ideas in the spatial form shown in Figure 12.2. The picture it provides of party-elector interactions is so concise, neat and powerful that it has been accepted over a long time period without much questioning of its basic assumptions. These include the idea that parties will jettison all their policies and ideological principles by moving to the middle to get votes; that electors will be concerned only about party policy in general elections rather than (also) record, competence or candidates; that all think in left-right terms about overall issues rather than, for example, about each issue separately; and that issue space is always a straight line. As we have seen, none of these ideas is upheld in actual party or electorate behaviour. Even in the purest two-party system in the world (the US) parties are highly ideological and do not converge in left-right terms either in single presidential elections or over time (Figure 6.3). The wonderful neatness and clarity of Downs's two-party model has thus exerted rather negative effects on representational studies by orientating them towards policy voting and party vote seeking as the main causes of policy-preference correspondence rather than crediting the evidence against them and looking for other mechanisms like party alternation in government (Chapter 7).

Such continuity has two effects so far as current elections are concerned. First, it renders parties reliable carriers of their core policies into government. A party committed to strengthening public services (generally socialist and left-wing) is going to enhance them – or at any rate reduce them to a lesser extent than right-wing parties. This is even truer for the concerns of parties like agrarians or greens. Indeed, these parties are often accused of being single-issue parties, whose only concern is to promote farming interests or reduce climate change. As we shall see, this may be a bit exaggerated: parties in the long run pick up additional policy concerns and carry these in to government. To maintain credibility, they have also to produce a comprehensive programme for the whole range of current problems facing the country and not just promote their own interests. But long-standing policy concerns remain their distinguishing feature, as Table 12.1 demonstrates.

Party reliability on policy is one thing; sensitivity to popular concerns is quite another. The very commitment to certain ideological principles and concerns which makes them reliable in carrying out 'their' policies in government means that they will stick to them whether or not the public turn against them. Of course, parties will try to persuade voters to adopt their own particular point of view in the campaign. But the process is 'top-down' rather than 'bottom up': parties will attempt to draw electors towards their own position rather than modifying it to conform to theirs.

If defeated in the general election, a party is unlikely to alter its core policy much (though it may modify its emphasis on it – see Table 12.2). Mostly, it will simply wait for circumstances to change in its favour. Similarly, if elected to government on its non-policy appeals, a party will claim electoral support for its pre-existing policies rather than make any attempt to go deeper into what electors really think and modify them in light of that.

Without shifty and unreliable parties willing to trade principles for votes, how can democracies provide their fundamental guarantee that public policy will reflect popular preferences? Clearly if parties – each of them based on a minority of supporters in the electorate – simply pursue their core concerns in government, there is only a chance that these will meet majority demands rather than any cast-iron guarantee that they will do so. Indeed, the probabilities are rather against public policy meeting majority preferences under such circumstances.

This democratic dilemma has already been raised in Part I, where we discussed the processes that *do* bring policy and preferences together. There is (1) an ameliorating influence and (2) a definitive process at work which resolve the problem:

1   A 'thermostatic' effect is an ameliorating influence which shows up in the inter-election period. Public support for government proposals diminishes steadily as they take up more extreme positions. When cuts to a policy are proposed, electors want more of it, or when more is proposed, electors want less. Apart from anything else, the thermostatic effect provides additional support for the idea that the majority of electors place themselves in the centre, between the policy extremes represented by different parties.

However, in the present context 'thermostatic' reactions also, importantly, slow down governments as they try to turn their targets into actual policy on the ground. Popular disapproval always produces party misgivings about losing support in the next general election. It often provokes media campaigns, peaceful or violent demonstrations, strikes and refusal to co-operate on the part of affected groups. It is wiser to seek compromises with these, which may lead to the policy being modified and which at any rate slow down policy implementation. All this contributes to policy inertia and gradual, **incremental change** in policy rather than the immediate implementation of policy.

Incremental change

Only limited change from a previous position.

2   Alternation effects make up the definitive process that helps bring policy and popular preferences together. The thermostatic brake on rapid policy change feeds into the major adjustment mechanism at work – party and policy switches in government. We expect general elections to produce such alternation on a regular, if chance, basis. As one plurality party replaces another as the main dynamic force in government, it substitutes its own policy targets for those of its predecessor and seeks to pull actual policy back towards its own. Total policy change is rarely effected before the results of another general election change the party composition of government. The ultimate effect is to substitute different, often opposed, targets for those being pursued up to now. Hence, actual policy, halfway to change in one

direction, is pulled back across the centre, where the new popular majority is situated.

The long-term effect is to keep the policy actually being pursued reasonably close to centrist majority preferences, thus meeting the democratic need for a necessary guarantee of the correspondence. It does this even accepting that political parties are by their nature committed to fixed principles which they will pursue in government, regardless of popular reactions to them. Such ideological rigidity means that short-term incongruence – especially between government policy targets and popular preferences immediately after an election – cannot be ruled out. However, it will be rectified in the long run through the working of the electoral-governmental cycle.

For democracy to work, therefore, we do not need shifty and unreliable parties ready to sell their ideological souls for a few extra votes. If parties actually behaved like this, we would have constant flux, as parties changed not only policy but name, identity and supporters. Given the need for parties to engage in **framing** popular policy preferences to give them focus and structure – essential if they are to emerge as stable and settled over time – stability in the party system is a major requirement at the input end of the democratic process. That this is then able to guarantee their eventual match with public policy at the other end, given reliable and principled parties, is therefore crucial to fully understanding how it works.

A final point which stems from parties consistently 'carrying' certain policies is that their alternation in government produces policy-preference correspondence for all policies, not only mainstream ones. Any policy backed by a reasonable body of opinion will find a party spokesperson. This might be an established party which picks up a policy which fits with its general outlook and existing programme. Or it could be a party founded specially to promote the policy in question, which gathers weight and numbers over time. This process is aided by pressures even on single-issue parties to confront the whole range of societal problems, suggest solutions for them and carry them all through into government, alternating with parties opposed to their policy as they do so.

Framing

Defining the possible courses of action to be considered on an issue.

Left-right

Welfare, state intervention and peaceful internationalism on the left and traditional morality, freedom and internal and national security on the right.

How parties decide policy: change within stability

Given that all parties put forward election programmes covering most of the issues facing the country, we can use the most convenient summary of these – the **left-right** continuum – to show how far they change overall position on these and how far their policies remain the same. Given what has been said about the pervasive influence of ideology, it is important for parties to retain their relative policy positions. But this is not to say they are totally inflexible in the face of a constantly changing social, economic and international situation.

Measuring overall policy change as reflected in their manifestos then helps us see how far our ideas (on the driving force provided by the party ideology and factional disputes over its exact interpretation) fit the actual evidence. This is provided by estimates of the left-right movements of parties in a whole range of countries, such as the ones shown in Figures 6.3 and 6.4. Developing a theory about why, how and when policy change will take place and then checking it out against relevant evidence is a classic way of extending our political science knowledge. So this exercise is not only instructive because of what it tells us about political parties and their policy targets but also informative about how we can develop and extend our knowledge of politics in general.

Our factional or alternation theory of party policy change is summarized in Table 12.2, which states its five assumptions. These all emphasize the influence of party ideology.

An ideology, as noted above, is a theory about politics which helps its adherents choose a policy under uncertainty – that is, when not much is known about its effects or consequences. Socialist ideology, for example, will always favour state intervention to set matters right, while neo-liberalism would favour leaving things to private initiative.

The pervasive uncertainties in politics let ideology in to suggest appropriate party reactions to the current situation. But argument about its exact implications generates factions that develop ambiguities inherent in the ideology into different prescriptions for action (e.g. state regulation of the pharmaceutical industry as compared to providing medicines through a state agency). The debate about policy and the factional dynamics driving change are largely internal to the party. However, it cannot be wholly indifferent to electoral reactions. Policy is one factor influencing voters. Their support in turn affects the party's chances of getting into government and putting its policies into effect. So if a change in policy initiated by factional changes in control is followed by an increase in the party

TABLE 12.2 Assumptions of a factional theory of party policymaking

1. Ideology	Parties' position taking occurs within the limits set by overall ideology, so individual positions stay in or return to a particular segment of the policy space over time.
2. Factionalism	Parties are divided into factions distinguished by their attempts to impose their own version of the common ideology on the party and government.
3. Costs of control	Events erode support for the faction controlling the party such that a rival faction and its policy normally substitute for the previous one at each election.
4. Elections	This erosion of support can be offset only in the short run, by increased vote associated with the policy shift for the last election, which allows the controlling faction to continue for one election.
5. Magnitude of change	The magnitude of policy change is proportional to the relative strength of the factions at the time of the change.

vote, even the opposing faction(s) will continue with it for the following election. After that, however, the controlling faction will be weakened by the continuing compromises and concessions it will be forced to make, especially in coalition governments. So after two elections, even if it is successful in voting terms, it will be forced out; the other faction will take over; and policy will change direction.

The size of the change will depend on the relative strength of the two factions. If the incoming faction is markedly larger than the other, then the direction of change will not just alter but rather change quite markedly. If, on the other hand, the two factions are relatively equal in size, there will probably be a standoff, and policy will stay where it is with neither faction being able to move it further in their own direction.

These points are all spelled out in the assumptions of Table 12.2. Assumption 1 reaffirms the point about policy generally staying within the overall limits set by party ideology, particularly regarding the party position relative to its neighbours. (Socialist and labour parties are almost always going to be left of conservatives, for example. If, by accident, they 'leapfrog', then they will return to their old position at the next election.)

Leapfrog

Change policy positions with another party.

Assumption 2 in Table 12.2 then spells out what has been said about the existence of internal factions and their attempts to take control of policy. Assumption 3, on 'costs of control', postulates an erosion of internal support for the controlling faction, more or less rapid depending on election success (Assumption 4). Assumption 5 relates the size of the policy change to the relative strength of the factions – one has to be large relative to the others to pull policy substantially in its own direction. If they are relatively equal in strength, there will be a standoff, and party policy will not change.

Factional competition to impose their own version of the shared ideology as the official position of the party as a whole thus accounts for the main features of party policy change – both its direction and magnitude. Realistically, factions – with their ambitions to affect government as well as party policy – have to take election results into consideration. But these are difficult to interpret except through ideology. Thus, they only have a minor, short-term effect – interrupting policy alternation rather than replacing it.

These assumptions can be represented concisely in the 'decision tree' shown in Figure 12.3. This presents a four-election sequence of policy movements leftwards (down) or rightwards (up) on the vertical left-right scale. Starting with Elections 1 and 2, we see that at Election 2, the party tracks to the left, as shown in the figure unless there is a vote gain shown as a plus sign (+). In this case, as shown in the figure, the party continues to the right. Whatever the result of Election 3, however, the party will then reverse to the left – again as shown in the figure.

If the party encounters a vote loss (-) at Election 2, it reverses its previous move and goes left – again as shown in the figure. If Election 3 then registers a vote gain, the newly initiated leftward move will continue (and will then be reversed after Election 4). If not and the party loses votes at Election 3, policy will be reversed again to the right.

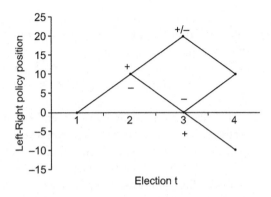

FIGURE 12.3 Postdictions of the factional or alternation model of party policy change, presented as a decision tree

Notes: Minus and plus signs indicate changes in the party's vote share during the election (i.e. the first change in vote takes place during Election 2). Downward slopes indicate leftward policy shifts, and upward slopes indicate rightward shifts. For ease of presentation, this version of the model assumes that all policy shifts are ten units in magnitude; there are only definite moves to the left and right; and policy does not 'stay put'.

The overall consequence of four-election, three-move sequences of this sort is to produce a policy zigzag between left and right. However, this is not a pure zigzag. Rather, it is an interrupted zigzag, where moves *may* continue in the same direction after a vote gain. But they will then be reversed.

In our model, each party decides independently of the others, so no mutual strategic adjustments are involved. This gives us the opportunity to put their decision trees together to produce a full-blown computer simulation, resting on the idea of party policy movement as an interrupted zigzag. What does the model look like when operationalized? And do the model's assumptions appear realistic when we compare them with observed patterns of party movement over time along the left-right continuum? We can decide this by comparing Figure 12.4, which shows the left-right moves that three parties would make as anticipated by our assumptions in Table 12.1 and the resulting decision tree in Figure 12.3, with the observed movements of the three main British parties over most of the post-war period, shown in Figure 12.5.

Figure 12.4 plots out a pattern of moves which would result if three parties decided in the way we anticipate on their policies – each of their policy paths taking the form of an 'interrupted zigzag' between left and right. We see that this 'map of movements' looks generally plausible – the right party stays pretty much on the right, the left party on the left and the centre party remains distinctly in the middle, though crossing occasionally with the other two.

Setting up a simulation like this is a first step in checking whether our factional theory of party policy change is true. Does it give reasonably plausible results? Of course, going from a general theory to such a detailed numeric representation does involve making supporting assumptions,

Briefing 12.12

Computer simulations as a check on theoretical ideas

The notes to Figure 12.4 show how you can detail and measure the consequences of theoretical assumptions like the ones in Table 12.2. Usually, the theoretical rules don't cover all the decisions you have to make in setting up the simulation, such as having to decide exactly what the central party position will be (-13 or +13, in this case, for left and right parties) and exactly how far the party can be allowed to oscillate around this (13 points). Vote gains and losses have to be made random. We can confirm the plausibility of these decisions against the manifesto-based data we have but not against the theory.

On the other hand, the theory does tell us under what circumstances a party will move left or right (though not how far, as we don't have data on the relative strengths of factions, so again the size of moves has to be decided randomly, by default). However, the theory does determine the overall patterns of movement we observe. We can thus look at the general picture given by the spatial representation which we produce on this mix of theoretical and data-based assumptions and try to determine whether they look plausible. We can also compare them with the 'real' observed picture of British party movements in Figure 12.5 to determine whether they broadly correspond – which they do.

None of this quite constitutes a test of the theoretical predictions against independent evidence, as too many other assumptions have been used to represent the ideas spatially. The simulation is nevertheless a first check that we can make on the theory – first of all on whether the theory is precise and clear enough to support a simulation and second on whether the results in the form of the spatial representation look plausible (which they do). Many theories in political science do not reach this first stage. Those that do, though, often can't go beyond it. In this case, we do go beyond it by checking out the theoretical predictions against observations.

which are specified in the notes to Figure 12.4 and Briefing 12.12. Nonetheless, these are simply supplements to the decision tree in Figure 12.3, which is the core of the simulation.

We need not simply rely on the general plausibility of the simulation, however. We can compare it with the actual left-right moves made by the parties in a three-party system – the main British parties over the post-war period (1945–2005) (Figure 12.5).

Comparing Figures 12.4 and 12.5, we can see that the theoretically derived moves in the simulation produce broadly the same patterns as the actual observed moves of the three main British parties over this historical period. We can, however, do more to check out the success of our theory, by seeing how far each individual party move in Figure 12.5 corresponds to our expectations about what way it should go (characterizing moves of four units or less as 'staying put'). Readers can in fact try doing this themselves as an exercise in checking out theories against evidence.

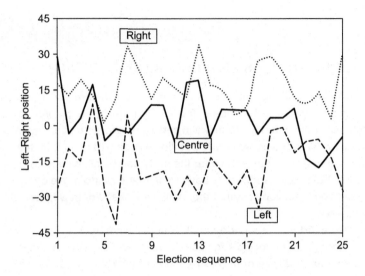

FIGURE 12.4 A simulation of the three-party policy dynamics from the assumptions of the integrated factional theory

Notes:

1   Create a large number (2000) of party positions with (a) left party, mean = -13 and standard deviation = 13 (normal distribution); (b) right party, mean = +13 and standard deviation = 13 (normal distribution); and (c) centre party, mean = 0 and standard deviation = 13 (normal distribution).

2   Each party has two factions, each covering half of the party's distribution: (a) left party faction 1 > -13.0. faction 2 < -13.0; (b) right party faction 1 > +13.0. faction 2 < + 13.0; and (c) centre party faction 1 > 0. faction 2 < 0.

3   To start the simulation, enter the large number of party positions at a randomly selected point, and apply the rules to generate the sequence: (a) accept as given the left and right party positions as the starting position of each of the parties; (b) let the sequence of position taking develop by picking out the party positions which conform to the rules for 25 elections; (c) with the constraint under the rules below that the left party cannot take a left-right position > 10 or the right party < -10; (d) a party's policy position alternates without regard to what other parties are doing between that of a left and right faction; (e) this holds except when there is a vote gain in the second election of an election pair, in which case the position in the third election becomes that of the faction in control at the second election; (f) each party gains or loses votes at random; and (g) this is under the constraint that a vote gain by one major party implies a vote loss by the other major party (right and left parties).

This procedure randomizes the size of left-right shifts and, therefore, by extension, the relative size of factions producing them.

What we find is that of the British parties, Conservatives and Liberals both move (or stay) as expected in 12 out of a total of 15 moves over the period and Labour in 9 out of 15. Labour thus seems to fit our rules less than the other two parties (though still in the majority of cases). Overall, 33 out of 45 moves by all British parties over the given period are in line with our assumptions: 73%. This is strongly in line with the success rate obtained by examining 1,737 party policy moves by 103 parties in 24 countries over the same time period of 60 years. In other words,

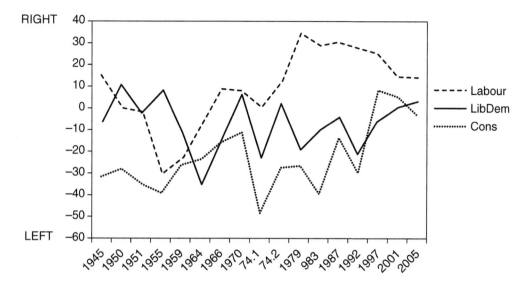

FIGURE 12.5 Left-right movements by British Labour, Liberal and Conservative parties 1945–2005

Source: Klingemann et al. *Mapping Policy Preferences II* (Oxford, OUP), p. 26

if we anticipate that any party's next policy move will be as our model says it will be, we are correct three out of four times. Odds of three to one on being correct would not be too bad in placing bets. So the theory improves substantially on anticipating moves at random or on assuming positions will stay the same from election to election – or change in the opposite direction every time. These are two other models of party policy behaviour that might be applied to predict party movements. But they perform worse than the idea of an interrupted zigzag. Even more importantly, the factional alternation model provides an *explanation* of why parties change position – one that fits in with previous arguments that parties are highly ideological and inward looking, with public opinion only impinging indirectly and as a marginal consideration in shaping their policy moves. This poses a paradox of representation. How can such parties adequately translate popular preferences into public policy? We then need the other model in Chapter 7 – party alternation in government and slow policy change – to explain how they can.

In both cases, their postdictive success is of practical use in giving us the ability to predict (reasonably well!) what parties will do in policy terms in the future. But it is even more important in reassuring us that we really do understand the process of party and democratic decision-making. The ultimate test of our understanding is whether we can predict the future on the basis of our theory and decide between opposing (sometimes radically different) theories by the success of their predictions. No doubt the one we have here will be improved and become even more predictively successful later on. But for the moment, it is the best in the field and yields important insights into party behaviour.

Briefing 12.13

Prediction/postdiction: the best way to see whether theories and estimates are precise and correct

We have used the terms 'prediction' and 'postdiction' fairly loosely and interchangeably in our evaluation of theories in the text. This avoids cluttering up our discussion with too many fine distinctions. Strictly speaking, predictions tell us what future outcomes will be, while postdictions tell us what past outcomes should look like. That carries a danger: in formulating the theory, we already know what has happened and thus tailor it to fit that. In turn, this would disqualify such previously observed outcomes from acting as an independent test of the theory as it was already formulated with them in mind.

On the other hand, if the past outcomes were collected independently and not known to the authors of the theory at the time it was formulated, they can then function as an independent check – first to see if the theory is clear enough to generate precise expectations about what they will look like and second to see if these match up to the independent observations. In this case, there is little practical difference between using (unknown) past outcomes to check the theory or unknown future ones. This is the case with most assessments of theories reported in the book.

Theories can have other strengths than postdictive/predictive success: clarity, conciseness, plausibility and fitting into the 'web of explanation' provided by other theories. However, the final and most severe check is whether they anticipate what has happened and what will happen in most of the cases they focus on. Only then can we tell if the explanation they offer is correct – provisionally at any rate, since it is always open to refinement by a more successful alternative theory.

End-summary

This chapter has demonstrated that parties, far from adapting their ideo-logically based policy targets to electoral preferences for them, tend to stick with them under most circumstances. They may as we have just seen, modify them slightly from election to election. But this is mostly the result of internal factional pressures – electoral reactions affect policy only marginally and indirectly. More substantial policy change comes from the parties' own adaptation to circumstances over time as they pick up new issues. Adding these to their repertoire reduces the salience of their older issues. But it does not eliminate them.

Parties are thus 'policy-carriers' of 'issue bundles'. They will try to effect these in place of their predecessors when they get into government. This alternation effect helps move the policies being implemented back across the centre in line with voters' preferences (see Chapter 7). It is not, however, a matter of responding to these preferences so much as coincid-ing with them temporarily as the party pursues its own targets. It does this in all policy areas as well as on the left-right 'super issue'. Parties are in this way essential participants in the overall process of democratic representation but not its guarantors. They simply stick to their ideology and pursue the policy targets it endorses (though there may be marginal factional conflict about what it implies).

This ideological and policy stability of parties – especially in relation to each other – provides a firm frame of reference for electors and voters in formulating their own preferences (Figure 3.1). The vague preferences of often apathetic and unsophisticated voters need to be firmed up by relating them to the acceptance or rejection of the policy alternatives on offer from the parties – or from party-dominated governments.

This kind of 'agenda control' by parties has often been criticized as mass 'mind control', ruling out certain policy alternatives from discussion and rendering the policy-preference correspondence tautological since parties and governments shape both. Naturally, they will coincide if parties simply characterize their own policy targets as the popular preferences.

How, then, can popular policy preferences be developed freely and autonomously, since they require party policy targets to be expressed in the first place? The answer lies in the freedom allowed under democratic processes for any popular grouping to form new parties to formulate different policies which represent its views and to run on the basis of these in direct or indirect elections. Political commentary and analysis have generally focused on elections and their outcomes one at a time. They have thus tended to see the party system as stable and unchanging and as constraining rather than extending choice.

However, this is true only if we ignore the long-term processes allowing for the foundation of new parties. If none are formed – as indeed may be the case over long periods of time – we may take it that all significant opinion groupings feel that they are represented adequately by the current party system and able to form and express their preferences relatively freely within it.

The relative ideological rigidity and stability of political parties thus, paradoxically, aids democratic representation in two ways:

1   By producing a reliable alternation of government policy targets that, over time, locates enacted policy at the centre of their joint policy space, where majority preferences also lie.
2   By ensuring that every popular voice can find expression in the electoral and government process by creating a reliable party representative in the long term. Popular preferences in this way make an independent input into democratic debate and do not simply echo parties.

The additional advantage is that parties can be both principled and popular – which is surely better from a moral point of view than making representation depend on parties abandoning principles in favour of popularity. In the next chapter, we shall see how this affects governance, where parties, as the key democratic actors, also dominate.

As a result of these processes, parties tend to acquire and 'carry' policies over a whole range of issues – not necessarily closely related. In government, they will pursue all of these, particularly if put in charge of relevant ministries. Party alternation thus carries with it changes in each individual policy domain, which have the effect of taking current implemented policy in it back across the centre, where the majority is to be found. Popular preferences can thus find fulfilment, eventually, in most areas of policy, not just on the big mainstream issues.

Extending the party programme to cover new issues inevitably renders older issues a bit less salient as the new ones are introduced and discussed. Similarly, the need to come to terms with new developments at home and abroad will modify programmatic priorities over time, even if these remain well within the bounds of the party's founding ideology. Studying the dynamics of policy change within the party in fact reinforces our earlier arguments:

1   Parties are always reliably committed to their original ideology and the policies it generates.
2   Any policy change takes place within these ideological limits.
3   Change is driven much less by responsiveness to electors than by internal party considerations.
4   These are powered by factional competition and disagreements over what the founding ideology indicates as the current situation.

The most direct way to see how these points play out in actual policy change is to look again at party movement on the left-right 'super issue' already discussed. For this, we can look back to Figure 12.5, which shows the changing positions of the three major British parties from 1945 to 2005 on the left-right scale as indicated by the statements in their election manifestos. The advantage of the scale is that it summarizes the policy in the programme taken as a whole. Thus, it provides us with a more comprehensive view of the adjustments taking place than if we looked at only one policy area. Change in overall party positions is clearly shown in the 1960s, when the Conservatives moved steadily rightwards and remained broadly in that position to the end of our period. Labour moved broadly right but returned left in the 1970s. After that, it drifted towards the centre and oscillated there. The liberals oscillated more than the other parties from left to right but returned to a more stable centrist position in the new millennium. Such long-term drifts are interesting but, importantly, leave relative party positions unchanged. Thus, Labour is always well to the left of the Conservatives, while the Liberals are generally between the two other parties. If you want rightist policies, you are always best to vote Conservative and vice versa for Labour. Liberals have been reliably centrist after the party re-established itself in the 1960s. Besides a long-term drift of all the parties from left to right, there are also minor policy changes between election and election that are captured by the zigzags in Figure 12.5.

Long-term policy change can be explained by the process just discussed of broadening and updating the party programme to cope with new issues. We have already accounted for short-term change, between one election and another, in the factional model summarized in Table 12.2. What is important is that we have change within relative stability, so that socialist or labour parties remain to the left, conservatives and neo-liberal parties to the right and progressive liberals (and Christian democrats where found) in the centre. Voters thus have fairly clear and consistent policy positions to choose between even if parties tinker with them in relatively minor ways over time.

The general considerations to take from this chapter are thus:

- The pervasive influence of party ideology over all aspects of party policy behaviour.
- This extends from the ideological 'families' they group themselves into to the policy changes they make in the short term.
- How to develop theories of seemingly contradictory behaviours: policy continuity on the one hand and change on the other.
- How to 'model' theories so that they can be directly compared to real-life processes and used to predict them.
- Building computer simulations as a tool for research.

Systematic working assumptions coming into this discussion

6   Policy targets and their implementation can be classified and measured far over time and comparative analysis on the basis of textual, survey, expenditure and other statistical evidence.

7   This allows them to be represented as points in spaces constructed on various measurement assumptions, with a centre and extremes, which can also relate the policy positions of political actors (citizens, voters, governments, parties, etc.) as specified from either data or theory.

8   Such spaces can have varying dimensions and measurements, the most common being a straight line running between left and right.

13 Ideally, political explanations should take the form of predictive theories consisting of propositions or equations which can be checked for predictive success against independently observed outcomes or behaviour.

14 The unifying focus of such theories – extending from preference formation and expression to policymaking and implementation – is on the extent of policy-preference correspondence and how it is achieved.

Sources and resources

Andrea Volkens, Judith Bara, Ian Budge, Michael D. McDonald, H.-D. Klingemann (eds) (2013) *Mapping Policy Preferences from Texts* (Oxford, Oxford University Press) pp. 49–68.

Alan Ware (1996) *Political Parties and Party Systems* (Oxford, Oxford University Press) Chapter 1, pp. 17–62.

Ian Budge, Lawrence Ezrow and Michael D. McDonald (2010) Ideology, Party Factionalism and Policy Change: An Integrated Dynamic Theory. *British Journal of Political Science*, (40) pp. 781–804.

Thomas Poguntke, Susan E. Scarrow and P. D. Webb (2016) *Political Party Database* https://dataverse.harvard.edu/dataset/xhtml?persistentID/

Suggestions for class papers

1 Is ideology good or bad for democracy?
2 Have political parties operated in much the same way over the last 150 years, or have they changed fundamentally in the new computer age?
3 Is left-right still useful in describing party behaviour today?
4 What is the role of the new social movements and their associated parties in modern politics?

Suggestions for class projects

1 Improve the predictive power of the factional theory of party policy-making by making more use of Assumption 1 in Table 12.2 to specify party priorities in making policy moves.
2 Characterize factions within one or more post-war parties, and relate their alternation in control to party policy moves.
3 Apply the factional model to specific issue movements by one or more parties over the last 50 years.

Chapter 13

Governments

Prime participants in policymaking

Chapter overview

Presidential governments and parliamentary governments

A presidential government is one where an elected chief executive forms the government, as opposed to a parliamentary one, where the government has to have majority support in parliament.

This chapter starts by putting party government in context, relating it both to the election cycle and the legislative arena within which it functions – not too differently as between **presidential governments** and majority **parliamentary governments**. The motivations which drive party behaviour in government are next spelled out as a predictive theory and then applied as decision rules, which explain the types of government which form. In turn, these are largely determined by the policies that parties want to pursue under varying political circumstances, which are specified in the following section of the chapter.

The alternation between one type of government and another over time is crucial in keeping public policy in line with centrist popular preferences. Central to this are the circumstances in which governments terminate – often closely linked to the way they formed in the first place. We consider termination – appropriately! – towards the end of the chapter, before concluding with our summary.

Key points to note are thus:

- The relative fragility of most governments which form, particularly in the case of coalitions grouping many parties.
- The leading role of the largest (plurality) party in government even where it does not have a majority of votes or of legislative seats.
- The decision rules determining which types of governments are formed.
- The dominance of ideology and policy in party behaviour, both in forming and running governments.

Governments in their institutional context

Governments have a dual role in democracies: as directors of the state bureaucracy and military, and as executors of the popular preferences expressed through general elections. Such preferences, however, are often unclear. So the party or parties in government can – and often must – take the popular vote as endorsing their own programme(s), which then define the government policy targets. Implementing these provokes increasingly negative 'thermostatic' reactions, which may lead to the defeat of the governing parties in the next general election and their replacement by rivals with opposing policy targets. The implementation of these, in turn, brings applied policy back across the centre, and thus the representational cycle goes on.

Thermostatic reactions

Expressions of popular support for or (more often) hostility to government policy proposals.

Governments are usually committed to more extreme policies than those favoured by the majority of the population. But the institutionalized cycle of elections leading to government and policy alternation over time ensures a long-term correspondence between preferences and actual policy.

Since the party composition of governments is the key element determining the direction and alternation of policy change, the chapter starts by considering party motivations and how these affect the way they form governments. The type of government which forms is of course automatically guaranteed in presidential regimes where the head of the executive branch is elected directly by a popular majority. The president then appoints a government (almost exclusively from their political party) and decides which nominee will hold each individual department, agency or ministry (the specialized parts of the government dealing with particular policy areas).

Briefing 13.1

The other policy-voting theory of policy-preference correspondence: the party mandate

Mandate theory assumes that voters decide between parties on the basis of the policy programmes for government which they present at general elections. In contrast to the convergence theory (Briefing 12.11), it therefore requires that parties *diverge* clearly on policy so that voters can make a clear choice between them. As we have seen, parties *do* diverge rather than converge on policy. However, the other key requirement of mandate theory is that voters then choose between parties purely on policy grounds. In this way, the majority or plurality party which forms the government will be implementing the policy preferred by citizens.

However, as we have also seen, many other factors enter into voters' choice of parties in the general election: past record, competence, candidates and so on. Indeed, general elections are deliberately designed so as to allow them to do so. Thus, the party taking the leading role in government may not represent citizen preferences well or even at all, likely taking a more extreme stance than they want. Alternation theory shows how a policy-preference correspondence can be achieved regardless, but the policy mandate does not.

However, both the government as a whole and individual ministers may need legislative approval in the first place and support for their measures later on. This increases the resemblances between presidential and majority parliamentary governments. Control by one party in both cases creates a more cohesive government united around its policy targets, which also holds a leading position in the legislature. This secures a fairly automatic endorsement of its programme and actions and enables it to claim a popular mandate for both.

Briefing 13.2

Is there really much difference between presidential and parliamentary governments?

In many democracies, the government (an executive president and the president's cabinet) are elected separately from the legislature, which, however, has to authorize laws and many government decisions. Under parliamentary systems, the majority or plurality party in the legislature (with its allies there) chooses the prime minister as the chief executive. Thus, the government, while it continues, can be sure of legislature approval for its measures. Under a presidential system where president and legislative have separate powers, this is not so sure. However, the entry of parties has weakened this 'separation of powers'. Where president and legislative majority belong to the same party, approval of the former's action is almost as certain as for a majority parliamentary government. Where the legislature is wholly or partly controlled by another party under a presidential system, negotiation, compromise and coalition building proceed as in a parliamentary system where the government is a coalition of parties or in a minority.

Parliamentary governments based on a single majority party have many similarities with presidential governments. However, only about 12% of parliamentary-based governments are actually based on a spontaneously formed popular majority. More usually they consist of two or more parties which have agreed to form a 'coalition' government together after negotiations about the policies they will adopt (or, in some cases, abandon!) and how ministries will be distributed between their members. Such coalitions usually have the support of a majority of members of the legislature and also of a popular majority, when we add up the votes for all the political parties composing it. However, this majority is 'manufactured' in the sense that the electors voting for each party were uncertain about the exact nature of the government it would participate in and might not have voted for if they had known what that would be.

Not only is the popular majority backing a coalition government a bit artificial in nature. The legislative majority on which it depends to get approval for its policy and general actions may be 'manufactured' too, depending on the way it was put together. If the parties composing it are

Briefing 13.3

Five laws of governments

These are inductive 'laws' about governments and their popular support, based on a large body of data going back in some cases to the nineteenth century. Methodologically, they demonstrate that extensive generalizations across countries and time can be made based on political science research. They also help to pull it together (see Part V). In this chapter, they provide a general frame of reference for our discussion of party activity in government. The laws are a unified body of knowledge consisting of five generalizations based on observations reported on Wikipedia:

1   The law of minority rule. All governments are minority governments in terms of the percentage of citizens who voted for them out of the entire population.
2   The law of incumbent advantage. In democracies, the governing party or coalition is returned to government in 60% of cases.
3   The law of shrinking support. All incumbents, however, face growing opposition during their tenure.
4   The 60% incumbent maximum in democracies. It is rare for the governing party in a democracy to be re-elected with more than 60% of the vote, and it never happens more than once within the same spell of office.
5   No one party or coalition of parties can encompass the whole range and variety of interests and ideas that make up a political community.

Source: Slightly modified wording from Alfred G. Cuzàn, *PS: Political Science & Politics*, July 2015.

opposed ideologically, the resulting government may not last long or get much done. (On the other hand, if the partners are not too disagreed, a coalition may function quite as effectively as a single-party government.)

However, no government, not even single-party ones, have overwhelming popular support. They are usually voted in by a minority of the population (as opposed to voters). Even the support they had at the election shrinks during their term of office owing to 'thermostatic' reactions and 'costs of governing', resulting in a regular loss of 2%–3% of previous votes. Their policies cannot satisfy all the preferences of a heterogeneous community. Incumbent parties, possibly owing to their greater visibility, have a slight electoral advantage over their opponents, and 60% get re-elected. However, the random events that often dominate election outcomes can easily cancel out such advantages. As noted at various points earlier in this discussion, random events render general elections relatively unpredictable. This does, however, accelerate the alternation of government policies, which we have seen to be the main guarantee that they will correspond in the end to popular centrist preferences.

Majority *legislative* support for governments is produced in two different ways, depending on the election system in use:

1   Under a SMDP system, the plurality party in each election district is privileged. If electoral politics are 'nationalised' – that is, if the local plurality party is generally also the national plurality party – its plurality of votes will be translated into a majority of legislative seats. This is because the largest party in each district wins the seat, regardless of its absolute size. If the percentages votes are 34%, 33%, 32% consistently across many seats, the first party wins them all (in spite of having only a third of the national vote) and gets a majority of legislators elected – who are all bound by party discipline to vote in support of their government.

2   PR aims to match the percentage of legislative seats that a party gets to its percentage of the popular vote. Such matching generally results in a legislature where all parties, both large and small, have only a minority of seats. The solution in terms of forming a majority government is to assemble a coalition of parties that together control a majority of seats (and who also in combination received a majority of popular votes in the general election).

The parties in coalitions generally must be compatible with each other, certainly in policy terms, to get together in the first place. They also expect some reward, primarily in regard to the government ministries which they will be allocated. In the following sections of the chapter, we go systematically into these questions of government formation and composition. The distribution of ministries between parties is also crucial but too complex to be fully considered here. So we go into detail about it in Chapter 14. If potential coalition members are satisfied with government policy and the share of ministries they get, coalitions can function well over a considerable period of time – *and* can claim a popular majority to base themselves on.

However, as we have noted, their majority has in most cases formed mechanically, from post-election party negotiations rather than spontaneously among voters. So it is far from providing an unambiguous majority endorsement of government policy targets. The same can be said of SMDP: the government's legislative majority does not genuinely reflect a popular majority, not even a manufactured one.

Plurality party

The party with most votes or seats.

In both cases, the **plurality party** takes the lead and lays down the main policy targets for government. As noted, these are likely to be more extreme than popular majority preferences. So immediate congruence between popular preferences and government policy is not guaranteed. However, the median party (the one in the centre of the left-right line) is usually included in the coalition. This moves policy targets more towards the centre, where electors are. Such 'centring' is even stronger where the plurality party is also the median party and supported by the median voter. It then has more clout in imposing its own targets, which will be more centrist than other parties' anyway.

There is, however, no automatic *guarantee* of median parties forming a part of governments and thus of the popular median being represented there. The only policy-preference correspondence built into democratic procedures and guaranteed by them is that brought about through party alternation, which over time brings implemented policy repeatedly back to the centre. This process works for the general direction of policy, summarized in left-right differences. It also applies to the mass of specific policies which parties commit themselves to at some point in time then 'carry' into government.

General government formation and functioning are best understood at the overall level of left-right differences and are discussed in these terms in the next two sections of this chapter. Specific policies are best promoted by individual party control of relevant ministries – the specialized government departments of permanent administrators and experts who devise and enforce regulations within particular policy areas (e.g. agriculture, justice, military, finance). The fact that administration is split up in this way – often with corresponding legislative committees to scrutinize ministerial actions and initiate administrative action – powerfully contributes to ensuring that different policy areas occupy their own space and are separated out, with measures in one area usually being undertaken without much thought for how they impinge on others except in general terms. This makes it necessary to consider policies and their implementation one by one as well as the way they fit into general left-right differences.

This also explains why parties in coalitions seek control of ministries in their unique areas of policy interest: to influence policy there. As all parties have unique concerns at the specific policy level – such as Christians with morality and schools, agrarians with agriculture and socialists with welfare – there is a basis for bargaining about the ministries that each will control. Only if parties get at least some of 'their' ministries are they going to join in forming a coalition government anyway. Along with policy, the

Briefing 13.4

Separate or separable policy areas and their implications for political analysis

Separate or separable policy areas (as they are sometimes termed) are areas of life like agriculture, welfare and so on which are separable in the sense that action in one area does not have immediate or obvious effects on the other. They can thus be legislated for separately and dealt with by separate government agencies, departments or ministries and overseen by different legislative committees. Government actions and policies thus proceed inside different frames of reference rather than in terms of the 'joined-up' thinking provided by left-right divisions. The single-issue or niche parties also encourage this separation of policymaking into different areas (Chapter 12). This also encourages electors and voters to think in terms of separate issue proposals rather than a joined-up left-right perspective (Chapter 5), where 'guns' (military spending) have to be paid for by less 'butter' (consumer spending).

distribution of ministries within a government is a crucial element in its formation. We deal with this in Chapter 14.

The way a coalition government is put together (e.g. with a larger or smaller number of party members) is vital to its survival and prospects of replacement. Greater numbers of parties with different aims and targets lead to more disagreements over policy targets, which over time build up to such an extent that they end the coalition. The three topics considered in this chapter – government formation, policymaking and termination – are therefore closely linked. So our discussion will move sequentially from one to the other, with the question of what parties want from being in government always at its centre.

One last point to remember throughout is the legislative arena governments operate within. Parties of course dominate in legislatures too – to such an extent that it is difficult to see parliaments or assemblies as collective actors in their own right. Rather, they constitute an arena within which parties in government interact with the parties outside it. Where single-party majority governments can dominate the legislature with a majority of seats, the parties outside government can do little more than use legislative procedures and committees to scrutinize government policy proposals and actions. Such critiques often form the basis of media campaigns and public demonstrations, which may result in policy compromises and withdrawals. These contribute to the slowness of new policy implementation ('inertia'), which is also crucial in securing a long-term correspondence between preferences and actual policy. Their more immediate effect, however, is to increase the 'costs of governing', which help erode the government majority in the next general election.

Where the government is a coalition of different parties, legislative scrutiny and debate may have a more immediate effect by breaking it up and either provoking a new general election or a new government. Although parties are the prime actors, the legislature is the context within which they make their most important inter-election moves. Here, as in elections (Chapters 9 and 10), rules and procedures influence the substantive policy outcomes, biasing results in favour of one party or another. The most important procedural resource is the number of seats that parties hold. This in turn determines the type of government – single party or coalition – to emerge from party interactions.

However, party policy concerns also affect the way in which they will deploy their legislative support, as we show in the next section.

Policy pursuit or office seeking?

Parties have to participate in governments to get their policies effected. But is it a place in government they really aim at, with policies simply adjusted to please electors and draw in their votes? The evidence is overwhelming that they stick to their policies. For one thing, it is hard to know how policy considerations affect popular voting anyway – and other strategies, such as choosing an attractive candidate, have more of a potential appeal. For another, abandoning policies characteristic of the party is rarely worth the cost in terms of blurring party identity and provoking internal tensions with members and supporters.

For all these reasons, parties are primarily concerned with pursuing and implementing their preferred policies. They form the governments which they see as most capable of doing so within existing limits (i.e. a hostile legislature in a presidential government or a fragmented one in multiparty parliaments). Factions within parties also favour their own interpretations of their ideology and policy. So government formation may also be influenced by which internal faction dominates within a party at a particular point in time – one inclining more to partnerships towards the centre and another more to parties at its own extremes.

These considerations are summarized in Table 13.1. The first simply notes the main constraint on government, obtaining legislative approval for their very existence, in the case of parliamentary democracies, or for the measures they undertake, such as budgets and legislation, under presidential regimes. In the latter case, the president's ability to appoint a government independently, without depending on a parliamentary vote of confidence, means that it is freer from legislative constraints. However, it would be foolish to appoint one which so alienated the legislature that it could not pass any policy or even get approval for its budget. This would soon lead to total paralysis of the whole administration.

In choosing between viable governments, parties will always try to form the one that is most capable of promoting their own policies. This consideration follows on from what we have said about the policy-pursuing nature of parties. Governments form the major instrument that parties use to effect policy. Parties have to create and participate in them. So governments have to be viable – but not at all costs. In extreme cases, parties will not participate in them at all if that would be counterproductive in policy terms. Short of that, however, they will enter into whatever viable arrangement best advances their most important policy priorities.

TABLE 13.1 Considerations affecting party behaviour in government

---

1. The party or combination of parties which can best obtain legislative approval forms the government.
2. Parties seek to form that government capable of obtaining legislative approval which will most effectively carry through their declared policy preferences under existing conditions.
3. (a) The principal preference for all democratic parties is to counter threats to the democratic system when they occur.
   (b) Where no such threats exist, but left-right differences are strong, the preference of all parties is to carry through preferred policies related to these differences.
   (c) Where neither of the preceding conditions hold, parties pursue their own group-related preferences.

That raises the question of which *is* most important, clarified by Consideration 3 in the table. This ranks defence of the democratic setup as a first priority for all parties. In itself, this is a natural prime priority. Since the end of the **Cold War** between the Western and Eastern blocs in the 1980s, democracies have not, however, been considered as being under severe threat – externally at least. However, it is clear that if an external attack seemed imminent, as in the 1940s in Europe, democratic parties would join together to form governments of national unity to counter it. Under presidential regimes, bipartisanship would involve non-partisan appointments to the government and co-operation with the non-presidential party or parties in the legislature.

More obviously, however, political parties will also join together in more normal times to counter internal threats from 'anti-system' parties perceived as challenging democratic procedures and institutions. Accusations of breaking the rules or acting 'undemocratically' are of course themselves part of the staple of political debate, often used by conservative parties against progressive ones and vice versa. However, there are enough neo-Nazi, revolutionary socialist and extreme right-wing parties around to make the threat a real one in some cases, as well as other parties advocating terrorism for religious or nationalistic ends. A natural reaction of the democratic parties under such circumstances is to overlook their own normal divisions and join together – most effectively by refusing all political co-operation with such challengers.

Where anti-democratic threats are absent or reasonably contained, more normal pursuit of party policy objectives resumes. The most pervasive form that these take is in terms of the left-right division, which encapsulates most of the argument and debate in modern politics, extending over the range of state interventions in economy, society and foreign affairs. Also pitting class and other social groups against each other across the country, it has, particularly in times of great social adjustment and change, the capacity to subsume or downgrade other potential sources of political conflict and to become the focus of division between almost all parties and party alliances. The policies that particular parties pursue thus become characterized as left or right, and this exercises a determining influence over their behaviour in government, as we shall see.

At other, more normal times of stability and prosperity, the intensity of left-right conflict tends to slacken. It always forms a convenient way of making sense of politics as a whole. But as it becomes blurred – for example, through the impact of **globalization** or breakdown of military alliances – parties begin to put more priority on their own specific policy concerns (see Table 6.6), often related to those of their supporting groups (Table 11.2). In spatial terms, politics becomes multidimensional rather than one-dimensional. This effect is compounded by the need for governments to confront many immediate problems, some of them in new areas, like the environment, which take time to be interpreted in left-right terms and assimilated to that overriding division.

Cold War

Confrontations (during 1948–1984) between the West (Europe and North America) and the Soviet Union (USSR), the predecessor of modern Russia.

Globalization

The increasing contacts and communication between countries in all areas of life.

Briefing 13.5

Issue dynamics: how do new problems affect old policy divisions?

Where issue areas can be separated out and actions in each pursued independently, the emergence of new situations and developments probably has less effect on established divisions and ways of thinking than where everything has been 'joined up' in left-right terms. The main effect in the case of separable issues is for new ones to take priority over the old ones (e.g. membership in the EU or in a new free trade area reduces the focus on climate change or the environment). In terms of left-right divisions, however, it may not be clear where the EU fits into the overall policy space: is it a capitalist plot to spread free trade and constrain state direction of industry or a force for upholding welfare and working standards against national attempts to reduce them? Until this becomes clearer, both left and right may split internally over membership. As the policy biases of PR election systems (Table 10.2) towards more progressive policies feeds into European policymaking, however, the left may swing towards support for the EU and the right against. Similar tendencies can be seen with green support for ecological intervention by governments, which have increasingly aligned the greens with left-wing parties. Until the new developments are combined with the old in an overall ideological argument to show how they must theoretically fit together, their alignment will probably remain temporary, however, and could change with further new developments.

Recognizing that different policy concerns may predominate at different points in time also helps explain why different types of government may form at these points, as we go on to see in the next section.

Government formation

Given the strong policy-centred orientation that parties share, it is no wonder that decisions about what government to form (or whether to participate in one, in the case of coalitions) are dominated by the policy priorities they want it to effect – leftist as opposed to rightist policies, where these are salient, or the policies uniquely associated with the party, when these come to the fore.

Of course, the most effective way to achieve all your policy objectives is to form a single-party government with enough legislative support to get all party targets accepted and approved. There is only one exception to this rule under parliamentary systems – when some kind of external threat prompts even majority parties to form a government of national unity as a show of general solidarity, even if not all its party members are essential to obtaining numerical support in the legislature.

Briefing 13.6

Electoral alliances versus government coalitions

Parties sometimes choose to endorse joint candidates at election time, particularly under rules which discriminate against smaller parties. By combining, the parties increase their chances of getting more support. To make such an alliance the parties have to be fairly close in terms of current policy proposals on the most important current issues; otherwise, they will simply turn off their own supporters.

Making such an alliance obviously predisposes the allied parties to go into a coalition government together. However, the reverse is not true. Most coalition partners have probably opposed each other electorally and only come together because a government cannot be formed without them – and because they get some policy concessions and their preferred policy-related ministries in the government which forms.

Single-party government is automatic in the case of presidential regimes when all the government needs is the president's support (with an eye, however, to its standing in the legislature). Where a legislative vote of confidence or approval is required for it, government formation is more problematic. If a party has managed to secure itself a legislative majority, however, it will form the government whatever particular policy goals it has at the time, since this is the most effective way of securing all of them.

Where no single-party majority exists in the legislature, the outcome becomes even more problematic and more dependent on the type of policy differences existing at the time. Where ideological tensions are strong and a right bloc of parties confronts a left bloc, concentration on common issues will induce all parties in the bloc either to join a government or to give it support from outside. (Any anti-system party excluded from the actual government for that reason will give ideological support from outside.) Such a bloc might well have in fact joined together as an electoral alliance in the general election.

Of course, such 'party-like' behaviour on the part of an ideological bloc will dissipate once the salience of the relevant divisions diminishes. In their absence, the plurality party –especially if it is large and gained substantially more votes than any other party – will seek to form a minority government on its own or dominate in a coalition with one or more smaller parties in the legislature (but not any anti-system ones). It will do so because it can count on getting enough of the necessary votes on an issue-by-issue basis from parties which share the same position with it. Provided that there is agreement across a range of such issues with another party or parties, it may be convenient to form a broader coalition to get more reliable support. But the plurality party will still set the overall policy targets for government.

In the absence of left-right glue to keep parties together, or of one large party around which they could cohere, situational factors will play the main role in bringing parties together. This is most obvious in the case of pressing issues requiring immediate action on which sufficient parties agree to form a government capable of getting legislative support. An international financial crisis threatening national banks would be a good recent example of when such action is required and coalitions form.

Of course, the main current issues may not be so pressing. So in a multiparty situation without strong focused issue divisions, governments may simply form to carry on administrative business without any ambitious or pressing programme of action. In that case, parties are likely to join together in a 'minimum winning coalition' which brings together the minimum number of parties able to get legislative support on votes of confidence, to minimize policy disagreement among the coalition members. The payoff for parties in this case is control of the ministries operating in the area of their particular policy concerns. Whatever governments as a whole are doing, party control of a ministry always means that a party's own specific concerns in the policy area will be favoured.

These regularities – summarized in Table 13.2 – render the formation processes of governments understandable and predictable.

They all follow directly from the policy-based considerations set out in Table 13.1. The limits imposed by institutional rules and political procedures (presidential regime versus parliamentary regime, legislative seats held after the last election) of course shape their behaviour. Within these constraints, however, parties always seek to advance their own policies. So

TABLE 13.2 Hierarchical rules for government formation implied by the assumptions in Table 13.1

---

i. Where the democratic system is immediately threatened (externally or internally), all significant pro-system parties will join the government, excluding anti-system parties.

In the absence of immediate threats to democracy:

ii. Any party with an absolute majority of legislative votes will (a) form a single-party government – except where such majorities are unusual, in which case it will (b) form the dominant party of a government, excluding anti-system parties.

Where no party has a majority of votes and left-right differences over current issues are salient:

iii. The left or right side with the majority will form a government either including or with support from all numerically significant parties on their side (anti-system parties can only provide support and are excluded from participating in government).

If no such left-right differences exist:

iv. The party which is manifestly larger than any other pro-system party will either form the government alone (in countries where single-party government is normal) or form the dominant part of a government (excluding anti-system parties).

Where left-right differences are not salient and no single party has sufficient votes to meet the criteria for Rules ii or iv:

v. Coalitions capable of winning votes of confidence form (a) to group the parties most agreed on the specific issues currently salient; (b) failing such agreement, to minimize the numbers of parties in government to those which will win legislative votes of confidence; (c) in any case, excluding anti-system parties.

---

if we know what these are at the time, in conjunction with the constraints, we can predict the outcomes. These then shape the policies which the particular government that has formed will pursue, as we see in the next section of the chapter.

We can summarize these rules even more concisely in a decision tree similar to Figure 12.3 on party policymaking. Whereas this involved choices between only two alternatives, (leftist policy moves versus rightist ones) the choice between different kinds of government is more complicated. Figure 13.1 lists on the left-hand side the different situations in which

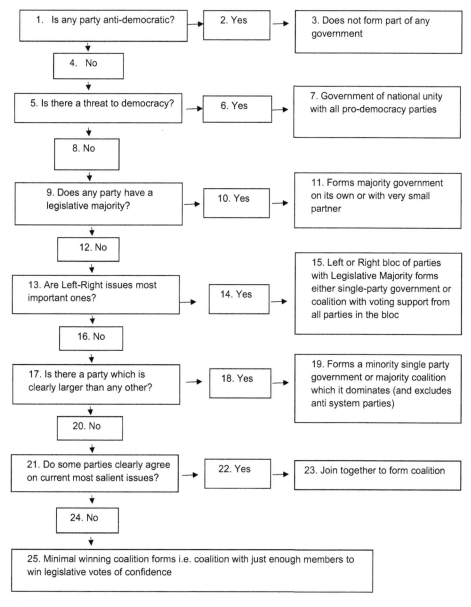

FIGURE 13.1 Government formation in different political situations

government formation may occur. Each situation triggers off a different kind of government response. If a given situation does not exist, we then move down the left-hand side of the figure to the next situation. If this applies, we can predict that a particular kind of government will emerge. If it, in turn, is not relevant, then we move down to the next situation.

This progression downwards is dictated by the hierarchical nature of the situational imperatives noted in Table 13.2. The higher-level situations produce more urgent and clear imperatives than lower level ones. For example, any threat to the democratic situation that parties operate in and that gives them legitimacy is more urgent for the moment than their own policy goals. So a government of national unity will be formed even if, constitutionally, a majority party could form a government on its own.

Further down, where the left-right division is at the heart of democratic policies, the imperative for the parties on each side is to line up in support of the leftist or rightist government. Where neither of these general conditions materializes, the largest party, whether with a legislative majority or simply the largest number of seats, will try to dominate government as much as possible, to get its own leading policy objectives effected. Wider coalitions have to form where no one party dominates, giving each partner scope to take over the ministries central to its own policy concerns, which it will pursue at all governmental levels. Each of these situations gives rise to specific expectations about what kind of government will form. These can be checked against the actual governments which do form to determine whether they are correct – giving us another example of a verified predictive theory.

Note that while parties pursue policies, they do not always pursue the same policies all the time. In particular their concerns may switch from the general orientation of the government policy programme towards left or right to a preoccupation with the more specific policy concerns they have (Table 6.6). To predict their behaviour, we need to know which is uppermost in parties' minds at any one time. How do we find this out? The answer is to check independent evidence, particularly parties' own statements of intent. These are set out in the only document authorized by the party as a whole – its **manifesto or platform**, published at each general election. By measuring the emphasis given to different issues, we can independently check the relative importance they attach to them, relate this to other relevant factors (e.g. number of legislative seats) and use the decision tree in Figure 13.1 to predict what government will emerge. We can then determine whether this works, in the sense of correctly characterizing the actual governments that emerged.

When the predictions in Figure 13.1 were checked for 20 parliamentary democracies from 1945 until the mid-1980s, they were correct in 81% of the cases examined. We can therefore conclude that the policy-based theory (Table 13.1) which generates them correctly characterizes party behaviour in forming governments. We go on from this to derive implications about how parties behave once in a government. We consider this in the next section.

Manifesto or platform

The published policy programme of a party in a general election.

Government policy targets

Parties enter governments to influence policymaking. They do this by setting targets dictated by both their standing concerns *and* priorities at the time and by getting the state administration to put them into effect. The most effective way of doing so is for a party to govern all by itself. Failing that, it can form a government around itself as the plurality party, where it exerts the main influence on overall policy. Even if a party is relatively small, so that it has little overall influence, it can take over ministries of particular interest to it and pursue those policy concerns unique to itself within the appropriate sector.

Government alternation thus ensures not only that general policy (usually linked to left-right differences) changes direction but also that a host of specific policies are also affected, as their party 'carriers' move in and out of ministries.

In discussing policy, we of course need to distinguish between government targets and their actual implementation. They will differ because of the time taken to change rules and expenditures and the obstacles to doing so, including popular resistance as the policy gets more extreme. Such 'policy inertia' often means that a policy will be only half implemented before a government terminates, helping to keep implemented policies close to the compromise positions favoured by electors.

Actual implementation is therefore to some extent out of any government's hands. Governments do, however, carry on with their declared targets, in the ways summarized in Table 13.3. These again follow on from the general characterization of party policy priorities in Table 13.1

Thus, a policy priority for all governments of any kind will be countering anti-democratic threats when they appear, either internally or externally. When these are absent, priorities shift and differences appear between different types of party government. The most obvious are between left and right governments, either formed by a single majority or plurality party on the left or the right or by coalitions of parties to the left or the right. These

TABLE 13.3 Policies expected to be pursued by governments following from the assumptions in Table 13.1

i.	All parties in government agree on countering threats to democracy.
ii.	To the extent that such threats are less evident, socialist-bourgeois differences over welfare, income distribution and economic management will become more prominent.
iii.	The direction of general policy in these areas will be decided by relative left or right dominance in government.
iv.	Each party in the government will have some of its preferred policies put into effect: for instance, governments including an agrarian party will pursue policies more favourable to farmers and rural interests than governments without an agrarian party; labour parties will favour the working class; conservative/liberal parties will favour business; and so on.
v.	The direction of policy in specific areas will be influenced by party control of the competent ministries.

will contrast quite sharply (depending on the saliency of left-right issues at the time) on welfare, the extent of state activity and questions of foreign intervention versus support for peaceful internationalism, involving bodies such as the UN. As we saw in Chapter 6, policies on these questions are at the heart of left-right differences, so they naturally carry through into the initial government formation and then to the different policies and actions it undertakes.

Even when general left-right differences are muted, and mixed coalitions form (often involving a centre party), we would expect the socialist or conservative or neo-liberal components to pursue their most characteristic concerns (welfare in the first case and a market economy in the second – see Table 6.2). All parties do so even in the presence of other, more general concerns – often through their predominance in certain ministries (see Chapter 14). Like agrarians seeking concessions for farmers or Christians wanting more support for church schools, socialists and social democrats will try to improve welfare provision regardless of the general salience of left-right differences. Any government incorporating them will therefore target that area just as its coalition partners will target theirs. Since the different parties' goals often conflict with each other, this will of course provoke clashes and tensions within the government, which will often bring it to an end, with another election making way for a new government to emerge, with a possible change in policy.

Table 13.3 sets all this out specifically. The formation of governments is therefore affected by the parties' policy orientations, as are their subsequent activities. As we shall see in the next section, this also extends to their termination and replacement. Parties' policy activity in government stirs up **thermostatic reactions** which cost them votes at the next election. And multiparty governments often end prematurely over policy differences between partners.

The UN (United Nations)

An organization of almost all the countries in the world, which discusses common problems.

Thermostatic reactions

Expressions of popular support for or (more often) hostility to government policy proposals.

How and why governments end – bases for alternation

Alternation between differently based governments (and hence between their policy targets and their partial implementation of these) provides the essential dynamic of the democratic process. The substitution of one relatively extreme target by an opposed one starts to bring actual policy back again to the middle and closer to the majority preferences of electors. Crucial to this development is the breakup of the existing party government and its replacement by a different one. This makes the forces promoting such change quite central to understanding the processes at work in democracies.

Most important among these are, appropriately, the democratic rules stipulating the length of time governments can remain in power before they have to face an election. These are particularly important in setting terms for presidential governments. Because these are normally formed by a single party, they do not face breakup through internal disagreements between different parties over what policy targets are to be set and how to implement them. Such governments are appointed in the first place to carry through presidential policy priorities, so any disagreement is likely to be contained and be more about the implementation of accepted targets and relatively minor. If resignations occur, they are likely to involve only individuals rather than a bloc walking out of government and bringing it to an end.

On their side, presidents – on whose support the government depends rather than on the legislature as in parliamentary regimes – are unlikely to sack the whole of the government that they have appointed. That would be an admission of weakness, which they are under no pressure to make.

The same is broadly true of a majority-party-supported parliamentary government. A party with a majority of votes in the legislature has every reason to support its government. So normally that kind of government is going to last the full term. The only exception is where there is no fixed minimum term specified by legislation and rules. Where a party leader can fix the date of an election before one is constitutionally due, this may be determined by the leader's favourable expectations of winning.

So election rules are crucial determinants of government duration, whether presidential or parliamentary in character. We would indeed be suspicious of the democratic credentials of any regime which did not have maximum terms, since holding regular elections is the hallmark of democracy and the essential element in the party alternation that keeps policy implementation in line with popular preferences for it.

Regular elections do not, however, totally guarantee party and policy alternation as such. After all, the same party with broadly the same policy may be re-elected to government and continue pursuing the same targets. In that case, it has more time to implement relatively extreme targets increasingly out of line with centrist preferences. The representational benefits from alternation in that case do not apply. We cannot, either, take the easy way out and say voters have simply gone for the relatively extreme policies. General elections are determined so often and so powerfully by non-policy-based considerations that we can never be sure that they reflect real changes of preferences. In any case, we know settled preferences lie in the centre and not the extremes.

Majority governments of the same single party following on from each other do therefore tend to weaken the democratic guarantee that policy will ultimately land up in the centre. There are, however, circumstances which ultimately restore that situation. One is the fact that government alternation between, for example, left and right can be successfully modelled as **random** for contemporary democracies (Table 3.1). That is, no government can ever be sure of remaining in office over a long period in the face of regular elections. The factors affecting election outcomes are so diverse and so out of anyone's control that they are bound in the long run to promote some party and policy alternation.

Contributing to this effect are the costs of governing. One of the best-known regularities in comparative political research is the observation that governments generally lose 2% to 3% of the vote they received just

Random

Governed
by chance
occurrences.

TABLE 13.4 Policy-related causes of parliamentary government termination

1. The less governments agree over policy, the more likely they are to terminate for internal reasons such as withdrawal of one of the coalition parties.
2. Hence, single-party governments are less likely to terminate for internal reasons than coalitions.
3. Of coalitions, the more ideologically mixed ones are more likely than those less ideologically mixed to terminate for internal reasons.
4. Governments which have been unsuccessful in implementing their policies are more likely to experience internal policy disagreements than others (and hence are more likely to terminate for internal reasons).

before taking office. This loss is produced by previous supporters reacting adversely to some current policy proposals and withdrawing support – the thermostatic reactions previously discussed. 'Governing costs votes'. That is to say, as more of a (relatively extreme) policy is proposed and effected, increasing numbers of a centrist electorate oppose it. Not all of this opposition translates into loss of votes, of course. But clearly some does, producing regular losses for the governing party or parties. In turn, this reduces the chance of a government returning to office after serving out a fixed term. Termination and alternation are thus partly driven by party pursuit of their policy targets while in office and the adverse popular reactions this provokes. Even in the cases where the same party or grouping of parties returns to office, this is likely to encourage some toning down and moderation of their original targets, favouring the more centrist faction as against the more extreme one. Elections therefore have effects extending beyond party alternation as such to policy alternation within the same government. All of this helps bring policy and popular preferences together over the long run.

Of course, not all governments last over the whole inter-election period. In multiparty parliamentary democracies where no one party has a majority or even a strong plurality, and left-right divisions are not strong enough to bind coalitions together or produce consistent support for the ideological 'standard bearer', multiparty coalitions typically form to get a majority of seats in the legislature. Since these are composed of parties with different policy objectives, however, quarrels over overall policy usually bring them to an end prematurely. Government alternation speeds up as two or three governments composed of different combinations of parties succeed each other between elections. These effects are summarized in Table 13.4 and upheld by comparisons of different types of government in the first half of the post-war period (1950s–1980s). The table relates ideological diversity, leading to disputes over policy, to the probability of termination and rapid alternation of governments. This illustrates again the importance of policy to parties and its consequent centrality in party-based governments. Even though policy is not so central or even determining of popular voting in general elections, it *is* central to governments, owing to party dominance there and its ideological importance to them.

End-summary

Policy rules within parties and governments if not in voting and elections. Parties carry their trademark policies into government and try to effect them there. This causes problems in coalitions where there are many parties each trying to effect as much of their own policy as they can. Only where there is one-party dominance and therefore a reasonably unified programme or strong ideological glue between leftist or rightist coalition parties is a parliamentary-based government even likely to survive the whole of the period between elections.

Even the greater ability of a unified government to pursue its policy produces problems for it, however. Pushing its targets through alienates some previous voters and provokes strong and growing opposition. This makes it likely even if a majority or plurality party is able to reform a government after an election that it will probably slow down the implementation of its policy or compromise more in other ways.

Where governments are more widely based – typically where two or more parties are relatively equal in terms of legislative seats and have to form a coalition – policy disagreements are more likely to occur and even finish off governments before an election. This makes it likely that policy will remain more or less stable near the centre, as this is the obvious compromise to adopt between relatively extreme positions. The centre party and the median party (if different) will be stronger in this situation, reinforcing tendencies to compromise towards the centre. The correspondence between popular preferences and public policy may thus be strengthened by party disagreement in coalitions in both the short term and the long term.

However, not all coalitions produce such moderate results; left and right differences (where they are salient) may keep individual parties focused within a firm alliance, quite capable of pursuing relatively extreme policies to left or right. A resulting loss of 2%–3% of the previous vote and consequent alternation between leftist and rightist governments may then take over again as the mechanism for conserving centrist representation in the long run.

The processes of government formation set out in Table 13.2 generate expectations based on party policy pursuit supported by comparative evidence about what kind of government is likely to emerge under particular circumstances. The rules apply to the formation of parliamentary governments; presidential ones are almost by definition single-party dominated. However, the need to get the legislative endorsement of government in the case of 'semi-presidential' regimes, where power between the president and the legislature is shared, or in any case to get a legislative endorsement for their most important actions, often causes the presidential party in government to act more like the plurality party in a parliamentary-based coalition than a majority party in a strong position in the legislature.

Tables 13.1 and 13.2, besides identifying important regularities in party and government behaviour, also provide a good example of 'model building' in political science – generating precise predictions from theoretical assumptions about how parties will behave in specified circumstances and the consequences this will have for policy representation. The basic assumption that parties each have distinctive policies that they will try to effect in government generates a series of expectations about what they will do there – which can then be checked against actual outcomes to determine whether they are right. We will discuss the nature of such 'postdictions' more generally in Part V of this book. But in the meantime, the successful rules and 'decision trees' in this chapter and the next (Chapter 14) provide concrete examples of how theory building in political science can proceed and how it can put itself on firmer evidential foundations.

Considerations to take away from this discussion are thus:

- The key role of ideology and the policies derived from it in determining what type of government will form and what it will do.
- Building a 'decision tree' (Figure 13.1) to specify such behaviour more precisely and check it out against independent evidence.
- Governments appointed by presidents and dependent on them do not seem to act very differently from parliamentary-based governments centred on a strong majority or plurality party or an ideologically based coalition.
- Policy agreement and relative success help governments last longer, while disagreement and policy failure bring them to an end prematurely, even without an election.

Systematic working assumptions coming into this discussion

6   Policy targets and their implementation can be classified and measured over time on the basis of textual, survey, expenditure and other statistical evidence.

7   This allows them to be represented as points in spaces constructed on various assumptions, with a centre and extremes, which can also represent and relate the policy positions of political actors as specified from either data or theory.

8   Such spaces can have varying dimensions and measurements, the most common being a straight line running between left and right.

13   Ideally, political explanations should take the form of predictive theories consisting of propositions or equations which can be checked for predictive success against independently observed outcomes or behaviour.

Sources and resources

Hans Keman (2006) 'Party Government Formation and Policy Preferences: An Encompassing Approach?' in Judith Bara and Albert Weale (ed) *Democratic Policies and Party Competition* (London, Routledge) pp. 33–35.

Jaap Woldendorp, Hans Keman and Ian Budge (2000) *Party Government in 48 Democracies: Composition-Duration-Personnel* (ISBN 978–90–481 5620–7) (Originally published by Kluwer (Dordrecht): distributed by Springer www.springer.com/authors).

Russell J. Dalton, David M. Farrell and Ian McAlister (2013) *Political Parties and Democratic Linkage* (Oxford, Oxford University Press).

Suggestions for class papers

1 How far do you think that parties are concerned with government office even if their main concern is making policy?

2 What influence do you think internal party factions have over parties' decisions about joining governments?

3 How far do the considerations listed in Table 13.1 as affecting party behaviour in government apply to presidential governments?

4 How far do the generalizations made in this chapter about party behaviour in governments apply to party factions under a presidential regime?

Suggestions for class projects

1 Check out the predictive success of the decision tree in Figure 13.1 against an updated data set on party government formation.

2 Construct a more precise predictive theory of government termination and a computer simulation based on Table 13.4.

3 Formulate other generalizations or 'laws of governments' like Cuzàn's (Briefing 13.3).

Chapter 14

Ministries

Separating out policy areas

Ministries

A section of the administration which deals with a particular policy area under a politically appointed head.

Ministries connect the government formed by politicians who decide overall policy targets with the administrators and specialists who implement them in detail at the different levels of society. A politically appointed head participates in general policymaking as part of government and in detailed decisions within the ministry about how to apply its specific policy directives.

Each ministry (sometimes called a department or agency) operates within a specialized policy area – a division of labour designed to maximize its knowledge and competence in the field it deals with (e.g. health as opposed to military). This has three major consequences. The first is that government policy plans are normally formulated in general terms. So most decisions about what is actually to be done within the policy area will be made within ministries rather than by governments as a whole. This is particularly likely under ideologically mixed coalition governments, where no one party is able to impose a clear programme over all policy areas.

The second consequence of policy specialization by ministries is how to co-ordinate their activities so that one does not negate the other. For example, health may want more detailed regulation of factory conditions to avoid workplace hazards, while business may want less regulation to reduce expenses for small firms. Such inconsistencies may continue for years, be resolved by factional alliances between ministries or go right up to government level. Resolution is easier where governing parties have clearly laid out their programme. Having clear government commitments also helps strengthen the minister (sometimes termed secretary of state or agency head) internally in regard to the permanent administrators, who may have their own views about policy.

Ministries are no more unitary actors than are parties and governments. Their various components may pull together at times – most obviously when the government programme coincides with what the administrators in the ministry want to do anyway. In the opposite situation, where the government has no plans for the area, both minister and civil servants may be happy to do business as usual and not cause trouble. In other cases,

Briefing 14.1

The 'departmental view' on policy

The specialized administrators and experts inside a ministry, who have been dealing with a particular area under successive governments for many years, often have strong views about the best policies to be pursued. For one thing, they would all want the area to be given a higher priority with more money being spent on it. The politically appointed minister leading the ministry is likely to agree with this objective as such expansion would enhance their own political importance. However, if the government has explicitly committed itself to cutting the ministry down or restricting its role, the minister is more likely to act on the general brief either from conviction or to strengthen chances of future promotion. This often leads to internal factional divisions within the department as junior members or dissidents are promoted to carry out the government plan and replace their current superiors.

ministers may try to impose their own party policy, so internal conflict may ensue.

The third general consequence following from the assignment of particular policy areas to ministries is to separate these out from each other, so relevant decisions are considered and decided within that area alone. The regulation of working conditions, cited above, is a good example. Inside the ministry of health, it tends to be considered primarily as a health problem and may be discussed solely in these terms. Outside the ministry, there will be a corresponding legislative committee which recommends and effectively passes legislation. If that requires debate and approval, there will be a special session of the whole legislature devoted to health matters, which will end with a full vote on appropriate legislation.

Policy space

One or more lines or 'dimensions' representing policy positions.

Where this situation of discussing policy areas separately prevails, institutionally rooted in ministry structures, it has to be mirrored theoretically and analytically by setting up separate **policy spaces** within which actors' positions and citizen preferences can be located and policy changes traced. We have already considered in Part I how this differs from linking up decisions on health to decisions on business – for example, through an overarching conception of 'right' versus 'left'. In the case of separate policy discussions in each area, no such linkage prevails, and different criteria and considerations apply in each.

In terms of representing preferences, we can still see parties as 'carrying' their differing issue concerns in each separate policy area into government and alternating them as targets. So having separable as opposed to 'joined-up' issues does not fundamentally alter the mechanics of representation. But the contexts in which these operate are different in the sense of being 'joined up' (usually in left-right terms) or separate and decided on their own.

This chapter goes into each of the questions raised by the structure and actions of ministries in turn, starting with the political context(s) they create and operate within. We can further clarify the effects of policy differentiation by seeing how and why parties want to control particular ministries in coalition governments – and how such behaviour can be generalized to factions within single-party governments.

The cumulative effect of these processes, as just noted, is to separate out policy discussions in each area (such as transport and culture) so that they focus on different questions which are rarely related to each other in any detailed way. This is particularly true for most inter-election discussion and for voting in referendums and initiatives. Such a separation has considerable implications for any attempt to analyse and explain what is going on from a political science point of view. We go into the wider implications towards the end of the chapter – having already pointed out, however, that the alternation model of political representation, with parties as 'policy carriers' into government, can cope with both 'joined-up' and 'separable' decision-making on policy. We draw all these points together in the chapter conclusions.

Key points to note in this discussion are thus:

- Ministries as the key meeting point between party politicians and professional administrators and experts.
- Their effects in separating out policy areas from each other.
- Their tendency to keep to existing routines and policies unless pushed in other directions by parties and governments.
- How policy stability is fostered by parties and factions staking claims to particular ministries dealing with their own particular policy concerns.

Carrying on as before: policy regimes, incrementalism and policy inertia – with 'punctuations'

The vast mass of policies, mostly inherited from the past, which have to be initiated or revised, implemented and co-ordinated by governments, requires some kind of administrative division of labour to carry them out efficiently – or even to carry them out at all. This in turn creates a need for some kind of overall co-ordination at the highest level, which is provided by party programmes and by party governments. These can operate only generally, however, typically by basing themselves on broad left-right differences.

When they get down to specific policy areas, such as agriculture, health or military, the details become much more important, and technical expertise and political direction is required. This is provided by a myriad of specialized agencies and ministries, staffed by career administrators and professionals (e.g. engineers and doctors), most of whom have no formal ties to political parties. Indeed, they are usually forbidden to have them by civil service rules. These professionals carry on in much the same

Briefing 14.2

Ministries and policy areas: an overview

The policy and administrative functions which modern governments have to cover are pretty much the same across countries, as are the policy areas they demarcate. The minister (the politically appointed party nominee who heads the ministry and has the final say in internal discussions) also generally serves on the cabinet, the inner core of the government. This cannot have more than 20–25 members to maintain its effectiveness. So the main ministries have to number around 20–25 too, again rendering their distribution across policy areas and countries fairly comparable.

The following lists the main ministries and the policy areas they cover:

Prime minister/president of the council (secretariat)
Deputy prime minister/vice-president of the council (office)
Foreign affairs (foreign office, state department, ministry of external affairs)
Defence (ministry of defence and/or ministries with related and/or subdivided remits
    such as navy, army, air force, defence production, etc.)
Interior (ministry of the interior and/or ministries with related and/or subdivided remits
    such as police, civil service, local government, citizenship, etc.)
Justice (ministry of justice and/or ministries with related and/or subdivided remits such
    as attorney general, solicitor-general, etc.)
Finance (ministry of finance and/or ministries with related and/or subdivided remits
    such as treasury, budget, taxation, etc.)
Economic affairs (the ministry of economic affairs and/or ministries with related and/
    or subdivided remits such as (regional) economic planning or development, small
    businesses, etc.)
Labour (ministry of labour and/or (un)employment and/or ministries with this particular
    remit)
Education (ministry of education (and science) and/or ministries with related and/or
    subdivided remits such as technology or technological development)
Health
Housing
Agriculture (ministry of agriculture (fisheries and forestry) and/or ministries with related
    and/or subdivided remits such as food, marine life, etc.)
Industry/trade (ministry of industry and/or trade and/or ministries with related and/or
    subdivided remits such as foreign trade, commerce, state industries, etc.)
Environment
Social affairs/welfare (ministry of social affairs, social security or social welfare and/
    or ministries with related and/or subdivided remits such as youth, family, sport,
    employment, women, industrial relations, etc.)
Public works (ministry of public works and/or infrastructure and/or ministries with
    related and/or subdivided remits such as (public) transport, energy, post office,
    telecommunications, merchant navy, aviation, construction, urban planning, etc.)
Religion
Regions

way regardless of changes in government. They will only occasionally be affected by these, when new policy targets require a modification in their routines. This is a situation which has been characterized as 'punctuated equilibrium': most of the time, policies carry on in the same way, so that next year's budget is much the same as last year's – a situation of 'incremental change' or 'incrementalism'. Occasionally, however, the government programme envisages major reforms to one or more of the areas being administered which carries with it drastically altered policies and budgets. These will take time to implement fully. But in the meantime, the ministry's activities will be diverted and altered.

Ministries are therefore the areas where party priorities meet, and may clash, with bureaucratic ones. This is not necessarily the case, however. Where governments are not contemplating change in the area, all they may want is for the ministry to carry on without causing trouble. In that case, the permanent administrators' natural tendency to follow established routines may be shared by the government party or parties. This all contributes to the continuance of 'policy regimes' inside each ministry consisting of bodies of interrelated policies carried out on the same general principles of action, such as a preference for direct provision of healthcare through state-run clinics or hospitals as opposed to contracting these out to private healthcare providers. Or in environment, conservation may be valued over food production, with specific policies and regulations reflecting this. In defence, planning may be directed to providing strike forces for interventions all over the world rather than simply safeguarding the national territory, requiring different organization and procurement programmes.

The existence of such slow-moving and change-resistant 'policy regimes' contributes to slowing down the implementation of new government targets. There are already many other factors contributing to such policy inertia – legally binding contracts and entitlements among other things (cf. Briefing 7.1). A slow rate of real policy change is of course one of the key factors in the alternation theory bringing about a policy-preference correspondence (Chapter 7). It is also at the basis of the predictive theory of budgeting incrementalism, noted in Figure 8.1 as feeding into and supporting this assumption of alternation theory.

The theory of 'incrementalism' argues that budgets are largely determined through interdepartmental bargaining. The bureaucrats within each department or ministry will seek to increase their own standing and importance by increasing its activities and spending. However, all the other ministries have the same aim. They all have to agree on the budget; otherwise, the politicians will step in with possibly unpalatable and certainly unpredictable consequences. The negotiators therefore have an incentive to reach agreement while safeguarding their own departmental position.

The easiest solution, therefore, is to start from the previous year's budget allocation and raise or lower it a little ('incrementally') – thus threatening no one too much by heavy cuts. In this way, agreement is secured, and budgets do not change too much. This reasoning is summarized in Table 14.1 in the same form as the other predictive theories encountered previously and referenced in the 'web of explanation' (Figure 8.1).

TABLE 14.1 The incrementalist theory of budgetary allocation – why each year's allocation will be much like the last

1. Each bureaucratic department or agency tries to maintain or enhance its funding in competition with all the other departments.
2. Where all departments have relatively equal standing, they all impede increases in each other's budgets but cannot substantially decrease them either.
3. The result is that departmental spending allocations remain much the same from year to year, so that the best predictor of next year's allocation/spending is last year's.
4. This limits the amount of funding available for policy changes, thus contributing generally to 'policy inertia'.

Source: Adapted from the reasoning of O. A. Davis, A. H. Dempster and Aaron Wildavsky (1966) 'A Theory of the Budgetary Process' *American Political Science Review* (60) pp. 529–547

This process can also be quantified in a predictive equation. This says that this year's allocation will be like last year's – mirroring the bargaining process which starts off from that allocation and only incrementally changes it. The equation takes the following form:

$$13.1 \quad \text{Allocation}_t = a + b \,\text{Allocation}_{t-1}$$

The subscripts $_t$ and $_{t-1}$ indicate current ($_t$) and past ($_{t-1}$) allocations. When actual allocations are inserted – either within countries or across countries – they work well, producing a high correlation between past and present allocations. This means that if you want to predict the money allocated for this year the best way is to say it will be last year's allocation.

This is a theory of budgetary allocations, not actual expenditure by the department. There may well be occasions and reasons for departments overspending or underspending in their area. However, the allocation ultimately decides what can be spent. So its pace of change will broadly determine the rate for actual expenditure. To the extent that it does so, incrementalism says change in expenditure will be slow as assumed by the general alternation theory. This is not to say, however, that it doesn't change sometimes; otherwise, democracies would be stuck in the mud. Sometimes crises call for big change – not to mention the occasions when a party stays in power over two or three elections with a programme for change in the policy area.

Incrementalism, therefore, does not explain allocation and expenditure change when it does take place. This may be rare, but it is often far-reaching. So although spending may be much the same over extended periods, it may change drastically at one point in time before continuing at the new level over many following years. To explain the pattern of long-lasting stability interrupted occasionally by drastic change, we can expand incrementalist thinking to incorporate the forces making for change. As summarized in Table 14.2, some have already been suggested (e.g. as a party coming into government with drastically new priorities for the relevant policy area or external developments such as wars or weather events associated with climate change, which change allocations quickly and for good).

TABLE 14.2 The theory of punctuated equilibrium in budgeting allocations – occasional events drastically change the allocation but then it stays stable for a long time

1. Each bureaucratic department or agency tries to maintain or enhance its funding in competition with all the other departments.
2. Where all departments have relatively equal standing, they all impede increases in each other's spending but cannot substantially decrease them either.
3. The exception is either where external events enhance a department's importance (e.g. military threats for the department of defence) and/or where a party platform promises increased spending or cuts in spending in its policy area.
4. These 'punctuations' change departmental spending sharply and quickly.
5. It then continues at the new level from year to year, achieving a new equilibrium relative to other departments.
6. Spending stability and continuity are thus the general rule, favouring a general 'inertia' with occasional 'punctuations' or changes.

Source: Adapted from the reasoning of Frank R. Baumgartner and Bryan D. Jones (2009) *Agendas and Instability in American Politics* (Chicago, IL: University of Chicago Press)

The theory of 'punctuated equilibrium' improves on incrementalism by taking both stability and change into account. It can be operationalized in an equation of the form already suggested but including the factors that cause change when it does occur:

13.2 $\text{Allocation}_t = a + b_1 \text{Allocation}_{t-1} \pm b_2 \text{Plurality Party Policy Priorities}_t \pm b_3 \text{Relevant External Development}_{t-1}$

Allocation_t is this year's budgetary allocation; Allocation_{t-1} is last year's allocation; current Plurality Party Policy Priorities$_t$ for the policy area are what the party has stated as its policy targets for the ministry's area; and external developments affecting it are e.g. new war or foreign intervention (e.g. for defence expenditures). The equation puts into quantitative and testable form the idea that allocations (and, by inference, actual expenditures) will continue at much the same level unless government priorities shift or external developments render more spending necessary in the area.

'Punctuated equilibrium' challenges the crucial assumption behind the general alternation theory that policy change will always be slow and incremental. Sometimes it will be rapid and large. As against that, incrementalism rules most of the time. Moreover, rapid alternation by plurality parties keeps actual policy changes, even large ones, in the centre zone, where the majority of electors are. Several concurrent factors are present (e.g. party bracketing of electors) – all working to move enacted policy closer to the centre even in the face of rapid occasional change (cf. Figure 7.4).

Tendencies to stability in policy and policy regimes are substantially reinforced by the special interest which particular parties may have in particular ministries. This derives from their unique policy concerns, as identified in Table 6.6. When they participate in coalition governments, these concerns drive parties to make control of relevant ministries a condition of participation. The clearest example is perhaps that of agrarian parties, which want the minister of agriculture to come from their party. If the party participates frequently in coalitions and thus controls the ministry most of the time, it will be able to slant agricultural policy and the way it is applied so as to favour farmers, its major supporting group and the one it was founded to help and advance. The permanent administrators are probably themselves agrarian specialists who favour farmers anyway and who depend on their co-operation to make administration easier. If the agrarian party also manages to increase support for agriculture and expand the ministry budget, that gives it more status within the administration as a whole and enhances career opportunities and remuneration for the individuals attached to it. Political and administrative interests may therefore often concur within the ministry.

On the other hand, where a single party (unlikely to be agrarian) takes over government, one of its members will become minister with no such guarantee of a cosy relationship – perhaps indeed with a mandate for policy change derived from the party election programme. In that case, the minister has to persuade or coerce administrators to change the policies they have been implementing – or which they may even have initiated. Paradoxically, the minister may depend on these very people to produce the changes the party wants – even cutting the budget. In that case, the minister may have to ally with some administrators against others within the ministry – possibly younger, more ambitious bureaucrats with new views on policy who see opportunities for promotion in the changes.

Policy disputes can involve career administrators lining up against elected politicians. Some interpretations of administrative behaviour therefore see policy disputes as a clash between new, democratic practices and older state traditions of administrative authority and autonomy. However, this view is undermined by the existence of opposed factions among the bureaucrats themselves – and possibly among the politicians too if the minister comes from one coalition party and the minister's deputy from another. Factional alliances transcending conventional divisions may readily form – going beyond one ministry to bring in allied factions from others. For example, bureaucrats from finance may favour cutting agriculture's budget. They may then find allies in doing so even within the ministry itself – for example, a non-agrarian party minister and environmentalist bureaucrats who want to see organic farming fostered by cutting subsidies for artificial fertilizers and weedkiller.

Nevertheless, the majority in the ministry, backed up by any agrarian party minister in charge, will seek to expand or at least maintain established programmes and budgets. Most of the time they will be able to do so, because routine is the norm and because no government can change more than a fraction of the policies in force. This means that rather than dealing with specific policies which can be changed or administered individually, we are really confronted by groups of related and interdependent policies – all having consequences and feeding into the others.

As we have just seen, the policies which ministries initiate and administer are best described as policy regimes – groups of policies based on one guiding principle (e.g. free healthcare) – provided by public bodies as a national health service. 'Policy regimes' such as this relate closely to structural features in the constitutional set up – for example, whether professionals like doctors are encouraged to organize themselves autonomously and negotiate with the state to provide services or whether such professionals are specialized bureaucrats in an appropriate ministry.

State constitution

A set of authoritative rules laying down political rules and procedures.

Such arrangements are generally embedded in the **state constitution**. So it is hard to change a policy regime based on the principle of state-administered public services to another, such as 'healthcare free at the point of delivery' (which leaves the way open for autonomous bodies or firms to provide treatment financed by the state). Changing policy regimes in one area may often involve changes in administrative attitudes and arrangements across the whole spectrum of policies. This is difficult and likely to be opposed by individual ministers and ministries committed to the policy regimes they have already established and opposed to change unless they are forced into it by budgetary or other crises. Within coalitions, opposition will spill over into clashes at government level between the parties which 'run' the ministry and others who want to enforce an overall programme involving change or cuts.

Party preferences for ministries thus stem from their policy and ideological commitments. These are themselves highly resistant to change, reinforcing the bureaucratic and structural impediments to it. How the party preferences play out in this context is what we shall consider in the next section.

The proportional distribution of ministries

From a political point of view, ministries have two aspects. First, they entitle their political head to a vote in government decisions about overall policy targets and any action the government may decide to take on them. Second, they give the minister an advantage in implementing policy in detail, which usually allows it to be 'tweaked' in line with the minister's own party policy.

From the point of view of overall voting strength in government, any ministry with a vote would do, although some senior positions like the premiership and finance and foreign ministries are seen as more important. Their ministers will be senior politicians, possibly party leaders, exerting more influence as a result – but still in the end with only one vote in the cabinet, the ultimate decision-making body in a government.

It is this institutional fact of collective policymaking in government which drives parties or factions to seek to maximize their share of ministries and hence their strength in cabinet votes. Because all the others also want to do so, they automatically limit each other's shares of a limited number of posts. To avoid prolonged conflicts over the allocation, they have to arrive at some division which all can agree to as reasonably fair.

One solution would be to give every party (or faction in a single-party government) an equal share of ministries. As all are equally essential in the government which has been formed, totally power-seeking parties might stick out for this. Differences in size and importance between partners are obvious, however (e.g. between a plurality party contributing 45% of seats to a coalition government and two small partners contributing 3% and 2%). Equal sharing is so obviously not going to be agreed to that it is a non-starter. Even two partners, one contributing 60% of seats and the other the remaining 40%, are unlikely to agree on an equal split. The larger partner can always make a better deal with other potential partners, moving back to a proportional share-out of ministries. These bargaining and strategic considerations then make proportionality the norm. In the case of single-party government, the dominant faction inside the party will wish to consolidate its position and is likely also to insist on a proportionate share-out of ministries.

The dominance of this rule is summarized in Equation 13.3:

13.3 $PM \approx PS$

PM is the percentage of ministries received by each party in each coalition government and PS is the percentage of legislative seats it is contributing to the government's total number of seats. The wavy equal sign ($\approx$ instead of $=$) indicates that there is not always an exact equivalence between the percentages. Each ministry – typically 20–25 ministries in all – makes up 4% of the total. A small party in a coalition contributing perhaps a crucial 2% of government seats out of 200 seats in all, has to get at least one ministry. This is twice its strict share in percentage terms but clearly in the spirit of proportionality. As the percentages on each side get larger, the equivalence becomes more exact.

The actual numeric equation shows that for every 1% in seats that a party contributes towards coalition support in the legislature, it receives on average 0.9% in ministries. This is one of the strongest general relationships found in political science research. It establishes that proportional sharing of ministries within coalition governments is the rule and the norm in setting them up. How far it extends to sharing among factions in single-party governments we shall consider later in this chapter. It is qualified there, however, by the dominant faction's disinclination to dilute its own power. Only where it confronts a faction of almost equal strength is it likely to agree to anything approaching real proportionality.

The proportionality finding has been taken to support the following arguments:

i   Parties are office-seekers.
ii   They therefore seek to maximize their share of offices in government.
iii   Since all are seeking to do this, the only rule that can be agreed on is to relate the share of payoffs (ministries) to contributions (seats).

iv   Hence, we get strict proportionality between offices and seats.
v   This implies that all offices (ministries) are equivalent in value for all the parties – which then goes against the idea that the latter have a substantive interest in which ministries they get.

As we shall see, however, the proportionality finding does not lead exclusively to the conclusion that all that matters to parties is getting a ministry regardless of what it is. The next section shows how it can be fitted into a policy-pursuing interpretation, where the nature of the ministry really counts.

Party policy preferences for ministries

Ideology
A set of assumptions about the world leading to certain kinds of political action.

Proportionality allows all parties in a coalition to get some ministries. So how do they decide which ones to go for? The answer lies in the particular policy preferences they have, as displayed in Tables 6.6 and 12.1 and applied to ministries in Table 14.3. Party policy concerns spring out of their **ideology**, which in turn is linked to the causes that they were founded to promote and the groups that came together to originally both finance and organize them. Minority nationalist parties, for example, have strong beliefs about their regions being able to express their distinctive culture and traditions through their own political institutions. Therefore, they want the ministry dealing with their regions or with regional affairs in general. Particular policy concerns and particular ministries go together seamlessly here as it would hardly make sense to pursue the one without the other.

The advantage in a party nominee occupying a particular ministry, is her ability to shape the details of policy even though its broad application has been agreed at government level. What a party has been forced to compromise on in general may be compensated in detail inside the ministry – subject to winning over the administrators. However, where a party has had its nominee in place over a long period, it has also had the opportunity to influence the appointment of administrators. So it can probably count on their generally favourable predispositions towards its own policy goals. Most of the time the policy regimes it administers will be in stable **equilibrium** rather than at a punctuation point signifying significant change. So the party in control, the majority of permanent

Equilibrium
A political process that tends towards the same outcome over time.

TABLE 14.3 A policy-based explanation of the distribution of ministries between parties in a coalition government

1. Parties seek to implement their core policy concerns at all levels.
2. When entering a coalition, therefore, they demand control of the ministries/departments active in their main area of concern – sometimes as a precondition of entering the coalition.
3. With the party controlling the ministry over successive governments, it adopts and implements party targets in its policy area, which policy inertia helps continue over time.

Briefing 14.3

Policy or office? Unrealistic contrast or real dilemma for political parties?

In some 'economic theories' of party behaviour (cf. Briefing 12.11), parties are treated as though they are business firms maximizing profits. From this perspective, all they are assumed to be interested in is getting into government and getting ministries – the more the better. To do this, they are prepared to abandon their own ideologies and policies for whatever is popular with the voters (more votes means greater chance of getting into government and holding office).

As we have seen, however, it is difficult to know which policy voters *do* want unless you first put a proposal to them, which necessarily reflects the party ideology and record. Abandoning these also means blurring party identity and undermining its cohesion. This doesn't mean parties are not concerned about being in government and office – they do want to be there – but so that they can implement their policies. The proof lies in the findings reviewed later in the chapter. Parties are not just content with having a proportional share of ministries and votes in cabinet. They want their share to consist of ministries relevant to their own policy concerns, which they can then use to advance these (Figures 14.2–14.6). This renders any contrast between 'office seeking' and 'policy pursuit' unrealistic for parties – the parties want ministries in order for the parties themselves to further their own policies.

administrators and the policies administered will all be in general harmony. All that is required is to take care of unexpected and potentially disruptive events as they come up.

Parties wish to control ministries because of their special policy concern with the field they operate within. We have already examined party policy concerns as revealed by the prominence that they give them in their own programmes (Table 6.6 and 12.3). This gives us a basis for specifying the priority that parties of each ideological family will give to control of different types of ministries. Table 14.4 ranks ministries in order of priority for each family. In the table, each kind of party family is listed across the top.

Under each family, the different types of ministries are ranked in columns, in their order of priority for the family. Looking at the first column, therefore, we can see that conservative parties, in line with their traditional concerns about state strength and stability, will want control of the more traditional state ministries concerned with maintaining order at home and abroad (interior, justice, defence and foreign affairs). They also, however, want to maintain a prosperous economy, which in itself is a guarantee of internal stability and security and where they can also safeguard the interests of their business supporters. So business, finance and economic affairs also appeal to them. The countryside is generally more traditional and conservative than towns. So conservatives have something

TABLE 14.4 Ministries preferred by party families in order to further their policy concerns ranked in order of preference

Conservative	Liberal	Religious	Socialist	Parties with main focus on a single-issue/niche parties
Interior	Economy/finance	Religious affairs	Health/social affairs/labour	Ministry related to issue*
Foreign affairs/ defence	Justice	Education		(Indifferent to other ministries)
Justice	Education	Agriculture	Economy	
Agriculture	Interior		Industry	
Economy	Trade/industry/ commerce	Social affairs/ health/labour	Education	
Education/trade/ industry/commerce				

* agriculture/fisheries for agrarians, regional issues for nationalists/regionalists, etc.

Notes: Ministries are ranked in their hypothesized order of desirability to the party family (e.g. conservatives most want the interior ministry (dealing with law and order) rather than agriculture).

of an interest in getting hold of the ministry of agriculture to consolidate rural support by getting credit for supportive policies.

Here, however, they have to reckon with interventions from the other parties that they may be in coalition with. For agrarian parties, one of the single-issue or niche parties belonging to the last column of the table, the ministry of agriculture will be the one they primarily focus on – naturally enough, given their rural ideology and support base.

Religious parties – primarily Christian democrats in the case of current democracies – may also want to favour the more traditional and religiously inclined countryside. They do, however, have even more pressing concerns with religious affairs (if there is a ministry in that area) and education. Not only do most religious groups maintain their own schools, as a way of passing on beliefs and traditions to the younger generation, but they also have an interest in getting or increasing state support for them, and ensuring that there is religious instruction in state schools.

Religious parties are also of course interested in maintaining their support among adults and fostering the stable families which pass on religious values. Such concerns dominate the social doctrines embedded in their ideology and support groups, like Catholic trade unions. This prompts them to go for the ministries dealing with welfare – social affairs and health. Improvements in living conditions through public service provision is, however, a top concern in socialist ideology and socialist party priorities. So again there will be competition among coalition partners for relevant ministries. When many ministries deal with the same policy field, one solution may well be to divide them up between the government parties which want them. Who gets what in the way of ministries may well in fact form the crucial part of overall coalition negotiations, which we will explore in more detail in the next section.

The fact that ministries do not always match up to policy fields – sometimes straddling several and sometimes proliferating within one – accounts for a certain lack of fit between Tables 6.6 and 12.1, detailing party policy concerns, and Table 14.3, ranking priorities for ministries. Neo-liberal parties, for example, quite strongly want to limit welfare and might want to cut social programmes. But coalition partners will go so strongly for these ministries as their first priority that it is hardly worthwhile for liberals to try to get them. As a result, they prioritize concerns with the market economy and individual freedom (the justice ministry) and content themselves with arguing the welfare question at general government level.

Parties, particularly when they get into government, are primarily policy pursuers. But they cannot just follow their own priorities, particularly where they do not have sole control. They may seek to achieve policy priorities under constraints both at general government level and in terms of implementation within existing ministries. They have to tailor demands for ministries to what their partners also want and operate within proportionality rules – limiting their share. Tables 6.6 and 12.1 give an overview of the policy considerations which drive parties. But these hardly allow us to predict exactly how the distribution of ministries will work out. To do so, we need to specify the exact processes involved, as we do in the decision trees of the next section. These deal with allocations only between parties in coalition governments. Generalizations to party factions in single-party governments cannot be exact. We may hypothesize, however, that something like the same processes operate there, giving left, right and centre factions within the party responsibilities conforming to their relative concerns.

Since ministries tend to be given the administrative and usually also legislative initiative in their own policy sphere, a major consequence of the match between party/faction and ministry means that ensuing discussion and debate is focused on one policy field at a time. Legislative committees and timetables are also matched to ministries and divided up between them. Rather than joined-up discussions, we get specialized ones, only dealing with the policies in question rather than how they all join up within the overall government programme. In fact, governments often encourage specialized discussions in one field at a time because it frees them from having to answer awkward questions like what cuts are to be made in one area to pay for others.

Note how this administrative and political policy separation into discrete areas mirrors and possibly shapes the way electors approach policy, which we explored in Chapter 5. Favouring expansion and spending in the social areas which benefit themselves, but advocating general cuts in taxation and in the spending necessary to pay for them, is a classic inconsistency eliminated by joined-up thinking along the left-right continuum. However, it is encouraged and framed by the institutional structures shaping government decision-making itself. So one can hardly blame electors and voters for reacting in precisely this way. Taking a long-term perspective, one can see that for both electors and parties general elections may join up everyone's thinking by focusing it on left-right concerns, particularly on service expansion versus tax cuts. But in inter-election periods, the focus of political debate may then shift to issue-by-issue concerns with individual policy areas, as illustrated in Figure 5.1. The division of policy responsibilities between ministries encourages this – particularly with their allocation to parties in line with their particular policy concerns – an allocation which we now examine.

Modelling the distribution of ministries between parties in coalition governments

Not all democratic governments are coalitions, but a high proportion of them are (65% – around two-thirds according to the latest figures on post-war governments). Visually representing how multiparty governments distribute ministries among their constituent parties has the potential to provide a complete explanation of how ministries get divided up in general. This is because it is the most difficult case. Where directly elected presidents nominate cabinets, or single parties form the government under parliamentary regimes, we can assume that one party takes all the posts. Seeing how they get divided up under coalitions thus arounds out the explanation at the party level. (Distribution among internal party factions is a different matter, which we consider in the next section.)

The way in which we transform the general characterization of Table 14.3 – of which type of party takes what type of ministry – into precise predictions about what will happen under particular types of coalition government, also has a methodological interest in the context of this book. Political science notably lacks predictive theory – that is, explanatory theories that generate exact expectations about past and future events. Most hypotheses are generally checked against the relationships which emerge from analysing accumulated past data like surveys. Rarely are these relationships explained at a level of detail that allows us to say exactly what will happen in the future under specified considerations. This is regrettable because without the ability to **predict** or **postdict** events, we are never entirely sure whether a theory really works – whether it is 'valid'. It will also be much more informative of course if it can predict the future. The 'decision trees' we present here are capable of doing so – and have actually been used to postdict the way governments were set up in post-war Europe, with an overall success rate of 0.70 (i.e. out of all cases of ministries going to parties, seven out of ten were successfully postdicted).

Ministries are of interest to parties not only from the point of view of implementing the specific policies they administer but also for their relative weight in general policy formation. The sheer number of ministries they hold contributes to a party's political weight, as it adds to its votes in **cabinet**. So parties will push to get as many ministries as possible, to a limit determined by their partners' desire to do the same. The only way to resolve this competition in an agreed way is to relate the number of ministries held to legislative seats through the proportionality rule. Where each

Predict

Correctly anticipate what is going to happen in the future.

Postdict

Correctly characterize what has happened.

Cabinet

The committee of a government making general decisions.

party reaches its due proportion, the distribution stops no matter how much the party covets a remaining ministry.

Possession of the premiership also gives an advantage to its holder in terms of shaping the general discussion of policy. As only one party can hold the post, numerical criteria again have to be called in, awarding it to the largest party in the coalition. Otherwise, argument would be endless. Doing so also acknowledges the plurality that the party received from the electorate. The deputy premiership, where it exists, may be awarded more flexibly to compensate parties which lost out in the overall distribution of other ministries.

Because of proportionality, the parties have to get their priorities right in choosing the ministries whose policy implementation they want to control because of their specific concern with the field. Combining general and particular policy concerns, we see that the distribution of ministries is a multistage process:

1   Parties assert their claims to specific ministries of interest.
2   Conflicts involved in claims to the same ministry are provisionally resolved by trading some ministries for others within the same policy area.
3   The resulting distribution is checked against the proportionality criterion and accepted when each party has got a proportion of ministries conforming to its contribution in legislative seats.

Negotiations may go between these different levels several times, leading to adjustments in original claims and failure because of the upper limits imposed by proportionality to gain some specific ministries of interest from the point of view of policy implementation. Distribution can be smoothed out with the aid of 'makeweight' ministries of no particular policy interest to any party and possibly by sacrificing ministries of lower priority in the interests of keeping those of higher priority.

**Operation-
alization**

Putting theories
into a form
which facilitates
prediction/
postdiction
of outcomes;
also called
'modelling'.

In this way, the proportionality criterion can be incorporated into a comprehensive, policy-based **operationalization** of the allocation of ministries. This combines three elements: (1) party attachment to particular ministries, as specified in Table 14.3; (2) the transference of concerns about getting particular ministries to related parties, where a particular type of party does not exist or at any rate does not participate in the coalition; and (3) proportionality. For maximum clarity, we have combined these elements in decision trees – direct representations of every step in the process of allocating ministries for each party type.

We start in Figure 14.1 with single-issue parties, as represented by the agrarians, because they form the simplest case. Since the decision tree, in specifying every step in the process of allocation, has to deal with all eventualities, it can become quite complicated. However, it is no more than a precise specification of our earlier reasoning, so the various steps involved should be reasonably clear.

We have said that participation is not worthwhile for agrarians unless they get their own ministry of concern – agriculture and possibly fisheries

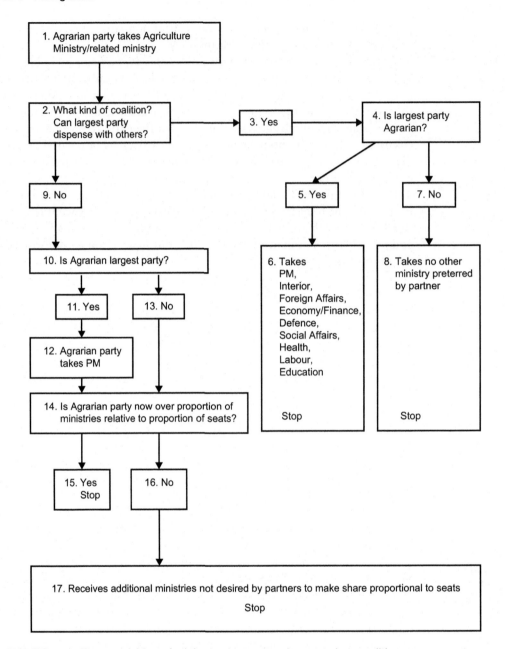

FIGURE 14.1 The acquisition of ministries by an agrarian party in a coalition government

or lands. Getting such ministries if they exist forms the first stage of the postulated acquisition process, as it is a necessary prerequisite to participation in government (though in itself it may not be a sufficient payoff, depending on the size of the agrarian seat contribution to the government's support).

The next stage is to review possible government situations. Looking back to the circumstances under which coalitions can emerge as described in Figure 13.1, we have seen that these can be varied. Three possibilities are particularly important from the point of view of distributing ministries:

1   There are situations in which one party *could* form a government on its own (because it has a majority or at least a strong predominance). As participation from the smaller partners depends on the goodwill of the largest, the latter can take all the ministries it wants almost without regard to the former (the exception being the proviso that agrarian parties would not participate at all without the ministry of agriculture). If the agrarians are the largest party in this situation, they will proceed to take all the important ministries, leaving to their partner or partners only one of the latter's preferred choices. If they are the smaller (and dispensable) partner, they will take (in addition to agriculture and fisheries) nothing which is preferred by their partner, as they are so completely dependent on its goodwill.
2   A second situation is where relationships between coalition partners are more equal but where agrarians are largest. In that case, they will be expected to take the premiership in addition to agriculture, which they have secured in their very first step.
3   Where parties are relatively equal but agrarians are not the largest, obviously they do not get the premiership, but they will secure agriculture as a sine qua non of governmental participation.

In any case, agrarians being satisfied on their major preferences (and if largest, on the premiership) now want no more specific ministries. It is at this point that the criterion of proportionality comes in. While for other parties there might exist a possibility of having too great a proportion of ministries relative to seats, and of being docked of those of lower priority, this could not be the case with the agrarians. To participate in the coalition at all, they must have agriculture, and if largest, must have the premiership. As these are indispensable, it is only if, having these, they still have less than their due proportion of ministries that any further allocation takes place; and this can be only upwards, carrying them into box 17 and gains of enough ministries not desired by partners to make their share proportional to their contribution of seats.

This review of the decision tree should clarify the processes involved and how they are represented by the diagram. We turn now to Figure 14.2, which at a similar level of detail specifies the processes of allocation for conservative parties.

Again, the three possible types of coalition situation recur. In the case of coalitions with a totally dominant party, the question is again whether the conservatives are dominant or dependent. If the former, then they will take all their preferred ministries, leaving to the partner only those not preferred by them. If they themselves are dependent, on the other hand, they in turn will obtain only ministries not preferred by the partner.

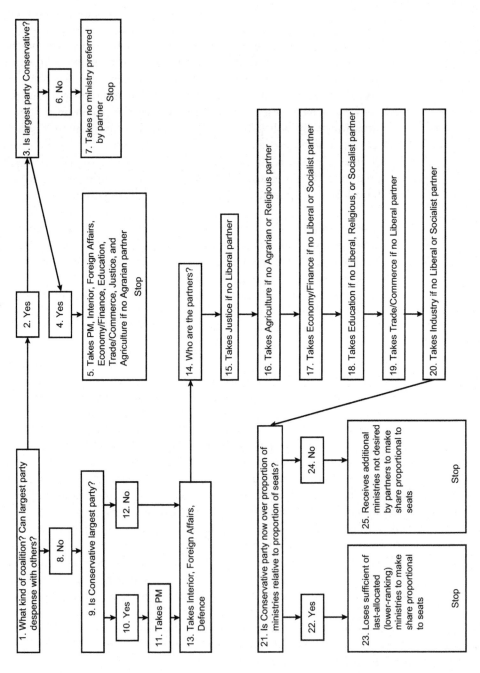

FIGURE 14.2 The acquisition of ministries by a conservative party in a coalition government

In a more equal situation but where they are largest, they will take the premiership, and even if not largest, they will bargain for their first priorities of interior, foreign affairs, and defence. At this point, however, they begin to compete for ministries also desired by other parties in the coalition. So whether they get justice, economy/finance, education, trade or something else depends on whether interested partners are asserting claims. If there is a clash between other parties' first-priority ministries and ones which rank lower for conservatives, the latter will obviously tend to give way.

The question of what other parties form the coalition is also of concern because the conservatives may 'inherit' an interest in certain ministries if a partner of a certain family type does not participate or possibly does not even exist in that **party system**. This is particularly the case with regard to agriculture if there are no agrarian or religious parties.

Party system

The number and types of parties in a country.

With desired ministries obtained, the equalizing process based on proportionality comes into play. If conservatives have too few ministries in relation to their seats, they will receive makeweights not especially desired by anyone else to make up their share. If too many preferred ministries have gone to them, however, they have to lose enough of their lower-ranked ones to bring them down to proportionality with regard to seats. This final, adjusting process therefore cuts across the earlier allocation in terms of substantive preferences and can reverse some of its results. This could account for some preferred ministries not being obtained.

Figure 14.3 lists the same processes but for liberal parties. Because the preferences of liberals for ministries have already been specified in relation to Table 14.3 and because distribution follows the same broad principles as those described for conservatives, we do not need to discuss the figure in detail. Because education is also a priority for religious parties – as the interior is for conservatives – liberals are not necessarily assumed to get them if they have partners of these types. Again, liberals have a nonnegotiable condition for entry to a coalition on relatively equal terms (economy/finance and justice), and again, the proportionalization of ministries and seats may knock out some substantively preferred ministries from their final allocation (in the case of small parties, entitled to only one ministry on proportional criteria, most of their preferred ministries would not in fact be obtained).

The allocation processes for religious parties (Figure 14.4) and socialists (Figure 14.5) are again similar, once essential modifications have been made to accommodate their different preferences and relationships with partners. Again, who is a coalition partner makes a great difference to the final allocation – also affected by proportionalization. Given this, the fact that parties get their preferred ministries in 70% of the cases covered by Figures 14.1 to 14.5, indicates a reasonable level of predictive success for the policy-based theory of allocations outlined in Table 14.3.

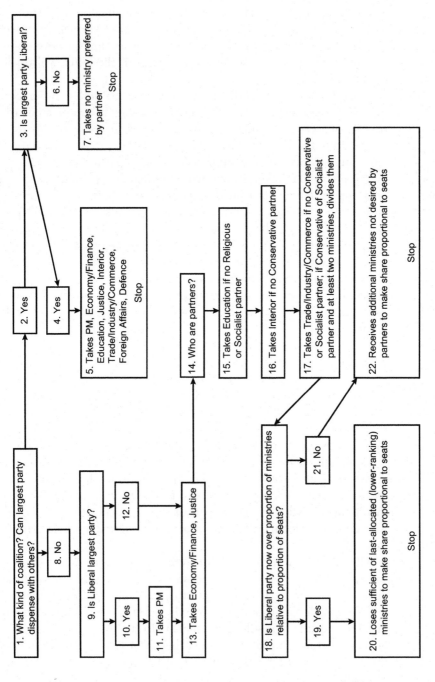

FIGURE 14.3 The acquisition of ministries by a liberal party in a coalition government

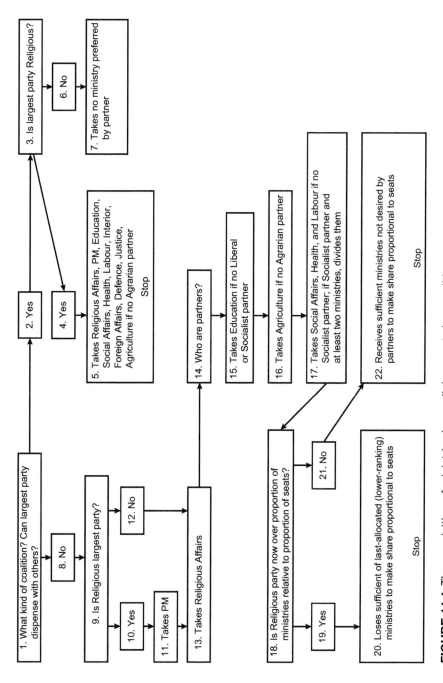

FIGURE 14.4 The acquisition of ministries by a religious party in a coalition government

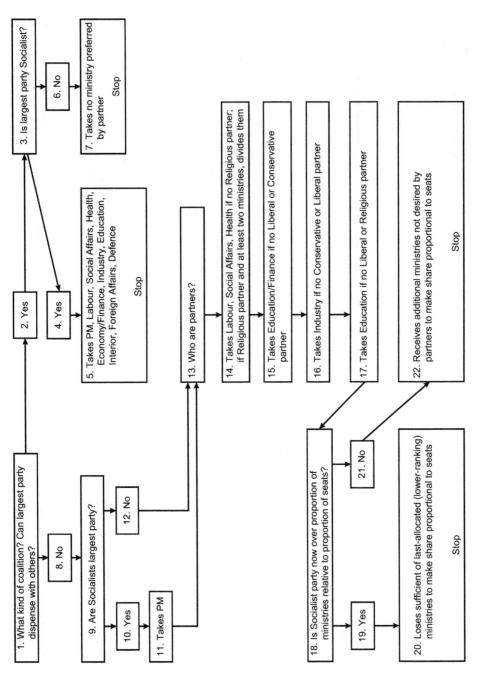

FIGURE 14.5 The acquisition of ministries by a socialist party in a coalition government

Distributing ministries among party factions under single-party governments

Faction

A grouping within a party with distinct views on policy and strategy.

NATO

The North Atlantic Treaty Organization.

EU

An economic, social and political grouping of most European countries.

Left-right

Welfare, state intervention and peaceful internation-alization on the left and traditional morality, freedom and internal and national security on the right.

Single-party governments are also widespread, if we take account of those which are presidentially nominated and the single-party parliamentary-based ones. By definition, a single party will take over all the ministries. However, we should not think that potential lines of conflict end here. Parties themselves are not unitary actors, and internal **factions** are sometimes as organized as the parties themselves.

Internal party divisions are often seen as running horizontally, pitting top leadership, at government level, against rank-and-file legislators and often against activists at branch and local levels. Opposition to the current party leadership and its policies will of course pick up support where it can locally and is by definition weaker in the legislature and government. To be effective, however, it needs to operate at all party levels, organizing itself as much as possible like a mini-party with a view to displacing the controlling faction everywhere it can.

This also implies that factions have to have a coherent policy position, both to criticize the party leaders and their policy and to motivate their followers. As noted in Chapter 12, almost all parties contain at least two groupings which divide on how to apply the overall ideology under current circumstances. One contains pragmatists, who want to compromise with other parties and social groups in order to get co-operation and more general acceptance of their programme. The other contains ideologues, who think that anything less than a full and rigorous application of their programme will not produce benefits.

These divisions may well occur on issues of particular importance: secession of one part of the country or adhesion to a larger grouping like **NATO** and other military alliances or the **EU**. In that case, factions lined up for and against are rather like the 'single-issue' parties in Table 12.1. Often, however, they divide on applications of the party ideology as a whole and are analogous to the programmatic parties discussed in Chapter 12. Factions of this type are likely to think in terms of the broad sweep of policy and are hence more easily classified in terms of a general ideological perspective, most easily summarized in **left-right** terms. The ideologues will be more left or right (depending on the party's own position). The pragmatists can be characterized as more to the 'centre'.

In distributing ministries, the controlling faction will of course take care to give the ones of most concern to its own supporters. The presidency/premiership will automatically belong to it, because otherwise, it could hardly be said to be in control. Generally, ministries important to effecting its overall programme – finance, defence and foreign affairs – will also go to its own leaders.

In the case of the other ministries, considerations of party unity, conciliation of opposition parties (particularly in the legislature under the

Separation of powers

A (usually presidential) setup that makes legislature and court approval necessary for major legislative and presidential actions.

separation of powers) and general co-operation both inside and outside the party and in the country as a whole all come into play. One way is to appoint other factional representatives to ministries not the subject of scheduled changes. The main concern there is to keep them running quietly. An opposing faction can well do that, while being conciliated by the appointment.

On a single disruptive issue not closely linked to its standing ideology, a controlling faction would naturally tend to appoint one of its own members to keep the issue under control. However, governments increasingly avoid splitting their own party on such matters by calling a **referendum** to 'let the people decide'. In that case, a neutral or even opposing factional member could safely be appointed as minister to conduct it while 'taking the issue out of politics'.

Referendum

A popular vote called by governments or courts to decide a policy proposal.

Overall of course, the controlling faction has to make sure it will have the majority of votes at government level. So a numerical constraint similar to the proportionality one operates for a factional distribution of ministries too. The controlling faction has to keep overall control. But that is not to say that the others do not get the specific ministries that are of most policy concern to them.

The fact that we can generalize to some extent about the factional distributions of ministries indicates that we could construct decision trees to explain and predict them just as we have done with the party distribution under coalition governments. In principle we could. What we lack, however, is any systematic comparative evidence comparable to what we have for party occupancy of ministries. Indeed, we lack much information about factions at all, apart from a few isolated country studies. This is probably the area of political science where collecting relevant data would produce a dramatic breakthrough in our knowledge. We already have the theories to guide their collection and testing. All we need now is actual comparative evidence to determine whether they are correct.

Ministries and policy spaces

Policy spaces

One or more lines or 'dimensions' representing policy positions.

At several points in our preceding discussion, we have brought in the question of how far political practice affects its (spatial) analysis. We already considered the question broadly and systematically in Chapters 4–6. The question usually boils down to asking, can we see every political decision in every area of policy as being linked to others (usually in terms of moving along a single line more to its left end or more to its right)? Or do we have to consider each major policy area in its own terms, with decisions made it without reference to any other area? This would involve representing preferences in each policy area on a separate line, as distinct from an overarching left-right line.

There is a third possibility which has not come up so much in this chapter: some policy areas might be so closely linked that decisions on one affect decisions on the other. However, the linkage falls short of the general left-right one which relates all the issues to each other. Short of that, the two (or more) linked areas would have to be represented in a two-dimensional graph where positions and movements are traced out in the common space (cf. Table 5.1). Where even more policy areas were closely linked, the common space might be defined by three or more dimensions. What our discussion of ministries shows, however, is that they generally consider issues within the context of their own specialized area. So they are not going to consider the effect of health increases on defence spending. If they *are* put together, it is in cabinet discussions in terms of the overall budget, generally in a left-right perspective. So government proposals frame public discussion generally within either single-issue contexts or left-right contexts.

Reducing all policy to one general decision about spending priorities means that it can be represented on a left-right dimension, as areas of leftist concern (e.g. welfare) are cut or expanded in contrast to areas of right-wing concern (e.g. military). Election programmes are often written in terms of these overall choices, to simplify things for electors. So they have successfully been put into numbers to map out general changes in party left-right positions relative to each other, as in Figures 6.3 and 6.4.

If, on the other hand, new issues like climate change and the environment come up, which do not fit into traditional left-right divisions, we may need to separate them out, along with related questions such as Third World development and how that is to proceed. In that case, policymaking will best be represented as a series of different one-dimensional single line spaces, each representing issues which have to be considered but separately from the others (Table 5.2).

Because governments usually have to consider the whole policy picture, they generally have to be considered as actors within a reasonably joined-up space, usually an overarching joined-up left-right one. Ministries, on the other hand, are dealing with narrower and more defined policy areas. They are expected to make decisions in their own area without involving others too much. Corresponding to the division of policy into areas defined by ministries, the corresponding structure of administrative and legislative committees will also deal with policy separately in this way, focusing on the ministry area and not generally querying decisions which have already been made at other levels. In this way, the institutional structure of ministries exert a strong influence on political debate and discussion, shaping it as a series of separate sequential discussions on one area of policy after another, without linking them up much.

Which type of policy space – unidimensional left-right, multidimensional clusters or separate individual issue spaces – is then the best one to conduct our analysis of representation in? The answer is probably in left-right and issue-by-issue terms. The overarching left-right dimension works best for locating electorates, parties and governments in terms of policy. It can always be disrupted, however, by a single unrelated issue which makes a big impact and inserts another 'dimension' into the political discussion. Over time, nevertheless, issues generally get joined up with right and left because it is such a simple and appealing way of looking at the political world.

On the other hand, when we get down to the day-to-day decisions of ordinary politics, issues tend to be considered one by one, on their own merits – reinforced by institutional structures, as we have seen. So the political world can be best seen as one-dimensional overarching, particularly at general elections, and as one-dimensional separate issue spaces in between elections, particularly if referendums focus attention on particular questions. An illustration of the way issues break up and join up at different points in the political process is given in Figure 5.1.

Of course, decisions about what type of spatial representation to use are always analytic, made by researchers because they seem the most appropriate representation of political reality – rather than being built into reality itself. The remaining question is how well electors' preferences are reflected in the public policy which emerges in one kind of policy space compared to another. Some accounts of political representation (cf. Chapter 5) depend highly on an assumption that the underlying policy space takes on one shape rather than any other – for example, that it is one-dimensional left-right with a clearly marked-out median position, so that the majority preference can be clearly measured (cf. Briefing 12.11).

The alternation model of representation, on the other hand, simply assumes that parties endorse many different policy targets, which can be represented in many different kinds of policy space – unidimensional or multidimensional, separable or joined up. At least some parties will take up contrasting positions in such spaces. As they move into and out of government, they will change the policies being implemented, pulling them across whatever segment of the policy space they define. Since the parties between them 'carry' all the significant policy positions citizen/elections endorse, the latter's majority preference will lie somewhere between the party positions in the region of the centre, around which actual public policy will oscillate. This process, carried on in the party-defined segment of all policy spaces, guarantees its correspondence with preferences in the long term – and most of the time in the short term too. This process will also operate in the policy areas which ministries tend to separate out and deal with sequentially – *if* parties alternate in possession of the ministries. This chapter has shown that at least some of the time they do, thus strengthening democratic representation in the detailed application of policy as well as in its general direction by governments.

End-summary

Subject to the overall direction which the party or parties dominant in government set, ministries have enormous discretion in the detailed application of policy. However, they are far from being unified actors. The party-political ministers in charge may or may not concur with their professional and administrative staff. In some cases, a long-standing connection may have been built up between the bureaucrats and the parties or party factions sharing the ministries' policy concerns. This may result in a stable policy regime over many years. It is always liable to 'punctuation' or disruption from changes of government and minister, however. Such changes can be charted and predicted in the case of coalition governments, with possible applications to party factions under single-party governments once sufficient information has been gathered about them.

The division of administrative labour between ministries also produces strong tendencies towards compartmentalization – the separation of one policy area, and discussion about it, from others. Doing so promotes the evolution of highly stable, long-lasting policy regimes. It also has implications for the way we analyse policy and represent it analytically, as a series of one-dimensional, separable spaces. This helps in defining the median popular position with party positions on each side of it and seeing whether public policy settles there. The alternation model also works in the other spaces which might be used to represent more joined-up policymaking, where ministries are only one type of actor involved in policymaking, along with parties, governments and the electorate. We now turn in Part IV to the overall context in which they operate: the state and its relations with other states, which strongly affect internal democratic processes.

Key points to take away from this discussion are thus:

- The internal structure of ministries, with a political party nominee influencing the policy direction taken by the administrators and professionals within the ministry.
- How this often lends to stability ('inertia') in the implementation of policy, given the 'claim' particular parties have on policy grounds to control the ministry.
- This is reinforced by 'incrementalism' in budgetary allocations which is only occasionally 'punctuated' by party initiatives or external events.
- Which parties have claims to particular ministries and how this works out for their distribution under coalition governments.
- How the policy specialization by ministries and corresponding legislative committees favours separate rather than joined-up policymaking.
- Leading to policymaking in a series of specific contexts, best represented analytically by separate straight lines.
- Which, however, sometimes get joined up – usually in left-right terms – in general elections.

Systematic working assumptions coming into this discussion

6 Policy preferences and their implementation can be classified and measured for over-time and comparative analysis, on the basis of textual, survey, expenditure and other statistical evidence.

7 This allows them to be represented as points in spaces constructed on various (measurement) assumptions, with a centre and extremes, which can also relate the policy positions of political actors (citizens, voters, governments, parties, etc.) as specified from either data or theory.

8 Such spaces can have varying dimensions and measurements, the most common being a straight line running between left and right.

13 Ideally, political explanations should take the form of predictive theories consisting of propositions or equations which can be checked for predictive success against independently observed outcomes and behaviour.

15 Popular policy preferences do not usually emerge spontaneously but rather are formed as reactions to policy proposals put forward by governments, parties or other political actors.

Sources and resources

Frank R. Baumgartner and Bryan D. Jones (2009) *Agendas and Instability in American Politics* (Chicago, IL, University of Chicago Press).

Ian Budge and Hans Keman (1994) *Parties and Democracy* (Oxford, Oxford University Press) pp. 89–131.

Jaap Woldendorp, Hans Keman, and Ian Budge *Party Government in 48 Democracies* 1945–1998 (Springer www.springer.com/authors/) – with various computerised updates. The one recommended by the original authors is https://fsw.vu.nl/en/departments/political-science-and-public-administration/staff/woldendorp/party-government-data-set/index.aspx

Suggestions for class papers

1 Why is the agrarian take-up of ministries better predicted and explained by their policy concerns (80%) than the conservative take-up (54%)?

2 Does the fact that parties (and factions) tend to take up particular ministries (or agencies or departments) promote a general correspondence between popular preferences and (implemented) policies or hinder it?

3 Is 'incrementalism' a good or bad thing for democracy?

4 Are coalitions better or worse in producing a policy-preference correspondence than single-party majority governments?

Suggestions for class projects

1 Identify party factions inside one or more parties and trace out their alternation. How far does your research support or discredit the factional theory of party policymaking (Table 12.2)?

2 Use updated data on party governments to further check out the theories of ministry allocation operationalized in Figures 14.1–14.5.

3 Having identified factions in the US parties for all or part of the postwar period, how far are departments and agencies allocated between them in the way ministries are allocated between coalition partners in parliamentary governments?

Part IV

States

Collective action without binding rules

Political science has traditionally focused on politics within each state rather than on the relationships between them. Even where states have been compared according to how their differing structures and decision rules produce different kinds of policy, each has been treated as a more or less independent unit. This approach has been summarized in Proposition 1 of the systematic overview (p. 136). 'States form the basic context/unit for most political research'. Interstate relationships are largely left to the separate discipline of international relations (IR), focused on the military and diplomatic interactions between independent states on a continental or world level.

However, as Proposition 2 of the overview makes clear, 'States are governments with supporting (quasi-)military, administrative and other institutions, recognized by other governments as providing public goods and services (including the regulation of non-state activities) within specified territorial boundaries'.

Such governments operate at many levels above and below traditional states, from local communes or parishes to cities and regions – all providing public goods and making policy within their own areas – and up to international bodies like the World Health Organization (WHO) and the United Nations Organization (UN or UNO) itself, which operates directly as a world body and through specialized agencies. All of these are in effect governments operating over a defined territory which raise and dispense resources for public goods, whose nature and provision they define through their policies. Besides a supporting administration (and sometimes armies, courts and police), such bodies usually have councils and assemblies chosen in a variety of ways, not unlike national legislatures.

On the other hand, not many international bodies are democratic in the sense of policy being tailored to the preferences of the population they regulate within their terms of reference. The more specialized international agencies are usually run and advised by professionals (e.g. doctors, engineers or military). The more general ones, such as the UN or military-political alliances like NATO, have assemblies nominated by the governments of the member states. Ultimately, any action or policy requires their unanimous agreement to be really effective.

This creates the same problem of supplying universal public goods which we examined in Chapter 2. If everyone can enjoy the benefits of world health or peace anyway, why bother paying for it? The solution inside traditional state boundaries has been for governments to raise taxes to pay for general goods and services, imposing penalties on non-payers. At international level, there is no such centralized authority to enforce payment, so the problem of doing so and funding the service remains.

Various expedients operate at international level to get around this problem. Most common is to try to get unanimous or nearly unanimous agreement among the traditional states which are members, on providing an obviously beneficial service or public good – such as health, particularly in tackling epidemics which threaten everyone. Climate change may be another area where growing perceptions of an immediate threat may generate near unanimity. Negotiations of this kind, seeking agreement on a common policy among independent protagonists who cannot easily be coerced, are a central focus in the study of IR.

Another solution to the problem of getting international agreement is to operate at continental level to create a central government to tackle common problems across previously independent states. These then become regional governments within a federal state or confederation. India, Switzerland, Canada and the US are examples, where not only have traditional states been brought together but a democracy created. The EU is an ongoing process of this kind.

The central question posed in Part IV – in line with the central focus of political science on democratic state structures – is thus on the extent to which a world democracy has been approximated, or could emerge, on this model. Increasing globalization seems to render it both necessary and possible, as we shall see. In that case, the processes and protagonists we have been examining up to this point – elections, political parties, governments and administrations – would all become relevant at world level, where we might also expect our predictive explanations to provide useful insights as well. We examine these possibilities in Chapter 15.

Chapter 15

Globalization and world democracy

Chapter overview: collective action without binding rules

So far, we have looked at public policy as the end product of institutional processes, rules and actors operating inside states. State governments, however, are not free to act independently of external influences – particularly in a world with massive economic ups and downs, where technological developments spread with amazing speed, carried by **multinational corporations** for whom territorial boundaries are entirely permeable.

Multinational corporations

Businesses which operate inside many countries.

Born of wars and conquests, states have always had to be wary of aggression from their neighbours and have sought to make military and diplomatic alliances which will protect them. Smaller and weaker states, in particular, need to forge ties with larger ones, who may in turn have an interest in building up international support against their own rivals. In the modern world, such alliances have become larger and more comprehensive, fostering cultural and economic ties between their members, as well as military ones. These extend into politics. One condition of alliance membership may be to have comparable civil rights and other freedoms (often enshrined in interstate treaties). The alliance and its dominant states may also put pressure on members to move towards democratic forms of rule and to adopt compatible business practices and media freedoms.

Supervising these developments often requires international councils and courts which operate across states. In turn, this blurs the distinctions between state institutions in the traditional sense – operating within territorial boundaries defined by citizenship and language – and international institutions, which also have responsibilities and jurisdictions inside and across these boundaries. The EU, for example, groups 27 states from the Atlantic Ocean to the Black Sea. It co-ordinates their political and military initiatives and their economies. Its overarching powers and responsibilities, administered by all-European institutions as well as an elected parliament, make it possible to ask if it has become a federal state in its own right. Certainly, it has transformed relationships so that its weaker members have become more like the subordinate states in a federal union than fully independent decision makers in their own territory.

The EU

An economic, social and political grouping of most European countries.

Traditionally, the crucial difference between a federal union and a confederation lies in the ultimate power of the member states to withdraw.

Briefing 15.1

Federations versus confederations – the US compared with the EU

In the late eighteenth century, the American colonies, each with its own legislative assembly and governor, which had broken away from Britain, formed themselves into a union whose elected president, congress and courts all exercised general powers across the constituent states boundaries (while they each kept their remaining powers and their constitutions). For their first 70 years (1790–1860), it was unclear whether these included the right to secede from the overall union of the US. The Civil War (1860–1865), when the southern states that tried to secede were decisively defeated, settled the question, defining the federal institutions as those that could decide on membership rather than any constituent state.

In contrast, the EU, still being enlarged through the endorsement of its basic treaties by yet more states, clearly rests on decisions made by its member states to stay in or pull out. In 2016 the UK did just that, pulling out of the EU as such, while retaining looser links with it (as do some other countries).

Groupings where individual states can decide on their own membership are generally thought to have a weaker form of association than the ones where central bodies decide on it, making constituent states rather than the central organization the ultimate representatives of their own population. The distinction is usually expressed as one between federations (no individual right of secession) and confederations. Confusingly, some countries like Switzerland call themselves confederations even if it is inconceivable that any constituent canton would withdraw. In other countries, like Spain or India, it is unclear whether the withdrawal of some regional entity requires a vote of the whole union or just of the area involved.

In a federal union, the federal government has the ultimate decision on whether they can, whereas in a confederation, ultimate decisions about membership rest with the members.

Formal, constitutional differences hardly matter, however, when external and internal pressures to remain together are strong. So many common problems, as well as flows of people, capital, technology and media-transmitted cultural influences, transcend state boundaries that the only way to confront them is to line up with other states, whatever the official name for the arrangement. Secession from such existing groupings, as opposed to accession, is rare. Even where regions of existing, long-established states, like Scotland (within the UK), Catalonia (within Spain) or Quebec (within Canada), threaten to secede, they cite continuing membership of international organizations as a major reason why they would then be viable on their own.

The problems which drive states into broader groupings continue in part to be external – military threats from stronger states on their borders

Terrorism

Violent action taken by one group against the others within a state.

Ideologies

Sets of assumptions about the world leading to certain kinds of political action.

(or at sea). However, the current main threat, **terrorism**, is less external than internal, driven by international ideological appeals to a section of the state population. Often this has originated from a spillover of some national or linguistic group across the political boundaries. This situation has produced the internal cleavages at the basis of many of the political parties examined in Chapter 12. Political frustrations and the desire for secession or union with a neighbouring state have also produced internal violence, however.

With extensive migrations across the whole world, more general **ideologies** – such as communism and militant Islam – have also been carried over formal state frontiers. They have found sufficient supporters inside existing states to produce acts of violence against civilians or even minor wars – sometimes provoking, as intended, counteractions by the army and police which is difficult to distinguish from the original terrorist violence and which may develop into a full-scale civil war.

Besides threats to order and civil rights, however, existing states also confront enormous common problems in the face of a dynamic and changing world economy, totally beyond the control of all but the two or three largest of them. This has also depleted natural resources and produced environmental degradation across continents and oceans. As a partial result, the world temperature is rising, melting polar ice and raising sea levels. Compounding threats which individual states cannot control, rapid travel also fosters the transmission of major diseases and epidemics worldwide.

Such developments may in part be countered or regulated through democratic processes at existing state levels. Solving them at source, however, demands co-ordinated action by a number of states – if not by all states – across the world. The problem is that such action has usually to be initiated by consensual procedures where every member state has a veto. But action is effective only if undertaken by all.

There *is* a proto-world government – the United Nations Organization (UNO) – which has been able to take decisive action to resolve some military conflicts and ameliorate others. It also provides a forum for world discussion and negotiation. It is limited, however, by the fact that five major states have a veto over its actions and in other cases around 200 separate states have to be persuaded to agree on them.

International policymaking between states thus suffers from the very collective action problems which were a driving force in the formation of existing states, when their territories were more autonomous and separate and collective action easier to take within them. The problem is that international action to solve existing problems will produce general benefits from which no one can be excluded. So who is to pay for them if **free-riders** cannot be forced to contribute by some world body?

Free-riders

Participants who take benefits without paying for them.

One current world problem – the immense disparities between states in their population, size, wealth, well-being and military power – may open the way to a partial solution. The ten or so most powerful states in the world – between them controlling more than half its land area anyway – could benefit so disproportionately from a solution to world problems that they might well pay for it themselves regardless of others contributing. It is easier to negotiate and reach binding decisions among a limited number of independent actors. The danger is that problems with collective action again appear even among this limited number if one sticks out against the others. Fewer participants may render problems easier to solve by negotiation. But it provides no guarantee of resolution or ultimate agreement, such as is provided inside existing state structures.

Accountability

The possibility of being punished if those you represent feel you should be punished.

The other political problem is that policymaking between states provides no guarantee of popular, democratic control over what is decided in world negotiations. The policies and policy regimes they agree on, as well as the bodies set up to administer them at international level, may have limited **accountability** even to individual states, let alone to their citizens. Lacking world elections either to a representative assembly or to decide directly on policy, the best that can be hoped for is that the citizens of

---

Briefing 15.2

Wars of the twentieth century, mainly in Europe

The history of the last hundred years has been determined by the experience and consequences of the First (1914–1918) and Second (1939–1945) World Wars, fought mainly in Europe.

They were both part of a continuing conflict in which a recently united and technologically advanced Germany sought to establish its military supremacy in Europe, in opposition to the traditionally dominant but declining France, Britain and Russia. In both cases, Britain was able to draw in the US to swing the outcome against Germany. The wars were complicated in that both caused horrific casualties (20 million in each case) and left a legacy of internal and territorial disputes. These produced a series of smaller wars and resulted in genocidal dictators being installed in Germany and Russia. The Second World War was more of a total world war than the First World War. Japan initiated a parallel war in East Asia and the Pacific, mainly against China and the US. It also took over European colonies in the area. This stimulated national movements which set up independent regimes there in the immediate post-war period. In China, the Communist Party established a one-party state which continued to flourish while Japan was occupied and westernized by the US.

In Europe, Germany was divided between a new Federal Republic allied to the US and an Eastern area dominated by Russia (then called the Soviet Union). Russia also dominated the other countries of Central and Eastern Europe. From 1948 to 1989 international policies were shaped by the Cold War, a military confrontation between Russia and NATO, a military alliance of largely Western European countries largely directed by the US. The Cold War ended when Russia, heading in a more democratic direction internally, allowed the countries it had dominated to go their own way, including those previously inside the Soviet Union itself. Meanwhile, France and Germany took the lead in forming the EU, designed to prevent them from ever going to war with each other again.

one or two more powerful states, which happen to be democracies, may exert disproportionate influence. But this in itself raises questions about popular preferences being weighted equally across the world, as would be required by democratic guarantees.

So far are world structures from even approximating to a recognizable state, let alone a democracy, that it may seem unrealistic even to consider the possibility. At continental rather than world level, however, developments do seem to be proceeding (slowly and with setbacks) in this direction. This is particularly true of Europe, the main cockpit of the two major world wars of the last century.

Briefing 15.3

The EU and its development

The EU was originally formed to unite the West European countries most seriously affected by the Second World War (France, Germany, the Netherlands, Belgium, Luxembourg and Italy) to guarantee they would never attack each other again. Political union was to be achieved in stages, first by integrating their national economies and trade. Increasing economic and social integration would ultimately create a need for international institutions to direct them, which would then form the basis for a political union (also covering defence). The economic success of the EU in the 1960s and 1970s made it attractive for Mediterranean, Scandinavian and, after 1990, Eastern European countries to join, as did Ireland and the UK (Britain).

In the meantime, central institutions developed at Brussels in Belgium: the Commission of national nominees to run everyday business; the European Court of Justice to adjudicate European legislative and citizen rights on appeal from national courts; and, more important from a political point of view, the EU Parliament, with increasing powers over the Commission. This was directly elected in elections across all member states and united members in multinational party family groupings, principally socialist, Christian and liberal. Overall policy, however, was still decided by a council of ministers from each member state, the most important being the European Council of National Presidents and Prime Ministers (now 27 in number).

The UK generally opposed closer political union but was the prime force in creating a single market with free movement of goods, capital and labour internally to supplement the original customs union, which had imposed common tariffs and controls over all EU imports.

The impact of these changes on economic and social life, particularly from immigration and free movement of individuals within the single market, stimulated resentment against the increasingly active EU institutions within member states – particularly in Britain, where governments were opposed to closer union anyway. This resulted in the UK formally withdrawing from the EU in 2019. This cleared the way for closer union among the remaining members, covering most of the European Continent from the Atlantic Ocean to the Black Sea, and the Baltic Sea to the Mediterranean Sea – a vast area which increasingly acts together like a united federal state.

FIGURE 15.1 Map of Europe showing EU member states and affiliates

Source: www.nationsonline.org/oneworld/europe_map.htm

The EU, as Figure 15.1 shows, has succeeded in creating state-like structures across most of the continent. These include a directly elected parliament, with considerable powers, including the approval of a government (the European Commission). It remains true, however, even in the EU, that any major initiative or crisis has to be handled by interstate negotiation, with each member having a veto. Europe has gone further than any other world region in developing international democracy and policymaking. Criticism of its continuing 'democratic deficit', however, shows how hard it is to achieve guarantees of correspondence between popular preferences and public policy at international level. On the other hand, its very emergence, and its creation of directly elected institutions, shows it might not be impossible either.

We pursue all these themes in this chapter, starting from the traditional 'hard-shelled' state setup; seeing how globalization has undermined this; and examining the response this calls for on the part of both traditional states and the international alliances and groupings to which they now belong. An important theme throughout the discussion is whether world democracy – or even world government – is emerging. Can such a possibility even be envisaged where states, both democratic and distinctly undemocratic, pursue their own foreign policies and handle their collective concerns through a series of multilateral negotiations which any one of them can block? (So no wonder many global problems go unresolved!)

Democracy

A regime with a guaranteed connection between public policy and popular preferences for it.

Three contemporary developments give grounds for thinking that a world **democracy** (or at least a partial form of democracy – a **republic**) may emerge from this situation. First, the leading world power – the US – is a democracy, as are the majority of leading states in the world. The media, communications and business arrangements that these states promote have inbuilt democratic features stressing above all free individual interactions and choice. Even controlling monolithic authoritarian regimes like China have had to introduce previously undreamt-of individual freedoms in order to benefit from new economic developments.

Republic

A regime where policy outcomes are decided between institutions rather than by popular voting.

Second, we have in the UN a set of institutions which could serve as a more integrated world government, within which state voting rights could be gradually transferred to individual citizens. As 'party families' are based on universal ideologies, they could take on the task of mobilizing and framing popular policy preferences across the world. Worldwide parties would facilitate direct individual voting to express and implement popular preferences universally.

Third, the EU provides a practical example of how international, broadly democratic institutions could evolve and bring together previously

---

Briefing 15.4

Leading world countries and their regimes

At the international level, countries and states are often described as 'powers', because size and force are so important in intergovernmental negotiations and relationships (sometimes through direct military action and wars). The leading state in the world because of its size, wealth, technological and economic development and military – is the US – a democracy, but it is closely followed by China, a single-party regime, and Russia, a recent and highly imperfect democracy. The EU is increasingly emerging as a power in the world, with its policy largely decided by agreement between two traditional states, France and Germany. Democracy is a condition of membership in the EU, so three out of four of the leading players in the world have largely democratic political arrangements ('regimes'). The second ranking 'tier' of countries in terms of current or potential influence are all democracies. These include the UK and Japan, both advanced countries technologically, with an effective military and sizeable populations, and India and Brazil, with large landmasses and populations but with major social and economic problems internally which impede international action. At the international level, therefore, almost all the most influential states are democratic. Many of the remaining ones are not, however, and those that are democratic are unstable and susceptible to military or other takeovers.

Briefing 15.5

Technological developments, individual freedoms and democracy

The major world development since 1950, producing immense changes in all areas of life across the world, has been the development of electronic technology, particularly of computer-based communications. Every individual can own a mobile telephone transmitting pictures and words through national and international hubs and platforms. These are difficult even for authoritarian regimes to control, and most democracies do not even try.

This has two major consequences. On the one hand, it enables individuals to express ideas and concert their actions more freely, facilitating democratic group action and discussion. On the other hand, it also facilitates spoiling and manipulative action by anti-democratic forces through their ability to spread fake news and propaganda anywhere in the world without being traced. Political parties and other groups often do this in attempts to influence their own national elections. But foreign governments can also intervene and, if they're really hostile, interfere with computer-controlled data banks or industrial activities (cyber warfare). Non-democratic regimes may also use such manipulative tactics for their own purposes to limit any demand for democratic freedom. Internally, on balance, technological and communications developments probably increase the scope for the free discussion necessary for democracy – particularly since technological development also depends on an ability to generate and develop new ideas freely. But like most new developments, communications technology also creates changes and threats, which need to be regulated and controlled to ensure proper democratic functioning. These include regulation of the multinational companies funding the new technology and the communication 'platforms' or hubs they provide.

warring nation states as an effective way to tackle regional and ultimately global problems.

This chapter accordingly starts with a description of the traditional system of 'hard-shelled' territorial states which developed over the nineteenth century and the first half of the twentieth century, until they produced problems which could only be met by international action. The second section goes into the processes of globalization, which have eroded traditional boundaries and jurisdictions to produce problems unresolvable at state or even federation level – suggesting that the only solution lies in something resembling world government.

This raises questions, the first of which (discussed in the concluding sections of the chapter) is, can a world government be a democratic government? A further question is, what role can existing state processes, particularly democratic ones, have when the major dynamic influences on their economy and society pass beyond their control? This question is particularly pertinent since they have a major challenger in the form of the multinational corporations operating in the global economy, who seem quite capable of taking on any of the existing democratic state governments and manipulating their policies to satisfy their own interests. But we conclude that ultimate power still lies with traditional democratic states if they wish to exert it. The reason lies in some of their features, which we now examine.

Key points in this discussion are thus:

- The fact that public goods and services must be provided universally.
- This creates the need to force individuals and corporate bodies to contribute towards their cost.
- The traditional role of the state in enforcing payments to pay for the policies which decide on and provide public goods.
- The need for democracy to ensure that such policies are what citizens actually want.
- How globalization raises precisely these problems at the international level, across the boundaries of existing states.

The traditional state system

There are precursors to contemporary state institutions to be found in the city states and empires of the ancient and medieval worlds. These came in the shape of territorial units with an army, bureaucracy, organized religion and some kind of ruler or governing council. These took varying forms but were recognizable forerunners of the institutions at the core of the early modern state.

This developed in Europe during the seventeenth and eighteenth centuries, especially in terms of a 'hard shell' of fortifications and defences around each state territory, safeguarding the 'sovereignty' of its rulers. Such entities provided a springboard for the emergence of the fully fledged nation states of the modern period, from around 1815 to 1940. The greatest changes compared to earlier periods were internal, consolidating – for the time at least – state independence, autonomy, self-sufficiency and, in some cases, democracy.

The most dynamic influence on state development was nationalism, in the sense of a spreading belief that each cultural and (above all) linguistic group ought to have its own state ruling its own territory. This proved disruptive for old multicultural empires like the Austrian and Ottoman (Turkish) Empires in Central and Eastern Europe, which had relied on religion as a binding force. Covering many different language areas, they began to break up. On the other hand, Germans and Italians came together in their own 'nation states', which gained internal coherence and support from promoting state nationalism – often against internationalist ideologies such as socialism.

Nationalism could, of course, also undermine states by prompting territorially concentrated linguistic and religious minorities to break away,

Briefing 15.6

Nationalism and the nation state

Most of the territorial groupings of the eighteenth century brought together different areas often speaking different dialects or languages and with different histories and/or cultural traditions. Sometimes they had been independent themselves before being absorbed into the larger grouping. The ideology and beliefs which held disparate areas together were more religious than linguistic. In the nineteenth century, linguistic and cultural ties began to be stressed equally or more strongly than religious ones, giving rise to a new ideology: nationalism. This centred on the belief that states had a mission to promote and defend their own culture and language rather than tolerate diversity within their borders. This had two consequences. First, it led existing states to seek to impose the majority language on everyone, principally through universal compulsory education and by using it exclusively in politics and administration. Second, minority groups mobilized against such assimilation and tried to create state structures to promote and defend their own language and culture. These movements gave rise to the minority ethnic parties within states, which are considered in Chapter 12. Sometimes these succeeded in creating their own political structures, either as a region within an existing state or as an independent state in its own right – often after violence or civil war. Though states are often called nation states, implying internal linguistic and cultural homogeny, this ignores their internal diversity and tensions due to such cleavages.

following the logic of expressing themselves through their own political institutions. A solution was to promote consistency between language and state by insisting on use of the majority language at all levels, in administration and media and above all in universal education, so that the entire population ended up reading and speaking it while minority languages died out (a policy also followed in countries of European settlement in Africa, the Americas and Australasia).

In elevating the political importance of the 'nation', governments put themselves under a certain obligation to give 'their' people a political voice. How could it be important for a 'people' to have their own political institutions if they could not influence the policies these were making for them? Nationalism thus went hand in hand with some degree of democratization. This led to new state institutions such as elected parliaments being grafted on to the traditional bureaucracy and army. However, it was rare to have these under total democratic control.

Nation states were also strengthened by technological developments, which governments fostered for military as well as purely economic reasons. Railways and roads were essential in mobilizing armies as well as transporting goods. Coal and steel were necessary for manufacturing weapons and ships, as to a lesser extent were textiles for uniforms and tents. Telegraphs and telephones facilitated military communications. Government sponsorship and subsidies for all these developments meant

Briefing 15.7

Protection as a means of fostering nation-state economies

The First Industrial Revolution, centred on Britain and based on coal and steam power, also transformed world communications and trade through railways and steamships. Cheap mass manufactures were carried through the world, driving out local goods produced for local markets.

These developments also had political implications, since reduced local economies meant smaller state revenues and left governments dependent on foreign imports for their military needs. From about 1850, therefore, the more technologically developed states, particularly the US, Germany and France, started to impose heavy import charges on British goods that they could produce themselves and encouraged other developments internally (roads, canals and shipbuilding), plus the new chemical technologies. Such policies, designed to project, regulate and develop home markets and manufacturing, were collectively described as protectionism. By limiting external competition, protectionism increased costs for the general population. But it also guaranteed employment and enabled governments to bring together banks and industry to foster long-term planning for economic development.

that the First Industrial Revolution, based on steam and heavy industry, developed interlocking activities inside existing states, making them to some extent autonomous in economic and political terms.

War was always the ultimate tactic that militaristic states had to deploy against each other. Peace was maintained in Europe over most of the nineteenth century, however, by an **equilibrium** between states known as the balance of power. When one of the major states seemed likely to become more powerful, the others started to gang up against it, thus counteracting its increased strength and forcing it to act in a more moderate way, even towards weaker neighbours.

Equilibrium

A political process that tends towards the same outcome over time.

In practice maintaining the balance of power was helped by other developments. The first was the exposure of most of the world to European conquest and colonization, which superior weapons and organization made possible. This made takeovers of underdeveloped areas around the world a more attractive option for most states than attacking well-armed neighbours. The second was the fact that internal consolidation, including institutional modernization, was more of a preoccupation for many states than external expansion inside Europe, at least until late into the nineteenth century.

The balance of power was, however, upset by German reunification and rapid industrial development, which rendered Germany increasingly stronger than counter-combinations of other states. Instead of shifting alliances, maintaining an international balance, states divided between a stronger

German-based, permanent alliance and a weaker lineup of the remaining states. The two alliances confronted each other in a series of territorial disputes and eventually drifted into two world (though mainly European) wars. The second of these (1939–45) can be regarded as a continuation of the first (1914–18), with 20 years of instability in between. Germany was decisively defeated in both, owing mostly to its overextending the conflict into Russia and the intervention of the US against it in Europe.

Permanent interstate groupings and hegemonies

The world wars were both the climax and ruin of the traditional state system in which hard-shelled states mobilized their armies and defended their own frontiers with help from shifting allies. By the middle of the twentieth century, technological advances in the form of tanks, airplanes and missiles had rendered fixed territorial defences irrelevant and created a war of movement over vast distances, with occupation and resistance within overturned states internationally co-ordinated.

The obsolescence of traditional state barriers at all levels – military, political, economic and psychological – created a new set of relationships

---

Briefing 15.8

The Cold War (1948–1989)

The 'Cold War' is the term used to describe the confrontation between the Soviet Union (USSR) – that is Russia with the territories it incorporated around its borders – and the US. Both were equipped with weapons and delivery systems capable of destroying the other, and both were supported by alliances of other states. In the US case, this was NATO, grouping most states of North America, Western Europe and the Northern Mediterranean, plus West Germany. In the Soviet case, it was the Warsaw Pact, grouping the Central and Eastern European states. NATO mostly consisted of democracies and the Warsaw Pact of communist party–dominated regimes. Thus, Alliance membership produced pressures towards having a particular kind of political regime internally.

Despite recurrent crises and confrontations, the prospect of 'mutually assured destruction' through nuclear and chemical war induced both sides to keep the peace, though they each backed opposing sides in wars elsewhere. The Cold War ended in the 1980s as the Soviet Union increasingly failed to keep up with the US technologically and moved towards a more open political system internally. In the process, it withdrew from Central and Eastern Europe and allowed its own fringe territories to secede. US failure to consult with the reformed Russia from 1990 to 2010 led to a more assertive foreign policy on its part. Increasing confrontations resulting from this led to the possibility of a new Cold War, with China emerging as a third international player.

after 1950. The US emerged as the leading state throughout the world – militarily, technologically, culturally and economically. It was challenged only by Russia, which, however, collapsed under the strain of the unequal competition in the 1980s and substituted a limited form of democracy for its former one-party communist rule. Only China, under the latter system, remained a rival, boosted by phenomenal technological development and economic growth – all based, however, on American models and inventions.

In a bipolar world, where war could be carried on by nuclear missiles and automated planes patrolling states thousands of miles away, traditional state boundaries were increasingly eroded. 'Mutually assured destruction' by each other's weapons prevented large-scale confrontations between the superpowers. Their pursuit of relative advantages tended rather to focus on backing one side or another in proxy wars on their borders or in civil wars within underdeveloped countries. Instead of wars between states, conflicts were increasingly carried on inside them, rendering the distinction between external and internal security meaningless. Mass migration from less-developed countries to the richer ones and the spread of sometimes violent international ideologies such as left socialism, the new right and militant Islam also shifted the focus of security from outside to inside traditional states.

The response of smaller (and even medium-sized) states was to group together in sometimes overlapping alliances to tackle common problems – not only of physical security but also of economic reconstruction and

Briefing 15.9

International political ideologies in the twenty-first century

One reason why states are increasingly 'permeable' across their territorial boundaries is the mobilization of different groupings within their population behind different 'ideologies' (theories about the way society and the world work) which they have in common with similar groupings in other states. We have already seen how this works out in political parties and party families. Internationally, however, it may lead opposition groups within one country to line up with the government of another; with other opposition groups within it; or with non-state organizations which operate across many countries. Sometimes these are peaceful, as is the case with ecological movements seeking to protect the environment and prevent climate change, or with Zionist groups defending Jews and supporting Israel. Sometimes they advocate violence and practice terrorism, as with militant Islamic groups advocating holy war against non-believers. Sometimes the same ideology may support both peaceful and violent actions within and across countries (Marxism and socialism, or nationalism in various forms). In any case, such movements spread so easily across the state boundaries that they render them increasingly irrelevant and shift the focus even of national politics to the international level.

development after the world wars and increasingly of international regulation and responses to world developments. Western democracies were largely grouped within a US-led alliance, NATO, and in the EU, which brought together Western and Central Europe in an increasingly federal arrangement.

This international system of interlocking alliances was different from the 'hard-shelled' state system which preceded it. However, the 'soft-shelled' states of the modern era were far from being reduced to practical insignificance. The policies they administered, though heavily influenced by outside developments, were still the ones of most significance to their citizens, particularly in the areas of health, well-being and culture.

Most important from the viewpoint of translating popular preferences into policy was the fact that traditional states were the major practitioners of democratic decision-making. International organizations, with the important exception of the EU, were answerable only to their state members – sometimes only to their stronger ones. Even the EU, with an influential parliament elected directly by citizens across the continent, still had mostly state-based decision-making centred increasingly on German initiatives and vetoes. This substantially increased its 'democratic deficit' even if it was the most democratic by far of international organizations.

While not the sole regulator of life within their borders, traditional state democracies remained the most important decision makers if they cared to use their powers. How they might do so remains controversial between different ideologies of right and left. Before coming to these, however, we need to examine the overall context in which they find themselves. This is shaped above all by the processes summarized as globalization, which we examine in the next section.

Globalization and the traditional state

Globalization is a summary term for the interrelated developments which have transformed life from the 1990s onwards, principally in terms of a growing interdependency between all areas of the world. What goes on in the remotest regions now has an effect everywhere and is recognized and reported as having an effect almost immediately, owing to developments in public and private communication.

Trends towards greater world interdependency have of course been evident for centuries as trade routes developed and colonial empires sprang up. Particularly with nineteenth century industrialization, raw materials were sought all around the world and technology exported in exchange. However, the modern development of electronic communications and automation – less and less dependent on land-based physical installations – has facilitated instantaneous interaction across the globe, which has played out in largely in economic and political terms.

On the economic side, autonomous national and regional economies have been swallowed up in a unified global one. National governments

Briefing 15.10

Colonial empires and settlements

Empires large and small have always existed, in the sense of one territorial group expanding and encompassing other groups and areas on its borders. Many modern states originate in this way. Some were so successful militarily, however, that they spread over continents and across seas to a quite colossal size, joining up many areas and cultures under one central authority.

The development of naval technology enabled West European countries to conquer large areas of the world, physically separated from each other by the oceans. The British Empire of the 1920s 'on which the sun never sets' was the major example. In Africa, the Middle East and India, huge areas were brought together and subjected to British administration. In others that were more thinly populated, the native population was largely exterminated and the land settled by Europeans (e.g. Canada and Australia).

To avoid the kind of conflict which had developed with colonies in the Americas, which produced the independent US and in the case of Spain the Latin American Republics, British governments granted independence to their colonies of European settlement immediately any significant support for autonomy emerged. In the 20 years after the Second World War, a weakened Britain also got out of the non-European colonies – mostly peacefully and leaving friendly governments behind. The Netherlands, France and Portugal became entangled in debilitating colonial wars, which ended up with independence for the native peoples.

Land-based empires had also developed in parallel to the sea-based ones, in the case particularly of the US, Russia and China. Such expansion usually involved parallel processes of settlement with incorporation of subject peoples – a continuing process that has gone on until the present day (though, as noted, Russia has conceded independence to many territories around its fringes, both in Europe and Central Asia). Since they cover such a large area, these three countries have evolved into the super states of the modern world, in contrast to the countries with sea-going empires. The exception is Turkey, which ruled the Middle East and the Balkans up to the First World War and whose dissolution has been more like that of the sea-borne empires.

may remain the largest economic actors inside countries. But the dynamic influences producing innovations and development come from outside, from a global economy centred on the US – but with many other protagonists.

Organizing and directing flows of trade and technology are multinational corporations ('multinationals') operating across the world and largely unaccountable to any national government. In terms of size and assets, indeed, they are bigger than most governments and well able to exert political influence (through controlling television and newspaper outlets, for example, not to speak of financing political parties).

Like other businesses, multinationals are dedicated to pursuing profits for their international shareholders – who, however, have little control of the company and little desire to exert it, provided that profits continue. Decisions affecting billions of investors, producers, consumers and less direct 'stakeholders' tend thus to be made by a narrow unaccountable group sitting at the top of a hierarchical organization. Technology businesses keen on innovation encourage active participation of their employees in the economic activities of the company. But this does not extend to control of their wider political or social impact. Multinationals, as largely economic entities, tend to be insensitive to these anyway, unless they stand in the way of their expansion and development.

These processes have had a generally positive impact in fuelling growth in many world regions, providing employment and income and even leading in some contexts to an improvement in health, safety and working conditions. The multinationals' need for predictability and stability in business dealings have also been found to reduce corruption and obvious political misconduct by state governments.

However, within democratic states, the more general political accountability of governments to citizens has decreased. This is because global 'economic imperatives' are often used by politicians to justify unpopular domestic measures like 'austerity' (i.e. cutting public budgets and services) – which are often demanded by international banks and lending organizations such as the International Monetary Fund (IMF) and the World Bank. The growth of such financial organizations, beyond the control of any one state, is another aspect of globalization. The most important social effect of multinational activity has been the increase in inequality, which has now reached staggering proportions. This shows up in the disparity of income and wealth between nations and world regions, where it has exacerbated the earlier contrast between the 'developed' countries, in Europe, North America and Australasia, and the rest of the world.

More obviously associated with multinational activities and globalization, however, is increasing inequality within countries, where it is common for the top 1% of the population to own as much wealth as the poorest 50%! Globalization has spread inequality for several reasons. The first has to do with the link between globalization and higher levels of unemployment. In richer states, labour is relatively expensive, so geographically mobile global firms are likely to relocate and hire cheaper labour elsewhere. The large transnational corporations that characterize the contemporary global economy can also realize considerable economies of scale, thus reducing staffing needs. Moreover, large corporations have the ability to develop technological solutions to many tasks that would otherwise have been done manually. This leads to machines replacing human labour in many areas of manufacturing and production. Unskilled workers, in particular, are marginalized. Globalization also fuels income inequality. Anyone with a good idea can sell to millions of customers in a globalized marketplace. Thus, successful businesses make more out of their innovations than was possible in the past, generating a super class of extremely wealthy people.

The opening up of markets and the computer revolution have, it is true, created considerable opportunities for the less-developed world in the new knowledge economy. At the same time, new opportunities for generating profits have consolidated the wealth of the richest, exacerbating levels of inequality between and within individual societies. The increasing differential between higher returns on capital investment and lower returns on labour in a globalized world also widens the gaps between rich and poor. This effect is intensified further when, within states, corporation tax is kept low and taxes on labour and consumption rise. These are all 'objective' effects stemming from the way a global economy has to organize itself to get the best return on investments. They are, however, also promoted by the politico-economic manoeuvres of multinationals. These take advantage of their global spread to store money and assets in states with lax regulation and low taxes. In many cases, these are tiny states whose main revenue comes from hosting secretive banks which allow firms to avoid tax payments in the large countries where they actually do their business.

These countries themselves are also responsible for inequalities by maintaining a legal system which facilitates tax avoidance by rich individuals and corporations. A refusal on the part of state governments to tax multinational profits made in their country, in order to attract their investments, has produced budget deficits. Instead of taxing multinational profits, such deficits tend to be tackled by raising levels of individual taxation and cutting public services for the citizens. One of the effects is growing inequality not just in wealth but in living conditions between rich and poor.

The reasons for democratic inertia in response to this 'fiscal crisis of the state' (and of many of its citizens) are twofold. First, political lobbying by multinationals and their supporters stresses their ability to move out of any country which taxes them effectively, in favour of countries which impose low rates of tax or none at all. This argument is often used by democratic politicians to persuade electors that the only alternative to tolerating multinational privileges is a national economic crisis and massive unemployment.

In point of fact, there is little economic evidence for the idea that multinationals base decisions about where to operate on low rates of tax. Infrastructure, education, political stability and an absence of corruption are all more important reasons – as well as the location of the natural resources they extract or need. It is also unlikely that they would abandon their largest markets in favour of mini-states offering only low taxes as an inducement.

Secondly, arguments against effective taxation have a strong internal buttress within traditional states in the ideology of neo-liberalism and of the parties (conservatives and liberals) supporting it. This ideology argues against taxation on the grounds that all money which goes to governments to pay for universal services and public goods removes choice from consumers and investment from business. Taxes and public spending should thus be kept as low as possible to maximize choice and investment. Ultimately, these will stimulate demand within a country and (by providing money for innovation) also encourage flexible and innovative ways of meeting it. In turn, this will generate more employment and wealth and thus increased demand, in a self-generating virtuous circle. This will be cut if governments increase public goods and services and raise taxes to pay for them.

Such an argument rests heavily on the assumption that there *is* an autonomous state economy within the traditional territorial boundaries which can be stimulated (or depressed) by government action. This goes against the points made above about globalization. The dynamic forces in any national economy are now global – to the extent that national action, particularly by governments, has little long-term effect on economic activity.

As against neo-liberalism, it could be argued therefore that the main policy mission for state governments at the present time is to protect their citizens against the vagaries of the global economy. They can do this by providing reasonable health and social care, paid for – without raising taxes on individuals – by dealing with tax avoidance, particularly on the part of multinationals. Are traditional state governments strong enough to deal with multinational free-riding however, within the bounds of democratic rule? Or is world government – and world democracy – the only answer? These are, however, distant and possibly unrealizable alternatives, while current problems accumulate in the here and now. We deal with political possibilities in the concluding sections of the chapter.

National policymaking under globalization

The traditional and new 'nation states' – most of them at least – are the main havens of democracy in the modern world. But globalization, in terms both of its external and internal effects, has a negative impact on country democracies. No longer do they have full control over what is going on in their own territory. Multinational decision-making proceeds secretively inside the corporation itself, with minimal consultation. Externally, one government can be played off against another with threats of relocation – which also reduce possibilities for international regulation and control.

The prospects for individual action by each state government are also diminished by the fact that they are often dominated by political parties subscribing to a neo-liberal ideology of non-interference with business. This is certainly opposed by other parties which put cultural or welfare considerations above presumed economic advantages (cf. Table 6.6 and Chapter 12 on parties' basic issue concerns). However, there is no guarantee that these other parties will attract the plurality vote in general elections or dominate or control governments. The two global economic crises of the 1970s and 2008 seem indeed to have strengthened the parties favouring business freedom and reduced social care, as popular concern shifted to immediate job prospects. Most governments in the established

Briefing 15.11

The oil crisis of the 1970s and financial crash of 2008

The global economy into which countries are increasingly integrated spreads the effects of 'booms and busts' across all of them. The two world crises with most extensive effects occurred with 25 years of world prosperity and economic growth between them. In the 1970s, the Muslim countries of the Middle East, which produced most of the world's oil, restricted their production in protest against Western (largely American) support for Israel against the Arabs expropriated by (largely European) Jewish settlement. This vastly increased the price of oil, essential for world production and trade. Other oil-producing countries joined to form OPEC (Organization of the Petroleum Exporting Countries), which left production low and prices high. A long slowdown in world economic activity followed, until the more efficient use of oil and discoveries elsewhere eased the situation for oil users.

In the following world boom, banks and lenders of capital increasingly operated as multinational firms on a world basis, buying and selling business shares with borrowed money in the confidence that they could sell them on to make a quick profit. When market confidence collapsed in 2008, some banks also collapsed. But most were bailed out by their national governments in the belief that their failure would cripple economic activity in the country. Banks were given massive loans to counter their losses and stimulate them to lend again. This was paid for by cutting public goods and services over a 15-year period after each boom.

democracies seem to have bought the argument that jobs can be provided only by attracting multinational investment through lax regulations and cutting taxes and public services.

The weakness of this reaction lies in the assumption that the national economy *can* be stimulated independently of the global one. Increasing globalization will surely show that this is wrong. Policy also bases itself on the idea that the national government is a significant player in the global arena, which (except for the US, China, Russia and possibly Germany) is also wrong. Once democratic electorates realize that the actions of their state government are only marginal to the globalized economic activity going on in their country, their concerns may well shift to safeguarding themselves against its ups and downs. Securing citizen well-being and freeing it from the vagaries of market-driven employment was the step which consolidated democracy in many states in the immediate aftermath of the Second World War (1945–1980).

The problem facing traditional states under globalization, however, is that their tax base has shrunk (at least proportional to needs) as multinational business profits are sent elsewhere to be left untaxed. The obvious solution, examined in the next section of this chapter, is to reach an international agreement on taxing them. However, this encounters the familiar problem of getting agreement on collective action between something

Briefing 15.12

Building the post-war welfare state (1945–1980)

The First World War, the Second World War and the period of economic depression and high employment between them led to economic and social interventions by post-war Western government, to protect their citizens' living conditions and general health and well-being. Massive investment in low rent public housing were accompanied by comprehensive health services for individuals and guaranteed monthly payments to them when unemployed, sick or old. Support while being educated and free education at all levels were also thrown in. These arrangements were collectively termed the welfare state, to underline traditional states' expansion of their activities and responsibilities to most aspects of individual well-being. These were cut back under the impact of world economic crises and neo-liberalism from 1980 onwards.

like 200 states, with no one authority to enforce the rules. Small states, who gain much of their revenue from banks and multinationals avoiding national taxation elsewhere, will impede government action by the larger states, which lose out. Countries where multinationals operate are likely to be pressured to delay action.

In a situation of international deadlock, there does, however, seem reasonable latitude for national democracies to tax all profits made on their territory whether by purely national or by multinational firms. This would increase the resources available for government action on behalf of the citizens without imposing any additional tax burden on them. Framing issues in this way shows that the popular preferences for more services and reduced individual taxation are not unrealistic. The main barriers to doing so are political and ideological: a belief that it is in some sense wrong to tax efficiently. As argued above, national levels of taxation are a minor consideration for major multinationals deciding where to locate. Much more cogent are education, research, infrastructure, (lack of) corruption, stability and order – as well of course as the presence of raw materials like oil deposits and of markets.

In the absence of decisive international action, therefore, party democracy can provide its own remedies at the level of traditional state structures. There are, however, problems other than multinational taxation and domestic well-being which can only be solved by international action. Can that have a democratic basis? We go on to this question in the next section.

Democracy at world level

Above the country level, political action has generally to be negotiated between individual state governments, where each has a potential veto.

The great exception is the EU – the European Union of 27 states covering Western, Central and parts of Eastern Europe and – the European Union of the Balkans. The European Parliament is directly elected by citizens across all member states. Parties of the traditional families (Chapter 12) are active in elections and in the European Parliament itself, organizing its business. This involves quite extensive powers of veto and approval of personnel and policy.

The main limitation is, however, that these powers are reactive – reviewing other bodies' nominations and policy initiatives. This is of course true of parliaments in relation to governments in the traditional states as well. However, inside traditional states, the party balance – either in terms of votes in elections or seats in parliament – does help determine what president and/or government will make policy. In the case of the EU Commission, members are nominated by the member states even if approved by parliament. Also, the main decision-making body is the European Council, composed of the heads of member governments (or councils of their government ministers in specialized areas).

It is easy to see how, over time, the EU might develop into a European federal state. It already has all the institutional bases for this (Figure 15.2) and only needs to extend parliamentary powers to transform European elections into contests covering all-European questions (rather than a series of country-by-country contests fought on national issues). The European Commission could then become a government wholly appointed by – and subject to votes in – the European Parliament. The European Council could then become an upper house of parliament representing the member states (like the German Bundesrat or the US Senate). The US indeed was a precursor in uniting independent states under such a federal constitution two centuries ago. However, these states had a culture and languages in common, which provided a solid basis for political union. The EU, bringing together many states mostly with their own language, provides a more relevant modern example of how a federal democracy could be created out of previously existing, and often warring, 'nation states'.

Even the EU, however, operates simply as one state among others in the international negotiations where it has authority. Mostly, international problems are the subject of negotiations between states, rarely ratified by their citizens and only slightly more frequently by their parliaments. It is true that the UNO (United Nations Organization) and its specialized agencies provide an institutional venue for such negotiations with a secretariat and arbitrators and negotiators. However, all matters are decided by state by state voting, and implementing resolutions is difficult or nonexistent except where all agree. Matters are further compounded by the fact that the supreme UN executive – the Security Council – has five permanent members (the US, Russia, China, the UK and France) any of which can veto any action.

The other factor affecting interstate agreement is the overwhelming influence of the US on world negotiations (though frequently challenged by China and Russia). US policy is ultimately laid down by elected politicians and parties, so must be regarded as corresponding to the popular will of a substantial slice of the world population. In this highly indirect way,

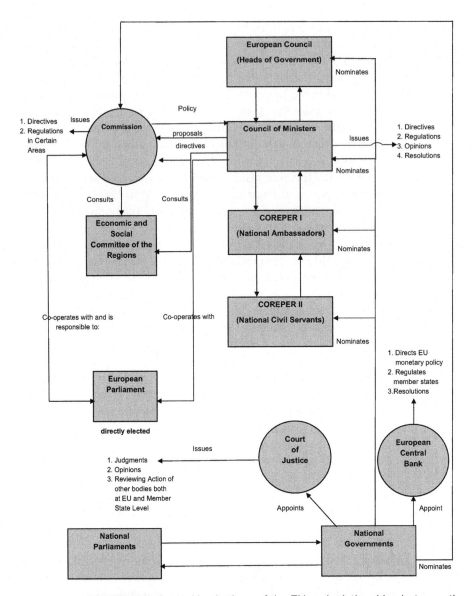

FIGURE 15.2 Central institutions of the EU and relationships between them

Notes: The figure charts the main central bodies of the EU – the Commission and the European Parliament, on the one hand, which act like member state governments and parliaments on a short-term basis, in parallel with a set of bodies bringing together ministers and administrators of member states, which decide on long-term policy. These are the Council of (relevant) Ministers in Member Governments and COREPER (the Council of Permanent Representatives), bringing together national ambassadors. Most important is the European Council, consisting of the 27 member state presidents and prime ministers, which makes the final decisions on long-term policy.

popular opinion does get some chance to influence world policy. And to the extent that other democracies such as India, France and the UK have influence, one could say the same for them. It is also true that most of the large states in the world and more than half of all states are democracies. So popular opinion there has some chance of being translated into global policy.

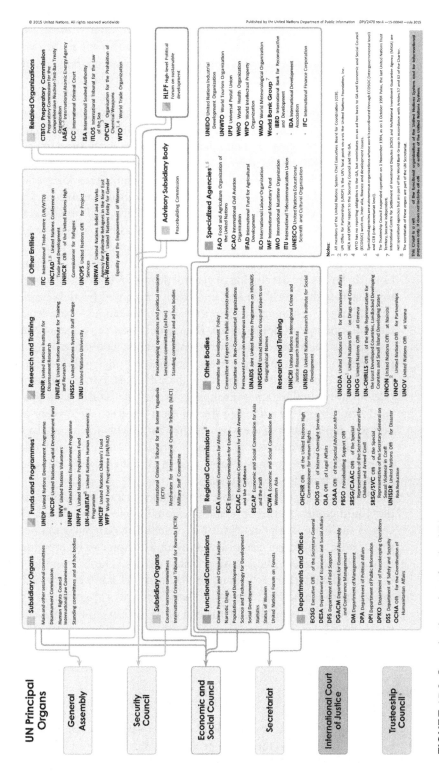

FIGURE 15.3 Organization chart for the UN

However, these are only the first stirrings of popular influence in world affairs and far from the way democracy works within traditional states. There is no voting equality, for example. Even in diluted form, American citizens have much more influence over world affairs through their vote than citizens of other democracies. Moreover, there is no guarantee that world policy on various problems will conform to world public opinion. It is even difficult to know what that is, given the absence of an election or party framework within which to express it. World surveys, properly designed, may give some indication. As yet, however, they are not conducted regularly and would be blocked or manipulated in the more authoritarian countries.

On the positive side, there are today a set of world institutions (Figure 15.3) which constitute an agreed venue for interstate negotiations and sometimes make effective policy decisions on pressing problems. These are usually problems of great public concern and practical impact across the world, and UN action can often be a basis for reaching agreement. As world problems mount and the action to be undertaken and its practical impact are increasingly debated at world level, there are more interstate negotiations. So habits are developing of general debate and discussion on common topics across the world. This is immensely facilitated by globalization and particularly by instantaneous electronic communications – between individuals and opinion groupings rather than simply between governments.

There is therefore an incipient world public opinion emerging. This provides a basis for clear preference formation, once political parties are in place to mobilize and **frame** it on shared issues. Parties themselves fall into broadly similar family groupings across the world. This provides a worldwide frame of reference for political choices. Were there a world political arena which made it worthwhile for worldwide parties to operate (by forming a government or electing a president, for example), one could expect them to perform the same role in world elections that they have assumed in traditional democracies.

Framing
Defining the possible courses of action to be considered on an issue.

The EU is a practical example of how nation-state institutions and parties could come together in a supranational democracy (though the process is far from complete). India, in somewhat different circumstances, shows how a common electorate of about a billion can be presented with reasonably coherent choices by political parties. The UN and its institutions are already there to provide an institutional framework which could evolve in a democratic direction. Democratic world government is not with us yet. But it could be by the end of the century, on a basis similar to the traditional state democracies we have examined in most of this book.

End-summary

This chapter has investigated democracy at state and interstate levels in terms of its ability to tackle the problems produced by a global economy. These are twofold. On the one hand, there are domestic problems caused by world economic fluctuations beyond any one actor's control – the defining feature of a free market. These create a need to safeguard citizens by providing them with support services where necessary. A second is the ability of multinational corporations to avoid paying domestic taxes, which has undermined the traditional state's ability to pay for public goods.

There is, however, no 'objective' barrier to existing states regulating all economic activity on their territory and taxing the profits derived from it. The barriers to doing so are ideological, enshrined in the doctrines of **neo-liberalism**. Ultimately, this is a party-political battle that can be carried on by democratic means within existing states.

Other modern problems, however, such as **climate change** and environmental degradation, can be confronted only through co-operation between the 200 or so states in the world. This raises problems of collective decision-making (making agreed decisions stick and preventing free-riding) which only a single authoritative state structure can solve.

There is, however, no single state structure encompassing the world at present. Even approximations like the UN are far from having the powers to come near to it. The contested global hegemony of the US enables it to exert pressure on many other states for action and to sanction free-riders in a limited way. This goes a little way to enforcing international agreements, but it is clearly not enough. It leaves many problems unresolved, notably local wars, economic inequality and instability, international terrorism and environmental problems.

The multiplication of world problems caused by globalization and economic expansion creates pressures and possibilities of solving them by creating some kind of world federal state. That would not necessarily be a democracy, however. It is more likely in the first place to be technocratic and based on interstate agreements rather than direct popular voting for either world governments or policies.

There is reason to believe, however, especially with enhanced communications and education across the world, and daily pressures from common problems, that individuals and political parties cannot be kept out of world political processes forever. Exemplars for uniting previously hostile countries already exist (the EU), and mass electorates running to a billion and spread across a subcontinent have been successfully mobilized and offered clear choices by political parties (India). There have also been notable examples of peaceful transition from authoritarian rule to a passable form of democracy (Russia). Institutions for structuring a world democracy are already there in the shape of the UN and transnational federations of political parties. Nothing is ever totally certain in politics. But the odds on an effective world democracy functioning by the end of the twenty-first century are certainly better than 50/50.

Key points in this discussion are thus:

- The continuing pressure of public goods problems in the world today (i.e. how to pay for universal benefits for everyone when some can refuse to pay).
- The only effective solution to the problem, as at individual country level (cf. Chapter 2), is a world state.

Neo-liberalism

The belief that all policy initiatives and implementation should be left to private enterprise.

Climate change

World heating and rising sea levels.

- Institutions already exist which, if empowered, could become a world government.
- Like the EU, this would probably be run by administrators and technocrats at first but could become increasingly democratic, with worldwide elections on a universal franchise.
- Democratic processes, centred on elections and political parties, would then probably evolve across the world as they have in existing states.
- And these processes could be explained in the same way, through the predictive theories outlined in the preceding chapters.

Systematic working assumptions coming into this discussion

1   States form the basic unit or context for most political research.
2   States are governments with supporting (quasi-)military, administrative and other institutions, recognized by other governments as providing public goods and services (including the regulation of non-state activities) within specified territorial boundaries.
3   Public goods and services are those provided universally so that no one can be individually charged for them or excluded from benefiting.
4   Only states can guarantee the provision of public goods and services through their unique ability to finance them by taxes and other means.
9   States vary in the extent to which decisions about policy and who is to make it are shared widely among citizens.
10   The most extensive sharing occurs in democracies, since by definition, these have to guarantee that public policies necessarily reflect the preferences of citizens for them.
11   This guarantee is provided by free, regular and competitive elections of governments and/or policies open to all groups and individuals, where votes reveal citizen preferences and authorize them as either policymaking governments or directly as state policy.

Sources and resources

Jesper Roine *Pocket Piketty: An Explainer on Thomas Piketty* OR Books www. orbooks.com/catalog/pocket-piketty/
Ian Budge, and Kenneth Newton (eds) (1997) *The Politics of the New Europe* (Abingdon, Routledge).
Ian Budge, and Sarah Birch (2014) *National Policy in a Global Economy: How Government Can Improve Living Standards and Balance the Books* (London, Palgrave MacMillan).

Suggestions for class papers

1 Assess the place of traditional states in the world today.
2 Would world democracy guarantee universal peace? Why, or why not?
3 What political alternatives are there to world democracy in solving the problems we face today?

Suggestions for class projects

1 Specify the policies which present-day democracies have adopted to tackle world problems by global action. Assess their effectiveness based on systematic evidence about their success.
2 Which party families, judged by their current party proposals, are more likely to succeed in the context of a world democracy? Would this involve modifying their current ideology? Why and how?
3 Why is collective action so hard to take in the absence of a unifying state context? Support your argument with concrete examples of successful and unsuccessful action on climate change.

Part V

Explanation

Explaining politics by specifying its processes more exactly so as to predict outcomes

Theory-driven data analysis

So far, this book has tried to explain how a correspondence between popular preferences and implemented policy can be guaranteed by democratic rules and processes, even at world level. These involve a whole series of collective actors, from electorates and political parties through to governments. Their motivations, and the ways in which they interact, can be examined systematically and represented exactly in spatial and other theoretical **models** – providing precise expectations about what the processes will lead to, in the way of preferences and policies corresponding (or not as the case may be).

Crucially, such expectations can be quantified and compared with the actual measured outcomes to see how well they match up. Only if they substantially match will the explanation be accepted as true. If it fails to meet available evidence, we have to reject it as an explanation of what is going on and build and test alternative theories.

Part V builds on the preference and policy measures introduced in Chapters 4–7. But it goes into more detail about the procedures involved in quantifying theories and checking them against the evidence. We start in Chapter 16 with the evidence itself, formed by estimates and measurements of political processes and events. These create both a need for explanation (for why processes such as elections and policy **targeting** turn out as they do) – and also a way of checking out its plausibility: do the expectations it generates conform to what actually happens?

Of course, explanations and evidence are never entirely independent of each other. Just as popular preferences need to have public alternatives on offer to **frame** them (Chapter 3), so too does the evidence need some

Models
Theories expressed in a form (spatial or otherwise) which will allow them to be checked against data.

Targeting
What governments want policy to be rather than what it currently is.

Frame
Defining the possible actions to be considered on an issue.

kind of theoretical structuring before it can be used to decide between the models on offer. For example, party election programmes ('manifestos' or 'platforms') would not figure as evidence for what parties intend to do unless we first had a theory that says they are important as indicators of party intentions. If we considered them to be merely promises made to win over votes but not seriously intended to be kept, then we would not go to the bother of collecting, quantifying and analysing them. Even to formulate predictions about what they will say, we need to consider them worthwhile, dealing with something important. Only if we start off from a theory that gives some reasons for considering that they are will we have both the theory and the evidence necessary to assess its predictions.

However, more dramatic events – notably the general-election outcome and the governments that form as a result – must make an impact regardless of the exact theory one has about them – unless it is to dismiss them all as a sham. (Even this extreme view is held by some Marxist and conspiracy theorists, so even what seem important events in their own right are not wholly independent of theories about their impact on politics).

Briefing V.1

Agenda control and 'non-decisions'

From an extreme Marxist point of view, all political participants and agencies of the capitalist state, including the media and the political parties, are committed to upholding it and only diverge on the precise tactics and strategies necessary to do so. Elections, even if freely conducted on a universal franchise, simply decide between trivial issues, because the important ones (such as the abolition of private property) never get raised and are thus never available to frame mass opinion and preferences. Such 'agenda control' renders it necessary to change current democratic structures totally and probably violently, allowing the really fundamental political questions to be discussed and voted on. 'Conspiracy theorists' of all political persuasions tend towards this view although the 'issues' they see as being suppressed may differ.

To say that evidence is theoretically framed is not, however, to say that it is entirely shaped by theory. If it were there would be little point in comparing the two as we would know in advance that they would match up. Theories should always exclude some future possibilities of what will happen. Otherwise, they become tautologies – true but uninformative in telling you what to expect from politics (e.g. that Party A will either be the majority party after the next election or not). This hardly lets you anticipate the result or evaluate the underlying explanation by seeing whether it anticipates what actually happens.

We can characterize political generalizations as either inductive (observation based) or deductive (theory based) in nature. We can check out all known election results and generalize about them to produce an inductive 'law' or generalization. Possibly the best-supported inductive 'law' in political science is that government parties will lose around 2%–3% of their previous vote in the following election. This regularity is based on results from elections over a long time and across the world. So we are pretty sure it is true. Another inductive regularity is that coalition parties get a share of government ministries corresponding in percentage terms to their share of pro-government supporters in the legislature. (For an excellent example of how inductive 'laws' extend and clarify research findings, see Briefing 13.3).

Inductive generalizations like these summarize available evidence and certainly tell you what you can expect to happen under prevailing conditions. Their weakness from being based on observations of what is currently going on is that they do not usually *explain* it. They simply tell you what generally happens. Thus, if prevailing conditions change (e.g. by becoming much better) induction cannot tell you for certain that things will go on as they are, since in itself it has no explanation of why they should do so. Its implicit assumption is simply that what happens today will go on happening tomorrow.

Briefing V.2

Necessarily true but uninformative theories versus contingently true and refutable theories

On the face of it, it seems better to have theories which we know to be true under all circumstances rather than ones which could be wrong. The trouble is that a theory which says that everything is equally probable is not going to let you say with any exactness what is going to happen next or what the cause of a particular outcome is. For example, if we say that party policy will either stay the same or move to left or right, we have covered all the available probabilities and whatever theory underpins the prediction will necessarily be true. If on the other hand, we say that the relative strength of 'centrist' and 'extreme' factions drives change from left to centre to right (within certain ideological limits), then this allows us to anticipate outcomes and (importantly) say what causes the change. Understanding the dynamics of the faction-based forces at work is more important theoretically than simply being able to make the prediction. But the two go together, as we do not know if the theory is (provisionally) true unless it makes reasonably successful predictions.

If you do have a theory as to why things should go on as they are, then that is more informative. For example, one might attribute loss of governing party votes to the fact that governments always have to make decisions which some electors dislike, contributing to 'costs of governing' which erode its support. In contrast to the inductive, observation-based generalization about governing parties always losing votes, this is a more speculative, 'hypothetico deductive' (**H-D**) **theory**, which could be shown to be wrong by collecting further evidence (e.g. by seeing if electors who lose out from government decisions actually do switch votes). An H-D theory does not rest solely on observation but draws on various assumptions about how individuals react to events and applies them to a particular situation. If electors' reactions remain negative even when surrounding conditions improve, we could expect governments to go on losing votes. We can then check the truth of the idea by seeing whether this actually happens when we compare votes over elections. If not – if governments actually keep up their vote when surrounding conditions get better – we would reject that theory.

Ideally, we should make predictions before the actual events happen, so that there is no fudging on the matter of whether the theory has been successful or not. At the moment, real prediction is rare in political science. Theories are mostly tested based on **correlations** between the explanatory **variable** (in our example, discontent with government decisions) and the outcome (loss of votes in elections). If the correlation is positive, then the hypothesis is upheld.

The trouble with the political (and indeed the social) world is that almost everything correlates weakly with everything else, particularly if you use powerful statistical techniques to make the connection. Having found a correlation, an ingenious analyst can always find a theory to justify it. Thus, there is quite likely to be a correlation between governing party vote and the national team's success in football. This can be explained theoretically by popular enthusiasm over the football result translating into vote rewards for the national government. In this case the correlation is likely to be weak – but possibly not weaker than that between discontent at government decisions and loss of votes for governing parties.

One solution might be to see how things change over time, so that prior contentment, say six months or a year before the election, is related to later vote. This makes contentment more clearly antecedent to vote and establishes a stronger **causal connection**. The problem is again that all sorts of weak over-time correlations are also likely to emerge – for example, between national team results last year and vote this year.

Another solution is to see whether a lot of individual variables go up and down together to such an extent that they can all be regarded as imperfect measures of one underlying 'dimension' that will have a stronger and more direct relationship with what we want to explain (cf. Figure 4.4). Various 'data-reduction' techniques we can use to identify and measure such an underlying dimension are discussed in Chapter 17. This harks back to our earlier discussion of the left-right dimension. This L-R dimension constitutes just such an underlying dimension to which specific policy preferences can be reduced – perhaps the most general and informative political dimension of all (cf. Chapter 5). We have already discussed its importance in identifying a stable middle position around which a policy

H-D theory

A theory in which assumptions are made independently of the data to be examined.

Correlations

Two 'variables' (e.g. preferences) going up and down together.

Variable

A concept, process or behaviour that has been measured.

Causal connection

A relationship in which one event regularly produces another.

majority can form. We expand on this in Chapter 17, demonstrating again how closely linked questions of conceptualization and measurement are to theoretical explanation.

The problem of endemic weak correlations linking almost every social, political and economic variable to each other (which can only partially be solved by data reduction) has given rise to the joke that any political scientist who can't find at least ten explanations for any given correlation should leave the profession. Such a proliferation of weakly supported and often vaguely formulated explanations muddles thinking about political events just as much as if we had no explanations at all.

One way of cutting through this tangled mass is to recognize that all estimates contain some error. By making allowances for this, we can eliminate some of the bothersome weak relationships that emerge. An increasing recognition of error both in measured variables themselves and in ways of estimating relationships between them has spurred major growth in methodology and methodological concerns in the last 30 years. We consider methodological approaches and solutions in more detail in Chapter 18.

Focusing on methods rather than substantive theories of politics has its dangers, however. If our ultimate goal is to explain and predict political events, methodological refinements can easily become over-refinements. Theoretically expected relationships should be sufficiently strong to shine through the murk of irrelevant and weak correlations surrounding them, without too much methodological manipulation. If they do not, we may conclude that the theories are on the wrong track.

The natural sciences like physics and biology are saved from much of this confusion by their ability to stage experiments (Figure V.1). A chemist

EXPERIMENTAL OBJECT (EXP)		CONTROL OBJECT (CON)
SELECTION ← MATCHING → SELECTION		
FIRST MEASUREMENT ($t1$)	EXP$t1$	CON $t1$
ASSUMED CAUSE INTRODUCED FOR EXP ⟶		
SECOND MEASUREMENT($t2$)	EXP $t2$	CON $t2$
PREDICTIVE SUCCESS MEASURED AS		

$$(EXPt2 - EXPt1) - (CONt2 - CONt1)$$

FIGURE V.1 The classical experiment

Notes: This says that the change in the experimental object or sample after the assumed cause is introduced must be (substantially) greater than any change in the matched object or sample over the same time period if the theory is to be upheld.

may have an explanation for a reaction between two substances, for example, which stresses the need for a presence of a third element to produce the reaction. To check this explanation out, the chemist can observe what happens in the absence of the third substance and then what happens in its presence, holding all other conditions constant in the laboratory by 'controlling' their effects. If the reaction happens only in the presence of the third substance, the chemist can conclude that its presence causes the reaction, upholding the theory that says it does. In publishing the findings, the chemist describes the experiment itself in sufficient detail that others can set it up and check whether they get similar results. In this way, the result and the supporting theory can be generally replicated and the new

Briefing V.3

Experiments in political science

Experiments involve manipulation and control, both of the objects of investigation and the surrounding environment which might affect them. That is why they are normally conducted in laboratories under easily controlled conditions. A typical experiment takes two exactly matched objects or samples and holds both under exactly the same conditions except for one crucial difference: the experimental object is subjected to the unique condition (e.g. heat) that the theory says will change it. Then the state of the experimental object is compared with what it was before. If the experimental object has changed while the control one has not, then the theory that predicts this will be the case is upheld. (If both stayed the same, it is rejected). Crucially, predictive success is measured as

$$(EXPt2 - EXPt1) - (CONt2 - CONt1)$$

EXP is the object which is the subject of the experiment; CON is the matched object held as a control on the results; and $t1$ and $t2$ are the times at which their state is measured. Only if the subject of the experiment has changed in the anticipated direction more than the matched control held under the same overall conditions would we say that the prediction and the theory behind it had been upheld. This is because there is always the possibility that surrounding conditions change in some unanticipated way and affect the results, so that change due to the presumed cause has to be measured by taking into account both the change in the control and in the actual subject of the experiment.

Experiments of this kind in political science are often done with matched groups of individuals when, for example, one group is subjected to a propaganda film and one is not. Change in the experimental group's opinions before and after seeing the film can then be measured through a survey before and after and confirmed with results at the same times for the control group. Because of expense and other difficulties, however, there is often no control group. Changes in the experimental group are informative but not as conclusive as comparing change in both groups. A further problem is that groups are often formed from students rather than the general population, and it is difficult to generalize from their reactions. Most data analyses in political science truncate the experimental approach even further in that they compare two groups at the same point in time while assuming they are distinguished from each other by having different characteristics picked out by the theory as having political effects (e.g. working class in one case and middle class in the other). The investigators then compare party votes in the two groups, for example, and estimate the effects of class by the vote difference between them. More refined analyses of this kind try to impose 'controls' for other factors at work by relating class to vote in subgroups of the same gender, with the same place of residence, the same occupation or some other characteristic. While these procedures are inspired by experimental ones and so far as possible copy them, it is clear that they are much less conclusive in eliminating other extraneous influences. At another level, countries can be divided into different groups based on a key variable identified as having policy effects (e.g. different electoral systems) and compared to see what policy differences there are between them (cf. Table 10.2 for an example). Even fewer 'controls' for extraneous influences are present here, however, so the results from such a comparison are even less conclusive, though informative so far as they go.

knowledge applied either in developing further theoretical explanations or anticipating events.

It is obviously difficult if not impossible to apply the experimental approach in most of political science. We cannot, for example, in checking out the factional theory of party policymaking (Chapter 12) substitute one faction for another in control of a political party and see whether policy switches left or right as predicted. All we can do is postdict – that is, determine whether the policy moves made in the past after each factional alternation are as expected by the theory. We can also, more powerfully, *predict* (say what will happen in policy terms when a given faction takes over). If such predictions are generally successful when made by the original investigators and by others with differing data sets under varying conditions, then we can accept the theory as reasonably validated. We can then go on to use it as a basis for further theory building (cf. Figure 8.1) or for predicting events, as with scientific theories validated by experiments.

A further use for well validated theory, often overlooked because systematic theory building and testing are rare, is in confirming the correctness and applicability of estimates and measures. This sounds paradoxical because in checking theories we generally take the estimates and measures (having made allowances for error) as authoritative. The process of validation, however, is reciprocal in the long run. We can never be entirely sure that even error-adjusted estimates are valid, in the sense of measuring

Briefing V.4

A rare example of a field experiment in political science

A 'field experiment' is an experiment conducted outside the laboratory under actual political conditions. For the reasons mentioned in the text and the other briefings, it is difficult to stage a classical experiment under these conditions. However, in the late 1960s, two political scientists in the Scottish city of Dundee decided to test the theory commonly held by political parties that canvassing supporters will stimulate them to turn out and vote ('canvassing' is having party activists visit electors at home, leaving pamphlets and brochures that encourage them to vote and, if possible, talking to them in person).

They set up the experiment by selecting two apartment blocks next door to each other which were public housing for lower paid workers. So they were pretty well matched on the social conditions likely to affect voting, as in the experiment described in Figure V.1.

The experimenters were in control of the Labour Party committee organizing the canvassers, the only ones to call there, so they ensured that one apartment block was intensely canvassed (the experimental block), while the other was given the minimal attention which both blocks had had in the previous election (resulting in both cases in poor turnout at $t1$). As party representatives at polling stations record who votes from where, there were measurements of turnout at $t1$ and $pt2$ for the blocks. So the investigators could estimate the overall effects of canvassing on turnout to vote, as in Figure V.1.

$$(EXPt2 - EXPt1) - (CONt2 - CONt1)$$

Turnout in the control block with no canvassing did not change much from the last time. In the experimental block, it went up by around 10% – upholding the theory that party canvassing does make a real difference.

With clearly defined objectives and procedures and lots of imagination, therefore, true field experiments are possible in political science – even if up to now they have been rare.

Source: J. M. Bochel and D. T. Denver (1970) Canvassing, Turnout and Party Support: An Experiment. *British Journal of Political Science* 1, pp. 257–269, https://doi.org/10.1017/S000712340000911X Published online: 1 January 2009.

what they should be measuring. If the substantive theory has gained a lot of credibility from repeated trials but some measure then produces results which go against its predictions, we would tend, at least initially, to distrust the measure rather than the theory.

Validation, in the sense of results conforming with reasonable expectations and being open to replication, is thus as important for estimates and measures – the evidence – as it is for theories. It is the ultimate guarantee of their usefulness, overriding other criteria such as reliability (do they consistently produce the same results?) and robustness (are they easy for other investigators to apply?) We will explore such measurements, concepts and procedures in more detail in Chapter 16.

Validation in turn results from repeated confrontations of theory and evidence. The evidence may be **qualitative evidence** (selected historical narratives) or quantitative evidence in the sense of demographic, survey, textual, expenditure or government collected statistics. These may also be analysed in various ways – spatially, statistically, experimentally or in simulations.

Confrontations of theory and evidence culminate in theoretically derived predictions of future events. Only then can we be really sure, first that we have a theory precisely enough stated to produce a specific prediction and second that it provides a correct account of the processes involved – attested by its ability to make correct predictions. We need evidence from outside the theory itself to determine whether it is true or not.

A useful way of developing predictive theories is to simulate them. We already put this approach into practice when we considered party policymaking in Chapter 12 (Figure 12.4). A simulation draws out the assumptions of a theory by using them to create estimates of the way actors will behave. In Chapter 12 the actors are political parties, and the behaviour in question is how they will react to vote gains or losses, given the length of time one faction has been dominant. The resulting changes in policy position from left or right (or lack of change) can be estimated using the theory's assumptions about how the background factors interact.

From these estimates, we can then plot out expected party policy movements over a given time period. These estimates do not all derive from the theory, since relevant data necessary to entirely quantify its assumptions may be missing. In the case of Figure 12.4, this is information about the relative strength of internal party factions, which the theory relates to the size of the policy moves made by the parties. The simulation gets over this by assuming that such fluctuations occur by chance, within reasonable limits.

Generating expected policy moves of this type helps advance theory formation in two ways. First, it helps develop the theory itself by making it more precise. Making such an explicit spatial representation as shown in Figure 12.4 requires that the assumptions have to say exactly what form each party policy move will take – to the left, the right or not moving at all. It also has to specify the circumstances surrounding a move in order to generate the simulation.

Besides improving the theory, analysts can secondly examine the overall pattern of results to see if they look plausible – which might, as in Chapter 12, involve comparing them with spatial mappings of actual party policy moves derived from what they have stated in manifestos and platforms. If the simulated results match up plausibly with the observed

Qualitative evidence

Unstandardized evidence (e.g. descriptions of events made by different commentators without a common frame of reference).

ones, we can conclude that the theory which generates them is reasonably supported by existing evidence and worth testing postdictively or predictively.

Sometimes we lack the data to go on from here. So we have to accept the theory (for the moment anyway) as probably correct since it has survived the simulation and the general comparisons and assessments of the overall results. Such a result is a second best, however, since we are concentrating on a virtual reality rather than actual reality.

It is much better if we can move beyond broad simulations to **postdictions** of individual events. Again, Chapter 12 does this by examining the individual policy moves actually made by parties in 25 democracies over five to 15 elections. These conform to theoretical expectations in a majority of individual cases (72%). The **model** also does substantially better than other postdictions, such as anticipating a change of policy direction at every election.

With such support, the theory can be used with some confidence to predict future party moves that have not yet taken place. Until better theories come up which have more spectacular success rates, we can also take the factional theory as the correct account of how parties decide on moves. It displaces other theories which assume that parties adjust policy entirely in line with popular preferences for it, to win over votes and gain office. There is only a secondary effect of votes in the factional model, where their loss weakens the dominant faction's monopoly of policy.

The conclusion that party policymaking is largely inward looking and dominated by long-standing ideological concerns does, as we have seen, sharpen the democratic dilemma of how to guarantee the correspondence between preferences and public policy – the eventual solution to which is found in the theory of party and policy alternation in government (Chapters 3, 6, and 7). From this example, we can see how establishing the validity of one theory can lead on to changes in others and to a better understanding of the whole pattern of democratic decision-making. The key to all this lies in the development and testing of predictive theory.

There are many more nuances to theory building and testing than appear in the summary here. The following chapters fill in some of these details. The point to focus on throughout is the primacy of prediction, both as a criterion for the kind of theory we aim to produce and for the utility of the evidence we collect. However complicated the techniques we employ to evaluate measures and individual hypotheses, the statistics they produce should never constitute the final stage in explanation. The ultimate criterion must always be how far they facilitate the predictive formulation and checking of theory. With this as our guiding light, we now go into the evidence available for checking theories (Chapter 16) and the techniques we bring to bear on the relevant data (Chapters 17 and 18) within the overall context of systematic political science (Chapter 19).

Postdiction

Correctly characterizing what has happened in the past.

Model

A theory expressed in a form (spatial or otherwise) which will allow it to be checked against data.

Sources and resources

The following provides an overview of the topics covered here and in Part V as a whole:

Keith Dowding (2016) *The Philosophy and Methods of Political Science* (Basingstoke, Palgrave MacMillan).

Williams Roberts Clark, Matt Golder, and Sona Nadenicheck Golder (2012) *Principles of Comparative Politics* (Washington, DC, CQ Press).

Gary King, Robert O. Keohane and Sidney Verba (1994) *Designing Social Inquiry: Scientific Inferance in Qualitative Research* (Princeton, NJ, Princeton University Press).

More generally, see:

Shively W. Phillips (2016) *The Craft of Political Research* (Abingdon, Routledge).

Chapter 16

Generating 'Big Data'

Sources, procedures, error checks

Chapter overview

To assess the standing of theories, we need an independent criterion of whether they work. This has got to be (at least in part) based on evidence outside the theory itself. If, as in computer simulations, the evidence is produced by assuming the theory is true, it can only be of limited use in checking it out (though useful in specifying it more exactly). Most commonly, independent evidence is provided by events or processes in the real world reported elsewhere. If the theoretical expectations match (or, better still, predict) independently observed outcomes, we can accept the theory-based account as correct, at least until a better one comes along.

This chapter reviews the different kinds of evidence which are commonly used to assess political science theories. It starts with the most obvious contrast – between qualitative and quantitative evidence. Qualitative evidence usually comes in the shape of non-standardized descriptions of political events. Quantitative evidence puts numbers on the events which are reported using a standardized description across countries and time, thus rendering more exact comparison possible. We have already drawn on quantitative evidence in assessing the predictive theories of Parts I and III.

Both kinds of evidence have their weaknesses. Numeric data provide a 'thin' description of any individual case, confined to what are assumed to be the essentials associated with it. Qualitative descriptions can be so rich that in the end readers are left with confused ideas about what is supposed to have caused what and whether this event is not surrounded with such particular circumstances that it is absolutely unique and not available for comparative analysis.

The contrast between these two kinds of evidence can be overdrawn, however. Not all the detail surrounding a particular event, like an election, is necessarily relevant to its outcome – its exact date, for example. Complexity can be stripped away without necessarily oversimplifying. And elections can be described generally in terms of the number of electors voting, parties competing, issues discussed – none of which appear trivial even when applied to an individual case.

Demographic

Data that describe territorial units (wards, cities, countries, etc.).

Aggregate analysis

Pooling information on individual cases (e.g. over an area or social grouping).

Quantitative evidence

Evidence (data) expressed as numbers.

Frame

Defines the possible actions to be considered on an issue.

Measurement error

The extent to which an estimate will give wrong information.

The chapter fleshes out these points by seeing how **demographic** data developed out of qualitative descriptions by converting the salient recurring features of these to numbers. This development also allowed analysts to compare elections which occurred in different places and at different times within the same countries.

We shall look at the development of surveys as a way of examining individual beliefs and behaviour lacking in **aggregate analyses** and how textual analysis developed out of classifying written reports of what survey respondents said. Government documents and statistics also provide another source of information and evidence, particularly for examining public policy, across and within countries and over time.

Table 16.1 provides a systematic overview of the main types of data (i.e. **quantitative evidence**) available for political research. Evidence may sometimes be useful for its own sake, as a basis for inductive generalizations based on regularities or common features across a set of similar events (e.g. elections or government formations). However, it is most useful as an independent criterion of whether theories are valid – that is, can predict outcomes which match up with actual ones. Hence, this table lists not only the different kinds of data available for political science research but also the 'unit of analysis' they use (e.g. individuals, areas, events of particular kinds), the way they are prepared and the source of the information. It also covers the areas of research that they are most relevant for and the kind of theories that they can be used to test.

While all such evidence provides an indispensable basis for political investigation, it cannot be taken entirely at face value. Survey responses are always **framed** by the questions which elicit them, and the same is true for measures based on data which has previously been collected by someone else. They are framed by the purposes for which they have been collected. A first question indeed is whether the data available *are* the best evidence for checking your theory. One difference between qualitative and quantitative evidence is that analysts can systematically try to estimate error in the quantitative case by applying statistical techniques. By definition, however, these cannot be applied to qualitative data, which is not generally numeric.

Measurement error is also a major concern for the techniques used to analyse data and evidence, which are the focus of Chapter 18. There are various approaches which can be applied to correct for both measurement and analytic error. The overriding test for both theory and estimates, however, is correct prediction. Bearing this in mind prevents the measurement discussion from assuming a life of its own separate from political analysis proper, and links it firmly to the explanation of actual political events, where it properly belongs.

Key points to take from the discussion are thus:

- Using theory to select and structure the data we want to examine and to guide its analysis.
- The approaches we can use to get systematic, quantified estimates of political events from descriptions and reports (qualitative evidence) of individual events.

TABLE 16.1 Main types of quantitative data available for checking theories

	Demographic	Survey	Text based	Events based	Government and public statistics
Source	Published census reports and political statistics (e.g. party votes)	Respondent answers to questionnaires in polls or academic surveys	Published documents e.g. party manifestos, parliamentary proceedings, institutional minutes	(Mostly) newspaper reports of elections, governments, legislation, issues and so on	Economic figures, social statistics, expenditures, published budgets
How quantified	Individual information aggregated for area units	Answers either recorded or put into general categories	Words or sentences put into general categories (cf. Table 6.3)	Events of interest counted for time periods (e.g. years) or areas (e.g. countries) or both	Collected as actual or estimated numbers by relevant agencies
Basic unit of analysis (which can be aggregated upwards)	Areas (local wards, towns, cities, regions, constituencies, countries)	Individual respondents	Text or document (e.g. party manifesto)	Individual events (e.g. new government formation with membership)	Published statistics generally at state/country level
Most relevant research area	Elections and voting behaviour	Voting preferences and opinions on policy for representational research	Organizational preferences and policy targets	Government functioning and behaviour	Policy analysis of various kinds
Examples of theories which can be checked against them	Social group theories of voting: 'the index of political predispositions' (IPP) (cf. Briefing 16.5)	Alternation theory of party representation (Table 7.1) – thermostatic theory of preference – policy interaction (e.g. Table 7.2)	Factional theory of party policy formation (Table 12.1), alternation and thermostatic theories	Government formation theory (Figure 13.1) Distribution of ministries (Figures 14.1–14.5) Salience theory of elections (e.g. Table 6.1)	Incrementalist theory (Table 14.1), punctuated equilibrium (Table 14.2)

Notes: Some theories put together different kinds of data (e.g. survey evidence on preferences with textual data on policy targets and expenditure data on implemented policy). The availability of the different measures and the ability to compare them enables us particularly to check on representational theories which predict correspondence between them. Such theories (e.g. alternation and thermostatic theories) are therefore listed as relevant under several types of data.

- The likely presence of error in such estimates and how to measure it.
- Reliability in the sense of measuring fluctuations in estimates not due to real change in the political events they describe ('random error').
- Reliability in the sense of the systematic over- or under-reporting of true values for political events or processes (bias).
- Validation as the final check on estimates, in the sense of their 'fit' with other independent estimates and with theories about political events and processes which have already passed tests and checks of their own validity.

Quality and quantity

Political discussions have always drawn on history to make their case, such as using conspicuous examples of democratic failure in order to advocate a balanced rather than a democratic constitution. A favourite example is the well-documented history of disordered democracy in ancient Athens (515–325 BC) which could be contrasted with the successful balancing of powers between aristocracy and citizens in Republican Rome (300–50 BC). This contrast figured largely in the 'federalist' debates on the American constitution in 1786–1788 and was highly influential in promoting the 'separation of powers' between the presidency, the senate, the house and the courts (now subverted by the political parties operating within all of them and co-ordinating their actions). The American constitution-making process itself emerged as an important example and precedent for others.

The EU (European Union)

An economic, social and political grouping of most European countries.

Qualitative evidence consists of non-standardized descriptions of single events or processes. These are often major historical occasions, such as the adoption of the US constitution just cited or the negotiation of the Australian and Indian constitutions as the basis for federal unions. The tortuous evolution of **the EU** has also given rise to many books and articles which regard it as a unique case. The adoption of a historical form of narrative based on a chronology of key events leading up to the ultimate outcome does indeed seem an appropriate way of explaining individual events. Such an approach can also be applied to regularly occurring events such as individual election campaigns or government decisions.

One can pick out common elements from such accounts of important decisions and generalize about them to a limited extent. But each is written up individually, usually without much reference to the others. So they contain certain information in common but also a lot of surrounding detail related to the unique features and context of the event being described. In the end, it is difficult to compare such accounts. Thus, the extent to which they really provide examples or parallels for action in other contexts remains in doubt.

Another problem which arises from non-comparability is how to decide whether an account is really correct or not. It often happens that different authors will come up with different explanations of why events (e.g. elections) produced the results they did. The problem is not so much that the accounts disagree on recorded details. Rather, one account tends to bring in *different* details and thus comes to different conclusions about the factors which produced the end result. This is particularly true if the two accounts were written at different points in time, ten or 20 years apart.

This is because any account of collective action has to make some assumptions about the motives that the people involved have; how these connect to the actions they take to implement them; and the surrounding constraints on these. All are made explicit in theories of the kind we have considered earlier in this book (e.g. in the 'factional theory' of how parties come to decide on leftwards or rightwards shifts in their declared policies – see Table 12.1).

Historical accounts, however, often leave such assumptions unstated. Nevertheless, they are there – and indispensable to first picking out the details relevant to the account and afterwards coming to conclusions about them. For example, was the nineteenth century drive to abolish slavery throughout the world driven by moral and religious considerations, stemming from the spread of evangelical Protestantism in the nineteenth century? Or was it based on a growing recognition that plantation production with a large labour force had reached its limits and needed to be replaced by more efficient agricultural arrangements such as individually rented freeholdings?

Adopting a 'moral' interpretation of these events involves collecting certain evidence (e.g. on churchgoing and the involvement of evangelical personalities in anti-slavery campaigns). Adopting an 'economic' interpretation involves research on plantation conditions and outputs and on commodity market reactions.

Thus, theory pervades descriptive accounts from the beginning – selection of evidence – to the end – conclusions about what factors produced the final outcome. As one theory becomes more fashionable, it tends to be applied by more historians and descriptive writers to their accounts, leading to differences from previous ones. This 'revisionist' process is summed up in the well-known saying 'History gets rewritten in every generation'.

Of course, quantitative analyses are just as dependent on theory to collect evidence and draw conclusions from it as qualitative descriptions are. The need to clarify standards and procedures for first identifying relevant evidence and then measuring it tends to make analysts more self-conscious about what they are doing and puts pressure on them to justify their procedures. This often involves citing relevant theories. Growing awareness of the pervasiveness of theory and the way it shapes evidence has led to political science journals insisting in recent years on **hypotheses** being stated at the start of each article and conclusions being explicitly related to them. This renders the theory underpinning descriptions and analyses clearer, although such hypotheses rarely add up to a complete account of the processes under examination.

Hypotheses

Succinct statements of relationships which produce a given outcome.

Even when theory remains unstated, though, it is still there. Different theoretical underpinnings lead to different descriptions being produced of the same event – adding to the non-standardization and non-comparability of qualitative evidence. The difference with quantitative evidence is, however, more a matter of degree than an unbridgeable chasm, as we shall see.

From qualitative to quantitative evidence

One factor further accentuating differences in qualitative accounts, even of the same event, is that they often rely on what newspapers report about it or what prominent persons or their biographers have said. This is often second- or third-hand evidence about other people's behaviour, such as how the public are reacting to events. Hence, it is often shaped by the biases or purposes of the reporter.

This disjunction between different accounts is most obvious in mass events like elections, where commentators often make quite different inferences about what drives public reactions. The first major steps towards collecting and using quantitative evidence, therefore, occurred as a way of finding out what was really happening on the ground in elections. This exploited the fact that quantitative evidence had already been collected as part of the process of registering the vote, on the one hand, and as a basis for conducting everyday government business, on the other (e.g. getting details about the population and their social conditions from a **census**).

Census

A collection of relevant information from a population within a given area.

The brilliant innovation was to put the two together so that analysts could check for example on the idea that Catholics were more inclined to vote for church-affiliated parties. The characteristics recorded in the census for each area were broad social characteristics of this type: religion, church attendance, occupation, type of housing and so on. So there was no general information on, for example, what electors thought about the issues of the day. Or rather, there was only selective information on this from newspapers, biographies and books – classic qualitative information of the kind the new quantitative investigators were trying to get away from in favour of 'harder' evidence. As the latter consisted mostly of the social characteristics of the population, together with their votes, within separate territorial areas of the state, the new evidence and analyses (developed largely between 1910 and 1950) were termed the demographic approach (from 'demography', i.e. mapping the population through the census).

An alternative name was 'electoral geography'. This derived from the fact that the unit of analysis was not the individual voter or elector (on whom background information was not published) but the constituency, county, commune or prefecture – the smallest area for which both voting and social background figures were available together. These could then be examined systematically to see, for example, if constituencies with high proportions of industrial workers produced higher votes for socialist parties than areas with lower numbers of industrial workers. One could also

Briefing 16.1

National censuses and their use in explaining political behaviour

From the beginning of the nineteenth century, state governments responded to the accelerating industrial and social changes in their territories by instituting a national 'census' of every household unit living in it, recording households' occupations, religion and other socioeconomic details. These replies were reported and published for units such as city districts or wards, counties, prefectures and communes – whatever seemed the appropriate area from the point of view of governing the country. It was natural to use political units for aggregating individual-level information. So for areas at a certain level of aggregation, the census information could be matched with election and other political information. By doing so, you could see, for example, whether areas where a high proportion were manual workers had voted more for socialist parties.

Analyses based on such 'matchings' of background and political variables over districts ('electoral geography') supported the first quantitative analyses in political science (though prone to the inferential errors described below as the 'demographic fallacy').

estimate the effects on vote of high numbers of farmers or peasants living within the constituency boundaries, or of concentrations of small businesspeople, Catholics, Protestants, rich or poor.

Using 'demographic' data of this kind permitted, for the first time, a systematic analysis of political events based on precise figures and statistical generalizations from distributions and **cross-tabulations**. You could say with confidence, for example, that 79% of constituencies with a high proportion of manual workers were won by the socialists compared to only 20% of constituencies where they were few. At a more sophisticated statistical level, using a graph which related proportions of manual workers in each commune to its socialist vote, you could make the generalization that socialist voting increases with industrial employment.

With such information on what happens over a large number of constituencies, it is possible to check out theories more systematically than one can from qualitative, descriptive accounts, which tend to be highly selective in what they report. The quantitative evidence is clearly much more 'given' from outside the investigation. Thus, it forms an external check on theories such as the Marxist one, which would claim that social class as determined by your relationship to the means of production determines both social and political behaviour. With demographic data, we can actually check this claim by seeing the extent to which working-class constituencies vote for socialist parties. As pointed out above, the theory frames the investigation by suggesting in the first place that social class is related to vote and is then 'tested' against the evidence gathered independently on this.

Cross-tabulations

Relating characteristics (e.g. class and vote) numerically by comparing the support given by one class to particular parties with that given by another.

While demographic data have the strengths of being external to theory *and* capable of generating widespread, clearly supported generalizations, they also have weaknesses. The most obvious is the limited range of information they supply about individual motivations. People can rarely be entirely characterized by class, religion or even gender. A lot depends both on their other characteristics and also how they react to them. Marx recognized that 'class' is not just a case of the work you do but also of how you think about it ('class consciousness'). That cannot be measured only on an occupational basis, even though you can start out from there.

These limitations lie at the root of the traditional contrast between qualitative and quantitative evidence, which we discussed in the last section. On the one hand, we have rich and detailed accounts of events, each treated as being determined by a unique concurrence of factors. On the other hand, we have generalizations over a large number of events based on a limited number of factors and often seeming just to confirm what we already know. Of course, low-paid workers will tend to vote for redistributive parties which promise to give them more money. So what's new?

Things have moved on, however, since such sharp contrasts between the qualitative and quantitative approaches were first made in the 1930s. Descriptive accounts are now much more likely to set the event they are describing in a wider context of similar events and even to discuss competing theories of what influences them. This is particularly true of democratic elections, given the vast amount of both statistical and other research done on them during the last 70 years.

On the other hand, 'demographic' research has moved away from an approach based exclusively on comparing geographical areas – an indirect and potentially misleading way of explaining voting (for reasons we shall go into at the start of the next section). It is now just as likely to draw data from the descriptions of individual elections which have appeared in newspaper and other accounts. From these, one can record the types of parties competing, the votes they received, the major issues of the election and other characteristics which almost always have to be features of a descriptive account. (If it doesn't report these, then it would be an odd description.)

Such information is more closely related to the election outcome than the traditional demographic characteristics. It also marks a transition to a more dynamic form of over-time analysis, as differences in outcomes from one election to another can be explained, for example by differences in the political issues relevant to them (see Briefing 6.1).

How would we use such information in a quantitative analysis? Based on the information we have about voters and parties (Chapters 11 and 12) we know that parties are closely linked to certain recurring issues and ideological stands. To the extent that issues to which they are linked, and which favour them, come up in an election, we would expect them to gain votes. By classifying individual issues in an election into broader types (e.g. a specific proposal to privatize a state-owned utility company into a broad category of 'economic initiative and freedom') and linking this to vote gains or losses for conservative-liberal parties, we can calculate what 'mix' of issues current in each election will favour each party. Thus, potentially we can predict what each party vote will be in the next election. By then, checking whether the predictions are correct in a variety of contexts (i.e. finding out whether predicted vote percentages match the actual election results) we can also see whether the salience theory underlying this approach is valid (see Briefing 6.1).

This example illustrates that area-based research is still relevant, even though within countries it has been largely replaced by survey-based research on individuals. Countries themselves, however, are what studies of 'comparative government' use as their basic unit of comparison. Thus, the qualifications made in the next section about generalizing from one unit of analysis (the country) to another, such as the actors within them (perhaps individuals but more often institutional actors like political parties, governments and bureaucracies), also apply to this modern and developing branch of political science. We go into this 'demographic fallacy' or 'unit of analysis' problem in the next section, after reflecting a little more on the relationship between qualitative and quantitative research.

We should note that recent developments in both have made them increasingly interdependent. The results of comparative, quantitative

Briefing 16.2

Cross-sectional over-time analysis

The classical experiment discussed in Briefing V.3 forms the ideal for most data-based checks on theories, even if it cannot be fully realized with the evidence in hand. At the most basic level, areas or events can be compared at one point in time to determine whether the proportion of manual workers in the population is associated with a difference in socialist vote. This is analogous to simply comparing outcomes in the experimental and control groups at t_2 without the other refinements that the experimental setup is able to introduce (Figure V.I).

A closer match between data analysis and experiment would be to record fluctuations in both manual workers and votes in the same area over time. Are fluctuations in the population of manual workers then followed by the expected changes in the socialist vote? This is equivalent to measuring change in the experimental group before and after the crucial condition (increases/decreases in manual proportions) occurs.

Of course, one could emulate the experimental setup even more closely by combining the over-time and cross-sectional approaches and observing fluctuations over time in class and vote in a number of areas. Then the control group would be areas where the manual proportions did not change, and the experimental one would be those where it did. Of course, these might not be matched on all other relevant characteristics, thus still falling short of the full experimental setup, but the results would still be informative. Combined over-time and cross-sectional analysis of such types are now common in political data analysis.

analyses based on a number of descriptive accounts of individual elections now feed back into new descriptive accounts of individual elections. One effect is to include the full range of election issues in qualitative accounts as important factors influencing the election, instead of only focusing on one or two thought to be important. In this way, quantitative analyses can influence qualitative narratives by providing possible explanations of the individual event they are describing, at least to the extent of suggesting the range of factors that they should take into account.

The general lesson is that we should be wary of drawing too sharp a contrast between 'quality' and 'quantity' in terms of the evidence we are dealing with. One can easily be transmuted into the other particularly where a number of individual accounts of fairly similar events exist. The qualitative focus will always tend to remain descriptive rather than theoretical, and individual and specific rather than generalizing and comparative. But each type of approach can draw on the other for its own ends. As generalizing theory changes, history gets rewritten. But theory also needs historical descriptions of events both to suggest new ideas and to put them together as quantitative data to check out its hypotheses and predictions.

From demographics to surveys

Surveys

Standardized questions put to individuals in a section of population selected by a polling organization with answers recorded and processed.

The years from 1910 to 1950 were dominated by electoral geography in terms of quantitative research, whereas 1950–1980 might be described as the age of **surveys**. These rapidly took over from demographic analyses of area characteristics as the main way of examining political behaviour and testing theories and hypotheses. The reasons for this are clear. Individuals are able to provide much more detailed accounts of their motivations and behaviour than can be inferred from area comparisons. Indeed, the indirect inferences we are forced to make from such 'demographic' evidence may be positively misleading when it comes to individual behaviour. For example, constituencies with higher proportions of recent immigrants and ethnic minorities often produce higher proportions of votes for extreme, anti-immigrant parties. Are immigrant voters therefore drawn to support hostile parties and policies like moths to a flame, willing their own self-harm? This would undermine most theories of voting behaviour, which would certainly not envisage electors voting so blatantly against their own interests.

The answer to the puzzle is found in the possibility that it is the *settled* residents in these areas who vote for anti-immigrant parties. It is they who find their neighbourhood disrupted and public services suffering from the influx of immigrants and who therefore vote for the parties who want to restrict their entry. One could, however, only *speculate* about this on the basis of demographic analyses of constituency behaviour in the absence of evidence on what individuals do and think. Surveys at individual level are necessary to check out theories which attribute various motivations to voters to explain their behaviour.

Briefing 16.3

The 'demographic fallacy' is a general problem of inferring from one unit of analysis (e.g. area) to another (e.g. individuals)

Once pointed out, it is obvious how different individuals within a given area might react politically in different ways, giving rise to seeming paradoxes like high-immigration areas supporting anti-immigrant parties. Less obviously the same problem also occurs wherever we generalize from one unit of analysis to another. For example, if we survey individuals in a given constituency, we might find the majority-supported anti-immigration policies and therefore infer that a candidate proposing them would get elected. But such an area might well in the end elect a pro-immigrant candidate because the minority supporting that candidate might be active and to turn out to vote, whereas the anti-immigrant majority were rather apathetic and didn't turn out to vote in large numbers.

Making inferences from one level of aggregation to another, while sometimes correct, is often prone to error. This is particularly true of individuals in organizations where official policy may often diverge from majority views, owing to the kind of procedural biases, voting paradoxes and cycling discussed in Chapters 9 and 10. As noted in the text, the problem may particularly affect studies of 'comparative government' today.

Briefing 16.4

Conducting political surveys

Surveys and polls can cover an almost infinite number of topics, but the basic procedures for managing them to produce the information you really want are basically as follows:

1   Before you do anything else, work out what you want to use them for, and if possible, specify what you want to explain (e.g. support or opposition to foreign immigration) and what factors you think explain it (i.e. residence in areas of high or low immigration). If possible, state each hypothesis clearly and express it as an equation, graph or table. Then link up their constituent variables to the questions you are going to ask.

2   These theoretical concerns will then frame the questionnaire you compose, including whether you want 'more' or 'less' questions or self-placements on numerical 'ladders'.

3   Deciding on what information you want should also help you decide on whom you want to put the questions to. You will almost never be able to interview all the people you are interested in, but you might have to decide, for example, whether

you want only to compare residents in areas of high immigration with residents of low immigration, leaving aside the middling cases. Or you might want to find out how citizens across the whole state are reacting.

4   In any case, you will have to interview a representative sample of the people you are interested in, rarely having the resources to interview everybody. The usual method is to draw names randomly (i.e. by chance) from the most comprehensive list of names with contact details that you can get – usually published lists of eligible voters. The reason for drawing names by chance is that there are established procedures for estimating 'sampling error' around the estimates you get from your survey when you apply them to the whole underlying population you are interested in.

5   Contacting and interviewing the potential 'respondents' in your sample used to be done by interviewers going to the appropriate address and asking the sample member to respond to the questions in the questionnaire. Now that most people can be contacted by telephone or email, interviewing is done in this way, which is much cheaper.

6   'Coding' and preparing answers. Formerly, most survey questions asked for 'more' or 'less' responses, or even invited people to give their own answers to 'open' questions about their feelings (e.g. What is the most important problem facing the country?). This involved a lot of 'coding' – that is, classifying answers into general categories to make them comparable. With increasing reliance on the 'self-placement' of respondents on 'ladders' or 'scales', the need for such 'coding' has diminished. Computer programmes can also pick out key words or phrases from answers to characterize the positions they take. This also simplifies data preparation.

7   With results from the survey questionnaire classified or quantified, data analysis can now proceed, guided by the theoretical questions clarified in Stage 1 above. These should guide you through the mass of potential information which surveys normally produce.

Two important considerations arise with regard to the procedures just sketched:

1   These require a lot of effort and work. So before undertaking a survey of your own, you should always ask yourself if you could not use an earlier one already available from a data archive or website, which will give you the information you want. Better still, you might be able to analyse lots of surveys from different times and places, which might give you a better and wider basis for generalization.

2   Error creeps in at every stage of a survey, from ambiguities in questions, biased sampling and the inability to contact all respondents to data preparation and analysis. It must be allowed for in making estimates and testing hypotheses in the ways illustrated below.

Going down to how *individual* voters behave by getting them to report on themselves, as in surveys, solves this problem. However, it can of course operate the other way round – black voters' support for pro-immigration parties does not necessarily translate into higher support for them in the constituencies where they live, since this may be balanced by white voters not voting for them. As noted at the end of the last section, these problems of inference for research which draw conclusions from one level of analysis and apply it to another may be a problem for studies of comparative government using country differences as their basis for generalizing about institutional behaviour within countries.

However, many of the questions we want to ask about influences on voting do relate to individual behaviour. It was thus immensely liberating for analysts in the 1950s to get direct answers on these from the people involved. As with all measurements, however, the answers depend on how questions are framed. This will vary depending on the theory started from. Surveys allowed innumerable types of questions to be put to voters, going far beyond their relatively fixed characteristics such as class, religion and area to influences more closely related to the election context voters found themselves in. Psychological factors such as **party identification**, candidate

Party identification

The emotional attachment to a political party felt by an individual elector.

Briefing 16.5

From the 'index of political predispositions' to the 'funnel of causality' as the explanation of vote choice

The first election survey was of voting in the US Presidential Election of 1940 in Erie County, New York State. The market researchers who organized it expected individual voting to be heavily influenced by the amount of advertising the presidential candidates got in local newspapers and radio, so they measured this as well as getting information from their survey. To their surprise, they found no relationship at all between advertising and vote. They did find, however, that vote was heavily influenced by social factors not particularly emphasized in the election campaign – notably religion, occupational class and urban or rural residence.

Based on their findings, they switched to the view that vote was largely determined by social location and devised an index (the IPP) running from a Protestant rural farmer (almost certain to vote Republican) to a Catholic urban manual worker (almost certain to vote Democrat).

The first national US election surveys of the 1950s had to deal with massive changes as voters switched from Democrats to Republicans in the Presidential Elections of 1952 and 1956. As a result, election analysts abandoned the idea that vote was 'fixed' and grounded in social characteristics. Instead they envisaged a 'funnel of causality', in which voting choice was immediately influenced by the issues and candidates of the relevant election. Views on these were affected, but not wholly determined by the individual's 'party identification' (party ID) – a long-standing psychological attachment to a political party which could be distinguished from current vote. Party ID in its turn was then influenced by the socio-demographic factors stressed in the IPP, as the 'funnel of causality' widened out and brought in more explanatory factors as it went backwards in time.

appeals and the impact of issues could be related to vote. This in turn shifted research interests from broadly Marxist-, class- or cleavage-based theories of voting behaviour to more dynamic, psychological ones.

The general lesson one can draw from this is that theory and evidence have a strong mutual influence on each other. Theory may shape ideas about what data to collect and how to collect it (in the case of surveys how questions are to be phrased). But theories and hypotheses are devised to explain the data available. Thus, a change at the evidential level is likely to produce changes in theories and explanations, certainly in those at the focus of research attention.

Surveys started off by gathering evidence on mass voting and related preferences from individual electors – and have of course continued to do so, primarily through **opinion polls**. However, one can ask questions of anyone, so surveys were soon extended to cover specialized groups such as legislators, party strategists, government ministers, bureaucrats, lobbyists, reporters and many others more directly engaged in the shaping of policy. Questions could go beyond the individuals' own preferences and reactions to their perceptions of how other political actors behaved and where they stood.

Such multilevel investigation facilitated studies of correspondence between electors' preferences and public policy. However, measures of the

Opinion poll

A sample of voters asked various questions, some on politics.

Briefing 16.6

Be careful what you're measuring! Public perceptions of policy, policy targets and implemented policy

Survey questions are so easy to ask that the temptation is to use them to measure everything rather than confine them to what they are best suited for. Clearly, if you want to know about popular policy preferences, the best way is to ask individuals themselves and then aggregate their responses (making allowance for errors along the way).

The temptation, however, is then to go on to ask individuals where they think the parties stand on these. Such perceptions of party policy may affect the individual's voting and other behaviour, so those factors should be taken into account in explaining it. But they are not necessarily the same thing as what the party has declared its policy to be, though they may be influenced by this. To know what national policy is, we need to go to party declarations and texts like its election manifesto. In turn, this, like government declarations and proposals, only states policy *targets*. To know how far these have actually been implemented, however, we need to go on to direct indicators, such as expenditure on different programmes and policy areas.

If we don't use the independent measurements appropriate to each of the things that we want to relate to each other, we will never know if the summary relationships between them are real or simply a carryover – for example, electors may perceive their party's policy position as similar to their own because they favour it on other grounds.

latter tended to be indirect: what electors *thought* each party's policy position was, either in broad left-right terms or on specific issues. The great flexibility of surveys, however, also enabled them to question specialists and experts – asking them to locate national parties along a left-right scale, for example (see Chapter 4). This allowed parties to be independently and precisely located in terms of their ideological and policy distance from each other. In this way, analysts could also see how close the parties were to electors. With this knowledge, analysts could judge which sets of voters would be likely to shift to another party – on policy grounds, for example – if their own party was not running in that particular election. Or they could see which party was closer to another on policy and thus more likely to go into a government coalition with it.

Surveys are so flexible and applicable at so many levels of political activity in different areas that their influence on research was like that of the telescope in physics. So much that was previously unmeasured or even unrecorded could now be observed. This produced an explosion of research, including many of the studies of representation and policy alternation considered in Parts I and III.

These qualities also had their downside, however. Surveys were so quick and easy to conduct that they tended to be used to measure everything, even where they provided second-hand or third-hand measurements of something that could be measured more directly at source. For example, why measure party policy based on electors' perceptions (or even of experts' perceptions of it) when parties actually state their policies explicitly in the shape of an electoral programme (a 'manifesto' or platform) – which is moreover officially approved by a party gathering legally charged with doing so?

You cannot simply assume that electors' or specialists' perceptions correctly catch what the party states as its policy. Indeed, it is an interesting research question in its own right to ask if the two coincide – whether a party is getting its real message through. If you use electors' perceptions to measure actual policy, you cannot ask this question. You simply *assume* that they coincide.

From surveys to other measures

Surveys are therefore excellent at measuring individual perceptions and preferences, but they are not necessarily best at characterizing bodies which act collectively. This forms another twist in the 'level of analysis' problem of making inferences from estimates based on one kind of unit to another. Getting a non-survey-based measurement in this case depends on developing techniques for the analysis of documents and texts, since it is in writing that collective actors tend to express their decisions about policy (among many other things). Indeed, practically everything in politics and society tends to be recorded in documents and other texts. This makes the ability to measure their content ('content analysis') highly important in the future development of political studies.

Fortunately, survey technology provided a springboard for doing so. Surveys themselves produced texts, in the form of written interview schedules or transcriptions of recorded interviews. **Coding** was necessary to place the sentences and words respondents used into general categories (i.e. 'positive' or 'negative' reactions towards certain parties). It was easy to apply the same technique, with similar coding categories, to a written text. We need not stick to simple categories. For example, sentences could be placed in one of a large number of categories covering all the major areas of policy (see Table 6.3). By counting the number of sentences in each and seeing how they vary between manifestos in different elections, you can get an idea of parties' shifting policy concerns. Or the categories can themselves be classified as left, neutral and right and parties compared on their left-right movements traced over time. (This approach to analysing texts has already been applied in Chapter 6.)

Word or sentence-counting into such categories thus offers a valuable new source of evidence tied down to specified documents stating actors' positions and intentions at a particular point in time. These 'public' statements can replace or supplement surveys of preferences and intentions at individual level or be related to them (as where we ask whether a party has successfully got its stated policy through to voters' perceptions of it – a crucial point in some election situations).

As with electors' perceptions and self-defined policy stands of parties, we should not, however, make the mistake of thinking that party policy intentions are necessarily the same as the policy being actually applied – even when the party is in government. Indeed, the whole process of policy alternation at government level and the slowness in getting targets translated into the policy actually being implemented on the ground are crucial elements of the democratic processes described in Part I. If we just assumed that policy targets automatically get implemented, we would lose a key factor in the explanation.

Coding

Classifying verbal information (e.g. sentences) into general categories.

From intentions to implementation: government policy statistics

Fortunately, we need not make indirect, and possibly misplaced, inferences from government policy targets to what is actually being implemented by the bureaucracy. For that, we can move on to direct indicators, such as what is being budgeted for (or, better, what has actually been spent) in various 'policy areas'. These may contain some **measurement error**, as all indicators potentially do. (We discuss how to measure error in the next section.) For example, there have been policy areas where large-scale spending has produced little in the way of concrete results – notably on large-scale computer systems or weapons development. So spending and

Measurement error

The extent to which estimates give wrong information.

outcomes do not always match up. In terms of established areas of policy, however, increased expenditure usually implies an expansion of responsibilities which require more personnel, more offices and other equipment and hence increased activity in welfare, economics or other policy areas. What has actually been spent is obviously a better indicator of policy activity than budgeted expenditure, which may not be spent in the end or which may be diverted to other uses.

Expenditures are thus the most general measure of policy activity and the one most easily related to policy preferences as measured by surveys. These latter are most usually expressed as a desire for government to do 'more' or 'less' in particular policy areas, which can be easily related to

---

Briefing 16.7

Big Data-sets useful for research

All the types of data mentioned are publicly available in 'cleaned-up', edited form, often with contextual and qualitative information included. Some 'such data-sets' contain different types of data, saving you the trouble of putting them together yourself. All the ones listed here cover a number of countries. The following are some major data sets:

- *Contemporary data on economic development and public expenditure (OECD)*
  http://stats.oecd.org/Index.aspx?DataSetCode=BLI
- *University of Berne: Politics and Society (1960–2014)*
  www.cpds-data.org/
- *Composition, Personnel and Duration of Party Government in Democracies*
  https://fsw.vu.nl/en/departments/political-science-and-public-administration/staff/
  woldendorp/party-government-data-set/index.aspx#
- *Party Programmes and Elections, Science Centre Berlin (1945–2019)*
  http://manifestoproject.wzb.eu
- Eurobarometer left-right self-placements
  http://ec.europa.eu/commfrontoffice/publicopinion/index.cfm
- Gallup Public Opinion Polls
  www.gallup.com/analytics/232838/world-poll.aspx
- Roper Public Opinion Data Archives
  https://ropercenter.cornell.edu/polls/
- Global Public Opinions Project
  www.gpop.eu/
- CSES (Comparative Study of Election Systems)
  www.cses.org/
- EES (European Election Studies)
  http://europeanelectionstudies.net/
- ISSP (Initiative for Science, Society and Policy)
  www.issp.center/

increases or decreases in spending. General 'left' and 'right' preferences are also reflected as support for 'more' or 'less' state activity, reflected in greater or less government spending overall.

Governments publish statistics on many aspects of their own activity, which may also serve as measures of policy implementation. Legislation, for example, has to be put on public record (otherwise, the population would not know what the laws were). Numbers of laws dealing with different areas can be counted. Or a more refined investigation that uses the techniques of 'content analysis' to examine reports on actual policy implementation may be used to estimate directly how far targets have been met in various areas and how this relates to preferences.

Besides reporting their own activities, various government agencies will normally monitor economic activity in a country, providing regular figures on levels of employment, trade flows, manufacturing output and a variety of economic activities and social problems. Insofar as citizens regard economic activity as a responsibility of government, these also enable us to see how far such responsibilities are being met.

Besides their own policy measures, governments also publish social, election and voting statistics by area, which we discussed as 'demographic' or 'area' statistics. Regional and local governments also publish reports for their areas covering both what they are doing and socioeconomic developments within them.

Most government information is already provided in numeric form. Emanating from largely political bodies it is usually relevant to the concerns of political scientists. It constitutes the major source of information on the end product of the democratic process: implemented policy. Describing this in terms of numbers makes it easier to feed directly into our research and to compare it with survey or textual information about preferences. However, the latter have often to be categorized and scored in some way before quantitative analyses are undertaken.

Estimation and error

A possibility of error exists at every stage of data collection and preparation. We examine it here. In the next chapters, we go on to error in the process of theory testing and in the techniques applied to it. The ultimate check on error is of course whether measures and techniques produce expected or at least plausible results. If they do, we can accept them as true – at least until they fail later checks. There is a catch, however, in that we need *independent* evidence to check out a theory with at least some possibility of disproving it. Otherwise, there is no point in putting theory to the test, since we are going to accept it anyway. But the theory in turn is based on our reasonable expectations about how, for example, party policy will change under certain conditions. So nonconformity with the theory may cast doubt on the standing of the measure. But measures which show theory to be wrong are not necessarily themselves wrong, even if these go against seemingly reasonable theoretical expectations. They are just doing their job of checking the theory.

We can get out of this circularity problem in various ways. First, where we have great confidence in the theory (especially if it is supported by other evidence), we might want to re-examine the measures we are using or substitute better ones if those measures go against the theory. Indeed, it is always better to rely on a number of different indicators rather than rely totally on any one given the possibility of error. If most measures go against the theory, even a well-established one, we have to accept the result.

Second, the reasonable expectations which we can check the outcomes of our measures against may not simply be embodied in the theory we are testing. We can take as an example the graphs in Figures 6.3 and 6.4 showing left-right movement by important parties over the post-war period. These are based on counting sentences from party manifestos into various policy areas and adding these up as 'left' or 'right' emphases. Party swings from left to right, as charted by this measure, can be compared with general judgements by historians and others on whether parties *did* move left or right in given elections. If the party movements shown in the graph correspond with these judgements, we are on fairly good ground in regarding them as correct estimates. On this basis, we can accept what they tell us about predictions from the theory being upheld or rejected.

Checking for error: end estimates versus production procedures

Validation generally takes the final estimates produced by the whole data collection and preparation process and checks out whether they are doing the job we want them to do. This seems the best test to apply to estimates, not only because it is the most relevant to our purposes (we use the final estimates to check theory) but also because it involves the whole measurement process, rather than any particular element in it. This is important because the error introduced at one stage of preparing estimates may be compensated by error going in a different direction at another stage, leaving open the possibility that the final estimate may be correct after all.

For example, in assigning individual sentences of manifesto text to policy categories, one coder may have a tendency to over-assign sentences to 'right-wing' categories. Of course, there will be many precautions against this happening, from initial training and checks on assigning trial sentences to categories, to continuing consultations by supervisors. Even so, applying the general rules to individual sentence assignments is difficult and mistakes may creep in.

At the same time, another coder may well be biasing results in another direction, by over-assigning sentences to 'leftist' policy categories. If we then assessed error by checking out the percentage of sentence assignments on which the two coders disagreed, we might then find that it is high. Hence, we might conclude that the resulting estimates had a lot of error and were unfit for purpose.

However, the cumulated error at the individual level of coding might not affect the overall estimate of a party's left-right score to any great extent. This is because the opposing biases on each side, left and right respectively, would largely cancel out, leaving the overall estimate similar to what it would have been if both coders had made unbiased 'correct' judgements.

The tendency for biases and mistakes to cancel out as you go up from individual sentence by sentence judgements to aggregate ones, parallels the 'level of analysis' problem. That raised the possibility that findings made at one level of analysis do not necessarily carry over to another. (Individually ethnic minority voters support pro-immigrant parties, whereas the constituencies where they live in large numbers may show disproportionate support for anti-immigrant parties.)

Similarly, error at an individual level of data preparation may not be reflected in the final estimates since individual errors can balance out when aggregated into overall estimates. This could happen if the errors reflected systematic but opposing biases, as with the case of the two coders. But it could also be the case if the errors were unsystematic and random – that is, each coder made wrong assignments say in 20% of cases – but these just divided between left and right assignments without unduly favouring either. In that case too, misjudgements could balance out, leaving final estimates of how much a given manifesto leaned left or right relatively unaffected.

It is, after all, these final scores that investigators wish to use in order to check out theories. Running checks on the accuracy of the procedures used to produce them are useful as data collection and production proceed. These are the best precautions one can take at these points against the final estimates being inaccurate. Once we have these, however, it is direct checks on the amount of error in the final estimates that become most relevant to the ongoing investigation.

The ultimate check on the final estimates is how well they perform within the theoretical context to which they are relevant. Relatively few predictive theories have been developed in political science up till now. At the present time, therefore, measurement performance can only rarely be assessed with their aid. So substitute tests have to be found. One of these has already been suggested: checking out the measure against other evidence or consensual beliefs about what has happened in the area they cover and seeing if the new estimates conform to these. The example we cited was whether graphs of estimated left-right movement by parties in various countries agree with historical accounts of ideological shifts by parties.

A more precise way of checking up on measures (though based on the same idea of comparing agreement between different bits of evidence) is to systematically assess one measure against another, as in the multi-measure multi-variable matrix displayed in Table 16.2.

TABLE 16.2 Checking measures systematically against each other for error: the multi-measure multi-variable matrix

	Manifesto L-R		Survey L-R	
	Socialist Party Scoring 1	Conservative Party Scoring 1	Socialist Party Scoring 1	Conservative Party Scoring 1
Manifesto L-R Socialist Party Scoring 2	**90**	△ 21	□ 74	◯ 11
Manifesto L-R Conservative Party Scoring 2	△ 21	**95**	◯ 11	□ 72
Survey Socialist Party Scoring 2	□ 74	◯ 11	**96**	△ 15
Survey Conservative Party Scoring 2	◯ 11	□ 72	△ 15	**94**

Notes:

Entries are percentage agreement between coders and respondents. Reliability diagonal (heavy type) reports percentage agreement between the same coders and respondents assigning scores to the same object (socialist party in 1995 or conservative party in 1995) on different occasions (Scoring 1 and Scoring 2).

Squares surround numbers for percentage agreement between survey-based and manifesto-based scoring of the same party positions. Triangles indicate agreement when the same method is used to score different parties. Circles mark out agreement when the different methods are used to score different parties. Figures in heavy type in the diagonal should be higher than ones in squares, which should be higher than ones in triangles, which should be higher than ones in circles.

Source: Adapted from D. T. Campbell and D. W. Fisk (1959) Convergent and Discriminant Validation by the Multitrait-Multimethod Matrix. *Psychological Bulletin*, 56(2), pp. 81–105

Theoretical variables

Concepts, processes or behaviours that have been measured, so scores can 'vary'.

This relates two **theoretical variables** and two ways of measuring these variables. The two variables are the socialist party's and the conservative party's left-right positions within a country in 1995. The two ways of measuring position are, first, deriving a left-right score by coding their election manifestos and, second, using electors' answers to a question in two identical surveys, staged at different times around about the 1995 elections about what the party's left-right positions are. Electors' perceptions of where parties stand may not be the best indicator of where they actually do stand. This is probably better provided by looking at what they themselves say about it in their authorized and published election programme. However, before the development of content analysis electors' placements of parties *were* the best indicators of party positions in each election that we could get, even if they were rather indirect ones. So we should expect a reasonable correspondence between the survey-based and the manifesto-based measures. Figures on their correspondence can be used to assess their degree of error within the general pattern of correspondences revealed in Table 16.2.

First, however, we should note that party positions need to be measured twice, using exactly the same method used to code and measure the party positions on each occasion. So the same coders code the same manifesto on two separate occasions by using the same instructions (Scoring 1 and Scoring 2). This gives us the opportunity to assess how reliable the measure is, by finding out whether it yields the same score on both occasions. It should, of course, since exactly the same measure is being applied to exactly the same party though at different times. We can also compare estimates of the party positions obtained from the identical surveys staged at two different times around the election.

Allowing for small errors, a general cross-time agreement is what emerges in the table. The reliability diagonal relates Scoring 1 and Scoring 2 on each measure to each other (with numbers shown in heavy type). Agreement is in the 90% range, reflecting some but limited error in the measurements. Essentially, they give the same result, showing that the two measures (survey and textual) are stable ('reliable') between different applications. So we can use Scoring 1 and Scoring 2 interchangeably in the table and expect there to be little difference in what they show. (We actually use Scoring 1 to define the columns in the table and Scoring 2 to define the rows. The high agreement between them in the reliability diagonal indicates that doing so gives much the same results as using Scoring 1 throughout. But we need both scorings to generate the reliability figures in the diagonal in the first place.)

The important part of assessing the measures' all-round performance is not, however, the diagonal figures in themselves but how they fit into the whole of the table. Where the same measures are being used to estimate the left-right positions of the parties, we should expect the association between the two to be higher than where different measures are being used. Figures for correspondence in this latter case are reported within the small squares in the table. We expect the agreement here, given the different text and survey-based measures being applied, to be smaller than where the same measure was being used two times to estimate the same party positions. And they are – in the 70% range as compared to the 90%–99% in the diagonal.

If measurement differences actually predominated to the exclusion of the real differences between the parties, we should, however, expect the square numbers to be smaller or just about the same as the other numbers in the table, contained in the triangles and circles. The triangles report the correspondence when the same method is used to measure the different party positions. If the measures are really giving the correct results, we naturally expect there to be a difference. The two parties are at opposite poles ideologically, so there should be little overlap between their real positions, which should be reflected in the estimates. The fact that these were done using the same technique on different parties should not obscure the real differences if the measure is functioning properly.

Therefore, the numbers in the triangles should be substantially lower than the numbers in the squares. The same should apply even more strongly to the numbers in the circles, where different methods are being applied to estimate different party positions. The overall pattern to emerge from the matrix should therefore show the figures in the diagonal to be highest, followed by those in the squares, showing up in their turn as substantially higher than those in the triangles and circles.

Of course, since two estimation methods are involved, we are not sure which (or both) might be at fault if the expected pattern of results does not emerge. We might in this case suspect the survey-based perceptions to be pulling everything down since they are more prone to error as more indirect measures of party positions. It is, however, up to investigators to choose reasonable measures for the comparison in the first place; otherwise, there is no point in making it.

The multi-measure multi-variable matrix gives powerful results because it combines and focuses several ways of assessing the error in estimates produced by measurement techniques. The figures in the squares relate to convergent validity: if the two different measurement procedures are actually measuring what they are supposed to be measuring – that is, the party positions – then their estimates should largely agree with each other on what the party positions are.

On the other hand, the triangles and circles in the figure rest on ideas of 'discriminant validity': the fact that different parties' positions are being measured by the same technique should not obscure the real differences in their actual positions. They should show up as different. Being able to compare figures for the agreement between different estimates helps us avoid setting arbitrary thresholds for results – for example, refusing to accept proof of convergent validation unless agreement in the squares is over 80%. But this is an arbitrary threshold. What matters, instead, is the overall pattern of results, including the convincing numerical gap between the figures in the squares and those in the triangles and circles.

Table 16.2 also introduces the concept of reliability into the comparisons. As we have noted, validity is overriding as a test of measurement and estimate quality. If a measure is working as it is supposed to do (i.e. giving accurate estimates of party positions), then it must also be reliable in the sense of always giving broadly the same results when applied to the same object. Nor can it be unreliable in the sense of being biased – that is, giving the same results over time, but ones which constantly favour one alternative over another (e.g. right over left). Neither of these defects can be present if the measure meets expectations and works well in a theoretical context – that is, is valid.

Validity thus overrides reliability by guaranteeing it. How can you get valid (consistently correct) results with unreliable measures? In our preliminary investigations, we may not know enough to have reasonably based expectations or a good theoretical basis for knowing what the numbers should show or whether the measure is stable and consistent across its various applications. This is where reliability comes into its own. The dearth of clearly formulated predictive and explanatory theory in political science at the present time focuses most current methodological discussion on questions of reliability rather than validity.

Of course, it is sensible and necessary in the early stages of investigation to check consistency to be sure as far as possible of the quality of the procedures and indicators we are using. Precisely because of the lack of substantive theory and knowledge to guide us, however, later assessment of overall reliability is fraught with difficulty, as we now explain.

Estimate error

The matrix provides an overview of how far the available evidence gives a consistent message and is to be trusted for that reason. However, just as the dearth of predictive theories limits their role as a criterion for the validity of estimates, so too does the lack of good alternative measures of the same concept restrict the use of the matrix. In the example in Table 16.2, we had to use a measure of *perceptions* of party policy positions as an indicator of their *actual* policy positions. We know it is a second-best measure. In the context of the matrix, its deficiencies are likely to drag down values for the more direct manifesto-based scaling, since lack of agreement is more likely to be due to error in the less direct rather than more direct measure. Lacking better alternative measures, however, we have to use perceptions of policy positions in the comparison rather than a more direct one.

These difficulties in measuring reliability mean that we are often driven back to single measures of procedural error in assessing the performance or potential of evidence. Such measures tell us, for example, what level of changes in a measure over time are true changes (e.g. in a party's real policy position) and which are simply error. The latter may stem from different samples – giving somewhat different estimates – being drawn from the same underlying population or from the same measurement technique being applied by different investigators in different ways at different times.

Table 16.3 summarizes different ways in which error might arise and how it may be estimated. The classic source of error, differences between different sample estimates, stems from the fact that large numbers of actors cannot all be questioned and counted, even with electronic aids like telephones, email and computers. Only the census covers whole populations but at wide intervals of time, because of the administrative effort and cost involved. Instead small representative groups are interviewed (as in the opinion polls), to provide estimates for the whole population from which they are drawn.

Even if such groups are made as representative as possible of the general population in terms of demographic characteristics (gender, class, ethnicity, education, area, etc.), their composition and responses will differ in many ways. So estimates may vary due to the peculiarities of particular samples. If the sample is a random sample of the population (each individual in it drawn purely by chance), statistical theory allows us to calculate what the likely error variation around each estimate will be and thus to

TABLE 16.3 Types of estimate error and suggestions for getting true values

Type of error	Possible solutions
1. Random sampling error	Assuming estimates are from a (nearly) random sample of cases from an underlying 'population', calculating a 'confidence interval' around estimates within which differences between them should be ignored
2. Selection error (where all available cases are included but they could still be regarded as a sample out of larger population)	A) Calculate confidence interval for each estimate, e.g. by seeing how similar it is to an estimate based on the most similar case not selected B) Assume it is (nearly) the whole population, so no allowance for sampling error required
3. Processing error (commonly this is coding error)	Calculate disagreements between independent applications of measure, and put them together to calculate confidence intervals around each estimate
4. Final estimate error	A) Calculate stability of each estimate in face of random substitution of other estimates B) Calculate boundaries within which most estimates produce similar scores, assuming that any variation within them is due to error (possibly leaving out any externally validated variation from the calculation and also large differences between estimates as likely to be accurate) C) Demonstrate that error is limited and can be ignored by showing that estimates meet external truth criteria (e.g. support successful predictions from relevant theories)

create a 'confidence interval' giving the range of values within which differing estimates cannot be trusted to reveal true change or differences in the underlying variable being measured. (So estimates are often reported as e.g. 5 ± 2, indicating that the true value is probably somewhere between 3 and 7. Any seeming difference within that range, e.g. between scores of 4 and 6, is not to be taken as a real reflection of what is going on in the underlying population.)

The problem in the social sciences is that samples are never truly random. Even if names are initially drawn on a random basis, unavailability and lack of response undermine a random draw. Even when you are sampling events or documents, some are likely to be missing. We can therefore estimate error on the assumption that the sample is more or less random. But adjustments will be correct only to the (unknown) extent that this 'near-random' assumption is correct.

These problems have led investigators to treat sample results as reliable if all reasonable precautions have been taken in drawing the sample (e.g. ensuring that there is good representation of all the major types in the population). Even more confidence can be placed in the figures if all the estimates from samples interviewed on the same subject at around the same time are aggregated, thus cancelling out possible mistakes in the individual sample surveys and revealing which is out of line. During election campaigns, for example, a 'poll of polls' is often used as the most reliable indicator of voting intentions. Aggregating estimates from the individual polls cancels out the variation due to the different types of processing error and has a better chance of producing an accurate estimate.

Sampling assumptions are often extended to other data sets derived by coding and scoring texts or events. On the face of it, these cover all relevant cases, such as all post-war election programmes in a country. This would imply that the estimates derived from these could be taken as they stand, without the need to allow for sampling variation, because they cover the complete set of party programmes for a country for a specified time period. An argument can be made, however, that the finished programmes are more or less randomly selected from a series of drafts, all making the same arguments with only minor stylistic and presentational differences. We could calculate the effect of the latter by, for example, comparing estimates from the manifesto texts that we have with estimates from their nearest equivalents (e.g. party leaders' speeches during the election campaign) to see the possible differences between them. We could use this to infer the range of values the original estimates could take on a result of sampling error rather than 'true variation'.

This seems like a lot of work merely to meet speculative doubts about whether a seemingly complete set of cases may actually be a sample. More concrete than selection and sampling effects are processing errors such as those produced by assigning survey responses or text units (words and sentences) to categories. Where assignment is not wholly computerized, there is always likely to be some variation in the way different coders apply the same instructions or even between the ways the same coder might apply the same instructions at different times. This can be calculated by the agreement between independent codings of the same document, done under strictly similar conditions, as shown in the reliability diagonal of the matrix in Table 16.2, for example. The range of different values taken on by the independent codings can then be used to calculate 'confidence intervals' that show the extent to which individual estimates vary purely from error rather than from true differences in electors' opinions or party behaviour.

There are, however, two problems involved in this approach. One is that it covers random error variation but not bias. In other words, if all procedures consistently favoured scorings as right rather than left, that error would go undetected. The second problem is how to get an overall measure of error from sampling, selection and processing in combination. After all, our main interest lies in getting correct estimates from the finished data rather than in seeing what has gone wrong with one process in their production.

From this point of view, there is no substitute for directly checking out the final estimates rather than assuming that all error is caused by sampling or coding respectively and calculating confidence intervals for this. As we have noted, coding errors in particular often balance out. So they are neutralized when it comes to effects on the final estimates. It is better, therefore, to base any final adjustments for error (e.g. calculating

Briefing 16.8

Computerized coding of texts

Computer programmes have the great merit of counting units and calculating related statistics at great speed. The basic units which make up a text – words and sentences – can therefore be counted and sorted quickly by computers once we know what we want to find out from the text. In the case of political parties, that might be 'policy targets' in the sense of knowing what it officially states as its aims on a particular issue or in general left-right terms. The main problem for a computer analysis is knowing what words/sentences indicate support for or opposition to a policy proposal or a 'left' as opposed to a 'right' position.

1   A first solution might be to prepare a dictionary of words/sentences used to indicate support for or opposition to proposals or indicating a general left-right position. Earlier attempts at creating such 'dictionary lists' were not successful in tracing out changes in preferences or targets, though current ones show greater promise. One problem is generalizing across different languages. All of these, however, can be translated (by computer) into English versions where a general dictionary can be applied in their quantitative analysis.

2   A variant on comprehensive dictionaries is to analyse texts for the whole of a given time period to see what key recurring words are used, such as by 'left' as opposed to 'right' parties. Then their policy changes can be traced out from election to election by the relative incidence of the key words or phrases they use in the associated election programme.

3   A more flexible approach is to select a key document (perhaps the most extreme manifesto agreed to have been produced by a political party) and compare the whole set of words in other documents with the ones used in the key document. The more they resemble each other, the closer the policy portions of the two documents are as reflected in the 'word scores' they receive. In this way, the parties' policy changes can be traced over time, or support or opposition to a policy proposal put forward in a legislative debate can be measured.

   The main problem here lies in the selection of the key document which provides the basis for the analysis. Should we estimate distances from the extremes or from the centre? How stable are the estimates if another document is taken as the key one?

4   An alternative procedure is to mix computerized with human coding, by creating a set of simple instructions for 'crowd coding' documents like manifestos by a set of paid volunteers contacted though a commercial website created for jobs like these. The problem is that both instructions and tasks for untrained coders have to be kept basic – for example, coding sentences into positive/negative or left/ right. While the average or mean judgement of the crowd sums up to produce valid results, there is a long tail of inaccurate judgements to each side, making for high variation across individual scorings. This is often used as a measure of error. Crowd coding cannot be used for long or complicated tasks, like coding whole documents into many categories. At the moment, this seems best done by trained coders under close central supervision (cf. Chapter 6 on the Manifesto Project).

confidence intervals) on the estimates themselves rather than on the way they were generated.

Several methods could be applied here. The first is related to the doubts already mentioned in regard to selection error. If the cases we have are simply a sample out of a wider population of drafts, each saying basically the same thing but with minor differences in wording, we could calculate the effect of these trivial differences on the final estimates by randomly dropping some words or sentences and doubling others. This simulates stylistic differences between the various tests which might have gone into the sample we have actually obtained.

Numerical estimates from longer documents keep their original values better in the face of such 'error' variation. Under this kind of error checking, therefore, estimates from longer documents will be more reliable and have smaller confidence intervals put around them than estimates from shorter documents.

As against this, it can be argued that the published election programme has been officially endorsed by the party leadership or convention as it stands. So we are dealing with a population of approved documents rather than a random sampling of drafts. Hence, estimates can be taken at face value. Attempts to 'correct' shorter documents may introduce distortion and error. For example, shorter documents can be more closely scrutinized by official bodies than longer ones and therefore could on this basis be regarded as more reliable indicators of party intentions.

Both assessments of document accuracy rest on arguable assumptions about what constitutes a sample as opposed to a population. Alternative 4.B in Table 16.3 adopts a different approach by arguing that, in any case, outstandingly large estimate differences between estimates have to be taken as correct if the data are at all credible. Variation between the remaining estimates is more likely to be caused by error. On the assumption that it is, we can then calculate the boundaries for confidence intervals around each estimate. Using our previous example where the interval was +2 to -2 around an estimate of 5, this would indicate that a change from the original 5 to a new one of 6 (e.g. in a party's left-right position from one year to the next) was not a real one. The seeming difference is due to error variation between one coder coding one programme and another the next year's programme. So what it indicates is that the party has not really changed its policy during these two years. However, if the differences between estimates were large (e.g. 10) we would take them at face value as correctly reflecting a real party policy change.

Any experienced investigator would probably discount small differences anyway. Calculating a precise confidence interval, however, does impose the same standard across different investigations, which helps in comparing results. Otherwise, one investigator might base conclusions on differences and changes between estimates which others might write off. This could lead to ambiguity in assessing whether the theory being tested has actually been upheld by all the evidence.

Table 16.3 demonstrates, however, that the questions of what standards to apply and how they should be calculated are often in doubt – no matter how precise they are in numerical terms. Whether a set of observations is only a sample of all those that could have been made or covers everything is a central issue that carries over to the statistical analyses discussed in Chapter 18. If it is a sample, then the main question is whether the differences or changes observed in the estimates really apply to the 'population' (of people, documents, events, etc.) from which it was drawn. This can be settled by 'tests of significance' applied to observations and relationships between them. If, on the other hand, the estimates are really made directly from the entire 'population' of cases, the question whether they 'really' apply to it is settled, and we are more interested in sorting out the strong relationships from the pervasive weak ones.

Whether or not we concur on this point, we can all agree on the existence of some measurement error in all estimates and data. Again, however, there are different approaches to it. One is to prioritize questions of reliability: we must be sure of the exact extent of error in any measure or estimate before we apply it. The other approach sees the application and use of estimates as *part* of the process of checking on them. If reasonable precautions against error have been taken in producing them, the overriding question is their validity. Do they work as intended within the theoretical context to which they are applied? If they do, this attests to their reliability and relative freedom from error. Such an approach cuts through the elaborate testing procedures which often slow investigations down and leave their conclusions uncertain. But it suffers from the dearth of precisely stated predictive theory in political science. In addition to its other advantages, this could offer a clearer context within which to validate estimates.

End-summary

The theory you start with indicates what evidence is relevant to any investigation and how it should be framed and reported. While influenced by theory in terms of selection and presentation, evidence reflects events and behaviour which have been observed independently. It thus provides external criteria on which to accept or reject the theory. This is particularly true where theories are clearly enough specified to generate predictions that can be shown to be true or false.

The chapter started with the traditional distinction between qualitative and quantitative evidence, showing that this is less hard and fast than often assumed. Descriptions of individual events can be summarized by numbers where there are enough of them, while theories and statistical findings feed back into descriptive accounts. We illustrated this point by contrasting the earliest quantitative data used systematically in political science – area or 'demographic' statistics – with descriptive accounts. The latter are rich and informative but difficult to compare outside their own unique context. 'Demographic' data do facilitate systematic comparisons. Their scope is limited, however, and they can be misleading when generalized down to individual behaviour. Surveys provide practically unlimited information on individuals, but this cannot be reliably aggregated to characterize collective actors like political parties. Texts and government statistics provide more direct evidence on their activities.

Mistaken inferences from one unit of analysis to another are only one example of the errors which affect all types of estimates. These may derive from the simple fact of being samples from some underlying 'population' and hence varying around the true value found in the 'population': or from biased or random mistakes in preparing estimates. To calculate the amount of estimate error due to such mistakes, assumptions have to be made about whether we are dealing with a sample or the complete set of source material and about what kind of processing mistakes occurred.

Such assumptions are themselves controversial. So adjustments made to the estimates on their basis may themselves compound errors. The most direct checks on error are those directed at the final estimates themselves – for replicability, internal consistency and above all validity (i.e. whether they fit with theory and/or reasonable expectations about what they ought to show us).

Error also crops up when we relate evidence to theory within a statistical framework. A main question again is whether we are dealing with samples or populations and whether tests of significance based on sampling theory or direct measures of the strength of relationships are the appropriate checks in testing hypotheses. Such problems might loom less large if we actually had theories which made predictions, where we could measure their success. Most advances here have been made using theories based on spatial representations – for example, to relate preferences and policy. Such representations (Chapters 4–6) accordingly form the central reference point in Chapters 17 and 18.

This chapter has covered a lot of points about the collection, nature and standing of the evidence we need to create policy series and to assess predictive explanations of political processes. Key points to carry away are:

- How qualitative descriptions and reports can be turned into numbers suitable for statistical analysis – that is, into quantitative estimates.
- How precisely their conversion into numbers can be carried out.
- The different kinds of data which can be related to each other to check out theories.
- The presence of error in all data and how to estimate it.
- The need to base error estimation on various assumptions about the type of error we are dealing with.
- So if the assumptions are wrong, 'correcting' data on their basis can make the data less rather than more valid.
- The best way of checking on error, therefore, is to apply the final estimates within a predictive and theoretical context to find out whether they work. This validates them and guarantees their reliability (at least until new theories and data become available to check them against).

Systematic working assumptions coming into this discussion

The assumptions reported as propositions here are particularly relevant in reminding you that the reported outcomes of many political processes are themselves estimates of what has happened and are therefore subject to all the warnings about error and its estimation made in this chapter. The most obvious political estimates affected by this are election votes taken as indicators of citizen preferences, which we have already shown to be subject to possible bias and misrepresentation (cf. Chapters 4–10 and Proposition 18).

The relevant assumptions are as follows:

6   Policy targets and their implementation can be classified and measured for over-time and comparative analysis on the basis of textual, survey, expenditure and other statistical evidence.

13   Ideally explanations should take the form of predictive theories consisting of propositions or equations which can be checked for predictive success against independently observed outcomes and behaviour.

18   However, all political – like other – measurements contain error (which can nevertheless be estimated and corrected on various assumptions).

Sources and resources

The best extended discussions of the points covered in this chapter is:
Andrea Volkens, Judith Bara, Ian Budge, Michael D. McDonald and H.-D. Klingemann (eds) (2013) *Mapping Policy Preferences from Texts* (Oxford, Oxford University Press) pp. 69–145. The discussion is focused on text-based estimates but generally applies to all forms of political measurement.

The framing and replicability of survey responses is concisely reviewed in the following:
Michael D. McDonald (2012) in *Organizing Democratic Choice* Ian Budge, Hans Keman, Michael D. McDonald and Paul Pennings (Oxford, Oxford University Press) pp. 202–207.
Stephen Ansolabere, Jonathan Rodden and James M. Snyder (2008) The Strength of Issues: Using Multiple Measures to Gauge Preference-Stability. *American Journal of Political Science*, 102, pp. 215–232.

Suggestions for class papers

1   What new information would you ideally want to more fully check claims about the policy-preference correspondence? How exactly would you use it?

2 What is the contribution (if any) that qualitative evidence and analysis can make to future political research?
3 What are the best checks for error in either quantitative or qualitative evidence? Why are they the best?
4 Is the validation of a measure or estimate the same thing as its replicability? Why or why not?

Suggestions for class projects

1 Check out the standing of the estimates used to validate any of the representational theories discussed in this book.
2 Measure the representational efficiency of governments in your country, at either the local or the national level.
3 How far would the level of analysis problem of extrapolating behaviour at one level of analysis to units at another level apply to comparative politics? Illustrate your response by comparing overall country behaviour to the behaviour of institutions/organizations within it.

Chapter 17

Simplifying 'Big Data'

Dimensions, majorities and the (missing?) middle

Chapter overview

This chapter carries on the discussion of indicators and estimates that began in Chapters 4–6 on the measurement of popular preferences and party policy stands. We generalized from this in the last chapter to wider questions of political measurement. A major problem identified in both discussions was how to cut through the tangle of indicators correlated with each other to a varying extent and reduce them to manageable proportions for analysis. This is a problem both for data analysis itself and the explanatory theories it tests, illustrating again the close relationship between the two.

That is particularly relevant here because both theory and data are most clearly presented in a spatial context. The point is underlined even more by the next chapter's consideration of graphs and the way they can be translated into numeric relationships by using regression analysis within appropriate policy spaces (cf. Figure 4.3). **Regression equations** can in turn be used as concise theoretical statements providing both an explanation of some political process and a prediction about its outcomes.

The question of how the variables are to be measured and represented as the 'dimensions' (lines) defining a space is crucial to both the formulation of the theory and our assessment of its predictions. Are the preferences and policies whose 'match' is at the focus of democratic theory to be taken as relating entirely to different policy areas represented by separate straight lines (cf. Chapter 5, Table 5.2)? This is likely to result in inconsistent overall preferences which governments cannot satisfy. Or can they be related in terms of a single overriding policy dimension such as left versus right, which will produce a stable and consistent majority preference?

This is a theoretical problem, but it is also a practical one for data analysis. To make the mass of information manageable, we have to boil it down in some way to a limited number of variables or dimensions. (Within the spatial context of most political analysis, these are broadly equivalent terms.) But we have to be sure that these condensed representations do

Regression equations

Relationships between variables represented spatially by estimating a best-fitting line between them.

not substantially distort the ways electors and parties actually think about politics or bias the observations used to check on theories.

Dimensionality (the number of lines defining a policy space) affects the possibility of finding a median position which reasonably defines the majority preference. Where all the individual party preferences can be ordered along one dimension, a median point can always be found at the middle around which a stable majority policy preference can form. But there is no guarantee of one overall median being found in a space with two dimensions and even less in spaces with more dimensions. So no stable majority preference can be guaranteed there. Theoretical discussions often take the absence of a *guaranteed* median as eliminating the possibility of finding any median position at all. In fact, there is still a high probability of doing so, particularly when dimensions, though distinct, are correlated with each other to some extent. Again, measurement procedures may have important consequences for political theory here, and vice versa. We go into these in more detail at the end of the chapter. There we suggest that stable majorities are more common than has been assumed in social choice theory.

Key points in this discussion are thus:

- The main techniques for combining and simplifying data: dimensional analysis, a priori scaling and discriminant analysis.
- What these reveal about the true nature and dimensionality of policy spaces.
- Possible limitations of such spatial representations.
- Consequences for the existence of a median and thus for the prospects of finding a settled majority policy preference.

Dimensional data analyses

Correlation

Two variables going up and down together.

Variables

Processes or behaviours that have been measured, so scores can 'vary'.

Where a lot of survey questions have been asked about providing healthcare or benefits and pensions to support people in difficulty, a question always arises of how closely responses are linked and how well they could be represented by various positions along an underlying 'dimension' of 'social concern' or 'support for welfare'. This might even extend to questions of providing foreign aid – but not probably to environmental issues. Some people might support action on all of these, producing something of a **correlation** between attitudes in the two areas and any dimensions underlying them. But unless analysts could predict most opinions in one area from opinions in the other, as in Figures 4.3 and 4.4, we would tend to see the 'welfare' and 'environmental' dimensions as distinct through related. The question of how closely they are related is an important one, bearing on the question of finding an overall median or 'centre' position, as we shall see.

There are well-established statistical procedures for combining 'indicators' or **'variables'** in terms of the predictability of positions on one from positions on the other – the extent to which they 'covary' with each other. In spatial terms, indicators which always go up or down together (so that a person holding a particular view on one will mostly hold a particular view on the other) can be represented by positions on a single straight line. The more that positions on the two indicators can be predicted one from the other, the better the straight-line representation will work and the less distortion it will introduce into the political relationships being portrayed 'spatially' in this way.

Of course, we must remember that some answers will be closely related to others in a negative way. If you support welfare benefits, you are not likely to oppose some provision for free healthcare either, and if you oppose them, you are unlikely to support other welfare measures. In 'reducing' all these responses to positions on a straight line, you are likely to end up with positive and negative positions defining each end, with 'undecideds' and mixed responses scattering between them along the length of the line.

As we noted, there are likely to be different opinion clusters emerging from any battery of questions included in a survey. These will hang together along different issue dimensions: welfare, environment and so on. An important dimension is usually **left-right**, given that distinctions between 'left' and 'right' positions (and the 'centre') structure so much political discussion.

Left-right

Welfare, state intervention and peaceful internationalism on the left and traditional morality, freedom and internal and national security on the right.

Dimensional analyses of this kind are not confined to survey responses. With any set of numerically scored 'variables', we can see how far values on one predict (positively or negatively) values on another. If such 'covariation' is high, we can represent them along a straight line, defined by clusters of opposing positions at each end.

For example, the 56 coding categories applied to manifestos (Table 6.3) produce numeric scores for each document in terms of the percentage of its sentences coded into that category. We can thus see how far one category is emphasized in each manifesto when another one is also stressed. Where the (positive or negative) association between issues is strong over all the manifestos, we can represent them by positions along one straight line – say a welfare dimension. We can then place each individual manifesto at a point along this dimension in terms of how it scores on 'welfare'. (The final score will be 'weighted', i.e. multiplied by a number representing the extent to which the particular issue on which it is being scored correlates with the overall welfare dimension.)

Other clusters and dimensions are likely to emerge, such as 'environment'. We can also place manifestos at particular points on these in the same way. If we have also analysed survey respondents' positions on a battery of questions corresponding to some or all of the manifesto categories, we can locate them on the similar dimensions that emerge and 'project' one space onto the other and then compare citizen and party positions directly on the same broad issues.

We need not make such comparisons separately along each line or 'dimension' taken on its own. We can put the separate dimensions together to form a two-dimensional, three-dimensional or even a multidimensional space. Even three dimensions are hard to represent in a graph, however, so comparisons are usually made in terms of two dimensions. An example of a two-dimensional graph comparing policy positions taken up by the US Democratic and Republican parties in the earlier part of the post-war period is shown in Figure 17.1.

For ease of reading the graph, party positions have been averaged where they resembled each other in contiguous years (e.g. 1948, 1952, 1956). Even with this simplification, they show movement over time, principally on the vertical dimension of regulation of social and economic activity. There is less movement, and there is a clearer distinction between the parties, in terms of their left-right positions.

We can project the average median elector positions on these two policy areas or 'dimensions' into their combined policy space, as shown in the middle of the graph. The median elector on the left-right dimension stands squarely in the middle, between the areas defined by the party manifestos. (S)he favours more regulation than the median elector on the vertical dimension itself. (S)he in turn inclines more to the right on the issues represented along the horizontal dimension than the other median elector does.

Because there are two independent policy dimensions, there are two median positions. The median electors on regulatory issues are more conservative than the ones on the horizontal dimension. Each group is not too far from each other but is still distinct. The medians *could* coincide on some occasions. But with two separate policy dimensions, this is not guaranteed. On the other hand, we can identify a central *area* of the space which includes both positions. If we were checking on whether

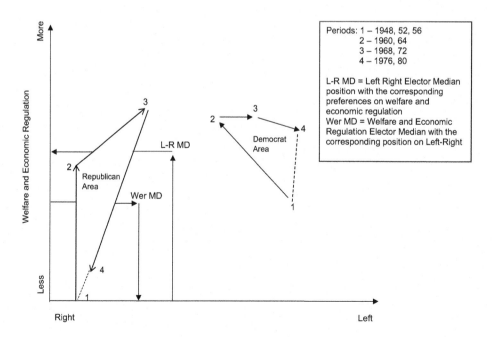

FIGURE 17.1 US party positions in a mapped two-dimensional space derived from factor analysis of their election platforms

government-implemented policy corresponded broadly to overall popular demands, we could find out whether it fell within this 'centrist' area or not. We shall discuss these possibilities in more detail below, but for the moment, we go into further detail about the data-orientated techniques which produce these policy spaces.

Factor analysis

There are many different ways to combine or 'reduce' an array of individual estimates to the lines or dimensions which constitute a policy space. They all provide criteria and statistics which can be used to distinguish the groupings of policy emphases or positions making up the separate dimensions. These can also be evaluated on 'substantive' criteria – that is, on whether they make sense in terms of what we know about their political context.

Figure 17.1 shows the results from summarizing the 56 policy categories used to code the election manifestos (platforms) of the US Democrats and Republicans for the early post–Second World War period (1948–1980). Assigning sentences to one of the 56 categories listed in Table 6.3 allows us to score these in terms of the percentage of sentences they contain out of the total in each individual platform. These percentages can then be examined for covariation (going up or down concurrently with each other). Those that relate can then be put together to form a policy dimension. Individual party manifestos can be located on each of the dimensions which emerge by the percentage of sentence references made to the issue areas associated with it, multiplied by the contribution of these areas to forming the overall dimension. (Areas are more or less strongly associated with each dimension and the degree of association is expressed by a decimal figure for its 'loading' on it.)

A first point of interest from such analyses is what these dimensions are, as they provide an insight into what policy differences separate the parties and what they might agree on. In Figure 17.1, the main division (the horizontal one) is the familiar left-right divide between a more moderate and more radical party. The secondary, vertical dimension seems to relate to disagreement on the extent of government regulation and intervention in socioeconomic matters.

This has often been assimilated into the pervasive left-right division in other analyses (in which case, we would have an overall median position). However, the more finely honed procedures here separate them out. It also picks out three other dimensions which each cover a more and more limited set of issues and which become harder to interpret in substantive terms as we examine their content.

Going from a one-dimensional analysis to two and then multiple dimensions – a common feature of factor analyses – has major consequences for identifying a policy majority. We have already seen this from the two different elector medians projected onto the figure. Both for presentational purposes and interpretability, a one- or two-dimensional representation is easier to handle and so is almost always preferred. As the basis for interpreting results, however, this choice is based on pragmatic and somewhat arbitrary criteria. It does not reflect a 'truth' that US policy divisions of their nature cover only two dimensions of conflict. One might just as well say 'one' or 'five' based on the analysis.

A spatial representation allows us to see what policy positions the parties take up in relation to each other and to measure their distance from each other. In this one, the Democrats are well to the left of the Republicans, as one would expect, given President Roosevelt and President Johnson's programmes of social reform. On regulation of the economy and society (the vertical dimension), the party positions overlap more. So we might infer that there is more substantive agreement between the parties here.

Had these two clusters of issues been put together and combined, as they often are, we would have a left-right summary of party positions. By putting less constraints on the analyses, we have allowed it to distinguish more issue groupings and dimensions. These are represented as independent of each other because the statistical procedures are designed to place them at right angles to each other in the resulting graphs. It is apparent from this dependence of the representation on these prior analytic decisions that even though the data are being allowed to 'speak to us' about what the key party divisions are, they can do so only under the constraints that we impose. A key consideration in evaluating results is whether they make sense in light of historical and other evidence. This justifies a concentration on the first two factors emerging from the analysis as the minor ones are generally difficult to interpret in historical terms.

What, then, are the two dimensions which emerge from factor analyses of party programmes across the world? Table 17.1 shows that world issues in the first half of the post-war period were mostly organized around left-right concerns. These emerge in 14 countries out of 20 and are almost always the dominant dimension where they appear.

Often the second leading dimension could be interpreted in extended left-right terms as well. This suggests that we could usefully reduce everything to a general one-dimensional representation with a determinate median around which a settled overall popular majority could form. This simplification would not only be beneficial in showing how a popular majority preference can emerge under democratic preferences but also provide a breakthrough methodologically (otherwise, we cannot check whether there is a policy-preference correspondence).

The qualification – as always – is that this result depends on prior decisions made by researchers as much as on purely data-based results. Moreover, the data themselves relate to the way parties and politicians choose to organize their discourse. This is almost bound to integrate policies and issues more tightly than electors do. Manifestos are written as an overall programme for government bringing numbers of issues together in a way which citizens are not bound to do (as shown in Chapters 4–6).

Despite these qualifications, strong general evidence seems to emerge for the existence of an underlying left-right dimension to policy and

TABLE 17.1 The two leading dimensions from a factor analysis of election programmes over 20 post-war democracies from 1948 to 1980

Country	First dimension	Second dimension
The UK	Left vs right	Liberalism vs class conflict concerns
New Zealand	Left vs right	Internationalism and welfare vs isolationism
Australia	Left vs right	Discipline and restraint vs free pursuit of goals
The US	Left vs right	Interventionism vs regulation
Canada	New leftism	Old leftism
Sri Lanka	Urban vs rural	Old left vs right
Israel	Nationalism and technological progress	Modernism vs democracy (associated with new issues)
Ireland	Authoritarianism and ability to govern	Capitalist economics and Irish unity
Northern Ireland	Pro– or anti–status quo	Socioeconomic concerns vs religious sectionalism
Sweden	Left vs centre	Left vs right
Denmark	Old left vs right	New left vs right
Finland	Socialist vs capitalist organization of the economy	Contrast between group norms and individual values
The Netherlands	Left vs right	New left issues vs social conservatism
Belgium	Left vs right	Progressivism vs clerical conservatism
Luxembourg	New issues vs isolationism	Social justice and freedom
Austria	Socioeconomic left vs right	New issues and internationalism vs social conservatism
West Germany	Organization of (world) society	Degree of concern with the social market economy
France	Left vs right (economic, social and foreign affairs)	Populism vs bourgeois liberalism
Italy	Left vs right	Social harmony (subsumes Catholicism)
Japan	Left vs right	New issues vs concentration on economic growth

Source: The table is adapted from Ian Budge, David Robertson and Derek J. Hearl (2008) *Ideology Strategy and Party Change: Spatial Analyses of Programmes in 19 Democracies* (Cambridge, CUP) pp. 390–391

politics. It is, however, worthwhile to revisit the question in the practical context of data reduction and analysis before returning to general theory. We do this in the next section.

A priori combination or 'scaling' of data

Induction

A generalization from available data.

Factor analysis has been jokingly described as a technique in which a researcher 'seizes the data by the neck and cries "speak to me!"' This emphasizes the **inductive** nature of the technique, which is designed to uncover patterns of covariation in the set of indicators (variables) being analysed and to combine them into a reduced set of dimensions ('factors').

What has also emerged, however, is that such dimensions, or at least the most important ones, have to be interpretable in terms of what we already know in order to be acceptable. Often what we know is expressed in theoretical a priori terms – not derived from the data themselves but thought up separately (e.g. left-right). A 'dimension' is classified by the indicators which define each end. So we have to interpret what each end cluster has in common, and why they should contrast with each other, if we are to say what the dimension really means. And of course, such interpretations need to draw on the wider context rather than be made from just the data-based patterns.

Data-based investigations thus require framing and patterning just as preferences and opinions do. They cannot 'speak' without help. On the other hand, what they say is not entirely dependent on their framing. They can 'speak' independently within it. This contrasts with the situation where a certain structuring is imposed on indicators on purely a priori grounds coming from existing ideas about what the world should look like. The most obvious examples follow:

1 The left-right scale, which has come into our discussion at so many points. The scale draws principally on Marxist analyses of social and economic relationships as a class struggle, which spills over increasingly into foreign relationships.

Briefing 17.1

Class, imperialism and globalization – Marxism and Leninism are still relevant!

In Chapter 6 and at various other points in our discussion, we have shown how Marx's nineteenth century analysis of socioeconomic and political relationships, extended by Lenin in *Imperialism*, underlies left-right differences as measured on the manifesto scale (Table 6.5). The core of Marx's theory was that industrialization creates an underclass which will be ground down by capitalist power holders if they do not organize politically to fight to improve their conditions. Lenin extended this thesis to a world level by arguing that workers' relative success in improving their conditions had led capitalists to exploit the more vulnerable inhabitants and resources of underdeveloped countries in order to maintain their profits. In addition to fighting for their social and political rights, socialists should therefore also support peaceful internationalism and the rights of all people in a globalizing world. Despite predictions of the 'end of (left) ideology' in the 1960s, such ideas still seem highly relevant today, and in measurement terms, they still render the left-right scale a useful context within which to map party and popular policy concerns.

2   Party families, based on 'developmental' ideas, which see parties with similar support bases and policy concerns developing from social and opinion groupings within and across countries. While some of these take up positions on the left-right 'cleavage', others derive from ethnic, religious and other divisions, which are reflected and fostered by the corresponding parties. From this a priori point of view, there are as many dimensions to policy space as there are family divisions and cleavages.

Both 'left-right' and 'party family' ideas have been used to put categories together and create policy scales and/or party groupings to organize the data before analysis or as a basis for analysing them (Chapters 4–6). One might say, in contrast to the dimensional analyses typified by factor analysis, that such approaches tell the data what to say rather than asking them to speak!

However, this contrast can be overdrawn. These a priori structurings are actually putting together categories which have emerged from reading the texts and grouping together sentences that seem to have a common focus and common concerns, like welfare, security and peace. The numeric scores then attached to them (percentage of sentences which go into the resulting clusters out of total sentences in the text: expert judgements of how party families relate to each other on some policy continuum) may be added up according to preexisting theoretical ideas about what is left or right (or what is needed for a party to belong to one party family as opposed to another). But the basic coding categories (cf. Table 6.3) have been pragmatically derived from the texts (though a starting point may well have been what policy concerns were expected to belong together in the first place).

We should therefore not view the various scaling techniques and the dimensions that they give rise to as totally dependent on theory on the one hand or totally devoid of preexisting theories and ideas on the other. Induction from data and deduction from theory are both present in data-reduction techniques, but to varying degrees. Factor analysis is simply more inductive and data based than a priori scaling – which in turn is more strongly dependent on preexisting ideas. The complementary rather than conflicting roles of induction and deduction are emphasized in the next section when we consider how various kinds of data-based dimensional analyses can be used to check out a priori scalings.

The greater ability of factor analysis and similar techniques to reveal existing data patterns ('letting the data speak') does have one great disadvantage, however: it can reveal only which dimensions exist in the data set currently being analysed. If more indicators are added in to update it over time or extend its geographical coverage, there is no guarantee that the same dimensions will emerge from the new analysis. If the original data set was pretty comprehensive anyway, it is of course likely that the main dimensions will remain with much the same interpretations. But there is no guarantee of this and interpretations of what the data is telling you may shift somewhat as a result.

This is a particular danger since the technique uses all the information available to make its placements. In the case of data stretching over many years and many countries (e.g. the manifesto data set), this may mean that cases separated by vast tracts of time and space affect each other's position. For example, the Italian Christian democrats' policy position on peace and security in 1990 might be estimated partly in regard to where the Finnish communists were on the same issues in 1950! Again, such linkages are not necessarily made in the factor analysis, but there is no guarantee that they aren't. From this point of view, the more heavily theory-based, a priori scaling of policy positions may be preferable as its characterization of party and elector positions comes from outside the data available currently and is invariant across different data sets.

Again, this contrast is a matter of degree and should not be overdrawn. A priori scales and dimensions may be theoretically derived. But we apply them to the data by using them to suggest relevant coding categories into which sentences can be grouped, in order to produce scorings of the party policy positions. Such categories also depend on particular sets of estimates hanging together plausibly within them, however. These tendencies emerge from the data in hand. On the other hand, if particular dimensions have emerged from factor analysing a large and extended set of relevant data and make sense in a theoretical perspective, it is likely that they will remain pretty stable even when new data are added to the existing set.

Contrasts in terms of stability and general applicability between theoretically and data-derived dimensions can clearly be overdrawn. But they are still there and need to be borne in mind when interpreting results.

Validating a priori scales and dimensions

Model

A theory expressed in a form (spatial or otherwise) which will allow it to be checked against data.

Data-based analyses have inbuilt criteria for saying when separate dimensions exist and how the original estimates and indicators hang together to structure them. A priori scales and dimensions lack these. So how do we know that they are measuring what they purport to measure (i.e. are valid)? The ultimate test is their ability to create a working **model** of the corresponding theory applicable to the available data which allows the theoretical predictions to be clearly specified in numeric or spatial terms and then checked out. Ideally, such predictions will anticipate future outcomes exactly enough to say whether they have been upheld or not. Thus, we should be able to predict a left or right movement by a political party in the next election or say what 'family' grouping it will join at the international level given its particular set of issue concerns.

If the scales work in these ways, we would certainly accept them (as well as the theory they put into numbers) as valid. We would also accept them if they went against a theory that we had some doubts about (e.g. 'convergence' ideas that parties will come closer to each other in policy terms over time). Well-specified predictive theories, however, are often lacking. Till they emerge, we can fall back on less severe checks on the plausibility of constructed scales – 'postdictions' about what already observed out-comes should look like or general 'fit' with historical accounts of what has happened. These 'softer' comparisons put into effect the 'convergent' validity checks of the multi-measure multi-variable matrix (Table 16.2). If two independent accounts of the same phenomenon do not match up, something must be wrong with at least one of them. With new measures, the presumption is that they will be wrong rather than the established ones. Thus, if our left-right measure showed the US parties agreeing more in the last 30 years than they did before, contrary to accepted accounts, we would be inclined to suspect that it is not properly measuring the main political disagreements that exist.

In the absence of theory or independent evidence to check up on a scale or dimension, there are still ways to assess it, drawing on the more inductive techniques already discussed. Thus, if we have picked out a set of indicators as cohering on theoretical grounds into a unidimensional scale, we can check this claim by feeding the variables that make it up into a factor analysis. This will show whether the ones picked out initially as likely to move up and down together (or in contrary directions) actually do so – by, for example, producing a single straight-line representation, with the original indicators placed at appropriate positions along it.

Where there is a broad correspondence between the original orderings and the factors produced, the analysis might even suggest marginal adjust-ments to the scale – pointing to the inclusion of one or two theoretically justified additions that had been overlooked – or dropping one that does not seem to belong. (Of course, we would only make these adjustments in preliminary testing and leave the scale unamended thereafter. If we altered the scale every time that we used it in research, we would be unable to make comparisons across time and space, because the measure itself would change. We would mean something different by left and right every time we used it, which would defeat the whole purpose of making comparable observations on its basis.)

These examples again show that the measures and scales constructed independently on theoretical grounds and the inductive dimensions which emerge (with some help) from the data in hand are not wholly different in nature. They may overlap to some extent in the construction and inter-pretation of measures even though their methodological foundations ulti-mately differ. This overlap is partly illustrated from a check we can apply to the other theoretically based measure cited in this discussion. This is the classification of parties into broader ideological 'families' which transcend their national context. The groupings are based on the developmental the-ory of how parties emerge at particular points of time from social and opinion groupings ('cleavages') in populations. These generate particular and long-lasting party policy emphases in line with the concerns of their core supporters.

A core prediction of developmental theory is thus that any party's 'family' can be estimated from their issue concerns, and vice versa. The prediction can be tested by applying the technique known as discrimi-nant analysis to the manifesto scorings of the 56 policy categories listed in

Table 6.3 (i.e. the percentage of sentences out of the total number of sentences in each document allocated to that category). The analysis searches to see which of these 'variables' (percentage of sentences in each policy category) best discriminates between 'party families' as indicated by an individual party's membership of international federations (socialist, liberal, etc.). As we saw in Chapter 6, they do sort individual parties into families as well, on the basis of the issues they uniquely emphasize.

The statistical techniques associated with discriminant analysis and applied to large numbers of variables and parties are inevitably complex. However, they boil down to looking for issue concerns that 'discriminate' well between groups. To assign individual parties to families, the technique averages the percentage mentions of a set of topics into one or more linear combinations which best separate them. Each combination is uncorrelated with the others, so in spatial terms, each is at right angles to the other. The combinations are set up so that each makes a maximum contribution to differentiating between one or more 'families' regardless of the others. Thus, if there is some correlation of original policy scorings that distinguishes between, for example, the communists and the liberals, with no particular relevance to differences between socialists and conservatives, the discriminant analysis will incorporate it.

It thus ends up with a multidimensional portrayal of family differences which emerges from the data themselves, with no preconceptions about what distinguishes the parties or how they should be ordered. So it forms a truly independent check on developmental theory, which says that the groupings should be distinguished by particular issue concerns. The affiliation of individual parties to the group should then be predictable from these.

We have already reported results in Table 6.6 which confirm developmental ideas. Each party family has a limited number of issue concerns which uniquely characterize its members. These may not be the ones that parties emphasize most in every election. But they are the ones it most *uniquely* emphasizes in contrast to the parties belonging to other families. Using just a limited number of key issue concerns to assign individual parties to a party family is successful in 80% of cases. This finding is important in confirming our general diagnosis of party policies as being ideologically driven rather than responsive to popular preferences, and divergent rather than converging on the median or centre positions. This leaves party alternation in government rather than convergence on policy as the major mechanism fostering correspondence between popular preferences and implemented policy. In this way, the developmental party-family theory combines with the other theories in the 'web of explanation' (Figure 8.1), support alternation ideas.

Here again, we should note the interaction between methodological techniques and preexisting theory. On the face of it, discriminant analysis is entirely inductive, searching for relationships among a set of data-based estimates and indicators without preconceptions as to which belong together. To do so, however, it needs the theoretically derived party groupings to discriminate between in the first place. This interdependency of theoretical and methodological considerations is less obvious – but perhaps even more important – in finding a middle position on which to base a stable policy majority. That is discussed in the next section.

Methodological influences on theoretical thinking: dimensions, medians and centrist majorities

Discriminant analysis needs independently derived groupings (like party families) to work on. Factor analysis and similar dimension-finding techniques can create policy spaces based on their own purely methodological assumptions, though the way we interpret them usually brings in theory.

A less obvious theoretical influence is on the way we structure the resulting space. We almost invariably require policy spaces either to run along one straight line, like left-right, or – if they have one or more dimensions – to be at right angles to each other (as in Figure 17.1). This is because right-angled dimensions have the useful property of not being related to each other (so positioning on one is independent of positioning on the other). Thus, when we do relate the two (e.g. in an equation), we can think of one as genuinely influencing change in the other rather than both simply running concurrently alongside each other over time or related purely by being parts of the same underlying dimension (Chapter 4).

We also like to think in terms of right-angled spaces because most of the mathematics used in the social sciences bases itself on this kind of space. Otherwise, the mathematics required becomes much more difficult to use. Hence, factor analysis and related techniques allow for the 'rotation' of the dimensions which emerge from the analysis of common variation among estimates and indicators, so that they will generate the best-fitting *right-angled* spatial representation rather than just the best-fitting spatial representation. In the latter case, the policy dimensions are usually correlated with each other, producing sloping (related) rather than strictly vertical and horizontal (unrelated) dimensions. (Compare Figure 17.1 with Figure 17.2 for examples of the two different kinds of policy space which emerge.)

In general, right-angled policy spaces fit with our theoretical thinking and are easier to work with. However, we always need to bear in mind that they may distort underlying relationships at least to some extent. This is vital to our discussion of the median position, the one occupied by the middle electors in any policy distribution. This is easiest to envisage in the case of a straight line. Taking the familiar case of left-right, we can see from Figure 5.2 that to have a majority (rather than a tie) on some proposal, you need to have 50% + 1 of the voters (going either from left or right). The decision of the '+ 1 voter' to support either left or right is crucial in swinging the majority decision one way or the other.

Because the median voters' support is crucial to passing any proposal, its proponents will be willing to compromise to get those voters' support.

Thus, the policy proposal is likely to move from the extremes towards the middle position in the course of bargaining. This is a better outcome for its supporters compared to the people on the other side getting the median vote and forming a majority by moving their rival proposal nearer to the middle. Such a bargaining process is likely to end up with the median policy preference being adopted by all sides – in other words, with a stable policy majority centred on the median (though some voters at the extremes may not support it because of the distance from their own preferences).

This reasoning makes the median position vital, theoretically and procedurally, for several reasons:

- It means that voting procedures can be guaranteed to produce a policy outcome which reflects the preference of a genuine popular majority (cf. Part II).
- Because of this, it will also be a settled and stable majority, which gives a clear indication to both policymakers and a researcher of where public opinion inclines.
- For representational theories such as party alternation in government, it provides a clear benchmark for when representation is working – the distance between the median policy preference and actually implemented policy should be small.

These considerations make the median a central reference point for almost all systematic theorizing in political science. Unfortunately, its existence is guaranteed only when the policy space can be represented by a straight line, as in Figure 5.2. Even in a two-dimensional space, with the straight lines at right angles to each other, the existence of a single median (a median in all directions, as it is often called) cannot be *guaranteed* (though it *may* often appear, of course). However, we can see from Figure 17.1 how this is rendered unlikely by the variety of positions on two different policy areas. There is only a limited probability of them actually coinciding to the extent of producing a common median position. It is thus quite probable that median positions in the common space which they define will differ on each dimension, producing unstable majorities (as in Table 5.1).

Voting cycling

Different majorities emerging, depending on the order in which policy alternatives are voted on.

The problems of instability and **voting cycling** which this creates for finding a settled majority policy preference have already been illustrated at many points in previous discussions (particularly in Chapters 5 and 9). It is no exaggeration to say that most systematic theoretical discussion in political science of the last 50 years has centred on this problem. Meanwhile, the bulk of data analyses and empirical generalizations have bypassed it by simply assuming that there is a stable point around which majorities can cohere.

One aspect of the theoretical debate is that it so sharply contrasts one-dimensional and multidimensional spaces with regard to the difficulty of finding one median position. This ignores an important finding on the methodological side: if the data analysis proceeds *without* imposing a requirement for spaces to be defined by right-angled (i.e. uncorrelated) dimensions, most of the ones which fit the data best have *correlated* dimensions (i.e. ones that are *not* at right angles to each other). When we have a space with slanted dimensions, producing a distribution more and more similar to a straight line as they are more and more strongly correlated, there are increasing chances of finding a common median around which a majority might cohere. This possibility is illustrated in Figure 17.2. Even if the medians do not come together at a single point, they will tend to lie within a fairly compact common area. So if implemented policy falls within that area, we know that it corresponds reasonably closely to what the popular majority wants, which is crucial for checking out representational theories against data.

Most policy dimensions, even if they are substantially independent of each other, are weakly related to some degree. The fact that even a small correlation between two policy dimensions substantially increases the possibility of finding a common median, has been passed over. This again illustrates the importance of evaluating the general methodological assumptions we make against the specific concerns of the substantive theories they translate into numbers and spaces and are then used to check. It also shows that a stable centrist policy positioning is more prevalent than has been thought – a crucially important substantive consideration in analyzing democracy.

A further complication in the 'hunt for the median' is that it has rather a different standing when opinion is sharply divided between two camps at the policy extremes – a bimodal distribution of opinions. In that case, the median point in the middle is not going to be one on which they can

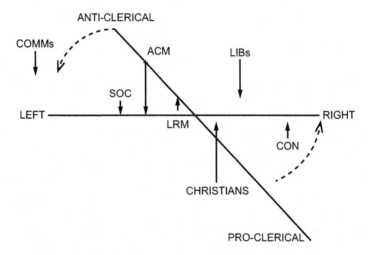

FIGURE 17.2 The increasing probability of finding one overall median as spatial dimensions are increasingly correlated

Notes: ACM is median on clerical dimension. LRM is median on left-right dimension. As the correlation between the dimensions increases and they align, the two medians come closer together.

Source: Adapted from James Adams and Ernest Adams (2000) The Geometry of Voting Cycles. *Journal of Theoretical Politics*, 12, pp. 131–154

easily converge. This contrasts with a situation where most voters group around the centre to form a 'unimodal' distribution. The two are directly contrasted in Figure 17.3.

Clearly, the median better summarizes the true distribution of preferences in the first case, where most individuals have moderate and centrist opinions. In the second case, there is really no agreement at all. Along with the median, we ought to report the dispersion of preferences (often termed 'polarisation'), to assess how well policy fits. We can see here too that alternation of policy targets and outcomes over time might be better at meeting preferences in a bimodal situation than simply staying at the median, which might leave people at the extremes all dissatisfied. A dynamic rather than a static **equilibrium** point for policy might well be the best representational solution, as the alternation and thermostatic theories suggest.

In general, electoral opinion seems to form unimodal distributions with their median located in the centre rather than bimodal ones (see Figure 4.6). Where dimensions have unimodal distributions – even where they are uncorrelated and at right angles to each other – they are likely to produce medians which are reasonably close to each other in policy space. This raises the question of whether we should not be looking for a central *area* rather than a central *point* in the space, to see how well representation is working to bring policy outcomes close to preferences. After all, if both end up reasonably close to each other, a fair degree of correspondence is being attained. Of course, there is again no guarantee in spaces of two or more uncorrelated dimensions of such an area (sometimes termed the 'core' or the 'kernel') being found. However, they do provide scope for

Equilibrium

A political process that tends towards the same outcome over time.

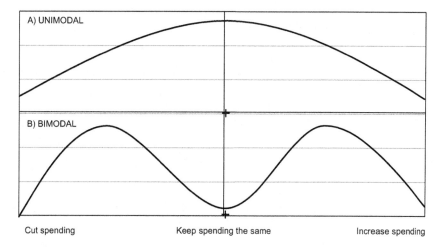

FIGURE 17.3 Unimodal and bimodal opinion distributions with the median at the same point

Notes: The crosses mark the median positions in the two policy spaces – which are identical. However, it would clearly be easier to get a compromise agreement in the use of A rather than B, given the differences in the distribution of opinions.

finding a centrist majority area, particularly if the dimensions defining the policy space are allowed to be correlated.

A further methodological consideration bearing on the question of finding a common centre ground is whether we regard policy spaces as dynamic – that is, as evolving and changing over time, so that at certain points there is more of a correlation or even an amalgamation of different policy areas over time, as illustrated in Figure 5.1.

There are factors promoting such changes, particularly between inter-election and (general) election periods. Between general elections, policy areas are split up between ministries and legislative committees and are considered on their own as different topics of legislation or debate under parliamentary procedures. In turn, this encourages opinion polls to present them as separate questions to electors and for the latter to consider them as separable issues. On each of the resulting separate, single distributions, we can find a median position. But as we discovered in Chapter 5, these are often conflicting and inconsistent with each other in terms of overall policymaking.

General-election campaigns and commentary, on the other hand, tend to reduce all these separate issue preferences into one overarching contrast – most usually between left and right – viewed as one single dimension where the important thing is to 'capture the centre ground' (i.e. the policy 'core' or 'kernel' shared by the majority).

In practice not everyone sees all of their preferences in left-right terms. Minority nationalists will stress decentralization or devolution, religious parties moral issues, greens environment – all issues which do not fit entirely into a unified left-right space. At the election, however, left-right issues will tend to dominate. Where they do, much more of a common area will emerge – for a time – which provides a basis for evaluating outcome policy-preference correspondence in terms of the distance between implemented policy and the position of the median elector.

Mention of elections brings the non-policy factors, which often determine their outcomes, back into our discussion, along with political parties. These move us away from multidimensional policy spaces, where it is difficult to find an anchorage point for a settled majority (or even a central area to contain it). Parties with their non-policy appeals (competence, candidates, past record as well as policy platforms) shift the yardstick for calculating representational correspondence from the median to the modal or plurality voter position. This is because the party with the largest vote and share of legislative seats can be said to have had its policies, if not exactly endorsed, at least not repudiated by voters who may have voted for it on both policy and non-policy grounds. Moreover, large plurality parties have been found to be the likely majority winners in any rerun of the election, as they attract more voters because of their ability to form a stable government.

The policy position of the largest spontaneous grouping of voters to emerge in an election (the modal or plurality party voters) thus has some claims to provide an alternative or at least a supplementary yardstick for evaluating the representational correspondence between policy outcomes and popular preferences. The choice of the median position as the measure of the majority preference rests on unrealistic assumptions: (1) only pure policy is being taken into consideration by electors or voters; (2) there is perfect information – that is, everyone involved knows everything about everyone else's position, so they can make strategic adjustments to their own position in light of the overall distribution of preferences; and (3) they so much desire even watered-down versions of their policy proposal to win that they are prepared to let it move a long distance from their own extreme rather than see the other side's proposal adopted.

The median position seems in this light to be a possibly arbitrary and artificial measure of majority preferences. Where there is a unimodal distribution of preferences over policy, it certainly functions as a reasonable summary of where the majority is located, being at the centre of the centre, so to speak. However, where the distribution is more dispersed and especially where it has two peaks, it gives a false impression of centrism where there is none. In such a situation, it might be better to conceive of the centre as a more extended area ('core' or 'kernel') – somewhat dispersed rather than concentrated at a single point. If a single point is required for measurement purposes, we might consider it the plurality position, as it is the largest opinion grouping to have emerged spontaneously from the population rather than being artificially calculated on fairly arbitrary assumptions.

Best of all might be to report policy-preference correspondence on several measures simultaneously, to find out whether we reach the same conclusions no matter which we use. Harking back to our discussion in Chapter 16, we would call this a form of convergent validation of the various measures of majority preferences. A further refinement is not just to look at the values of these measures year by year, or election by election, but to take their average value over the whole time period we are dealing with (i.e. their own mean value). Doing so provides some assurance that we are dealing with the really settled preferences of electors and voters. In fact, when we make a comparison between the mean and mean plurality positions over time, the two tend to come together since alternation between plurality parties and their policies brings their average closer to the centre and hence to the median position. In practice most spatial representations and indicators point to most citizens holding centrist preferences and sticking to them over time. So a reasonably close policy-preference correspondence seems to emerge in most democracies whichever measure we use as the hallmark to estimate agreement.

End-summary

Spatial representations of policy processes and outcomes are central to both theory and measurement in political science. However, the spaces produced by applying various techniques to the data-based estimates are too often taken as given, without bringing theoretical concerns into their production and evaluation. The disjunction has been illustrated here in regard to the median measurement of majority preferences. Doubts about the working of democracy have stemmed from the absence of a guaranteed median position in multidimensional policy spaces. In conjunction with the voting paradoxes uncovered in Part II, the absence of a guaranteed median position has been taken as a fundamental flaw in democratic procedures in terms of identifying the majority preference, ignoring the following:

1   The extent to which this depends on arbitrary methodological decisions about how to structure the relevant policy space.
2   The kinds of measures we want to employ – overall median, separate issue medians, plurality voter position or over-time averages of these. Many decisions on these points are really theoretical, but they get dressed up as methodological. Reviewing them critically indicates that it may be less problematic to identify a majority preference based on the median than has been assumed in the theoretical discussions of the last 50 years.

Key points in this chapter are thus:

• The way in which 'dimensional analyses' – particularly factor analysis – can reduce complexity among individual measures by putting them together to form the 'dimensions' of a policy space.
• A priori scaling where indicators are put together on theoretical grounds (usually to form one dimension, a 'unidimensional space').
• Discriminant analysis, with somewhat different concerns about testing the validity of theoretically based groupings of political participants.
• Theoretical anxieties about the nonexistence of a median 'anchor' for a stable policy majority in policy spaces of two dimensions or more, which are largely allayed when we recognize realistically that policy dimensions are usually correlated with each other.
• The wider measurement context which renders such concern about a 'missing middle' less acute, by showing how they emerge from the relatively arbitrary methodological assumptions we choose to make, often unconsciously.
• The solution, in terms of always bringing theoretical and methodological assumptions together in translating theoretical concepts into estimates and using the latter to test theory.
• When we do so, the likelihood of finding a stable centrist majority is increased.

Systematic working assumptions coming into this discussion

6   Policy targets and their implementation can be classified and measured for over-time and comparative analysis on the basis of textual, survey, expenditure and other statistical evidence.

7   This allows them to be represented as points in spaces constructed on various measurement assumptions, with a centre and extremes, which can also relate the policy positions of political actors (citizens, voters, governments, parties, etc.) as specified from either data or theory.

8   Such spaces can have varying dimensionalities and measurements, the most common being a straight line running between left and right.

Sources and resources

An excellent application of factor analysis to policy data which also brings in questions of measurement reliability is

Derek J. Hearl (2001) 'Checking the Party Policy Estimates' in Ian Budge, H-D Klingemann, Andrea Volkens, Judith Bara, Eric Tannenbaum *Mapping Policy Preferences* (Oxford, Oxford University Press) pp. 111–126.

For discriminant analysis, see

Hans-Dieter Klingemann, Andrea Volkens, Judith Bara, Ian Budge and Michael D. McDonald (2006) *Mapping Policy Preferences II* (Oxford, Oxford University Press) pp. 28–50.

A general discussion of the 'dimensionality' of policy spaces is in

Judith Bara, and Albert Weale (eds) (2006) *Democratic Politics and Party Competition* (Abingdon, Routledge) pp. 125–178.

Suggestions for class papers

1   What kinds of dimensional analyses are best for what research areas? Say what the advantages are.

2   Is the median policy position really as important as it is made out to be? Why or why not?

3   Can we do without spatial analysis in political science? Why or why not?

4   Which is more useful in political research – factor analysis or discriminant analysis? Why?

Suggestions for class projects

1   Do a number of dimensional analyses of the same data set on different assumptions, and report on the difference these make to the results.

2   Assess the relative advantages of a priori scales and dimensions compared to data-derived ones, by applying them both to party policy movements over time.

3   Search out two political variables that are totally uncorrelated with each other. Can one be used to explain the other? How?

Chapter 18

Managing 'Big Data'

Theoretical explanation and statistical analysis

Chapter overview

Factional theory

A theory that relates shifts in party policy to changes in factional strength within a party.

Variables

Processes or behaviours that have been measured, so scores can 'vary'.

Hypothetico-deductive theory

A theory based on assumptions made independently of the data.

Policy and other estimates can be used to check theories on their own, particularly if they come in the form of time series, recording changes (or stability) in party and government positions (as in Figure 12.5). From a simple inspection of this graph and similar ones, we can see, for example, whether the **factional theory's** expectation of an irregular zigzag movement between left and right is generally upheld (Figure 12.5).

To be really illuminating, however, theories have to go beyond such general characterizations, to explain why and under what conditions individual left-right shifts take place. This requires us to bring in other **variables**, such as vote gains and losses and relative factional strengths. Relating these causes to their policy effects (shifts between left and right) requires us to bring a number of different estimates together in a precise way to establish whether individual observed shifts in the policy effects are actually those anticipated by the theory. Focusing investigations on theories in this way helps greatly in reducing the complexities of Big Data analyses. These always tempt you to pursue interesting relationships with nothing much to link them up and no clear outcome. Where you have a backup theory, the unifying focus is always on whether the effects are actually those anticipated by the theory.

Most theories are causal in the sense that one event (e.g. factional change) is assumed to regularly produce another (party policy change) under specified conditions. Causal relationships have to conform to certain requirements to qualify as such. The chapter starts by exploring these since they set a framework within which quantitative analyses of political relationships can be carried through.

Much current political analysis is not directed at testing complete theories, which is relatively rare. Instead, it reverses the **hypothetico-deductive theory** to *generate* hypotheses from the observations and theories rather than check predictions from an existing theory against them. Causal relationships require that the presumed cause is regularly associated with the presumed effect. So if we find that two variables are regularly associated

Hypothesis

A succinct statement of relationships which may produce an anticipated outcome.

Elector turnout

The percentage of electors who actually vote in an election.

with each other when relevant data are analysed, we can take this as the basis for a **hypothesis** which describes how they are associated. Generalizing in this way from data to theory is termed an 'inductive' approach, as opposed to the 'hypothetico-deductive' one just described. Following our discussion of cause and effect, the second section of the chapter goes into deduction and induction and the differences between them.

Constructing and testing predictive theory is a more powerful way of generating political knowledge than induction, though in the absence of well-specified theories, we tend to fall back on inductive generalizations. These can be useful in focusing attention on possible theoretical explanations for observed processes and events. The great difficulty in going from observations to theory comes, however, from what we might describe as the 'curse of the social sciences' – the fact that every variable is related (but often weakly) to every other one. This gets in the way of identifying the really crucial connections between political processes and events. For example, the weather on election days has some impact on **elector turnout**. That does not render it particularly important in explaining it. The problem is that a variety of other concurrent factors also correlate weakly with turnout levels, obscuring what fundamentally *does* drive them. To find that out, we really need to build and test a complete predictive theory.

Compounding the problem, more or less plausible justifications can be provided for almost any correlation found in an inductive analysis – which gives rise to the joke that any analyst who can't find at least ten explanations for any given correlation should leave the profession. There *are* statistical procedures for eliminating irrelevant relationships which we discuss below, in the fourth section of the chapter. However, these often create their own problems of over-elaboration. With eight to ten variables brought into the equations as checks on the explanatory relationships (and, in some cases, interacting with each other) it is difficult to pin down what the equations really tell us at a theoretical level. This is an additional reason for first building a clear theory and then going on to test its predictions against data (when possible – but the relevant evidence is often not available).

One aspect of political analysis which eases the way is that processes can mostly be represented spatially. Spatial representations (e.g. those in Figures 4.3 and 7.3) are the common way of presenting both data estimates and theory. Most estimates are made in, or can be converted into, numbers. These can be expressed as points or lines in some kind of space. As we have seen throughout the book, this is also the easiest way to formulate and present theories which relate two or more processes and events. Political analysis – whether theoretical or directed by data – *is* mostly spatial analysis. This enables theory and evidence to be directly related, making the task of evaluating theory much easier. We deal with spatial analyses involving two or more variables in the fifth section of the chapter.

Going from a general discussion of cause and effect in the next section, to deduction and induction in the one following, on to statistical and other ways of evaluating evidence and then to spatial analyses helps underline the relationships between all of them and the impossibility of considering any one in isolation from the others. Theories generally explain and predict political effects by specifying their presumed causes, usually in spatial terms. Inductive analyses search for statistical correlations which suggest causal regularities, change in one variable being regularly associated with change in another. The tool for uncovering these is mostly regression analysis, itself summarizing spatial arrays of data by identifying their **central tendency** and dispersion of individual cases around it. It is not going too far then to say that political analysis is mostly spatial in form, a point addressed in the chapter conclusions. These pave the way to considering how far we have actually come with clear explanations of political processes, which is the focus of the next chapter.

Key points in the discussion are thus:

- Theory as a way of focusing and organizing analyses of large, complex data sets.
- The nature of explanatory theories, which is generally, but not always, causal in nature.
- Prediction and postdiction of outcomes as the main check on their standing.
- Spatial representations of both theory and data as the major way to link them up.
- Graphical presentations of spatial relationships, which can then be summarized numerically by using regression statistics.

Central tendency

The average relationship between two variables, often summarized as a line.

Cause and effect

In most political situations, we want to know what consequences will follow from some event (which might, for example, be a change in a particular party's leadership). Political commentary in the newspapers and on TV will then speculate about the consequences of the change for the party's election campaign and vote prospects, as well as on wider implications for the governments which may form and the policies they will implement. The mission of systematic political science is to move such discussion from the realm of speculation by providing clear and validated knowledge of exactly what changes in party policy targets the new controlling faction is likely to make and whom they will go into government with, in the event that the party gets more or less votes.

The theories discussed earlier deal with these points. Generally, they consider what outcomes a particular event like a change of party leadership from one faction to another will produce in the immediate or more distant future. This assumes that such events have broadly the same consequences wherever and whenever they occur – that is, there is a constant relationship between them, so that a particular type of change is always, or at least generally, followed by a particular kind of outcome. Thus, a leftist faction replacing a right-wing faction in control of a party will generally result in more leftist policies replacing rightist ones as policy targets, and a left-based rather than right-based government coalition (given appropriate conditions). We want to be able to state correctly what will follow on from what, when and how – not just by **extrapolating** from what has happened before but also by basing the statement on a plausible and validated theoretical explanation.

Extrapolating

Assuming that what happened before will happen again, without providing an explanation for the connection.

Such explanations usually take on a causal form. Factional change, as the cause, will be necessarily followed by certain policy shifts and choice of government partners under appropriate conditions (as spelled out e.g. in Figure 13.1). Relationships where one event is not just *generally* followed by certain outcomes but *necessarily* followed by them are called causal. Such a relationship is 'guaranteed' or 'validated' by (1) the fact that it has generally occurred in the past and (2) the fact that it will occur in the future because the supporting theory shows that it *must* happen. Given that factions are defined by their policy stances, substitution of one faction by another will necessarily result in a change of party policy.

This assurance of necessity in the relationship – certain outcomes will follow from a preceding event because it is in the nature of the process that they do so – is what distinguishes a causal relationship from a mere **correlation** or extrapolation. Thus, we are not simply saying that certain events will follow on each other because they have always occurred together in the past (i.e. are correlated). This is simple extrapolation from what is going on up to now. The theory is also saying that the follow-on is guaranteed by something fundamental in the conditions that surround the relationship, which we can specify and explain. The theoretical reasoning thus adds in the necessity of the relationship to its observed occurrence. The statistically observed relationship shows that the theory is generally correct in linking up the constituent variables. Causal connections thus have to meet three conditions if they are to be accepted as causal:

Correlation

Variables going up and down together.

1. One event has to be statistically associated (correlated) with the other.
2. The presumed cause has to precede (or at least occur simultaneously with) the presumed effect.
3. We have to have a good explanation of why the relationship exists (usually provided by a predictively validated theory).

A good theoretical explanation is required because two events could always occur together, and one could constantly precede the other, without actually causing it – particularly in political science, where correlations between all manner of variables are so common. For example, there is an increased probability for US presidents elected in years with a zero in them to die in office. Their election also precedes their death. So Conditions 1 and 2 are satisfied. There is, however, no plausible explanation of why election years ending in zero *should* affect a president's life expectancy. Therefore, this can be dismissed as an accidental conjunction of events rather than a causal connection, simply because there is no reasonable explanation of why it should happen.

The first condition – that when the presumed cause is observed, the presumed effect should usually be observed also – is of course inherent in the relationship. If they often occur independently of each other, we would assume they are not necessarily connected. Logically, we would also expect the presumed cause to occur before the presumed effect. We do not believe the influence could run backwards: in our example, a factional change in one year could not produce a left-right switch in policy the year before it happened. However, Condition 2 makes some allowance for the fact that observations can be rough and approximate, so that change in the events being observed might be recorded simultaneously (e.g. in the same year). Allowing for measurement error, we could accept this as evidence for causality, simply assuming that factional change came first although our estimates are too rough to record this.

Classic accounts of cause-and-effect relationships based on nineteenth century natural science assumed that causes must always produce the associated effect – a fully determined relationship. In the twentieth century, however, it became clear that many phenomena (even in physics at sub-atomic levels) – and in much of biology, ecology, medicine and the social sciences – had to be treated statistically, in terms of high probabilities of expected effects following from a presumed cause, but not always. Predictive success is thus measured in terms of 80% or 90% of observations – but not all – occurring as specified in the theory. The deviant outcomes might be due to deficiencies in the theory (other causes as well as those it specifies are at work), measurement error or the fact that some unpredictability is built into the process itself, by its nature (e.g. the jumps made by subatomic particles).

All of these factors are present in politics and political science. So we have to accept that expected effects will follow from presumed causes only in a majority of cases rather than in all cases: we are dealing with a probabilistic rather than a fully determined relationship. However, this still gives us a good basis for describing and anticipating political events, even if we go wrong sometimes in individual cases.

We normally think of causal connections as producing change. A change in the presumed cause (e.g. in factional control of a party) is followed by change in the effect (e.g. a party policy shift from right to left or left to right). This is not always the case, however. For example, a faction may take over control and shift party policy in its preferred direction. This is then associated with increased vote in the forthcoming election. Our factional alternation theory therefore expects that policy may remain the same *if* the party factions are relatively equal in strength. This is because the dominant faction is not strong enough to push policy further in its own direction even after an election success. Thus, stability in factional control can produce stability in policy – no change in the presumed cause will be associated with no change in the presumed effect. Of course, we would want there to be concurrent changes in both at some point. Otherwise, we would be inclined to think that neither variable had much effect on the other and that they just ran along together – a strong possibility given the mass of weak, accidental correlations in political and social life.

Briefing 18.1

How far can cross-sectional analysis reveal or test causal relationships?

Cross-sectional analyses concentrate on (e.g. survey or demographic) evidence at one point in time. Thus, they might divide up individual survey respondents into different social classes to find out whether these vote for different parties in elections. Or countries might be divided up according to the type of election systems they have (e.g. PR versus SMDP) and their different policies examined (cf. Table 10.2).

From the perspective of the classical experiment described in Figure V.1 cross-sectional comparison concentrates on comparing groups at the second stage (t_2) of the experiment. Moreover, these groups are not 'matched' in the sense of being similar in all the possible conditions that might affect the outcome, nor is the presumed cause introduced only into one group but not into the other. Rather, two contrasting groups (one middle class and one working class) are compared in terms of voting patterns. Of course, refinements ('controls') are often introduced into the comparison by extending it to subgroups (e.g. of men and women of different classes) to find out whether the class-vote relationship continues to hold.

Such 'cross-sectional' comparisons are often made as checks on theory (e.g. Marxist theories, which predict that class will be the major influence on voting behaviour). If the cross-sectional comparison shows that there is no relationship, this contradicts the theory. The observed relationship would, however, have to go through other checks closer to an experimental setup, and would have to bring in time, to be fully accepted as a causal explanation.

With large amounts of data, however, cross-sectional analyses can be suggestive in identifying relationships which can be either generalized as inductive 'laws' (cf. Briefing 13.3) or built up into causal theories which can be tested predictively. Causes, however, generally have to occur before presumed effects. So a cross-sectional comparison can go up to only a certain point in testing causal theories before time-based comparisons have to be brought in.

Policy stability or 'inertia' is an important consideration for many influential theories of policy processes such as budgeting. Incrementalist theory, for example, predicts that next year's budget will look like this year's in terms of departmental spending allocations – that is, the share of total government income which each ministry or department will receive to cover costs of personnel, accommodation, service delivery and so on. This is because each department wants more money for itself and thus keeps a close eye on other departments' budget shares. The others will strongly oppose any increase while each will fight strongly against any decrease in its own budget – possibly forming alliances with other affected departments to do so.

The end result of such collective decision-making is to keep budgeted departmental expenditures at much the same level from year to year. The

Briefing 18.2

A non-causal theory? The policy mandate

Theories generally take on a causal form. This may not be true of all theories in political science, however, particularly where they have prescriptive as well as descriptive implications – that is, tell protagonists what they ought to do as well as describing what they in fact do. A classic example here is the theory of the policy mandate which parties receive on being voted into government office. Mandate theory sees the vote as conferring on them both the right and duty to see that the policies put forward in their manifesto are being carried through. Mandate ideas were already described generally in Briefing 13.1. Put more precisely, they boil down to the following propositions:

1   *Party distinctiveness* – at least two parties have policy profiles distinct from one another.
2   *Voter information* – voters recognize the policy profiles of each party.
3   *Voter motivation* – voters cast their ballots based on the party profile that they prefer to see implemented by a government.
4   *Voter majority* – a majority of voters are revealed to have the same preference, given the choices available.
5   *Electoral system translation* – the election outcome clearly designates the party with majority electoral support to form a government that will carry out its policy.
6   *Government policy commitment* – the government follows the party policies that were announced at the time of the election.

The theory thus gives rise to a clear prediction (6) that parties which control government will in general preside over policies in line with targets contained in their manifestos. Correspondence between the two, therefore, is clearly the effect anticipated by mandate theory. But what is the cause? Is it the manifesto? But that in itself could be taken as simply a statement or signal of party intentions. Is it the moral commitment the party has made to electors to implement its policy targets? Or is it, as the factional alternation theory would say, that the faction in control of the party is pursuing its own ideological objectives, some of which it has written into the manifesto and which it would follow anyway.

These are not causal questions raised by the mandate theory itself. It does, however, make clear predictions about implemented policy following what is said in governing parties' previous manifestos. In turn, this has consequences for the checks we run on whether the theory is correct (see Briefing 18.10).

technical term for such a stable situation is that allocations are in equilibrium – that is, the departmental spending allocation has reached a point at which it broadly remains as it is. If there is any reason – like a war in the case of a defence ministry – which results in additional spending, the allocation moves back to its former equilibrium position in the long run.

In the case of such equilibriums, we cannot say that the presumed cause (departmental desires to increase their spending) is not operating, – just that each department's efforts to do so neutralize each other to produce a generally stable outcome. Because the theory predicts general stability, it cannot be said to have been falsified by the absence of change in the allocations.

A similar situation rises with party mandate theory, which stresses party commitments to carrying out their policy in government if they get a strong popular endorsement. Instead of advocating change in their election programme, parties often simply stress the importance of maintaining existing policy. Failure to change this once they get into government can hardly be taken as disproving mandate theory by showing that parties do not carry out their commitments, when their commitment *is* not to change. This creates problems for **regression equations**, where the general practice is to automatically include past values of the **dependent variable** to find out whether the presumed causes really have an independent influence on the presumed effects. However, this would eliminate any sign of incrementalist effects from the start because the theory itself predicts that past spending levels will correlate strongly with present ones.

One way of checking the usefulness of a theory is to compare its predictive performance with some naive extrapolation which has no theoretical grounding. In the case of the factional theory of party policymaking (Chapter 12), we can see, for example, whether it enables us to anticipate policy shifts better than (1) assuming that policy changes in the opposite direction after every election, producing a uniform zigzag effect and (2) assuming that it always stays the same. The assumption of stability has no theoretical backing in this context (unlike incrementalist theory, which gives *reasons* for thinking that budgets will be stable). In this case, stability, like pure zigzagging, is a way of assessing how much the proposed theory adds to our knowledge over simply assuming that what happened previously will happen again (or that the opposite will happen, in the case of a zigzag).

Naive comparisons of this kind take on a more specialized form in regression analyses under the name of the 'lagged dependent variable'. This extends beyond checking on specific causal theories to checking on claims of any causal connection at all. Two event series may often run alongside each other over time, showing broadly the same ups and downs, so that changes or stability in one may frequently parallel the same shifts in the other, such as national sports successes and failures accompanying the re-election or defeat of governing parties. To check on whether there actually is a causal connection between the two, we would want to see how well sports results predict governing party vote compared with the party's previous vote – a procedure known technically as controlling for the lagged dependent variable – in this case, the previous vote. If the correlation with previous sports results is then substantially weakened through the inclusion of previous vote into the equation, we would reject the idea that sports results generally influence subsequent votes.

Regression equations

Relationships between variables estimated from a best-fitting line between them.

Dependent variable

A variable whose value depends on the value of another variable.

This is a reasonable precaution to take given the large number of social and political processes that run alongside each other and show weak correlations. So the lagged dependent variable has come to be automatically included in regression analyses to eliminate spurious relationships. Some theories do, however, explain and predict a strong correlation between past and present values of the affected variable, such as budget allocations. Not allowing for stability in the presumed effect and focusing entirely on change may then seriously underestimate the strength of the causal relationship which does exist.

Using past values to take out the effects of stability in the dependent variable implicitly says that only policy *change* is to be counted as supporting evidence for a theory rather than the widespread 'policy inertia' that clearly exists. Of course, a more sophisticated theory might allow for both as with 'punctuated equilibrium' in the case of budgetary allocations. This expects allocations to remain stable over considerable periods of time but to be radically changed from time to time either by external events like wars or from parties entering government with radical proposals for change in particular policy areas like welfare. Both change and stability in presumed causes and effects are then incorporated into the theory, so it is only reasonable to consider both as supporting evidence when it is applied to the data.

These examples demonstrate, again, the importance of having a reasonably comprehensive and clearly stated theory to make predictions which can then be checked for their success over individual cases, rather than just on overall patterns revealed in the existing data. Extended theorizing is particularly needed because 'causes' often require supporting conditions to trigger 'effects'. For example, factional alternation is predicted to produce policy change after each election *unless* the party gains votes at the first succeeding election. In that case – but only in that case – policy will stay as it was or continue in the same direction. Allowance for such interactions can be made only through a fairly extended theoretical argument. This is another reason for stressing the importance of theory in improving the subtlety of the statistical assessments. These have to take into account that both stability and change are being theoretically predicted under certain conditions.

Generating theories: deduction versus induction (or is it retroduction?)

The importance of theories in providing a context for assessing evidence – and, through their predictions, a more decisive way of choosing between competing explanations – prompts a question: how do we develop theories in the first place?

The traditional answer is that we look for regularities in the individual events we observe and then think of how we can explain them. A well-known regularity, for example, is the loss of votes by governing parties between elections: they generally lose 2%–3% of their initial percentage vote when they come up for re-election. This has been described as the nearest thing to a universal law in political science.

However, the regularity does not in itself provide an explanation of *why* it happens or whether it will continue regardless of other developments. We are left to speculate about this. The most popular speculation is that the vote loss is produced by the 'costs of governing'. 'Stuff happens' beyond government control – wars, economic downturns, ecological disasters – and the government gets blamed for them. Governments themselves make mistakes and again get blamed – or scandals sap their credibility. These are all 'costs' of being in government and under the public eye.

A related but different explanation comes from psychology. This is that people react more strongly to losses than to benefits. The people who lose out under government programmes hold this against ruling parties more intensely and longer than those who benefit remember the gains. Hence, there is an inevitable tendency to lose more votes than they pick up between elections.

This reasoning might explain the 'thermostatic' reactions discussed in Chapter 7. Government policies generate more and more adverse reactions the longer they carry on. If a policy involves more expenditure on a certain policy area, for example, more and more electors want 'less' (and vice versa). This could lead to the observed loss of votes. Another explanation comes from economic ideas about satisfaction from a benefit declining as more of it is provided (and dissatisfaction increasing as less is provided).

Here, therefore, we have three different, though related, and plausible explanations for the observed government vote loss. Which is correct? Unfortunately, since all have been produced retrospectively to explain the already-known vote loss, that powerful observation cannot in itself be used to decide between them. That neatly illustrates the main dilemma of the inductive approach, which assumes that explanations will emerge uniquely and spontaneously from the observations. Instead, the second obstacle in the way of clear political explanation emerges, alongside the abundance of weak relationships – that is, the large number of plausible explanations for any relationship and the difficulty of deciding between them.

Broadening the traditional focus of political science on individual countries; identifying similarities and differences between countries; and finding possible explanations for these represent clear methodological advances in the discipline over the last 40 years. For one thing, they provide a better insight into national politics by letting us know what is unique to a particular country rather than being one of the general effects of e.g. the electoral system it uses (cf. Table 10.2).

However, the main concern of comparative politics, as currently practised, is describing politics in and across a set of countries; identifying their similarities and differences; and suggesting possible explanations for these. Comparativists can use the evidence they assemble to reject implausible ideas. Given their country focus, however, they rarely have time to decide which of the more plausible ones is best. Comparative politics is thus generally characterized by an inductive approach rather than a deductive, theory-centred one, though that may change as the subject develops.

The solution must be to expand each line of explanation into a more developed theory which generates other unique and testable predictions. The theory of declining marginal utility (decreasing satisfaction from a public good as more is provided), for example, supports the further inference that politicians become less and less concerned about office the longer they hold it. If that is not found to be true, that would rule out decreasing satisfaction with a good the more you have of it, as an explanation for adverse reactions to governing parties.

Developing a theory and then testing it against data takes us away from an inductive approach – first observe regularities which then suggest a theory – to the (hypothetico-)deductive (H-D) approach. This argues that theories are elaborated first and that the success of their predictions are then checked against evidence specially selected for this purpose.

Supporters of this approach make two principal points. First, we cannot just observe regularities and then generate theory from them. To know which regularities to look for, we need some theoretical idea of which are relevant. We cannot build a theory of political action based on the waxing and waning of the moon, even though these events are regular and in the past were thought to have psychological effects. From this point of view therefore the choice is not between starting investigations from theory or from observed regularities. Rather it is between starting from a well thought out and explicitly stated theory: or from implicit theories whose assumptions and expectations are unexplored and thus remain unexplained. There can be no doubt which approach is better.

Second, we need to eliminate weak theories by raising requirements for acceptability. Even the act of setting out assumptions and expectations explicitly helps eliminate theories which, on closer inspection, are internally illogical and inconsistent. However, theories which pass the test of consistency and clarity could still be unsuccessful in predicting or postdicting individual outcomes. In this way, the H-D approach helps us reject many of the superficially plausible but weak explanations that clog up political science.

In spite of its strengths, however, 'deductivism' overstates its case. Researchers are not in practice called on to conjure theory out of thin air, ignoring established regularities and observations which are only supposed to come in at a later stage. We are not confronted with a dichotomous world in which there is only theory and observation. This is to ignore the vast body of previous writings and research from which new theories can be generated and at least initially checked. Theory development seems much more a matter of developing tentative ideas – often slight modifications of old thinking – fitting these to existing data, modifying them if they don't fit and trying the new ones out again until they do. Only then do we reach the stage of setting out the theory in full with

Briefing 18.3

'Systematic political science' as theory generator and validator

'Systematic political science' has been defined at various places in this discussion (e.g. at the end of the Preface) as 'that body of political research on the basis of which a set of interrelated predictive explanations of political processes can be generated and validated'. Neither the earlier research nor the predictive explanations coming out of it emerge spontaneously out of political processes and events of course. Decisions need to be made about what to focus on and how to deal with it. Such 'working assumptions' are summarized and explicitly stated at the end of Chapter 8 and in Chapter 19.

The various data analyses, theories and hypotheses which constitute this body of research do not necessarily draw on all of the working assumptions stated there – for example, some are qualitative in form, so they do not have to make the assumption (Assumption 6) about measuring policies and preferences. Enough of the assumptions are shared across the main body of research, however, to make them generally relevant to the 'systematic' approach.

By its nature, all of this research is publicly available and can be drawn upon to formulate and evaluate theories such as the policymaking ones reported in this book. So no theorizing is going to start totally from scratch or as an unmediated reaction to the world around us. It is going to be prompted or guided by previous discussions and findings; or in many cases, it simply represents a slight modification of a previous theory, which then predicts or postdicts outcomes and processes better. Once this has been established against previous data and findings, it can be applied to predict new events, measured on the same basis as has been done by previous systematic research, to validate it even further (or of course to go back to the drawing board if it can't be validated in this way).

This all illustrates the existence of a 'third world' of recorded theory and observation which exists independently of both new a priori theorizing and direct observation of the physical and social world around us. This is true for all science, of course, not just the social sciences and politics – though these do have a 3000-year tradition of writing, observation and conceptual development behind them.

all its assumptions and expectations and then checking them against new observations.

This process of going between observations and old and new theoretical ideas to create a new synthesis has been termed 'retroduction' to distinguish it from induction on the one hand – all observation and no theory – and deduction on the other – abstract theorizing with observation brought in only to check it out. 'Retroduction' gives a better picture of the actual research process as being more fuzzy edged and eclectic than in the sharply contrasting traditional accounts. What we should take away from these, however, is the real need – particularly in political science with its forest of weak correlations and plausible but competing explanations – for theories to be explicitly stated, comprehensively explained in all their ramifications and assumptions and tested by successfully predicting new events, case by case. These are searching requirements rarely applied in contemporary political science. But they are essential if it is to generate more accurate and relevant knowledge about political processes.

Briefing 18.4

The need for comprehensive explanation: fully specified theories against single hypotheses

Most political science journals now require articles, particularly statistically based ones looking at data-based patterns and relationships, to specify their research hypotheses at the beginning of the article and to say at the end how far these have been upheld by the data analyses. This requirement does not generally change the research design or the nature of the analyses undertaken. It simply requires the authors to clarify in writing the expectations they had in undertaking the analysis. This is useful but does not amount to stating and developing a full theory like the ones presented in this book, notably in Chapters 7 and 8. These cover whole political processes and put them in context rather than focus on just one part of them.

We may take as an example the policy mandate theory described in Briefing 18.3. This lays down six conditions for a mandate to operate. In contrast, research on a single relationship, such as that between the policy emphasis in a party electoral programme and expenditures in corresponding policy areas once it is in government, may often rest on the main hypothesis – that there is a relationship – qualified by subsidiary hypotheses that this is weakened when the party is not in full control (e.g. through it lacking a legislative majority or being in coalition with another party). The hypotheses are perfectly reasonable and do clarify the intentions of the researchers. But they do not give a complete account of the conditions and processes involved in fulfilling a mandate, as the full theory does.

Relating estimates to theories – regression analysis

The lack of well-specified theories producing testable predictions has concentrated attention instead on analysing existing data, drawing on mathematical and statistical measures of error to distinguish true from false hypotheses and strong relationships from weak ones. We have already encountered this approach being applied to measures and estimates in Chapter 16. Rather than putting them to the test in a theoretical and predictive context, the tendency instead is to submit them to a battery of error tests. The trouble is that these are often based on controversial assumptions about the nature of the measures, such as that they constitute some kind of sample out of some underlying, wider set of potential indicators rather than span the spectrum themselves. We shall examine such assumptions more closely, after we discuss whether the main criterion in accepting a relationship as confirmed should be tests of statistical significance (showing how representative it is of relationships in a wider underlying set of indicators from which the ones examined may have been drawn) or measures of its strength, as shown in the estimates we actually have. We need to start, however, by examining the basics of regression analysis, the major context within which data estimates are deployed to analyse political processes at the present time.

For all the elaborate forms they may take, regressions actually start out from a simple graph relating two variables. We encountered graphs at several points in our earlier discussion, notably in tracing out left-right policies over time (e.g. in Figure 7.3). By inspecting such graphs, we can see whether party policy positions generally bracket popular ones and whether this in turn is associated with policy outcomes falling close to popular preferences – or in the case of non-bracketing, not doing so. In the case of seven countries, bracketing and policy closeness to preferences occur together, and in two, there is no bracketing and policy distancing from preferences. This patterning upholds the alternation theory of policy demand and supply, as we concluded in Chapter 7.

The graphs in Figure 7.4 take up a more analytical approach, enabling us to estimate the range of policy-preference correspondence that will result from different combinations of plurality parties' alternation in government and general policy inertia. Some of the variables which the theory expects to affect representational correspondence are assumed to remain unchanged, however. These are bracketing of the majority preference by the plurality parties and their distancing from each other (polarization).

Graphical representations provide a good basis for checking out theories. There is no substitute for looking directly at data at the start of an investigation or going back to it at various points to check whether summary measures are truly representing what the individual data points are telling us.

The danger from having too much information, however, is what we may miss the wood for the trees. In other words, so much detail can be provided in a graph like Figure 7.3 – US government and party positions; elector preferences year by year; and actual policy outcomes – that it is hard to grasp it as a whole. Rather than leaving it to the reader to follow the lines tracing out popular preferences and expenditures each year and mentally estimate the distance between these, we can calculate the extent of policy-preference correspondence and relate this directly to the other variables for the US from 1972 to 1992. An example is shown in Figure 18.1.

When we trace the correspondence in the US between the policy outcome and popular preference (policy mood) over time, as shown in Figure 7.3, we can see that it improves after 1980. That is, the distance between the outcome in terms of actual government spending and electors' preferences for it is less after 1980, indicating that the correspondence between them is greater. Within these two periods, however, year-by-year

Briefing 18.5

Keep an eye on the dependent variable!

Having identified what they feel to be the causes of some process or behaviour (the 'dependent' variable), researchers often spend a lot of time on the former (the 'independent' or 'explanatory' variables in technical language). They do so even though they have not fully checked out the relationship which focused attention on them in the first place.

Not doing so is excusable in the current state of affairs when relevant data may not be available or may be difficult or expensive to collect. It is also facilitated by the vague nature of much theoretical discussion which proceeds at a general and abstract level, leaving the exact nature of the postulated causes and their relationships unclear. This typically leads to research focusing on the nature and measurement of the independent variables, on the grounds that such clarification is essential before establishing their exact effects. Actually establishing that the latter exist recedes on to the research horizon. The exact nature and behaviour of what is to be explained (the dependent variable) – the original object of interest – then gets lost to view in an interesting and increasingly complicated discussion of the original explanatory design.

A concrete example here is the saliency theory of elections. Originally specified to an unprecedented degree as a predictive theory of election outcomes (cf. Briefing 6.1) and actually used to generate future predictions, it has latterly generated much discussion of saliency as an aspect of political rhetoric – a general approach rather than a refutable predictive theory. Certainly as a general approach, it has considerable implications for text-coding. Nevertheless, in this case, saliency has become noticeably less focused and effective than when it was just proposed as a predictive theory. This is a result of attention having been diverted from the specific outcomes that it was first intended to explain.

To follow up on this example see, the Special Issue ed. Anne Tresch, Jonas Lefevre and Stefan Walgrave (2015) of *West European Politics* (38) on *Issue Ownership: How the Public links Parties to Issues and Why It Matters*.

correspondence remains fairly stable and within the general ranges anticipated in Figure 7.4 B. This seems the best predictive graph to relate to the US given that the presidency usually alternates between parties after an eight-year tenure. Policy inertia may also be a bit less in the US than other countries given the president's extensive powers of initiative, so we would take it as nearer 0.15 than 0.10 in this case, anticipating the range of correspondence or non-correspondence between preferences and policy to be between +8 and -8. The actual average for the US over this period is 7.6 – within this predictive range.

Figure 7.4, however, shows only alternation and policy inertia at work, assuming that parties always bracket the median elector's preference and that distancing from each other (polarization) is limited and constant. When we actually look at US patterns from 1972 to 1992, we see that the stability assumption is broadly true for bracketing but not for polarization, which is quite extreme and variable.

To examine the effects of this, we can, on the basis of Figure 7.3, directly relate polarization scores to ones for correspondence or non-correspondence between preferences and policy. As the scores on this polarization measure increase, the distance between preferences and policy is hypothesized to increase. So it is a measure of *non*-correspondence rather than of correspondence as such. Polarization increases along the horizontal dimension, so we would expect scores for non-correspondence to increase on the vertical one. Actually, the opposite happens! As we go along the horizontal dimension at the bottom of the graph, non-correspondence decreases – that is, preferences and policies are shown to come closer. This goes against the implications derived from alternation theory, in Chapter 7. We explore the theoretical implications of this below, but for the moment go into the mechanics of this regression analysis, which can certainly be said to have refined our earlier analysis.

Regression analysis always starts from a spatial representation of the relationship between two variables in a data set, like that in Figure 18.1. This is termed a 'scattergram' because each case (in this application each year) is represented by a dot located in the graph by its score on each of the two variables or dimensions which define it. The dots 'scatter' over the space to a greater or lesser extent – hence the name 'scattergram'.

By inspecting this 'scatter' of dots we can see in general terms how far values on one variable go up or down along with the other i.e. whether or not there is a relationship between them. We can also see how strong the relationship is from whether the dots go up and down in a tight, bunched pattern or whether they scatter quite broadly over the whole of the graph bringing considerable inconsistencies into the general relationship.

We can summarize these general tendencies by drawing a line through the scatter of individual points in the graph to represent the average relationship between the variables (Figure 18.2). The line summarizes the central tendency over the whole scatter of individual year points. Its position is calculated as the line which most minimizes the vertical distances between all the individual points in the graph and the line (in technical terms, the sum of the squared vertical distances of each point from the line). This is known as the regression line. A 'correlation statistic' (r) summarizes the extent to which the points fit closely to the best-fitting line in terms of the sum of their squared (vertical) distances from it. The greater the scatter the less representative the line is of the true relationship between the two variables, as most of the individual cases deviate considerably from what it sums up as the central tendency.

The line in a 'scatter' of points in a graph such as Figure 18.1, relating two 'variables' to each other (in this case policy-preference correspondence and polarization) is called a 'regression line'. This name bears no relationship to its general purposes or mathematical attributes. It simply derives from the first use to which this kind of graph was put, which was to summarize the general relationship between body height and age, in a

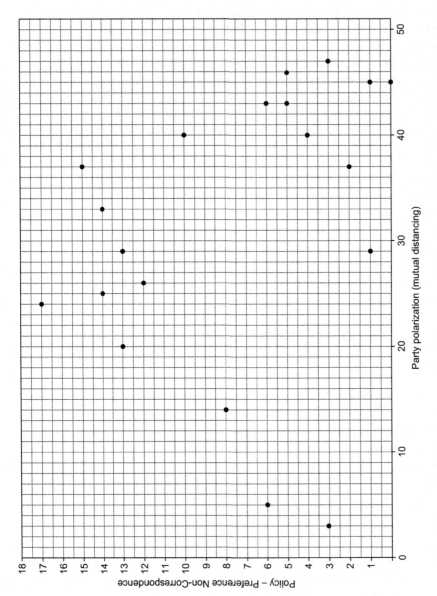

FIGURE 18.1 Correspondence between policy outcomes and popular preferences for them related to party polarisation (mutual party distancing) each year for the US 1972–1992 (see Figure 7.3)

Notes: The dots in the line relate correspondence or non-correspondence between left-right (policy mood) and total government spending to left-right distancing between US Democrats and Republicans (party polarisation) in the late twentieth century. Polarisation is supposed to be one of the factors (the 'independent variables' or causes) producing correspondence or non-correspondence between popular preferences and actual policy. So it is represented as the horizontal dimension of the graph. As we can see from the figure, however, it does not really seem to do this, at least on its own. As we move from left to right along the horizontal or base line of the figure – that is, from low to high polarisation scores, the non-correspondence scores get lower on the vertical dimension, showing that spending seems to conform more to popular preferences for it as party polarisation increases!

'bivariate' graph similar to Figure 18.2. Height diminishes or 'regresses' with age among adults. So this method of analysis acquired the name 'regression analysis' whether or not it showed a negative, diminishing effect of the 'causal' or 'independent variable' ('ageing') on the effect ('height'), or in our case polarization, on policy-preference 'correspondence'. In such 'regression' graphs or 'scattergrams' the 'independent variable' is always represented as the horizontal or flat line defining the graph and the 'dependent' variable as the vertical or upright one.

As we move along the horizontal baseline of the graph by one unit we can project this move on to the regression line as shown in Figure 18.2. By then projecting the interval on the line on to the vertical dimension mediated by the slope of the average relationship between them we can see what effect this has on 'correspondence'. A change of 1 unit along the bottom is associated with an approximately tenth of a unit reduction in distance between preference and policy outcome: that is a tenth of a unit increase in correspondence.

We can now summarize the average relationships revealed spatially in the graph in algebraic terms, basing ourselves on what the regression line tells us about the relationship between the two variables involved, namely policy-preference correspondence and polarization. The graph takes the form:

$$C = a - bP$$

where 'a' represents the point on the vertical dimension where the regression line starts off from (the 'intercept') and 'b' represents the shift in distance between policy preference and policy outcomes associated with unit changes in polarization. The important statistic is the 'b' because that measures the slope of the line and hence the effect polarization is having on correspondence. Its value in this case is almost −0.1 showing that preference-policy (non) correspondence generally decreases with polarization i.e. correspondence *increases* with greater party polarization!

Of course, none of the regression statistics show the relationship as particularly strong or as constituting a particularly good summary of the pattern of dots – from which no clear central tendency emerges anyway. But that simply reinforces the point that if polarization *had* strong effects, we would expect stronger regression relationships to emerge. We were expecting a clear relationship, but a weak reversal of it emerged from the analysis.

This paradoxical result cannot just be taken at face value, especially as other research has found substantial polarization effects on representation. If upheld, the finding has serious implications for the alternation theory and other explanations of democratic functioning. So a first check is to examine it for the eight other countries for which similar graphs to Figure 7.3 have been published. This would be a suitable project for students and other readers of this discussion to undertake. Sources and suggestions for this are given at the end of this chapter. Such an extension of the analysis constitutes a potentially major piece of research in its own

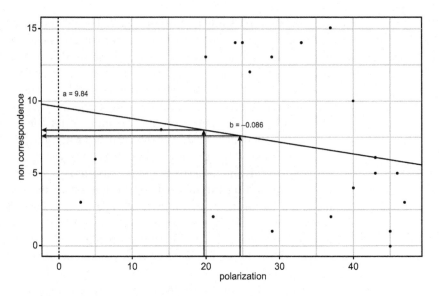

FIGURE 18.2 Fitting a 'regression line' to a 'scatter of points'

Notes: The general patterns which appear in the scattergram in Figure 18.1 are summarised in the line running from the left of Figure 18.2 to the right. This line represents the average or best-fitting relationship between correspondence or non-correspondence and polarisation shown by the dots in the figure. The fit of the line to the dots is estimated by the sum of the vertical distances between it and the individual dots. This in turn is summarised by the 'correlation coefficient' or 'measure of fit' which shows how closely the line comes to all the dots – not very well in this case given the 'outliers' in the corners. $r = 0.02$ which is very low in its range of 0-1.00 and shows that the line, though the best fit here, does not really represent any general pattern emerging from the scattergram.

In general the slope of the regression line shows the extent, on average, to which a unit move on the horizontal base line (measuring polarisation) produces a change in the correspondence or non-correspondence between preferences and policy. We can see this spatially by projecting a five-unit move on the horizontal dimension onto the regression line and then onto the vertical dimension as mediated by the slope of the line. A five-unit increase in polarization thus provides a 0.43 decrease in non-correspondence.

The slope thus shows what (if any) relationship exists between the 'independent variable' (the presumed cause – in this case, party polarisation) and the presumed effect (in this case, correspondence or non-correspondence). The whole relationship can be summarised neatly in an equation:

18.1 $NC = 9.84 - 0.086\ P$

where NC is non-correspondence and P is polarization.

As noted, this all adds up to a weak linear relationship. Actually, a curved line going from bottom left to the top of the graph and down to the bottom right would fit the scatter of points better. However, there is no obvious reason why both low and high polarization should increase correspondence, so there seems no real reason to go on to complicate this analysis further.

right and a suitable one to extend the discussion in this book. This is even more appropriate since the other country graphs constructed on the same basis as Figure 7.3 do not on first sight seem to show correspondence or non-correspondence between left-right preferences and expenditures having much of a systematic relationship to plurality party distancing from each other.

In the event of further analyses showing no relationship, we therefore have to ask what effects dropping polarization as an explanatory factor for preference-policy correspondence or preference-policy non-correspondence in the alternation model would have and how this affects the theoretical explanation of general democratic functioning given in Chapter 7.

To anticipate the theoretical re-evaluation to be discussed, the general conclusion is that while plurality party distancing (polarization) necessarily defines the potential range of values which correspondence or non-correspondence between preferences and actual policy *could* take, in actual practice the other factors emphasized by the theory – bracketing policy inertia and party alternation in government – all push implemented policy so firmly into the centre of the range that the party positions defining variation in the distance between them (polarization) has relatively little effect on actual correspondence. To elaborate, plurality parties alternating in government may adopt quite extreme policy targets and try to pull actual policy towards them. Policy inertia – practical differences in translating policy targets into actual policy – however, slows down their efforts to reverse what the previous, opposed government has done. So they succeed only in pulling back policy to their side of the centre before another government comes in and starts reversing the policy back to *their* side – but slowly enough not to move it irreversibly to the opposed extreme.

From this perspective of alternating governments bracketing the centre with their policy targets, their relative distancing from each other does not matter unduly, since inertia will normally prevent actual policy from moving too far away from a centrist position. Thus, the three other factors highlighted in the alternation model will normally keep policy in the centre if they are operative, regardless of policy polarization between the parties.

Polarization does, however, define the range of outcomes which *might* occasionally emerge from party interactions, such as the election of Trump to the US Presidency in 2016 with extreme policies. Thus it could have important effects when alternation does not take place and a relatively extreme party stays in government long enough to pull implemented policy decisively to its own side. In doing so, it might move the position of the popular centre towards a very extreme position, pulling the rival party over as well. If adjustments do not take place, increasing hostility between the parties might also decrease the tolerance and compliance needed to support a regular policy alternation, thus endangering the democratic regime itself. These extended consequences are crucial but go beyond the normal workings of democracy. So they are not covered explicitly by the theories discussed in this book, even if one can make extended inferences from the consequences of them ceasing to apply. These could well however form the basis of an independent theory of major policy change in democracies separate from the alternation theory we have been discussing, which covers its normal functioning. Creating and testing such a supplementary theory might well be another project which could be undertaken by readers of the book.

Briefing 18.6

What should we do when some evidence goes against theory?

Karl Popper revolutionized thinking about scientific procedures in his *Logic of Scientific Discovery* (1959) by suggesting that (1) theories were formulated a priori (i.e. before looking at evidence) and (2) the major concern was then to falsify them rather than produce supporting evidence. This thesis has been substantially qualified since. But it remains true that a theory which fails to explain new observations in its field will eventually have to be either substantially modified or replaced. Modification of existing theory rather than outright rejection is the preferred strategy, because it is obviously easier to carry through and because the existing theory already explains a range of other processes and events quite adequately.

This is what we see happening with the alternation theory here. A first concern is to check out the anomalous findings about polarization on the other countries for which data is available to find out whether the negative evidence about its relevance actually holds up. If it does, the next step is to modify the theory to take care of the anomalous evidence by suggesting that polarization (policy distancing between the parties) is not as important as originally thought and that the other factors emphasized in the theory – party bracketing of the majority preference, alternation of parties in government and slowness of policy change – are sufficient under normal conditions to ensure policy-preference correspondence. This modified theory can then be tested against further evidence. The scientific process of theorizing and testing is a continuous one. So every explanation has to be taken as provisional and always subject to further checks.

Back to methods! Multivariate regressions

Considering the interactions between evidence and theory in general, and applying them to the specific case of alternation theory, has momentarily diverted attention from the main focus of the discussion here, (1) the statistical methods used to check theories and (2) the assumptions underlying them. What the discussion *has* shown though is how useful regression analysis can be in directly confronting the main theoretical question: how far on the available data can the presumed cause be shown to influence the presumed effect?

The regressions in Figures 18.1 and 18.2 give a clear if negative answer in this particular case. A further check on the relationships involved is provided by multivariate regressions. We need not only look at the effects of one 'independent variable' (the presumed cause) on the dependent one (presumed effect). Instead, we can examine the combined effects of all the causal factors emphasized by the theory on the dependent variable.

This constitutes an even better check on theories in most cases. Theories, as opposed to single hypotheses, aim at providing a complete explanation

Briefing 18.7

Prediction and postdiction

The theories our discussion has been based on are predictive in form – that is, they say how future processes and outcomes will turn out under the conditions they specify. However, only one of them has actually been applied directly to anticipate future outcomes: the issue saliency theory described in Briefing 6.1. Otherwise, the theories have been checked 'postdictively' against already-existing data. The reason is that future observations (at least in sufficient numbers for statistical evaluation) are not generally available – at least for years after the theory has been published. So it is easier to check it out by showing that it fits existing evidence.

The problem with such 'postdictions' is that the theory might have been developed consciously or unconsciously to fit them. Even where the observations were unknown to the theorist at the time of developing the theory, the theorist still has some general inkling of what happened, and this again might lead to tailoring the theory to fit the known facts.

As things stand, there is no obvious way out of this dilemma. Theoretical claims need to be checked somehow, and systematic postdiction is a reasonable way of doing so – and better than just selectively citing evidence in support of the theory. Postdictive tests can be strengthened by seeing whether 'naive extrapolations' perform in them as well as the theory itself (see Briefing 6.1 again on this).

of relatively complex processes. This usually draws in a number of influences and qualifying conditions. To provide an overall check, we have to relate them all to the outcome rather than focusing on them one at a time.

In the case of the modification to alternation theory, we have three factors suggested as exerting an influence over preference-policy correspondence or non-correspondence: (B) bracketing of the median electoral position by the plurality parties; (A) alternation of these in government; and (I) policy inertia. All can be related to (C) correspondence or non-correspondence in the following equation:

$$18.2 \quad C = a - b_1B - b_2A - b_3I$$

Leaving aside a (the intercept), the equation says that non-correspondence between preferences and policy will go down (i.e. correspondence will increase) where plurality parties bracket the median, alternation is frequent and actual policy is slow to change. The b- coefficients show the extent to which B, A and I exert an effect on C independent of each other, thus telling us what added value each brings to the explanation. Putting the relationship into an algebraic form thus helps specify it more closely and provides other checks on the underlying theory.

Unfortunately, we do not have enough information from the time series provided in Figure 7.3 and the eight relevant graphs in the original report (see

Bibliography) to check the equation out. There are not enough alternations in government, estimates of policy inertia or instances of non-bracketing and its consequences to put flesh on the variables involved. Operationalizing the equation therefore has to be left as another project which readers of this book may undertake in the future. Suggestions for doing so are made at the end of the chapter. Meanwhile, we can comment on the methodology and assumptions underlying this and other multivariate regression equations.

What you are doing by introducing another variable into the regression analysis is adding another dimension into the underlying space. Instead of the two dimensions of Figure 18.1, representing polarization and distance between preferences and policy outcomes, you now have four (and if you wish, you could add more, up to five or ten). Of course, these are difficult, and in higher-dimensional cases, impossible to represent spatially. They can, however, be summarized algebraically in the shape of equations like the one shown in the notes to Figure 18.2.

By providing actual numbers for the variables involved for 90-odd elections across nine countries, we can determine, as with the bivariate equation, what the exact values of the b- coefficients are and thus how much independent effect each of the variables on the right-hand side of the equation have on preference-policy distance. We also have a measure of how well the central tendency in the four-dimensional space from which the coefficients in the equation are calculated fits the individual cases – that is, how closely they come to the central cube or scattering all over the space. This measure (R^2) gives an indication of the overall strength of the theoretical relationships involved.

Adding more variables into the regression equation gives us an even better appreciation of these relationships. However, this comes at a cost. Each new variable adds an extra dimension to the underlying (but unrepresentable) space. Only imagining an eight- or ten-dimensional space is difficult. Thus, interpreting relationships becomes more and more complex. Their effects and interactions are perhaps better represented by another kind of spatial analysis – flow diagrams of the sort used in Chapters 12 to 14 on which we can more directly base individual case predictions and check their success.

Because of these difficulties, analysts have been advised not to go beyond four or five independent variables when setting up regression models. If these are not enough to provide a good explanation and prediction of an individual case, perhaps researchers should think of other ways of modelling the theory and data. In the case of alternation theory, this would bring us back to the graphical representations and other modes of analysis applied in Chapter 7.

Error checks as the main form of assessment in statistical analysis

Every regression equation, whether bivariate or multivariate, provides a prediction for individual cases which can be found by taking the score

Briefing 18.8

Random sampling distributions and tests of significance

Mathematical probability theory tells us that if repeated random samples are drawn from the same underlying 'population' of cases or individuals under investigation, the estimates they give for its characteristics and/or relationships between them will form a symmetrical unimodal distribution. (To see what such a distribution looks like spatially, you can leaf back to Figure 12.2, though that comes from quite another context.) The mean or mode of the probability distribution of random sample estimates will give the true value for the population. But the distribution of estimates around this will eventually diminish into long tails of erroneous values.

Of course, the actual random sample we have is only one of the repeated ones which we could draw in theory from the relevant population. In using its estimates, therefore, the basic question is whether it belongs with one of the repeated samples clustered reasonably close to the true estimate at the mean/mode of the hypothetical distribution or whether it is one of the deviant ones at the tails which gives a false estimate, being so far out from the true value?

We can never answer this question with complete certainty. Probability theory does, however, inform us what percentage of the repeated samples would fall within given distances from the true estimate at the mean/mode of the distribution. We can then evaluate our own sample estimate in terms of whether it belongs with the majority of repeated sample values (95%, 99% or more of them), each giving a different probability of being wrong (5%, 1% or others). This is termed the 'level of significance' of the estimate and set at 0.05, or 0.01 depending on whether your sample is assumed to belong with 95% of repeated samples, 99% and so on.

What such 'significance levels' tell us, however, is whether the estimate we have from our actual sample is likely to be a correct reflection of actual estimates or relationships in the population from which it is drawn. It does not tell us if it is a weak or a strong relationship. That has to be measured by different statistics on the 'strength of relationships'. The trouble is that tests of whether relationships actually *exist* are often used as evidence of their *strength* in many analyses. This is quite misleading, because the two kinds of measures are not the same thing. Indeed, one problem for political explanation is that there are so many weak relationships around, and we want to eliminate as many as possible in favour of strong predictive theories. Another problem with significance testing is that our samples are seldom truly random, and therefore, we do not know whether sampling theory of this kind really applies to them.

of the independent variable at a particular point (e.g. the 22nd year). We can then multiply this by the relevant b to get a predicted value for the correspondence or non-correspondence score in year 22. This can then be compared with the actual known correspondence or non-correspondence scores for each observed position in every country in year 22. If the theory underlying the regression equation is a good theory, the fit between the predicted and actual scores should be close.

Perhaps because of the dearth of complete theories about the political processes involved, using regression equations to predict individual cases is relatively rare. The variables they include are not seen as covering all the influences which affect the outcome (i.e. the dependent variable). So the inability of the equation to correctly characterize all the cases is not to be taken as necessarily refuting the partial relationships being investigated.

More of an emphasis, therefore, tends to be put on summary measures of how far they are likely to be in error. Tests of significance assess the extent to which the numbers in the regression equation (the b- coefficients) can be taken as true reflections of relationships in the underlying population from which the presumed sample generating the equation has been randomly drawn. As we have noted, both the assumptions of randomness and sampling are controversial. It may be argued that every data set is actually a subset of some wider set which in principle encompasses it, even if we can never get hold of it (post-war manifestos cannot all be collected and in any case are a subset of all the ones ever issued, which in turn are only a subset of all official party documents, which in turn are a subset of all political documents and so on). This is a rather stretched sampling assumption: can we credibly assume that the actual post-war policy programmes we have are randomly drawn from these wider populations?

In spite of the strong assumptions necessary to generate them – which may or may not be applicable to the sample we have – tests of significance form a major if not the main working criterion for assessing the standing of b- coefficients in regressions. Doing so has downgraded strength measures such as the actual size of their effects: does a unit change in the independent variable result in moving the dependent value only a little or quite far? Along with the question of how well the average relationship fits observed relationships (the 'scatter' of points around the line summarized by the r^2 or R^2 statistics), this gives a preliminary indication of predictive success for the equation. So it is a bit odd that such measures of the 'strength of relationships' are so often passed over. Perhaps this is explained by the dearth of completely specified theories to be tested.

In the absence of validation through successful prediction, attention has focused on the range of error measures summarized in Table 18.1, putting acceptance of regression equations on a purely methodological footing. The table lists some of the main approaches to judging the extent of error in – and therefore the acceptability of – an equation. What is often not considered is that error tests generally rest on strong assumptions about the nature of the measures and relationships in the equation. If these happen to be wrong, adjustments for presumed error are likely to distort rather than clarify the true relationship.

We have already discussed the main acceptability criterion – statistical significance, based on random sampling assumptions. These can lend to misleading inferences if the data set is not a random sample. If taken as measures of strength as well as significance they lead to many weak statistical relationships being accepted as worthy of consideration, when the real problem is eliminating them in favour of the strong relationships.

TABLE 18.1 Types of error estimation in regressions and their possible downsides

Tests of acceptability – procedures for error correction	Associated problems
1. Tests of statistical significance	Irrelevant if sample can't be conceived as random
2. Measures of strength of relationship	As summary measures, may need to be qualified in terms of the shape of the underlying distribution (Are individual cases widely spread out, or do they bunch up near the middle?)
3. Introducing new variables to control for extraneous influences	May make regression equation more complex and difficult to interpret
4. Lagged dependent variable	May lead to mistaken rejection of theories predicting stability as well as change in dependent variable
5. Robustness checks by varying estimates and measures to see if broadly the same results emerge	Depends heavily on the alternative assumptions involved
6. Make adjustments for presumed error in certain variable(s) in equation but not all	Inflates estimates for adjusted variables' effects

Strong relationships, on the other hand, as confirmed by appropriate measures (2 in the table) are almost always significant ones. Strength measures inform analysts about the characteristics of the data they have, so they do not have to make extended assumptions about how these were generated or about their wider characteristics. Strength measures are, however, generally produced on the assumption that a straight line best fits the data rather than a curve (or a straight-edged shape rather than one with curves, in the multivariate case). This could be misleading as with the right-angled assumption in dimensional analysis (Chapter 17).

Other problems occur where the individual cases represented by the dots in the scattergram fall into distinct clusters which would be best represented by separate and distinct lines. These problems can be potentially resolved by always looking closely at the initial data distribution to see what measure best represents it rather than take the summary as the first and final word – as unfortunately tends to be done in too many cases.

Table 18.1 goes on to list other acceptability and error checks. There is always a possibility where so many social and political processes unfold alongside each other that a seeming effect is being produced by another process than the one being examined. This creates a need to bring in other variables as 'controls' to check whether they are not providing the real dynamic (see Briefing V.3). Controls perform the necessary job of getting rid of weak and spurious relationships. Introducing them rigidly and in large numbers in an equation does, however, run the risk of leaving it unclear what work the surviving variables are actually doing in explaining the dependent. Where the general advice is to operate with no more than four or five explanatory variables in the regression equation, controls may double the number. This renders a clear interpretation of effects difficult.

The key control generally introduced is the previous value of the dependent variable: the lagged dependent variable. (It could of course be

Controls

Holding all external influences constant to find out whether the relationship of interest is weakened.

'lagged' even further, to two or three years beforehand). Its use meshes with the general idea of evaluating the predictions of a newly proposed theory against 'naive' predictions – if the new theory cannot do better than simple projections from the variable itself, then it should not be seriously considered as an explanation of it.

Again, this strategy is admirably adopted to eliminating the weak explanations of which we have so many in the social sciences. However, it is less appropriate where the substantive theory behind the regression itself anticipates great stability in the process being explained. The best example is the incremental theory of budgeting (see Chapter 14). Because all ministries want to increase or maintain their allocated funding, they keep each other in check. Thus, few go down and few go up over time, in terms of their budget. The *prediction*, therefore, is that allocation will stay much the same from year to year.

Rejecting incremental theory, which explains *why* budgetary stability must prevail, as a naive extrapolation from one year to the next, would clearly be wrong. More generally, any theory which predicted much stability, with occasional change, like the punctuated (by events and party target changes) equilibrium theory of budgeting (see Chapters 14 and 19), would also have its statistical credibility undermined by including the lagged dependent variable as a control – only the 'punctuations' in the budget would count in its favour.

It is almost a law of contemporary methodology that a lagged control for autoregressive effects (i.e. stability in a time series) should always be included in any equation. But a rigid adherence to universal methodological 'laws' of this kind unfortunately leads to misassessments of the substantive theories being checked out, which in many cases predict stability as well as change in the presumed effect over time. (An example is given in Briefing 18.10).

Other robustness checks on theoretical predictions are numbered 5 in Table 18.1. Again, the general idea of seeing whether relationships can stand up to random changes in the estimates and measurement approaches adopted to test them is an excellent idea – in effect the same general idea as embodied in the multi-measure multi-variable matrix (Table 16.3). As we saw however, much depends on the assumptions on which the alternative formulations are based. In the case of the matrix for example, it had to be assumed that electors' perceptions of party positions were as accurate as the party's own statements of them in the manifesto. This is problematic. Low correlations were attributed to bad performance of the manifesto measure rather than to (more likely) electors' misperceptions of where the party stood. With robustness checks in general, it is important that all the alternative approaches and measures being applied are reasonable statistical representations of the substantive theory or hypothesis underlying them.

Comparability, in terms of measurement adjustments, is also crucial as between the variables that make up a regression equation. Focusing on one variable and adjusting it to take care of anticipated error can paradoxically lead to overestimating its influence and importance. This is because an exaggerated adjustment for error – when in fact the measure may be performing reasonably anyway – considerably boosts its performance

Briefing 18.9

Inferential errors – Type I and Type II

After applying measurement checks and tests, you may correctly judge that a theory, measure or equation is correct or incorrect. But you are also liable to make two kinds of error, known as Type I and Type II error respectively.

A Type I error is when you reject a true hypothesis. A Type II error is when you accept a false one. There is a trade-off in making these mistakes: the severer you make the tests and checks, the less likely (subject to the considerations discussed in the text) you are to accept a false hypothesis or theory as true (Type II). But at the same time, you increase the probability of rejecting a true one (Type I).

relative to other variables in the equation. The only safeguard against this possibility is to treat them all equally. Either leave them all unadjusted, or adjust them all on the same basis.

It is often assumed that error adjustments can only improve the quality of a statistical analysis. It is methodologically virtuous to make them as severe as possible because this provides a sterner check on regressions and the assumptions behind them. What is not taken into account is that adjustments carry their own costs in the form of debatable and perhaps wrong assumptions. Introducing error checks may paradoxically import more errors into the analysis.

Imposing checks certainly leads to more substantive hypotheses about politics being rejected. This is a good thing if these are misleading or weak. An overemphasis on error may, however, lead to true theories being rejected. Given the lack of good predictive explanations, this is a high price to pay for what at best are supplementary checks on the standing of theories and their measurements, compared to their predictive validation.

Most current methodological emphasis is placed on rejecting false hypotheses through strict error checks. This is understandable given the mass of weak theories and relationships in the field. With the emergence of more and better data and systematic theorizing, however, perhaps more emphasis should now be placed on the danger of rejecting true hypotheses and the consequences of doing so emphasized more in methodological training.

Reliability

The stability of a measure or estimated relationship across different contexts.

Of course, **reliability** and other checks on statistical formulations and measures, given that error affects all of them, are useful – even indispensable – as an element in systematic political research. Trouble arises, however, when attempts are made to make particular tests a generic requirement for all research, regardless of the theory behind it or of the substantive context within which it is located. We have discussed an example of such methodological 'legislation' in regard to the insertion of the lagged dependent variable (past values of expenditure and so on) as

Briefing 18.10

Better exactly wrong rather than approximately right?
A warning example

A leading mathematical statistician of the 1950s, John Tukey, satirized the practices of his social science colleagues in a series of 'Badmandments'. One of these forms the title of this briefing. It warns against Type I errors (rejecting true hypotheses) by imposing overly rigid statistical requirements for the acceptance of a reasonably performing theory.

A concrete example comes from a methodological critique of an early attempt to link party policy priorities, as set out in their election platforms, to actual spending on these policies when they were in government. This is a crucial hypothesis of mandate theory, which assumes (1) that voting for a party in some sense endorses their published policies and (2) that majority or plurality parties are therefore both required and empowered to have their government pursue them while in power.

The original analysis focused on this second point, on which there was considerable scepticism – especially regarding US party behaviour. As it happened, results for the first half of the post-war period strongly upheld the mandate hypothesis – US administrations *did* spend in line with their party's declared priorities, surprising many experts in the field.

But, said a published critique, the investigators did not insert previous values of the dependent variable into the equations that linked prior manifesto emphases to current spending. This left open the possibility that party priorities have as much connection with government spending as baseball scores. They might fluctuate in the same way but have no real connection. By inserting each previous year's spending as a 'control' variable, the critics substantially reduced the strength of the relationships between platform emphases and policy spending, in line with their initial scepticism about the ability or desire of parties to carry out their promises.

There is, however, a theoretical flaw in this reasoning. This is revealed when considering what mandate theory actually says about the priority-spending linkage. It predicts neither stability nor change as such. What it does say is that parties/ governments/administrations follow through on their parties' stated priorities, whether for change or continuity. Governing parties coming up for election often promise spending stability in order to continue what they describe as their successful policies.

Cutting out the cases where current spending does not change substantially – which is what controlling for past spending does – is therefore mistaken in the context of mandate theory (which, as noted in Briefing 18.2, may not even be causal in nature). By arbitrarily weakening its evidential support, this analytic strategy commits a Type I error (rejecting a true hypothesis).

In their draft reply to the critique, the original authors tried to make this point. It was, however, rejected by the journal's methodological advisers. Both they and the critics ignored what mandate theory actually said and claimed that the lagged dependent variable must be introduced as a control on relationships under all circumstances – a perfect example of the 'methodologism' that Tukey satirized. (Gary King and Michael Laver (1993) 'Party Platforms, Mandates and Government Spending: a Critique' *American Political Science Review*, 87, pp. 744–758.)

a check on other relationships in regression equations. Despite it being inappropriate for assessing theories which predict stability rather than (or as well as) change in the outcomes, its inclusion is required by almost all contemporary political science journals as an indispensable test of statistical standing.

At its extreme, such attitudes can harden into what we might term 'methodologism', a belief that there are general methodological 'laws' that must be observed in all contexts by everyone and that applying these is sufficient to establish the standing of hypotheses and theories as true or false, regardless of their content. The absence of well-formulated predictive theories to validate measures and relationships within a substantive context has encouraged this elevation of methodology to pre-eminence. On a wider view, however, methods of measuring, analysing and checking evidence should always be 'but the slave and servant' of the explanation, to adapt what David Hume, the great eighteenth-century philosopher of knowledge, said in another context. In other words, the role of methodology is to aid the quantitative formulation of theories and assess their standing in light of evidence. It is definitely not to dictate what they say or how (outside broad limits) they must say it.

End-summary

The chapter started off by reviewing basic assumptions about cause and effect, which provide a common basis for most scientific theorizing and analysis. Going on to show how these could be applied to political analyses, it also considered how causal theories can be built up on the basis of observed regularities (induction) or by a priori reasoning (H-D). A more realistic picture is probably one where theorists draw on previous ideas and observation, checking out their tentative ideas against the evidence and moulding them to fit (retroduction), before going on to prediction.

In the social sciences, regression analysis is the most common way to relate two or more variables, either to identify regularities inductively or to check out existing theories. Regression analysis is always heavily affected by its theoretical context, which specifies what variables are to be included in its equations and the extent of which they are independent of each other. It also indicates which are causes and which effects.

Although most regression analyses are specified only in an algebraic form, the fact that they describe underlying spaces always has to be borne in mind. The spatial context sets limits on how many independent variables should be used in regressions, with a maximum of four or five being advisable for clear interpretation.

Theorizing as well as analysis in political science largely operates in a spatial context. This makes it easier to represent many theories in regression form for testing and predicting. Where theories are more complex, they can be formulated (as in previous chapters) as decision trees or flow diagrams which generate predictions about what actions will follow under particular sets of circumstances. Flow diagrams can also be used to generate simulations, which form a first step in checking how a theory works out and whether it looks broadly plausible. One should not forget, however, that simulations provide only a virtual reality against which theory can be assessed. So we need at some point to predict actual events to be really sure that the theory is correct.

Validation through postdiction and (ideally) prediction of individual events is the ultimate test not only of theories but also of the appropriateness of the measures and statistical procedures through which they are operationalized. If theories, estimates and procedures all work together satisfactorily in actual research applications, such validation overrides more technical checks. It is of course only validation for the time being. Later theories, measures and evidence may supersede earlier ones, which is the cumulative way science works, by checking and extending previous theories and relevant results. At any one time, however, currently validated theory is king, its predictive success superseding or modifying other checks and measures and itself providing substantive explanations of why political processes work the way they do.

Key points from this discussion are thus:

- The importance of theory in focusing and organizing analyses of Big Data.
- Cause and effect as the conceptual framework for (most) explanatory theories and statistical analyses.
- The inductive, H-D and/or retroductive development of theories.
- Regression as the main way theories are expressed for checking against evidence.
- Bivariate and multivariate regressions – describing underlying spaces in algebraic terms in equations.
- Acceptability of theories and their related measures through error checks.
- Types of error checks and their limitations.
- Explanatory and measurement theories.
- Better to be approximately right with the best validated theory (up to now) than exactly wrong by rejecting it (unless you have a better theory).

Systematic working assumptions coming into this discussion

5   Government decisions about what public goods and services to provide and how to provide them are codified and recorded as state laws and policies to guide the actions of state and other bodies and the behaviour of individual citizens.

6   Policy targets and their implementation can be classified and measured for over-time and comparative analysis, on the basis of textual, survey, expenditure and other statistical evidence.

7   This allows them to be represented as points in spaces constructed on various assumptions, with a centre and extremes, which can also

represent and relate the policy positions of political participants (citizens, voters, governments, parties, etc.) as specified from either data or theory.

8   Such spaces can have varying dimensions and measurements, the most common being a straight line running between left and right.

18   However, all political – like other – measurements contain error (which can nevertheless be estimated and corrected on various assumptions).

Sources and resources

Ian Budge, Hans Keman, Michael D. McDonald and Paul Pennings (2012) *Organising Democratic Choice* (Oxford, Oxford University Press) pp. 175–280.

Michael D. Ward, Brian D. Greenhill and Kristin M. Blake (2010) The Perils of Policy by P-Value. *Journal of Peace Research*, 47, pp. 363–375.

William Roberts Clark, Matt Golder and Sona Nadencheck Golder (2012) *Principles of Comparative Politics* (Washington, DC, CQ Press) ISBN 978–16087 16791.

Suggestions for class papers

1   In view of the evidence against polarization having a direct effect on policy-preference correspondence, reformulate alternation theory to take this into account.

2   What other effects would you expect party polarization to have on democratic politics?

3   What role do you think the classic experiment (Figure V.1) might play in future political research? Go into practical applications.

4   Are there any methodological procedures that must always be used to check out theories, regardless of what the theories say? If so, what are they?

Suggestions for class projects

1   Analyse all relevant data to establish whether polarization has any effects on policy-preference correspondence. What are the wider theoretical implications of your findings?

2   Restate alternation theory to cope with the possibility that it deals with two dependent variables (actual correspondence and its potential range). Draw out the wider implications of your propositional restatement.

3   Set up data analyses to assess the role of the lagged dependent variable as (1) a control on hypothesized relationships and (2) an explanatory variable in its own right.

Chapter 19

Developing political science by explaining democracy

Chapter overview

This chapter moves on from the details of specifying and testing to the 'big picture' of how democracy works. This is also a vital question for the development of political science as a discipline. With an increasing mass of Big Data and a consequent outpouring of research, analyses and journal articles from all over the world, we always seem to know more and more about less and less. This is because we lack the unifying context (which economics, for example, has with supply and demand in the free market) within which to relate the new findings to each other. Such a unifying context can be provided for modern political science by developing an overall picture of how democracy works. Democracy not only has an inherent attraction as the most desirable political system to live under but is also the only one we can generalize about, giving two-thirds of world's states their defining characteristics and political processes. We can generalize about these states in ways impossible for non-democratic regimes which take on a variety of forms from traditional aristocracies to army-based dictatorships and single-party rule. The development of political science as a generalizing discipline and a better understanding of democracy thus go hand in hand – a fusion which underlies most of the theoretical and methodological concerns of this book.

This final chapter aims at drawing them even closer together by first identifying the assumptions which most research on democratic representation has to make. These have already been presented as systematic working assumptions at the end of most chapters, thus demonstrating concretely where they come into the general discussion. The propositions have also been presented together at the end of Chapter 8, following on from the various theories of democratic processes which draw on them in their 'web of explanation' (Figure 8.1).

This chapter turns the ordering of Chapter 8 around, first presenting the basic working assumptions of representational research and then revisiting the actual explanations of processes and outcomes which they support. Having already seen the contribution that these theories make to understanding democracy, readers are in a better position to appreciate the relevance of the methodological assumptions underpinning them.

After listing and commenting on their underlying assumptions – useful in filling in the details of what these are and how and why they are needed – the second part of the chapter then draws together the explanatory theories from previous chapters, to provide an overall, updated account of how democracy works. Hopefully this provides not only a better appreciation of democracy as a representational process but also an insight into how political science can provide a deeper understanding of its functioning across the world. We begin with the working assumptions which research has to make in order to do this.

Specifying a working context for cumulative political research

To develop systematically, science needs a common focus for research and a shared context, both of which enable us to relate specific theories and findings to each other. This is what makes research cumulative – that is, correcting and extending previous research rather than throwing up interesting but unrelated bits of knowledge. Sometimes, of course, scientific breakthroughs do put together seemingly unrelated observations, as when spontaneous motion in liquids was shown to demonstrate the existence of atoms, previously postulated in quite another field to account for the way steam engines worked. So we should never seek to prescribe or limit intellectual activity. The fact that political scientists work in many different areas of interest and often cross the boundaries into history and economics should be welcomed. It all makes for a fascinating and ever-expanding body of knowledge on which everyone can draw.

By the same token, however, it is useful to counter dangers of diffuseness, especially in the face of an ever-growing mass of unrelated information, by drawing together what we know to the extent that we can. Representational research – matching policy supply and demand – seems one field where research at the present time rests on a set of shared assumptions about the political context, actors and processes, and the way they should be studied. It also has a common focus – in this case, on the workings of democracy. The assumptions and approaches discussed below specify current practices more precisely to draw them together so that political scientists can build on them as a common frame of reference for cumulative research. This is presented in the next section in 20 related propositions (with supporting clarifications and explanations).

Systematic political science: a propositional summary

Collectivities

Groupings or organizations which can act together to further common goals.

Propositions are precise statements of relationships between political actors, whether individuals or **collectivities**, and how to specify and study them. They form a context within which to formulate predictive theories about how political processes work and what outcomes emerge under specified conditions. The propositions we review here are supportive of predictive explanations rather than predictive in themselves. When brought together as a context for the process theories presented in the rest of the chapter, they do facilitate explanation and prediction, however, as we shall see.

There are two ways to approach a propositional summary like the one here. The first, suggested in Chapter 8, is to read the propositions straight through so as to get the overall thrust of their argument. With this in mind, we can then go on to justifications and clarifications of what they are saying. That was the approach when the propositions were presented previously as a midway summary. The main purpose there was to provide a concise overview which readers could use to place each surrounding chapter in an overall context.

Here the second strategy will be followed – that is, following each proposition with a justification of why it is being made and takes on the shape it does. Having already picked their way through the book, readers can benefit from the summary provided for each proposition and the supporting comments. If they feel the need to reorient themselves through a quick overview, they can always go back to Chapter 8, where the same propositions are stated directly, without intervening comment. The two approaches complement each other and can be adopted as readers require. The propositions and supporting commentary are grouped in terms of the actors or processes they deal with. These proceed from the most fundamental question – what is political science about? – to the most specific one – how does democracy work? On the first front (what is political science?), a partial answer at least is provided by the definition of systematic political science already offered in the Preface and in Chapter 8. 'Systematic political science integrates the working assumptions of that body of political research on the basis of which a set of interrelated predictive explanations of political processes can be generated and validated – in particular for democratic policymaking'.

The 20 propositions summarizing the working assumptions on which our discussions and theorizing have been based fill in this general characterization. They are far from defining the whole of political science, of course, or even of policy analysis (as Proposition 20 makes clear). But they do consolidate the subject's dynamic core, where most innovative research is currently being done. In particular they guide us through the problems of Big Data analyses with their special emphases on predictive theory as the best way to cut through their complexities and understand the full significance of their findings. They also of course underpin the predictive theorizing reviewed in this book, which attempts to answer the second big question: how does democracy work? We consider this in the later part of the chapter. Here we first present the general working assumptions which form the methodological basis for answering that question.

Systematic working assumptions propositionalized

States

Propositions

1   States form the basic unit or context for political research.
2   States are governments with supporting (quasi-)military, administrative and other institutions, recognized by other governments as providing public goods and services (including the regulation of non-state activities) within specified territorial boundaries.

Comment

Political research often compares states directly, to establish the effects of their varying characteristics and institutions on outcomes. This is often termed 'comparative' or 'cross-national research' as opposed to analyses of politics within a single country. However, research undertaken within a single country can also be comparative in the sense of comparing devolved or delegated governments within an established state. The latter are also states in terms of the broad definition in Proposition 2, since they have a government providing public goods (see Proposition 3) within definite territorial boundaries and are recognized by other governments – even if their powers are formally restricted. All states (notionally independent or not) vary in terms of the powers they (formally or actually) have. An interesting research question is what political and policy effects legal or other limitations have. States are to political science what the 'economy' is to economics (though, curiously, economies are usually defined in terms of state boundaries as well). Having states as their basic unit of analysis gives political science a more directly relevant territorial context to work within.

Normative political theory often starts with the need for public goods (Propositions 3 and 4) as the reason and justification for having states. Here states themselves are given priority because political research focuses directly on them and because historically their rudimentary institutions seem to have imposed themselves first on a territory before providing public goods. Anglo-American and Continental European writers often differ on whether the state (with its continuing institutions) can be identified with the government currently in office. Proposition 2 reflects the general focus of research on governments as both spokespersons and executive committees for the state. Their pronouncements and actions *are* state actions during their term of office. The importance of mutual recognition acknowledges the influence which other states' actions have on internal politics, particularly with **globalization**.

Public goods

Propositions

3   Public goods and services are those provided universally, so that no one can be individually charged for them or excluded from benefiting.
4   Only states can guarantee the provision of public goods and services through their unique ability to finance them by taxes and other means.

Comment

Propositions 3 and 4 develop the concept of public goods (including services such as overall regulation and co-ordination of activities within the territory) and relate it to state functioning. The essence of a public good is that no one can be excluded from benefiting (e.g. from health provisions against epidemics). There is some question whether some services (notably defence but possibly public health and internal security) have by their nature either to be provided for all or not at all. Universal provision varies widely across policy areas, countries and regimes. The common feature is that all states provide *some* public goods and services, as Proposition 4 notes.

Proposition 4 also hints at the coercive power which states can deploy through the army and police to enforce taxation. A monopoly of the use or authorization of force is often a key element in definitions of the state. Most political science (as distinct from IR) research, however, is done on relatively peaceful democratic states. So the use of force is not strongly stressed here.

Policies

Propositions

5   Government decisions about what public goods and services to provide and how to provide them are recorded as state laws and policies to guide the actions of state and other bodies and the behaviour of individual citizens.

Comment

This proposition makes policy, its genesis and its implementation the general focus of state activity. It frames and regulates everything done in the state territory (possibly by leaving it unregulated). Records of past decisions, which continue in force unless explicitly repealed, create slow-changing '**policy regimes**', which resist major alteration by any one government. This sustains theories of administrative budgeting such as 'incrementalism' (last year's policy is the best predictor of this year's) and 'punctuated equilibrium' (change is incremental except where occasional and selective government intervention or external crises necessitate radical change, followed by a long period of relative stability).

Policy regimes

Bodies of established policies being implemented in a particular policy area.

Policy positioning and movement

Propositions

6   Policy preferences and their implementation can all be measured for over-time and comparative analysis, on the basis of textual, survey, expenditure, and other statistical evidence.

7   This allows them to be represented as points in spaces constructed on various measurement assumptions, with a centre and extremes, which can also relate the policy positions of political actors (citizens, voters, governments, parties, etc.) as specified from either data or theory.

8   Such spaces can have varying dimensions and measurements, the most common being a straight line running between left and right.

Comment

Fairly self-explanatory, these propositions recognize the progression from largely qualitative to quantitative methods over the last 70 years and the basis this provides for spatial analysis and mathematical theorizing (as explored in preceding chapters). By far the most extensive developments have taken place in a spatial context, in terms of regression for data analysis and various postulated spaces for theory building, of which the most common is the left-right continuum. Central to the analysis of democratic policy-preference correspondence (Proposition 10) is the ability of spaces to relate the policy positions of one political actor to another (e.g. citizens to governments) and to distinguish positions on the various extremes from those at the centre.

Policymaking and democracy

Propositions

9   States vary in the extent to which decisions about policy and who is to make it are shared among citizens.

10   The most extensive sharing occurs in democracies, since by definition, these have to guarantee that public policies necessarily reflect the preferences of citizens for them.

11   This guarantee is provided by free, regular and competitive elections of governments and/or policies open to all groups and individuals, where votes reveal citizen preferences and authorize them as either policymaking governments or directly as state policy.

12   Democracies are the only states with such key political procedures in common across the world. Hence, they are the only states whose policymaking processes can be analysed and explained at a general level by political science.

13   Ideally, explanations should take the form of predictive theories consisting of propositions or equations which can be checked for predictive success against independently observed outcomes or behaviour.

14   The unifying focus of such theories – extending from preference formation and expression to policymaking and implementation – is on the extent of policy-preference correspondence and how it is achieved.

Comment

Within the general focus on policy, these propositions move our attention to the crucial dependent variable in investigations of democracy – that is, the correspondence between popular preferences and the actual public policy that gets effected. (Not to be confused with party or government policy *targets*, which may or may not be achieved.) Democracy justifies itself as guaranteeing this correspondence. Empirical research tests this claim by measuring how far actual democracies produce it and can also guarantee it through the procedures they put in place. (We go into these in more detail in the next section.) The reason for stressing the guarantee provided by democracies for preference and policies matching, rather than simply their observed correspondence, is to exclude cases of benevolent despots who meet popular policy demands without providing any inbuilt institutional guarantee that this will carry on.

Note that the propositions are formulated so as to cover both direct citizen voting on *policy*, in referendums and initiatives, and general elections where they choose *policymakers* (governments), not necessarily on pure policy grounds.

Much research on democratic origins and stability looks at the purely internal factors promoting political competition and popular participation. External pressures to conform to general democratic norms (as exercised by the EU and the US) seem equally important in the majority of cases, however, especially given the need for governments to have external recognition (Proposition 2). Once they get an initial start, however, elections and party competition generate their own internal dynamics.

All this leads on to the key point that political science (excluding IR) has a natural focus towards researching and explaining political processes in democracies (like economic science towards (reasonably) free markets). This is because political arrangements vary so much across the minority of non-democratic states in the world in country-specific ways, which render generalization difficult if not impossible across different types of regime.

Hence, the central question in political science (excluding IR) is how policies get matched to preferences in free societies (as for economics, it is supply being matched to demand in free markets). There are of course many distinct research areas feeding into this concern – for example, preference formation, 'framing' and measurement; elections, voting and parties; government formation and functioning; and policy analysis, to name a few. All have the ultimate aim of clarifying the policy-preference relationship, sometimes by showing how it can go wrong.

Framing preferences

Propositions

15 Popular policy preferences do not usually emerge spontaneously but rather are formed as reactions to policy proposals put forward by governments, parties or other political actors.
16 The free formation and functioning of such actors is thus essential for estimating the full range of true popular preferences.

Comment

These propositions simply restate the points made – particularly in Chapter 3 – about the difficulty of relating individual preferences to public action. This is also heavily stressed by thermostatic theory. Public preferences are usually formed as reactions to proposals put forward by parties, governments or pollsters. Given the latent nature of citizen preferences, they have to be brought out as reactions to concrete proposals. Before they can be fully expressed, therefore, there needs to be a full range of political actors around to bring them out, to guarantee that they are fully voiced and to cover the whole range of possible alternatives to the proposals under consideration.

Estimating popular preferences – with error

Propositions

17 The popular preferences with which public policy must necessarily correspond in a democracy can be specified sufficiently to form a basis for public decision-making only if estimated from voting outcomes in free and open elections (or from election-like formatting of questions in well-conducted surveys).

18 However, all political – like other – measurements contain error (which can nevertheless be estimated and corrected on various assumptions).

19 This is necessarily true of election votes in their role as measures of popular preferences. The rules and procedures which structure votes (e.g. the order and wording of alternatives being voted on and the methods of aggregating individual votes to produce a collective decision) can all distort the final outcomes and have to be allowed for in estimating settled preferences.

Comment

Election votes are of course the only fully authoritative expressions of preference in democracies. But they are lacking in inter-election periods, when both politicians and political scientists draw on survey evidence to say what popular preferences are. Proposition 19 recognizes the central role such evidence plays both in political research and debate. However, neither votes nor surveys may properly reflect underlying preferences (as pointed out in Parts II and V of the book). Thus, they require checks and external validation of the extent that they do reflect underlying preferences.

Other analytic approaches to policy

Propositions

20 Alternative ways (among others) in which public policy can be studied are:

a Normative political theory, which focuses on the extent to which the democratic policy-preference correspondence can produce good public policy, as judged by the independent criteria of quality which it develops.

b Policy analysis, which assesses policies by their success in achieving their own stated goals.

c Class-elite analysis, which investigates who benefits from the policies which are adopted.

Comment

Traditional political philosophy focuses on developing criteria for a just or good state, in terms of the policy decisions it makes and the procedures for making them. The spread of democracy and semi-democracy in the modern world means that modern political philosophy is increasingly concerned with possible biases in democratic procedures and the policies they produce. This gives it many concerns in common with empirical theory, with which in any case it substantially overlaps (e.g. on 'cycling' in voting procedures). Despite a seeming disjunction, the many points of contact between normative and empirical theory and their increasing focus on democracy and its effects renders political science more unified as a subject than first appears. Normative theorizing needs in any case to make assumptions about the actual way democracy functions in order to critique it. To the extent that such assumptions are important to its reasoning, it opens itself to checks against observations and evidence, as empirical theories do.

Determining whether policies are effective in their own terms is also essential in informing democratic discussion, as is information about who benefits from them – temporarily or permanently. The latter question, of course, is at the heart of Marxist analyses of politics and society.

How the systematic working assumptions underpin specific process theories

The propositions just reviewed form part of the supporting web of definitions and assumptions that any specific theory needs to build on in explaining political processes. However, it would make no sense for every such theory to go back, every time it is stated, to the remoter fundamentals it rests on. The factional theory of party position taking, for example, does not have to always reiterate that the context it assumes is that of a democratic state; nor do specific theories have to go into spatial measurement assumptions too much (unless they are introducing radically new assumptions which affect their own reasoning). Mostly, such theories just take the general research framework summarized in Propositions 1–20 for granted and carry on from there.

This is an entirely proper way of proceeding. On the other hand, the fact that the general background is not precisely specified can lead to confusions and misunderstandings, as one theory may implicitly make background assumptions not shared by others. The solution is not to repeat everything in great detail every time a new theory is formulated. Rather, it is to concentrate on necessary clarifications while referring back to a commonly held inventory of background assumptions. This is what the overview here provides. From an inventory such as this, everyone knows broadly just what general assumptions each specific theory is making. In developing it, analysts can indicate any general assumptions they are accepting or changing and then proceed with their own applied assumptions and predictions. Each chapter in the book has tried to do this by explicitly stating the systematic working assumptions coming into its discussion, thus tying it in to the general framework laid out here.

How systematizing political science guides data analysis and political research

Big Data give us access to more and more information. However, its very potential for explaining the research questions we can ask, and the analysis we can do on them, creates problems of overload and complexity for researchers. Unless we can find ways of cutting through the masses of information they produce and the many – often weak – relationships which emerge from them, we are never going to be able to come up with clear conclusions from either a theoretical or a practical point of view.

A first step in focusing our research is therefore to recognize and clarify the assumptions on which the data sets are prepared, measured and used. The data relate mostly to states, and in particular their governments and other internal political actors and the policies their interactions produce. All can be measured numerically and represented spatially, which is what Big Data do.

Policy does not solely depend on the way the various actors are lined up but also on the rules defining majorities and linking their preferences to outcomes (Part II). Once we realize that spatial interactions within the rules are the essence of what Big Data describe, we can research them systematically to provide answers to the central questions we want to ask. These must surely start with ones about democracy. To avoid diffusion and vagueness, it is best to formulate such questions before proceeding with the data analysis itself. Research questions should always be put in the form of clearly stated theories whose expectations we can then check out – again, hopefully in pre-specified ways – against the data. This helps us to find a path through the wood in spite of all the trees. We can then check pre-formulated theories against many data sets and innumerable individual cases without getting lost in methodological details.

Theorizing is the path to follow. In the event that one theory does not work, we have to get back to the drawing board and think of another rather than blundering through the data searching out relationships. Sometimes induction works but rarely without some preconceived ideas to guide it. One purpose of this book is to convince readers that we can all develop theories to guide us (if only by modifying the ones we already have in plausible ways). Doing so will always require us to draw on some of the working assumptions we have laid out here. That is why it is useful to make them accessible through the propositional analysis.

If the working assumptions provide a framework for research on Big Data, the cutting edge is provided by the predictive theories presented in this book and other theories like them. Below we summarize their reasoning in a propositional form similar to the one presented above. This time, however, it is directed to the second big question: not how we study democracy but how it actually works.

From working assumptions to applied explanations – another propositional analysis!

The systematic working assumptions in the inventory above form an 'envelope' or overall context for the specific theories of democratic processes on which our chapter discussions have been based. Some of the latter have already been brought together in the 'web of explanation' (Figure 8.1). That dealt mostly with parties at the electoral level. Additional analyses of processes and behaviour have, however, been added, notably in Part III, dealing with party behaviour in government and in the individual ministries, departments or agencies. To flesh out the overall picture of how democracy works, we need to bring all the specific theories together here – at a more general level, however, than the propositions which have been the focus of individual chapters. We do this now in the same propositional form used for the methodological working assumptions.

General elections

Propositions

1   General elections, with political parties competing for votes and defining the alternatives to be voted on, bring other considerations to bear on voting choices than pure policy ones.
2   This is because at any one point, political parties – running blocs of candidates in the election and organizing them afterwards – may define themselves in terms of candidates, record and various situational factors as well as the policy bundle that they put in their programme.

Comment

That general elections are decided on numerous, often unpredictable, circumstances as well as on policy, is generally accepted in voting research. However, the implications of this for representational theory are often overlooked. General models of election outcomes are based mostly on the idea that policy determines the final outcome, either because other influences on voting are ignored in the supporting theory or because policy voters are assumed to swing cohesively in one direction or another while other types of voters do not.

If voters' policy preferences actually determined who would make policy in line with their wishes, this would of course provide the democratic guarantee of a policy-preference correspondence. But this is not supported by any evidence that policy voting has that effect. Were policies adopted by straight popular voting on them (initiatives and referendums), the link would be guaranteed, subject to error. Almost all democracies, however, rely on general elections to decide on policy indirectly by nominating a particular set of policymakers with known commitments to focus on a particular policy line. The two propositions make the point, however, that parties are often put in government to make policy for reasons unrelated to it (e.g. general competence).

Theories of the election process thus have to cope with a situation where the policy targets being implemented are not necessarily those which the majority would have chosen in a direct vote. How, then, can one achieve a policy-preference correspondence when the policymakers are almost randomly selected in policy terms by the general-election process? This is the paradox of democracy which the party alternation model, outlined below, seeks to confront.

Political parties

Propositions

3   Over time, parties' characteristic policies continue to distinguish them relative to other parties while their other appeals show no such continuity.
4   The free formation of political parties – as guaranteed in democracies – ensures that at any one time the policy preferences of all significant opinion groupings are contained in some existent party's policy programme.

Comment

The two propositions about political parties are important in themselves, characterizing parties as ideologically based policy carriers for all groups in the population. This does not imply, of course, that each opinion grouping necessarily has its own party. The policy stand taken by an existing party may appeal to new opinion groupings. However, where a grouping is sufficiently distinctive and does not feel well represented by any existing party, it is free to found its own party and contest elections. The practical problem, of course, is winning enough votes under the existing electoral system to give it a share in policymaking.

The continuing identity of any party is bound up with the characteristic policies that it originally started off with and the **ideologies** – stressing 'freedom', 'equality', 'tradition', 'religious values', 'environment' and so on – from which they derive. These may be more or less emphasized by different factions within the party but cannot be totally abandoned without threatening its continuity and identity – that is, the party's very existence. This reinforces parties' inward-looking nature and their delayed and restrained response to popular policy preferences – again raising the question of how such relatively unresponsive organizations can guarantee correspondence between popular preferences and public policy.

Ideologies

Sets of assumptions about the world leading to certain kinds of political action.

Popular centrism

Propositions

5 Unconstrained party formation implies that the majority policy preference must always be centrist relative to those of the parties – that is, the preferred policy position of most electors must either coincide with one party position or lie between two or more of them, therefore on the boundary or within the boundary of the most concise segment of any policy space which can be defined by the party positions within it.

6 Ensuring a correspondence between centrist popular preferences and enacted public policy thus requires that enacted public policy also be centrist most of the time. Parties are the alternatives that electors have to vote for in general elections. Each party carries with it a 'policy bundle', expressed in its programme, of policy priorities and positions. Electors may vote for a party on other grounds than policy, but they also get the policies associated with it as part of the package.

Comment

If parties define the policy-preference space for electors by carrying all significant policy preferences in their 'policy bundles', the popular majority preference must lie between them. Of course, not everyone will endorse any one party's set of positions; they may find policy targets they favour in two, three or more party policy 'bundles'. That means, however, that their preference in relation to the party positions must lie on or between them. Even extremists in any one party who spill out over the boundaries defining the party policy segment must be counterbalanced by an equal number within the boundary. Otherwise, the party would move outwards, thus extending the boundary and keeping the majority within it. This argument applies to any policy space, however multidimensional.

An alternative view is to regard issues either as all aligned along an overarching left-right dimension or as largely separable and best represented by a series of one-dimensional spaces where decisions are made sequentially. In both cases, there is a guaranteed median/majority preference, with the party or parties endorsing positions at one end of the continuum alternating in government with those at the other, again pulling policy to one side or other of the majority position.

An important implication of Proposition 4 is that electors' preferences are not irrevocably framed and set by the existing set of party policy alternatives, since they can always act autonomously to change these over the course of time. Both of these conclusions about a necessary centrist preference location of elector preferences relative to party policies, given the electorate's potential to form new parties to represent significant opinion groups, are simply reasonable conjectures at the moment. The processes producing popular centrist preferences do seem amenable to formal mathematical proof, however.

Party alternation and the policy-preference correspondence

Propositions

7   Unpredictable (i.e. random) election outcomes reliably alternate parties and their extreme (relative to electors) policy targets in government over time.

8   Alternations of plurality parties in government pull previously enacted policies, tending to one extreme, across the centre of the party-defined policy segment towards another extreme, during the current inter-election period.

9   Policy change is, however, usually incremental and slow, so enacted policy tends to be only part way to a new target before another government alternation takes place, when the process repeats itself in reverse, again pulling enacted policy across the centre.

10   Correspondence between popular policy preferences and public policy, the ultimate guarantee and justification of democracy, is thus mostly produced through its institutional mechanisms of party competition in general elections – which regularly alternate different party policy carriers in government – combined with slow incremental change in enacted policy. This process applies equally to overall policy orientations (e.g. left vs right) and to specific policies, provided that parties are differentiated on them and bracket the centre.

Comment

Given the inability of policy-voting theories to provide a validated explanation of policy-preference correspondence, we have to turn to other explanations of how it can (and does) come about under democracy. These explanations have to confront the following findings: general-election vote gains and losses seem almost random from a policy point of view; parties are not particularly sensitive to majority opinion and pursue their own objectives in government; and governments generally form on the basis of party strengths and ideological positioning in the legislature. These may not exactly reflect (or may even wildly distort) the popular vote distribution. All of these circumstances tend to strengthen the position of the plurality party (the one with the largest number of seats) relative to the party that the median elector voted for (though sometimes the same party will be plurality and median).

The one reasonably certain assumption we can build on within this setting is that uncertainties and instability in both the internal setting and the outside world will erode government support and lead to one plurality party replacing another reasonably frequently (or one plurality-dominated coalition replacing another). As government policy targets alternate under these changes, enacted policy will be pulled across the centre from their previous position and thus brought closer again to majority preferences. Such see-sawing in terms of direction of change makes for a dynamic centrist **equilibrium**, which slow policy implementation keeps from moving out of the centre before the next change of government.

Equilibrium

A political process that tends towards the same outcome over time.

Thermostatic reactions and slow policy change

Propositions

11 Policy-preference correspondence is also facilitated by hostile 'thermostatic' reactions to government policy initiatives during the inter-election period, which leads to the following:
   a Increasing 'costs of governing', which contribute to governing parties' loss of support at general elections.
   b Modification or withdrawal of party proposals.
   c Thus slowing down change in implemented policy, leaving it near the centre.
12 Slow policy change, which hinders plurality parties from completely changing actual policy when in government and keeps it in the centre, is also facilitated by the following:
   a Incremental or 'punctuated' change in ministries' budgets.
   b Same-party or same-factional control of particular ministries over time, which hampers policy change.

Comment

'Policy inertia' at the upper levels of government keeps implemented policy close to the centrist preferences of electors, by hampering plurality parties in government from totally meeting their policy targets. It is partly created by popular resistance to new policy proposals. But it also stems from the government setup, particularly from party or factional resistance to change in 'their' ministries. This also spurs on bureaucratic infighting, which constrains their budgets by preventing any one department or ministry from substantially increasing its own share.

When viewed overall, these processes slow down moves away from the centre, where majority preferences lie. Democratic, electoral and governmental processes thus foster and rely on policy alternations as the way to match public policy to popular preferences for it over time, overcoming the practical difficulties which render policy-voting theories unconvincing. We can demonstrate that they do so by generating predictions from supporting theories which prove reasonably successful in anticipating independently observed outcomes from democratic processes, as shown in the individual chapters of this book.

End-summary and conclusions

Prediction is not an end in itself, though it is clearly useful from a practical point of view to anticipate what is going to happen politically. The review of working models undertaken in this book demonstrates that they can be set up to permit general assessments of their plausibility, comparing overall patterns produced by the models and simulations with real mappings based on independent observation. Postdictions of individual events can also be judged against actual events and processes. The real prize, however, lies in making true predictions about future events. The models reviewed here generally achieve a postdictive success rate of 70%–80%. This is not overwhelming. But the models and theories all have a potential for improvement, which could eventually stand comparison with success rates in other sciences. Rather than making general affirmations that this is possible, our discussion has tried to illustrate in detail how models can be constructed and quantified so as to be compared with observations. The main tools for doing so are regression, decision trees, and flow diagrams, aided by simulations. All of these techniques are based on assumed or actual policy spaces. This is useful since most systematic theorizing makes similar spatial assumptions.

Whatever its practical uses, prediction's major role is to support theorizing and explanation. First of all, it improves the quality of the explanation. To even generate predictions, explanations have to fill in all the gaps in their reasoning (which can otherwise be glossed over). They have also to be stated precisely enough for it to be clear when their predictions are upheld or falsified; otherwise, the exercise is pointless.

Providing explanations rather than predictions is of course the major objective in building a theory. But prediction is the indispensable tool in deciding on current evidence whether the theory is valid. The abundance of plausible and competing explanations which can be produced retrospectively for any political happening means that we have to decide between them on clear, independent grounds. General assessments of plausibility such as those based on simulations are an approximation to this. But post-diction of individual events provides a sterner test. True future prediction is the ultimate criterion for acceptance (at least until alternative theories and more evidence become available).

What does more precise explanation do for us as political scientists? Hopefully the book has convincingly answered this question by providing a coherent overall picture of the way democracy works – and, ultimately, the way it guarantees a correspondence between public policy and popular preferences for it. This provides both a context for drawing together the findings from Big Data analyses and a basis for more informed public debate on particular policies – and for normative political philosophy, whose goal has traditionally been to distinguish good policy from bad and describe how the former may be guaranteed. Responsiveness to majority preferences may not be the best guarantee of ethical quality. But arguments about this ought to start from a clear understanding of how democracy works, which can be attained only through properly validated predictive theorizing.

Any theory draws on a web of assumptions about what to focus on and the proper approach to adopt to it, which it would be tedious and repetitive to detail in its specific reasoning. In theorizing about party policy movement, we do not always have to bring in the state as the context in which such movement takes place. However, the state setting is assumed in almost all the research that gets done. The propositional summary at the beginning of this chapter (and in Chapter 8) provides a convenient inventory of the methodological assumptions that systematic political research has to make (and generally does make) if it wants to be cumulative and build a convincing overall explanation of politics. Hopefully both the propositions themselves, and the detailed discussion of the theories which draw on them, will prove useful in furthering this aim.

Sources and resources

Hans Keman and Jaap Woldendorp (eds) (2016) *Handbook of Research Methods and Applications in Political Science* (Cheltenham, Edward Elgar) info@elgar.co.uk INBUNDEN Engelska.

Keith Dowding (2016) *The Philosophy and Methods of Political Science* (Basingstoke, Palgrave MacMillan).

W. Phillips Shively (2016) *The Craft of Political Research* (Abingdon, Routledge).

Suggestions for class papers

1 Are some of the systematic working assumptions listed in the chapter more important than others for political research? Which are they, and why are they more important?

2 In doing comparative research, do we need to make more methodological assumptions than those listed? What are they and why do we need them?

3 Do you agree with the characterization of political parties as inward looking and unresponsive? What evidence is there to support it?

Suggestions for class projects

1 Check out one of the general propositions about parties and elections towards the end of the chapter. Specify the methodological assumptions you need to make in order to do this.

2 State a convincing alternative to alternation theory as an explanation of democratic representation, and present it in propositional form.

3 How could political science develop in the future on the basis of the two propositional presentations in this chapter? Justify your 'vision'.

Index

Note: **Boldface** page references indicate tables. *Italic* references indicate figures and boxed text.

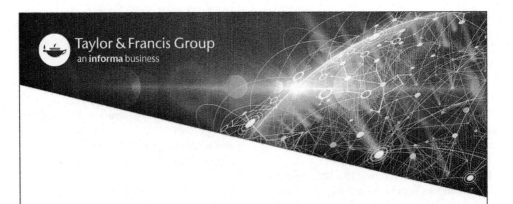